THE BUSINESS GUIDE
TO LEGAL LITERACY

*To my loving parents and husband
for their undying support,
understanding, and encouragement.*

THE BUSINESS GUIDE TO LEGAL LITERACY

What Every Manager Should Know About the Law

Hanna Hasl-Kelchner

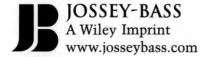

JOSSEY-BASS
A Wiley Imprint
www.josseybass.com

Published by Jossey-Bass
A Wiley Imprint
989 Market Street, San Francisco, CA 94103-1741   www.josseybass.com

Jossey-Bass books and products are available through most bookstores. To contact Jossey-Bass directly call our Customer Care Department within the U.S. at 800-956-7739, outside the U.S. at 317-572-3986, or fax 317-572-4002.

Jossey-Bass also publishes its books in a variety of electronic formats. Some content that appears in print may not be available in electronic books.

Library of Congress Cataloging-in-Publication Data

Hasl-Kelchner, Hanna, 1955–
   The business guide to legal literacy : what every manager should know about the law / Hanna Hasl-Kelchner.
      p. cm.
   Includes bibliographical references and index.
   ISBN-13: 978-0-7879-8255-3
   ISBN-10: 0-7879-8255-5
   1. Business law—United States. 2. Executives—United States—Handbooks, manuals, etc. I. Title.
   KF390.B84H37 2006
   346.7307—dc22

                                                              2006001083

Printed in the United States of America
FIRST EDITION
HB Printing   10 9 8 7 6 5 4 3 2 1

CONTENTS

Preface   vii

PART ONE: HOW TO CREATE A WINNING
LEGAL ATTITUDE   1

1   The Need for a Paradigm Shift   3
2   How Behavioral Economics Influences
     Decision Making   18
3   How Latent Legal Liabilities Escalate the
     Cost of Doing Business   36
4   How Legal Leverage Creates Value and
     Competitive Advantage   63

PART TWO: HOW TO ACHIEVE LEGAL LEVERAGE:
DEVELOPING TOOLS TO MINIMIZE RISK
AND MAXIMIZE OPPORTUNITY   79

5   How to Integrate Legal Literacy into the Enterprise
     Value Chain: Who Needs to Know What   81
6   How Miscommunications Create Liabilities:
     Avoiding Smoking Guns   98
7   How to Keep the Wheels On: Managing and
     Mediating Expectations   134
8   How to Transform Legal Obstacles into Strategic
     Opportunities: The Role of Good Decision Making   156

PART THREE: HOW TO MAINTAIN LEGAL LEVERAGE:
DEVELOPING A SUPPORTIVE CORPORATE CULTURE   175

9   How to Stay On Course: The Role of Continuous
     Learning and Knowledge Management   177

10	How to Stay In Synch: The Role of Lawyers	198
11	How to Stay On Message: The Role of Communications	215
12	How to Stay Centered: The Role of Ethical Leadership	230
	Epilogue: Winning from the Beginning	251
	Appendix A: Legal Literacy Toolkit Chart	257
	Appendix B: The ABCs of Legal Literacy	260
	1. International Law	260
	2. Contracts	269
	3. Product Liability	281
	4. Employment	287
	5. Unfair Competition	295
	6. Intellectual Property	303
	Appendix C: The Lessons of Sarbanes-Oxley	312
	Appendix D: Excerpts from Federal Organizational Sentencing Guidelines, 2004	318
	Appendix E: Excerpts from the Sarbanes-Oxley Act of 2002: Table of Contents	325
	Appendix F: United States Attorneys' Manual: The Thompson Memo	329
	Bibliography	347
	Acknowledgments	355
	The Author	356
	Index	357

PREFACE

When I first began practicing law in 1981 I was struck by the way smart, seasoned business professionals could significantly underestimate the legal consequences of their business decisions. A minor course correction early in the process could make the difference between hitting a bull's eye or missing the mark altogether. It could prevent corporate meltdowns and protect profits. Yet I quickly learned that legal issues and lawyers were something managers preferred to avoid. At best, we were viewed as a necessary evil. Like patients who visit the dentist only when the pain becomes unbearable, business professionals consulted lawyers reluctantly. They waited.

At the same time, I learned why many managers and executives held a dim view of lawyers. I met lazy lawyers who found it easier to say no and kill a deal than to work through the issues and find solutions that were both practical and legally sound. I also met lawyers who never met a legal issue they didn't like. They rendered very good legal advice, but in their zeal to leave no stone unturned they'd lose sight of the big picture—the client's overall business needs. Both camps made every issue sound like the sky was falling. After a while their Chicken Little pleas were ignored. Worst of all, their lopsided *weltanschauung* alienated clients.

There was clearly a tension between law and business, a tension that the textbooks, the classroom, and the bar exam had not prepared me for. Yet, as a young lawyer with a master's degree in business administration who had grown up in an entrepreneurial family where dinner-table conversation inevitably turned to business and family outings often included customers, I viewed law and business as a natural fit, not as natural enemies.

Nonetheless, there was a standoff between the two. More time was spent fixing problems than avoiding them. If only these business professionals could envision the law as a tool for achieving business objectives rather than an obstacle to be avoided, I thought to myself. Similarly, if only these lawyers could master the art of a balanced response. Together they could create a tremendous, unparalleled partnership. They could manage legal issues in their infancy while problems were small and comparatively inexpensive to fix, instead of at the more rebellious adolescent stage. They could also open doors to new opportunities by securing their legal rights early, before those rights were compromised. Such partnering would save a lot of horseshoe nails, horses, riders, and corporate kingdoms. Staying in the saddle would also make it easier to conquer new realms. *If only they knew.*

It was these early perceptions of law and business that were the genesis of *The Business Guide to Legal Literacy.* From my perspective, law and business are the yin and yang of commerce. They are complementary sides of the same coin. Harnessing and synchronizing them is the key to business sustainability. Yet too many managers viewed the synergy between law and business as counterintuitive. Until that tension was harmonized, the full potential of this tremendous partnership would remain untapped and unfulfilled.

My desire to bridge the gap between law and business heavily influenced my legal practice: how I counseled clients in transactions and how I managed litigation. My goal was always to translate legalese into language that made business sense—to use the law as a business tool. To help facilitate this goal I developed legal training programs for corporations that directly related the law to people's everyday work responsibilities and decisions. These training successes evolved into "Legal Leverage," a course I taught in the graduate programs at the Duke University Fuqua School of Business, and they contributed significantly to the evolution of *The Business Guide to Legal Literacy.*

While I was busy building bridges one case and one class at a time, the gap between law and business unfortunately continued to widen. Over the years more civil liabilities were criminalized, retroactive liabilities were imposed in the form of environmental compliance laws, and more regulations and stiffer penalties were necessitated by assorted scandals, beginning with the insider trading and the savings and loan debacles of the 1980s.

The legal environment of business was growing increasingly hostile. Ironically, the gap was growing at the same time that missteps were becoming more expensive than ever before. A bridge urgently needed to be built between the two disciplines. To encourage the U.S. business community to be more proactive about its legal compliance efforts, the U.S. government stepped in and adopted the Federal Organizational Sentencing Guidelines in 1991. The law offered sentencing leniency *if* organizations had an *effective* compliance program in place.

The new guidelines were a roundabout way of aligning business practices with the law, but they were not much of a marketing coup. In some corporate corridors lawyers asking for more compliance resources were faced with a tough sell. After all, how do you convince an organization to devote resources to effective compliance if all anyone gets out of it is reduced sentencing? I mean, who *plans* on getting sentenced? Sentencing is a disincentive. Reducing the disincentive doesn't make it more attractive.

That would be similar to my telling my husband I'll save money by spending more when my favorite dress shop is having sale. "That's right, honey, the more I spend, the more you save." You can imagine his reply. All he'd have to do is open the door to an overstuffed clothes closet to make his point.

Selling managers on less jail time and smaller fines met the same kind of enthusiasm. More compliance was a want, not a need. Effective compliance was a good thing, management acknowledged. "We have a program, we'll look at it again, but there's no need to get carried away," they reasoned, particularly if they experienced no serious compliance problems.

The "no harm, no foul" approach meant that effective compliance did not rank high when competing against revenue-generating projects for limited resources. From management's perspective, increased compliance would be a smart investment only if they thought the company could land in serious hot water—that is, if noncompliance were *probable*. Otherwise, added compliance was seen as little more than an insurance policy, another lifeboat on what was perceived to be an overcrowded deck of overhead costs.

As a result, many corporate compliance programs are perfunctory. The sentencing guidelines' backhanded benefit generated very little deep-seated commitment or passion for compliance. It just wasn't much of a marketing platform. The consequences of sentencing were too far removed from the event that could cause *or prevent* the legal mishap. That's why more than a decade after the guidelines became law some general counsels are still unnerved by their company's ad hoc approach to compliance and worry about their compliance program's effectiveness. They wonder whether it would really pass muster if a meltdown led to sentencing.

The fresh wave of business scandals, including Enron, World-Com, and Parmalat, that hit the U.S. and international business scene near the turn of the century created a new level of concern and awareness about compliance in the business community. Suddenly the unthinkable became possible. Executives who were once heralded as corporate heroes, who had graced the covers of business magazines, were now being led away in handcuffs and disgraced in "perp walks" on the evening news. The scandals created a buzz about compliance. When the enactment of a new financial transparency law in the United States, the Sarbanes-Oxley Act, paired the disciplines of law and business in a shotgun wedding, the hastily arranged marriage pushed the role of compliance and corporate governance further toward the top of corporate agendas. It was a major stepping-stone in bridging the gap, and it created new impetus for reexamining business legal risk.

Another plank fell into place in 2003, when the fast food and snack food industries, concerned about obesity lawsuits, began to tout the virtues of healthy eating and began reformulating recipes. When a spokesperson for a major food company defended the practice, saying, "It was the right thing to do" and adding that if it "discourages a plaintiff's attorney because he or she would have an even tougher time trying to portray us as a company that doesn't care, that's OK with us," I realized that the stage was set for *The Business Guide to Legal Literacy*. Fear of the legal anaconda in the corporate chandelier was causing more businesses to become proactive. They now needed a comprehensive road map to maintain the momentum.

Even though a number of books have been written about business law, *The Business Guide to Legal Literacy* breaks new ground by offering a different way of thinking about this intimidating subject. It is the first book of its kind to connect the dots between law, decision-making psychology, quality management, organizational change, and leadership. It is also the first to explain how these disciplines influence legal risk exposure.

The purpose of this book is to cut through the fear factor of "The Law" by offering practical solutions to help you avoid lawsuits and embarrassing perp walks. It also shows you how to transform latent business legal risks that threaten growth and profitability into opportunities for developing more constructive business relationships that deliver sustainable shareholder value, more competitive edge, and greater excellence.

In twenty-five years of legal practice experience and through extensive research I have watched smart executives and managers unwittingly make the same types of mistakes over and over again. In the process I have seen patterns of cause and effect emerge, the kind of patterns that lead to the missing horseshoe nails that jeopardize transactions—and companies. *The Business Guide to Legal Literacy* identifies these patterns and shows you how to steer clear of the speed bumps and potholes. It puts you, not your lawyers, in the driver's seat of legal risk management.

More specifically, this book gives you tools and solutions that have been honed and polished over time. In the chapters that follow you will learn how to anticipate legal problems and use the law to your advantage. For ease of reference the book is organized into four key sections:

Part One sets the stage by showing how decision traps keep us stuck on a decision-making hamster wheel, how being stuck is costlier than ever before, and how legal literacy lets you pick and choose your legal risk, thereby avoiding unnecessary liability that detracts from your business objectives.

Part Two focuses on what individual employees can do: how you can improve your legal literacy and how you can use that knowledge to identify problems early. It shows you how to avoid the creation of smoking guns that fuel litigation, and how to manage expectations that strengthen business relationships through sound decision-making processes that balance business and legal risk with integrity and fairness.

Part Three takes the matter to the organizational level and identifies the infrastructure and the techniques necessary to support legal literacy and legal leverage. Effective knowledge management is the key to establishing an institutionalized reservoir of legal literacy, and effective communications are necessary to broadcast the role of legal literacy throughout the business enterprise. Business-minded legal counsel can provide coaching and act as a vital sounding board, while ethical leadership breathes life, legitimacy, and trust into the entire process.

Finally, the Appendixes offer several resources, including a legal primer that will serve as a quick reference guide to assist you in connecting the dots between core legal concepts and their business applications. It is not intended to be legal advice, but rather to provide a baseline of information that helps you ask the right questions sooner, rather than later.

The Business Guide to Legal Literacy will help you develop a better understanding of the law and a more structured approach to legal risk management. It won't turn you into a lawyer or be a substitute for one, but if it helps you avoid losing even one horseshoe nail and keeps you on the right trail—instead of en route to trial—I will consider the book to be a success.

January 2006   Hanna Hasl-Kelchner
Chapel Hill, North Carolina

HOW TO CREATE A WINNING LEGAL ATTITUDE

CHAPTER ONE

THE NEED FOR A PARADIGM SHIFT

A company uses aggressive accounting techniques and financial engineering to boost its earnings per share. On Wall Street, its market value soars and its senior management are among the most admired business leaders of their time. They reap huge salaries, even bigger bonuses, and lavish perks. One day the company's stock price falls and continues to drop precipitously. A subsequent investigation uncovers a financial rats' nest laced with conflicts of interest and self-dealing. The revelation rocks the marketplace to its very core and leads to federal criminal investigations, charges, individual indictments, and civil suits against the company, its accountants, and its bankers.

What went wrong here? What combination of decisions could create such catastrophic blindness and inertia? Was it an accident? Or were these results foreseeable and avoidable?

A textile manufacturer creates an innovative synthetic fleece fabric prized by the fashion community for its warmth and light weight. The company brands the product and obtains trademark protection for its brand name. Unfortunately it does not seek patent protection for the manufacturing process. Competitors are soon able to make the same fabric and sell it under a different brand name. The stiff competition ultimately drives the manufacturer into bankruptcy.

What do these two companies have in common? They both failed to manage their legal risk effectively. One tested the limits of the law, straining like a puppy on a leash. The other failed to take advantage of the law's scope. Both miscalculated the legal consequences of their business decisions. Both failed to develop their business sweet spot—and both lost shareholder value. It was a tremendously heavy price to pay.

Classic economic theory teaches us that organizations make rational decisions. It further defines a rational decision as one that maximizes *utility*—economist-speak for what the rest of us call maximizing value. Decisions that fail to maximize utility represent lost opportunity and *opportunity cost,* a cost that in accounting parlance is both variable and avoidable. Economists further reason that if maximizing value is rational, then decisions generating opportunity cost are irrational—at least that's what classic economics teaches us.

When applying classic economics to our two management examples, calling all the decision makers who contributed to the scenarios irrational sounds a bit harsh and simplistic. It's unlikely they were intentionally playing Russian roulette with their company's future. They no doubt thought they had good reasons for making the choices they did. But the quality of their decision making was ultimately flawed.

Business is a complex endeavor. These scenarios did not materialize overnight. They evolved gradually through a series of decisions. Numerous motivations and factors contributed to the end result. But something blinded these managers and executives to the ultimate consequences of their actions. They could not foresee how the legal aspects would play out. As a result, the cause and effect of a series of small miscalculations snowballed and buried them.

ELIMINATING THE BUSINESS BLIND SPOT

Even smart, seasoned business professionals can significantly underestimate the legal consequences of their business decision making. I noticed this phenomenon early in my legal career and at first thought this behavior was a bit odd, if not irrational. After all, if these business professionals had adopted the law as a tool for achieving business objectives rather than defining it as an obstacle to be avoided, the majority of their legal problems could easily have been eliminated or reduced. If only they had a better understanding of how business and law are intertwined. If only they had asked the right questions earlier. *If only. . . .*

At the same time, however, I recognized that traditional legal training and business training stem from different pedagogy and paradigms. The young manager is taught to embrace risk, the young lawyer to banish it. One is the curious puppy eager to jump on the next deal, the other a curious cat looking to toy with it. Both are curious. Both are eager and both appreciate risk, but they approach it from totally different angles. Without some mechanism for rationalizing the two temperaments, putting them together in the same room could only make the fur fly.

Eliminating business blind spots is not necessarily about zero risk tolerance. It's about taking smart risks, calculated risks, and managed risks. It's about capitalizing on mutual strengths and finding a business sweet spot. It requires a sense of balance. Lawyers need to recognize that not all legal risks are created equal, that is, that distinguishing the severity and likelihood of a given legal risk and prioritizing it in business terms is more valuable and leads to better joint problem solving than overwhelming clients with legalese.

By the same token, managers need to be able to recognize potential legal hot spots. They need to develop a better understanding of the law and how it affects their business, so they can ask the right questions sooner. Fostering an interdisciplinary approach improves the organization's ability to foresee problems and manage them effectively. It eliminates predictable surprises, saves time and money, and allows the company to be proactive instead of reactive. Eliminating the business blind spot is therefore about making smart choices.

If only they *knew*.

Translating Legalese into Business Speak

Our frame of reference plays a critical role in determining how we perceive and analyze the world around us. A Cornell University finance professor once told me that he would not grade the most brilliant financial analysis higher than a C if it failed to include tax consequences. He reasoned that whether an investment was profitable or unprofitable, or even *how* profitable, was determined by tax law. *All* of the relevant factors need to be considered.

While the financial impact of tax law on the bottom line is direct and easy to trace, the impact of other laws is more indirect and insidious. It's fragmented and scattered throughout the organization. But the cumulative trickle-down effect can nonetheless wipe out net earnings just as easily as a direct tax hit. The key difference between the two is that the cause-and-effect impacts of tax consequences are easier to identify and measure.

Business issues do not land on your desk with prelabeled solution sets or answer keys. And they certainly do not come with a legal road map. Even if they did, the worlds of business and law speak different languages. How we frame the issues therefore greatly influence our success in managing them. Tax is one of the few legal topics that translate easily to the bottom line. But without the ability to connect law and business directly and systematically to financial consequences, the significance of the legal aspects easily gets lost in translation.

Traditional business education focuses on accounting, finance, marketing, and operations management. It does not focus on managing the legal risk associated with these functions. As a result, it is difficult for most managers and executives to recognize the avoidable opportunity costs the legal system imposes on them. It is simply not part of their vocabulary or analytical skill set.

Since 2001, the business environment in the United States and abroad has been rocked by multiple scandals, and the regulatory backlash has left many managers fearful of lurking liabilities. Although the wave of ethics training intended to respond to these management lapses is useful as far as it goes, it is no match for the intricacies of the legal system. Thus we are left with too many of today's managers learning about legal risk management the hard way, through expensive trial and error—or worse, error and trial.

According to quality guru Philip Crosby, it is cheaper to build quality into a process than to catch mistakes later and then fix them. Therefore, incorporating legal considerations at the beginning of the decision-making process in a systematic and thoughtful way can make the difference between turbocharging or overcharging your bottom line.

Competitive organizations are constantly looking for ways to improve their processes. They want to excel, to be the A Team, not the C Team. Yet when it comes to managing legal risk, many managers leave it to chance. It makes you wonder: *Who is responsible for the legal health of an organization?*

Many managers would shrug their shoulders and say, "That's what lawyers are for." Yes, indeed. But their answer simply raises another: Who calls the lawyers? Or more important, How do you know *when* to call them?

TIMING

All too often, lawyers are called *after* a legal risk has escalated into a full-blown problem. When a 2005 survey of CEOs asked where the general counsel adds the most value to the company, 58 percent of the respondents answered managing legal issues. Only 12 percent responded anticipating legal risk. It means lawyers get called in more often to fix problems than to avoid them. The focus is on being reactive rather than proactive.

The results speak volumes about how CEOs perceive and apply their company's legal talent and how they view the role of law in their operations. In any other area of business a function expected to devote more than half of its time to firefighting would come under intense scrutiny. Inquiries would be made regarding what types of problems are being managed, and how the issues could be eliminated or reduced. A quality improvement program would immediately be kicked into overdrive.

Imagine for a moment interviewing a new vice president of manufacturing or sales and telling the candidates that most of their talents are to be focused on managing "issues." They would no doubt walk away thinking the system was out of control. A task force would be created to study processes and customer complaints. Recommendations would then be made on how to reduce defects, improve efficiency, and increase customer satisfaction rates. The recommendations would be reviewed, evaluated, prioritized, and implemented. Simply stated, the objective would be to squeeze out avoidable costs and rationalize the process.

Why doesn't the same thing happen with legal problems? Why does more than half of counsel's time need to be devoted to fixing problems instead of eliminating or reducing their causes? Why is more time spent on getting out of trouble than on staying out of trouble? Why do we accept these inefficiencies?

Unfortunately, when it comes to law and lawyers we carry baggage. Our perceptions influence our decision making. We might ask for legal help with litigation, complex financial transactions, mergers, acquisitions, and other high-profile events, but we prefer to handle routine transactions ourselves because the cost of a legal review is generally perceived to outweigh the benefit. *That's the way we've always done it* is often enshrined in the corporate culture along with a perception that *it's more trouble than it's worth*. As a result, legal risk is often trivialized and treated like an inevitable fixed overhead item, a mere cost of doing business.

A NEW FRAME OF REFERENCE

In recent years legal risk management has been given new prominence due to a string of high-profile business scandals in the United States and abroad. In 2001, just as some of the major scandals began to erupt, another survey of CEOs conducted by the Association of Corporate Counsel revealed that only 23 percent of the respondents identified legal risk management as a "critically important" role for their general counsel. Two years later, as the magnitude of the scandals unfolded and after the U.S. Congress adopted the Sarbanes-Oxley Act, a law intended to protect investors by improving the accuracy and reliability of corporate disclosures, the number of CEOs who thought legal risk management was important nearly doubled, to 44.2 percent.

Even though legal risk management was rising to the top of business agendas, the same Corporate Counsel survey also found that approximately 61 percent of the CEO respondents wanted their general counsel to focus more on corporate governance, the issue du jour, while only 37 percent ranked *anticipating* risk as the most value-added service provided by their chief counsel. As the memories of scandalous business headlines dwindle, so too does the perceived value of anticipating risk. By 2005 only 12 percent ranked it as the most value-added activity. What appeared to be the start of a paradigm shift has slid backward. Much legal risk is still being managed *after* a liability-triggering event has occurred, rather than in *anticipation* of it. The focus is still skewed toward getting out of trouble instead of staying out.

While a focus on corporate governance is commendable, from a risk management perspective it only addresses a small, albeit powerful, group of decision makers within the organization. Senior executives are, both figuratively and literally, only the tip of the legal risk iceberg. Below the waterline are hundreds of nongovernance decisions, large and small, routine and nonroutine, made throughout the organization each day. Each decision represents an opportunity to advance or detract from the bottom line. Each decision represents a link in the value chain of activities conducted by an organization to deliver goods or services.

THE VALUE CHAIN AND LEGAL RISK MANAGEMENT

The value chain concept was first used by Michael Porter, professor of business administration at the Harvard Business School, to describe the relationship among all the activities an organization performs to do business. More specifically, Porter says, "A business is profitable if the value it creates exceeds the cost of performing the value activities. To gain competitive advantage over its rivals, a company must either perform these activities at a lower cost or perform them in a way that leads to differentiation and a premium price (more value)" (Porter, 1985, p. 150).

When viewed in legal terms, the value chain lets us develop a better understanding of the organization's risk profile. It acts as a prism, refracting responsibility for the legal health of an organization across the full spectrum of employee activity. Identifying how, when, and where these legal risks are embedded in the value chain gives us a better understanding of our vulnerabilities. Best of all, it allows us to reverse engineer these processes and helps us develop a road map for improvement, for filling in legal potholes and improving our legal risk profile.

As a result, the legal leverage corollary to Michael Porter's definition looks like this:

> A business is *more* profitable *and more sustainable* if the value it creates exceeds the cost of performing the value activities *and the cost of the direct and indirect legal liabilities generated by the value activities.* To gain *and maintain* competitive advantage over its rivals, a company must either perform these activities at a lower cost or perform them in a way that leads to differentiation and a premium price (more value) *and eliminates or reduces unacceptable legal risk while simultaneously maximizing business success.*

We all know from experience that a chain is only as strong as its weakest link. What is tougher to see is how several slightly weak links can be just as dangerous to the organization as one spectacularly compromised link. Pinpointing these cause-and-effect relationships allows us to control the impact of legal risk on the value chain. It identifies when and where we need to install controls to protect ourselves.

Take, for example, the experience of Huntsman Chemical Corporation. In the early 1990s certain types of specialized compliance information resided in the environmental health and safety (EHS) group, while manufacturing process knowledge resided at the plant level. Both of these links in the value chain went about their business independently as separate silos.

Their failure to communicate meant that the plant was unaware of how changes in manufacturing processes could alter effluent discharges and lead to violations of the plant's various environmental discharge permits. Similarly, the EHS staff was unaware of forecast changes and other operational issues that could affect permit requirements. Only by appreciating the relationship between these links in the Huntsman value chain could the organization build a more constructive relationship between the two. Once the disconnect was identified, improving the timeliness of the information led to more compliance and better accountability. A small adjustment created a much better overall result.

Maximizing and capitalizing on interdependencies in the value chain requires a holistic approach that goes beyond the corporate governance requirements inspired by the Sarbanes-Oxley Act. Unfortunately, when organizations try to examine legal inefficiencies they often focus only on the links with obvious legal tie-ins such as the Legal Department or regulatory compliance areas. Such an analysis is good but not great.

Regulatory compliance, like corporate governance, *does* play a significant role in helping to maintain the legal health of an organization. But beginning and ending the analysis there misses important links whose decisions create the risk in the first place. That's why cracking down on the legal or regulatory compliance departments as a method of managing legal risk does not address the source of the problem. It manages a symptom. It's like mopping up around the edge of the shower instead of turning off the spigot. Mopping more efficiently makes you feel productive, but it does not address the underlying source of the problem.

THE MALDEN MILLS LESSON

Remember the competitive edge lost by our synthetic fleece manufacturer at the beginning of this chapter? That manufacturer was Malden Mills of Lawrence, Massachusetts, maker of the high-quality surface-finished fabrics Polarfleece and Polartec. Malden's legal failing was not a result of breaking the law but rather of failure to secure its legal rights early and to capitalize on them.

The company obtained trademark protection for Polarfleece and Polartec but neglected to patent the manufacturing process. Traditional compliance programs would not have caught that error because no law requires the patenting of inventions. The law merely provides the opportunity. It is up to the company or the individual to recognize the opportunity, seize it, and use it strategically.

What is even more heartbreaking about the Malden Mills story is that it happened to a company whose owner, Aaron Feurstein, was heralded for his altruism. He was named "CEO of the Year" by George Washington University and his folk hero status earned him recognition during the 1996 State of the Union address from President Bill Clinton. In September 2005 he was awarded a Leadership in Ethics Award by the Washington, D.C.–based Ethics Resource Center.

Why? On December 11, 1995, a boiler explosion at Malden Mills triggered a fire that destroyed three of the factory's historic buildings and a substantial amount of its manufacturing capacity. The operations meltdown put 2,400 jobs at risk in an economically depressed area of Massachusetts, just two weeks before Christmas. Many speculated that the seventy-year-old owner would cash in his chips, collect the insurance proceeds, and retire to a sunnier climate, or relocate his operation overseas to take advantage of lower labor cost.

Instead, three days after the fire, a company press release announced that Feurstein's first priority was to help his employees and return them to their jobs "as soon as humanly possible." To make good on his promise he kept everyone on full salary and health insurance benefits for thirty days following the incident while working to rebuild the plant in Lawrence. Feurstein's generosity would ultimately continue beyond the original thirty-day window; and, true to his word 80 percent of Polartec production was churning out warm, wooly fleece by the end of January.

The salary and benefit continuance program during the reconstruction period cost Aaron Feurstein $25 million. But rebuilding the factory cost $400 million, $140 million more than the insurance proceeds from the fire. The shortfall forced Malden Mills to borrow heavily. Unfortunately, the crippling debt load combined with increased competition in the marketplace proved to be too much. The insurmountable financial burden pushed the company into bankruptcy.

Had Malden Mills owned the Polartec process patent, the company's history might have been written differently. The near-monopoly conferred by a patent would have given Feuerstein the option of stopping competitors from using his process or requiring them to enter into a license agreement and pay royalty fees. Either path would have eased competitive pressures. One would have stopped the competitors cold in their tracks. The other would have had the added benefit of generating sorely needed cash flow. Either way, the patent would have been a strategic asset and contributed to the sustainability of the business.

A traditional compliance program would not have flagged the patent opportunity. Traditional compliance deals primarily with meeting existing legal requirements. It operates as a gatekeeper rather than a gateway for capturing legal opportunity. As a result, companies that take a narrow, compliance-oriented perspective on legal risk management are unaccustomed to the idea of recognizing and seizing legal opportunities, and ill equipped to do so when the occasion arises.

Managing a legal risk portfolio requires vision similar to that of financial portfolio management. It requires quality decision making and shrewd evaluation of performance processes. Risk needs to be anticipated and hedged as part of a systematic and progressive risk analysis process, which also needs to be synchronized and aligned with overall business performance objectives. It is a dynamic, not a static process. It is a process that is part of *everyone's* job.

LEGAL LEVERAGE: WINNING FROM THE BEGINNING

Courts use hindsight to judge business performance. Keeping courts out of your business therefore requires foresight. Recognizing the nexus between law and business sooner rather than later will put you ahead of the game. Better decision making lets you decide how much legal risk you want to reduce, transfer, or avoid. It lets you take smarter, more calculated risks and manage problems while they are still small and relatively inexpensive to deal with. It lets you leverage the law for competitive business advantage and start winning from the beginning.

Legal leverage offers unprecedented strategic value for building sustainable shareholder value. With fewer black eyes to defend in court, organizations can reallocate scarce resources previously used for litigation defense and other claims. Balancing legal risk in a thoughtful and responsible way thus creates a business sweet spot.

Legal risk is not a random event. It can be anticipated and mitigated. One of the key factors to success, however, is timing. The longer you wait the less options you have available, and instead of helping to shape the facts as they unfold you are forced to play the hand that is dealt you. Timing can work either for you or against you.

If you want to start winning from the beginning you need employees, particularly executives and managers, to take a greater ownership of legal issues early in their business decision-making processes. Employees are strategically positioned within the organization to avoid or minimize the vast majority of organizational legal problems simply because they are the business decision makers. It does not matter whether the employees function in senior or entry-level positions or whether their decisions are large or small. The legal literacy of all employees plays a role in an organization's ability to exercise legal leverage. *Employees* shape the deals at each step of the value chain and create the goods or services that the enterprise is based on. They know what is going on long before the lawyers do.

Managing legal risk well adds value to the value chain. To be effective at the process, however, employees need to be equipped with the proper legal tools. Unfortunately, most are unprepared to recognize routine legal risks in their embryonic stage.

For example, one junior scientist, proud of his patentable breakthrough, bragged about it in a scientific Internet chat room. Thinking that patents were already applied for, the scientist acquiesced to his online colleagues' curiosity when they pressed him to reveal details. Little did he know that his Internet chitchat was a public disclosure that started the one-year deadline ticking for protecting U.S. patent rights. When the scientist's employer de-layed its U.S. patent filing to conduct more tests, the one-year dead-line slipped by unnoticed until a patent was issued to a *competitor* for the same invention. Imagine the inventor's surprise. His lack of legal literacy translated into lost patent rights for his employer and lost competitive advantage. It probably detracted from his an-nual performance review, too.

Seemingly routine decisions can have a disproportionately large impact. A simple software agreement, for example, can pre-sent a serious business threat if the software happens to play a crit-ical role in your business and vague warranty language leaves you without recourse if defects subsequently crash your servers and strangle your daily operations. "I would have thought the contract would be fairly standard, but evidently that's not the case" is what one manager told me once he realized that the simple business transaction had legal implications that in turn carried operational risk and huge financial implications.

Connecting the dots from a boilerplate contract to the bottom line helped motivate this manager to negotiate the deal further. It broadened his frame of reference and led to better protection for the company and a better deal. Instead of glossing over ambigu-ous or unfavorable contract language, he was able to seek clarifi-cation with the vendor and avoid the kind of misunderstanding that could later escalate into conflict or a lawsuit. By managing ex-pectations well at the beginning of the transaction and reflecting them in the contract, he was able to shift unwanted legal risk while maximizing business objectives. He negotiated a fairer deal, trans-forming potential warranty liabilities into an asset. Such is the power of legal leverage.

IGNORANCE IS NO EXCUSE

Many employees and managers underestimate the complexity of the law and the risk that well-intended actions will later haunt them and their employers. They believe that if they act with integrity and simply follow their bosses' or customers' instructions, their good intentions will keep them and their companies out of legal trou-ble. Unfortunately, good intentions are not enough to keep you out of court, particularly in the United States.

Expecting vindication because you "didn't know" is a losing strategy. It's your business to know what is going on within your sphere of responsibility. When A. Alfred Taubman, the chief executive officer of Sotheby's, the renowned international auction house, was accused of participating in an antitrust price-fixing scandal he tried the dumb-CEO defense; the jury didn't buy it.

"Hey, the law's the law," shot back the Taubman jury foreman shortly after the verdict was announced. The juror's message is clear: ignorance is no excuse. If you work in a position of responsibility you are *expected* to know the score.

When investment banker Frank Quattrone was convicted of obstruction of justice for e-mailing colleagues and telling them to "clean up those files" after his firm had already received a subpoena investigating the firm's process of allocating shares in initial public offerings during the dot-com boom of the 1990s, one of the jurors said afterward, "We felt he had risen to the top of his profession: he was too smart to let this happen." The crux of the case was the defendant's intent, but the jury's inference about Quattrone's competency led them to believe that he knew or should have known that instructing a clean-up of company files relevant to the investigation was a problem and that the document purge was no accident.

Having employees develop legal literacy and understand the legal aspects of their roles is good business. Most legal problems start small, with nothing more than missed signposts and missed opportunities. The inability to read those signs is like driving down a one-way street heading the wrong way. Misinterpreting street signs flirts with disaster. To strengthen the value chain, employees must be able to read and follow the legal warning signs that appear like pop-up Internet ads but are drowned out by the drone of the daily grind.

Creating a higher level of vigilance throughout the value chain requires a systematic approach. Unfortunately, formal legal risk training, to the extent that it exists within an organization at all, is often limited to an occasional compliance course taken to satisfy a policy or performance review requirement, or to the faint memories left by a college business law course. Most employees learn about the law on the job through trial and error, by rote, or not at all.

We make dozens of decisions every day at the office and well over a hundred thousand decisions in the course of a career. Exactly how expensive our legal risk management mistakes are will depend on the business ramifications of our decisions. The opportunity cost, or potential for negative business impact, as illustrated in Figure 1.1, includes much more than the direct cost of a lawsuit, the court-ordered judgment, or a settlement (discussed further in Chapter Three). It also includes lost goodwill, ruined reputations, and negative public opinion that destroy market valuations as well as interfere with the sensitive windows of time that can make or break a new product launch. Without a proactive approach to identifying, prioritizing, and managing legal risk, employees are doing nothing more than gambling with their piece of the value chain.

FIGURE 1.1. POTENTIAL NEGATIVE IMPACT OF MISMANAGED LEGAL RISK.

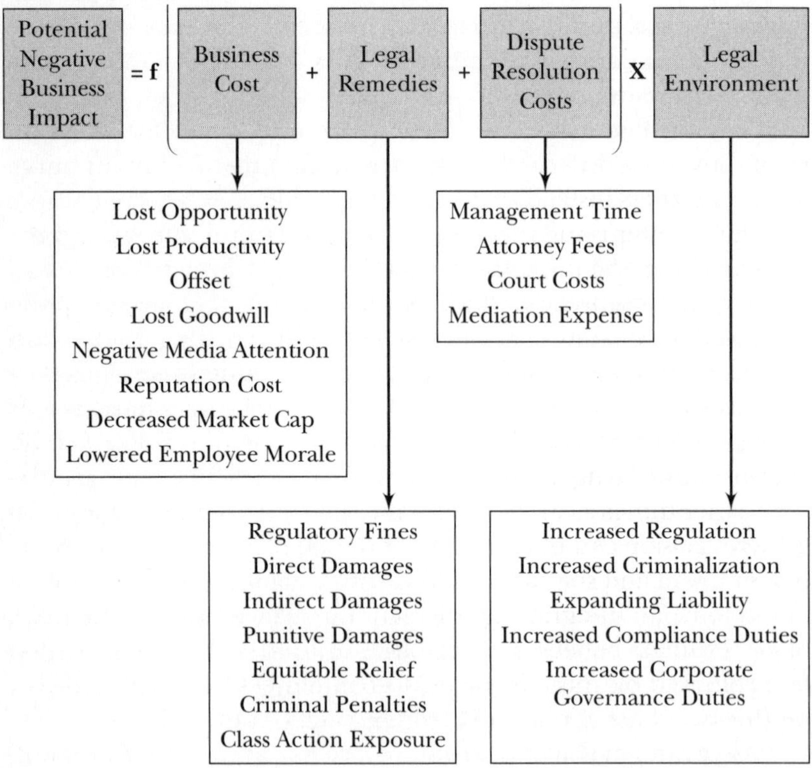

$$\text{Potential Negative Business Impact} = f\left(\text{Business Cost} + \text{Legal Remedies} + \text{Dispute Resolution Costs}\right) \times \text{Legal Environment}$$

Lost Opportunity
Lost Productivity Offset
Lost Goodwill
Negative Media Attention
Reputation Cost
Decreased Market Cap
Lowered Employee Morale

Management Time
Attorney Fees
Court Costs
Mediation Expense

Regulatory Fines
Direct Damages
Indirect Damages
Punitive Damages
Equitable Relief
Criminal Penalties
Class Action Exposure

Increased Regulation
Increased Criminalization
Expanding Liability
Increased Compliance Duties
Increased Corporate Governance Duties

LEVERAGING THE LAW FOR COMPETITIVE ADVANTAGE

Legal leverage seeks to systematically identify weaknesses in the value chain that threaten the company's legal risk profile, capture those missed opportunities, and translate them into profits. It is a process that assists decision makers in anticipating legal problems. It lets them use that knowledge to manage expectations, avoid lawsuits, build constructive relationships, and influence better business outcomes. The objective is to minimize, transfer, or avoid unwanted legal risk and to maximize business opportunity. It is not about hardball tactics, loopholes, or winning in court but rather about avoiding the courtroom brawl altogether if possible.

Anyone who has ever been involved in a lawsuit in the United States can testify to the fact that legal battles are no fun. At best, the process is time-consuming, expensive, and a diversion of scarce resources. At worst, in a criminal proceeding, it ruins careers, destroys families, and threatens the very existence of the organization. There are no winners, only those who lose less. The process can be expensive, unpredictable, and downright dangerous.

Few businesses have the luxury of generous legal budgets and even those that do are better off spending those resources building the business instead of defending it. Better resource utilization, including better return on investment, is one reason why smart decision making and doing what's right (instead of what's easy) make good business sense. Prevention is always a cheaper solution than going to trial or settling cases out of court.

Unfortunately, many managers discount the legal aspects of their business and brush them off as a cost of doing business. As with good nutrition and exercise, most of us know we should do better. But we struggle. It's not that we don't care, it's just that we treat other things as more important. We brush off the risk and justify the decision as a trade-off. But if we want better results, we need commitment and solutions—not casual trade-offs and excuses. Law needs to be an integral part of corporate life, part of the bedrock of our business belief system and operational protocol, not merely embroidered on mission statements. We need to change the way we think and act about legal risk and legal risk management. We need a paradigm shift.

CHAPTER TWO

HOW BEHAVIORAL ECONOMICS INFLUENCES DECISION MAKING

If we get the lawyers involved they'll find some legal issue that will delay the project. They always do. I think we can handle it ourselves. We've never had a problem before. Besides, we don't have time to get bogged down in detail. We need to make this project happen.

In my years of counseling clients and teaching MBA students I have learned that many managers are quick to discount legal risks and treat them as a cost of doing business, even before they know what those legal risks are. For them, embracing the law as a strategic tool is counterintuitive. It diverts their attention and is perceived as interfering with their business activities.

Take, for example, the situation involving an engineer under a tight deadline who was trying to fix a quality control problem on a production line. The product being manufactured would be subject to new government regulations within twelve months. Drifting specifications needed to be reined in by then. Time was short. He thought his chances of success in developing instrumentation would improve if he entered into separate joint development agreements with two vendors offering different technology solutions. His plan was to develop both of them simultaneously and use the prototyping phase of the project to determine which one worked best.

He had already fleshed out the project with each vendor and invested a significant amount of time and effort when he learned of patents that might be infringed by the projects. Instead of meeting his business targets, he was suddenly turning the company into one.

In twenty-twenty hindsight, it's clear that it would have been faster and cheaper to consider the legal aspects of the project sooner rather than later, instead of barreling along and then backtracking to design around the patents and evaluate patent licensing options. But since the law was not a part of the engineer's day-to-day frame of reference, he didn't factor it into his decision calculus. Nonetheless, once he saw how law and business are related he began to realize how managing legal risks *was* part of his business objectives. "Initially we treated this as *just* a technical issue," he acknowledged. "In the future we need to have more people, including the legal department, involved earlier doing things simultaneously."

Education appears to be an effective way to increase knowledge of legal issues and improve legal literacy. It raises awareness. But education by itself is rarely enough to create sustainable legal leverage. Unless the awareness is translated into practice and made part of a functioning skill set, it will disappear. It's a lot like learning a foreign language: you either use it or lose it.

One college professor tells of an undergraduate student who was a star performer in her business law course and later continued on to medical school. The student, now a young doctor returned to campus one day to visit the professor. The discussion turned to the doctor's hunt for office space to house her new medical practice. The former student recounted how at one office complex she visited the leasing agent remarked: "You're not one of those doctors who advertises, are you? Because if you are, we can't lease to you. We have a policy against it."

Instead of being outraged by a policy that was anticompetitive, the former star pupil missed the legal implications of what the leasing agent said altogether. Too much time had elapsed since her business law class. Her awareness level had faded. She was experiencing a learning paradox even though the course had been taught "by the book."

The phenomenon is not unique to law. Believe it or not, management guru Peter Drucker experiences the same phenomenon with his students. He says he is always appalled by how little statistics his business students know, even though it is a required core discipline. Marketing professor J. Scott Armstrong, of the Wharton School at the University of Pennsylvania, echoes the same concern. "I usually spend some time on the first day of a course by asking students to anonymously provide written descriptions of techniques that they learned," he says. "No matter how I word the question or how much time I allow, few students can report any techniques learned in a course, or even in a year or more of courses." Sadly, according to one university dean, "lots of students look at a course syllabus and ask themselves 'what do I need to pass?'" Once the requirements are met the information mysteriously evaporates. The course has been successfully completed. Graduation is one step closer. The material no longer has context and is no longer relevant. Mission accomplished!

These student examples demonstrate that it's possible to acquire lots of information yet learn very little. Organizations experience a similar learning paradox. They collect information and manage it, but translating that storehouse into institutional knowledge—and translating the knowledge into smart decisions and actions—takes more than a database. To appreciate this curious contradiction we need to examine *what* we allow ourselves to know, *when* we allow ourselves to know it, and *how* we allow ourselves to apply it. More specifically, we need to take a look at behavioral economics.

BEHAVIORAL ECONOMICS: AVOIDING DECISION TRAPS

Unlike economists, who study how decisions *should* be made, behavioral economists look below the surface at why we do what we do and how decisions are *really* made. They examine the birth of our habits by examining how and why we selectively filter information. According to the research, we are typically unaware that what we regard as "knowledge" is often based on tenuous assumptions, assumptions that cause us to accept or reject certain information, assumptions that lead to faulty judgment and to poor conclusions (Kahneman, Slovic, and Tversky, 1982). As a result, our decisions may not be as rational as we think.

The implications of this research for legal leverage are mind-boggling. It means that without systematic checks and balances to neutralize decision traps, we can often misjudge the nature and the magnitude of legal risk. Consequently, much of our effort to manage it may be misdirected—a result that is inefficient and costly in today's highly scrutinized business environment.

Behavioral economics first gathered momentum in the 1970s with the early work of Amos Tversky and Nobel Prize winner Daniel Kahneman. Together they identified thirteen decision traps that influence human judgment and decision making. Their scholarship is noteworthy for isolating cognitive biases and recognizing their systematic power to significantly affect our thinking.

Since business is forced to operate under conditions of uncertainty, it's essential that we recognize and sidestep the biggest decision traps if we want to tap into the power of legal literacy and select wisely among complex choices. With that objective in mind, consider the three areas most likely to contain traps that sabotage legal leverage: availability, overconfidence, and loss aversion.

AVAILABILITY

Behavioral economists have determined that experiences play a vital role in shaping perceptions of risk and coping with uncertainty. In particular, we draw on the past to predict the future. Behavioral economists call this coping mechanism "availability" (Kahneman, Slovic, and Tversky, 1982). In other words, how real is the risk? Is it believable and easy to imagine? Is it "available" to us? After all, it's tough to deal with abstract concepts that we have not experienced and that we believe we're immune to—just try warning a teenager about anything and you'll know what I mean. They tend to believe danger exists only after they've tasted it firsthand.

Although reliance on past experience is perfectly reasonable, further research has revealed that we do not weigh our experiences equally. The more explicit, dramatic, or sensational the event, the more emotional weight we give it and the higher we perceive its probability of occurring (Tversky and Koehler, 1994).

Do you remember where you were on September 11, 2001, during the terrorist attack on the World Trade Center in New York

City? Some events, like the tragedy now referred to as 9/11 or the assassination of President John F. Kennedy in November 1963, are so shocking and sensational that years later we remember not only the event but also the exact time and place we heard the news and what we were doing at the time. Yet we typically can't remember a more recent event, for example, what we had for lunch on Wednesday two weeks ago.

Did the World Trade Center attack affect your short-term travel plans? Did you hesitate when making airline reservations? Did you postpone or cancel any trips? Did it make you more cautious? If you answered yes to any of these questions, then you experienced the emotional tug of war between availability and rational logic. Statistically the risk of loss from a terrorist attack was the same the day before the twin towers' collapse as it was the day after; but emotionally it was worlds apart.

Prior to 9/11, the use of a highjacked commercial airliner as a guided missile was unthinkable to all but a few in the military intelligence community. What changed for most Americans was our *perception* of the risk of a terrorist attack. Concrete experience had transformed an abstract scenario into reality. The unthinkable became thinkable. Furthermore, the extensive media coverage ensured that the topic stayed top of mind. As a result, a low-probability event *appeared* more likely than the evidence would support (Slovic, Fishhoff, and Lichtenstein, 1982). That's the power of availability and an example of how information overload skews perceptions.

When dealing with legal risk, the challenge for any organization is finding the business sweet spot, a healthy balance between respecting the law and not letting business operations be subject to analysis paralysis, an endless stream of "what-if" scenarios. Too much information saturates decision makers and overweights risk, whereas too little information underweights the risk and emboldens risky behavior. Unfortunately, the increasingly hostile legal environment of business means that underweighted legal risks, the ones that are out of sight and out of mind but get triggered due to our own ignorance, can spiral into a full-blown crisis in a heartbeat.

The Denny's Lesson

Take, for example, the case of the Denny's restaurant chain in the early 1990s. A group of high school and college-aged African Americans entered the Denny's in San Jose, California, in the early morning hours on New Year's Eve 1991. Before being seated they were advised by the manager in an unfriendly tone that they were subject to a $2 cover charge in addition to Denny's prepayment policy. In other words, they would need to prepay their checks before being served. Denny's had allegedly experienced late-night problems with young people skipping out on their checks, but when the group asked to see the written policy, the manager refused.

Only African Americans were subject to Denny's late-night prepayment policy, even though the Civil Rights Act had made discrimination based on race illegal since 1964, nearly thirty years earlier. Regrettably, the connection between this law and the prepayment policy was "unavailable" to the wait staff twenty-seven years later on that fateful New Year's Eve. Had it been available, they might have recognized that such prepayment discrimination was illegal.

The San Jose incident escalated as the young people complained and then sued. More reports of Denny's discriminatory prepayment practices began to surface. Hundreds of calls poured into the company reporting similar incidents. The National Association for the Advancement of Colored People (NAACP) started to get involved, then the U.S. Department of Justice (DOJ). Privately, Jerry Richardson, the chairman and chief executive officer of Denny's parent company, TW Services, was horrified anyone would think he was a racist who ran a racist company.

Comedians referred to Denny's in their opening monologues. "Denny's is offering a new sandwich called the Discriminator," quipped Jay Leno in May 1993. "It's a hamburger, and you order it, then they don't serve you."

The DOJ later concluded that there was "evidence of a pattern and practice of intentional discrimination in a place of public accommodation" and demanded the company enter into a consent decree in lieu of being sued. Denny's was totally stunned.

Determined to set things right, Denny's signed a fair share agreement with the NAACP that set specific goals for how Denny's would expand the presence and participation of minorities in its business. It also entered into a consent decree with the DOJ setting forth an aggressive five-prong antidiscrimination program. Unfortunately, the very day the DOJ agreement was signed more trouble surfaced.

Twenty-one U.S. Secret Service agents, part of a detail assigned to meet President Clinton at the U.S. Naval Academy, had an hour to spare before the president's arrival and stopped at a Denny's restaurant in Annapolis, Maryland, for a quick breakfast. Identifiable in their uniforms (sporting the official presidential seal, badges, and gun belts), seven members of the detail were African Americans; six of them sat together at one table. After thirty minutes it was clear that no matter who ordered what, the six black officers had not been served while the rest of their group had. After forty-five minutes some members of the detail were enjoying second helpings of the All-You-Can-Eat Breakfast (a popular promotion at the time) and Caucasian customers who'd arrived a half hour later were already eating.

When the hungry table again asked their server about the status of the order she rolled her eyes as she walked away. Running out of time, they got up to leave just as one of their orders arrived. But it was too late. They could not keep the president of the United States waiting.

Unfortunately, the Annapolis incident, following so close on the heels of the DOJ consent decree, was a lawsuit and a public relations nightmare waiting to happen. Sure enough, shortly after the incident a letter arrived at Denny's headquarters from a plaintiff's lawyer demanding $10 million in three days. If the demand was unmet, it said, three simultaneous press conferences would be held to announce the filing of the biggest discrimination suit Denny's had ever seen. Unwilling to cave in to the pressure and believing that the new diversity pledge with DOJ adequately addressed the problem, the company declined the $10 million offer.

Suit was filed, only this time the story stayed in the news much longer than the San Jose incident. Two years later and after more than $75 million in fines and legal fees, Denny's eventually settled the case for $54 million.

To Denny's credit, in the years that followed, it has become a poster child for diversity and inclusionary practices. The NAACP voted Denny's chief executive officer CEO of the Year. *Fortune* magazine ranked Denny's among the top ten companies for minorities. People of color occupy a significant number of seats on Denny's board of directors, and minority suppliers provide goods and services. But Denny's newfound fame came at a heavy price.

The Denny's experience is a cautionary tale of how the concept of availability unintentionally influences decision making and legal risk management. In the *Denny's* case it interfered with employees' ability to adequately assess the nature and magnitude of their legal exposure and precluded early detection and timely resolution. As a result the smoldering problem flared into a crisis—not just once but twice.

Framing

A subjective lens of good intentions and the desire to protect its business interests defined Denny's frame of reference. The issue was not viewed through the eyes of the customers, the NAACP, or the DOJ. Denny's did not mean to discriminate against anyone, yet it happened. The dilemma pinpoints the fundamental problem of assessing availability: the need to consider *unavailable* possibilities and the need for an objective perspective. Without a process for self-evaluation, Denny's management simply didn't know what they didn't know. Their unintentional ignorance torpedoed availability and made it impossible for them to be proactive.

Research has shown that people prefer to act in situations where they feel knowledgeable or competent rather than in situations where they feel ignorant or incompetent (Heath and Tversky, 1991). The preference for staying in our comfort zone thereby serves to reinforce our existing frame of reference and feeds overconfidence.

In the *Denny's* case the management team's overconfidence about their commitment to the newly signed antidiscrimination program with DOJ just as the Secret Service crisis was unfolding caused them to misread the litigation tea leaves brewing in Annapolis. They miscalculated the magnitude and severity of the pending lawsuit. In the process they turned down a $10 million offer in 1993 in exchange for paying $54 million in 1995—not a good return on investment by any standards—particularly when you add in the fines and defense costs.

OVERCONFIDENCE

Overconfidence is a failure to appreciate the limits of our own expertise or available data. It silently dispatches availability by toying with our ego. Like car drivers who—despite tailgating and driving too fast—nonetheless complete trip after trip without mishap, we develop overconfidence that leads us to believe we're *good*. We owe our success to *superiority*—superior experience, superior knowledge, or superior skills.

Confidence is good, but overconfidence causes smart people to take unnecessary risks, risks that can trigger legal liabilities ranging from negligence to brazen malfeasance. Famous examples of disastrous overconfidence range from the "masters of the universe" who led the Wall Street insider trading scandals of the 1980s and the living-large culture of Enron and WorldCom to the information cover-ups by Wall Street superstar Frank Quattrone and domestic diva Martha Stewart. As illustrated in Table 2.1, the lack of availability, whether triggered by ignorance, overconfidence, or design (including self-serving interests), carries legal risk.

Even the most accomplished and celebrated business leaders can be seduced by overconfidence. In 2001, when General Electric's Jack Welch was negotiating the $42 billion acquisition of Honeywell, the deal was scuttled at the last minute because it failed to pass antitrust muster with the European Competition Commission. Certainly the need for European review had been anticipated, but the European response was not anticipated at all. The parties as-

TABLE 2.1. LEGAL CONSEQUENCES OF UNAVAILABILITY.

Unavailability	Characteristics	Corresponding Legal Risk
By ignorance	• Complacency • Don't know what we don't know	• Negligence • Strict liability
By overconfidence	• Invincibility and denial • Discount contradictory information	• Negligence • Strict liability
By design	• Willful blindness • Intentionally avoid or rationalize contradictory information • Conflicts of interest	• Negligence • Strict liability • Criminal liability

sumed that if the deal passed muster under U.S. standards it would pass under European standards too.

No one bothered to check the pulse of European competition law until the deal was nearly done. Had they done so they would have learned that the European interpretation of antitrust law differed significantly from the U.S. interpretation. The Europeans favored protecting competitors rather than competition per se. As a result, the GE-Honeywell deal that had sailed through U.S. review hit the wall in Europe. Had the deal structure been explored earlier with European competition lawyers they might have been able to restructure it to everyone's mutual satisfaction before the parties became too vested in their strategy. But they didn't and the deal died.

Regression

Overconfidence is a decision trap because statistically, over time the highs and lows of experience, like the ups and downs on a graph, continuously regress toward the mean—toward average. If we continue past practices because that's what we've always done, regression suggests our bad habits eventually catch up with us. One day we out-drive our headlights, lose the road, and crash. Our luck runs out. We encounter the prospective plaintiff who won't put up with a discriminatory meal prepayment practice, the one who sues us for big bucks. At that point the only risk left to manage is damage control.

Take, for example, the case involving hotel employees who were told about knee injuries that occurred during a "Sumo" style wrestling match at a hotel convention center. Apparently, the heavily padded suits designed to make contestants look like Japanese Sumo wrestlers did not always protect the contestants from injury. The hotel briefly considered the use of waivers to warn participants about the physical hazards of playing the game but decided against it. The game had been played before without incident and they didn't want to scare off any contestants.

Regrettably, the hotel's decision did not have a happy ending. Several days after the knee injuries occurred a man was paralyzed and later died from injuries sustained in a Sumo match. In the wrongful death case that followed the jury returned a $9 million verdict against the hotel.

Regression happens. Unfortunately, overconfidence works to our detriment, blinding us to inherent risks until the principle of regression slaps us in the face. Overconfidence shackles us by diminishing our desire for more information, blocking the amount of data available to us, and creating a false sense of security. It creates an information disconnect that shuts out more information than it shuts in. In the process we short-circuit our ability to avoid or mitigate unwanted risk.

In contrast, the availability of unbiased information *increases* competency. Better information through improved legal literacy allows us to consistently avoid or mitigate unwanted legal risk. It thereby creates a new set of behaviors and habits that consistently raises our level of performance to a new "average" high. It reduces the likelihood of erratic results and *hedges* the impact of regression. (See Figure 2.1 for a sketch of the effects of information disconnects and information flows.)

LOSS AVERSION

We love to win and we hate to lose. Actually, we *really* hate to lose. We value gains and losses asymmetrically and hate losing almost

FIGURE 2.1. THE EFFECT OF BIAS ON AVAILABILITY OF INFORMATION.

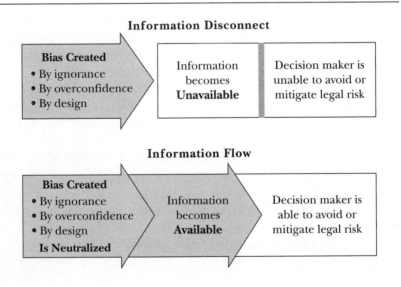

twice as much as we enjoy winning (Kahneman and Tversky, 1979). We are unhappy, for example, when a store charges us extra for using a credit card, but we are willing to accept higher prices if the store gives us a discount for using cash. Mathematically both scenarios yield the same result, but the way the offer is phrased makes one feel like a benefit and the other an unfair "take-away," or loss.

Context counts. We seek risk and are willing to overweight a small probability of success, for example, when we focus on the idea of winning the lottery, but at the same time we are risk-averse when it comes to losses and we hedge those losses by buying insurance. How we frame business issues, whether the glass is presented as half empty (loss) or half full (gain), can therefore make a world of difference in determining how much legal risk we ultimately assume.

When the owner of a family business was looking to sell his business and retire, the final negotiations started to stall over some environmental testing that needed to be done on the property. It involved the removal of an underground storage tank and some minor soil remediation. At issue was who would pay to yank the tank. The owner felt that he had conceded enough during the course of the business sale negotiations and was unwilling to budge any further even though the remediation cost was only $5000. To the owner it was a matter of principle. It was a loss, and he was stubbornly determined to avoid it. However, when a family member reminded him that he was letting $5000 stand in the way of retirement—a gain—he changed his tune.

In business our infatuation with loss aversion is personified by cost-benefit analysis. Although cost-benefit analysis is a valid exercise, it's only as good as the strength of the numbers it's based on. *All* relevant costs and benefits need to be included. The Dow-Corning breast implants, for example, only accounted for less than 1 percent of the company's 1991 revenues. Unfortunately the product liability issues surrounding that tiny portion of the bottom line served to plunge the company into bankruptcy four years later, when a number of class action suits alleged that the silicon implants caused serious health problems. If we allow overconfidence to gloss over the soft or missing numbers associated with latent legal liabilities, the math is self-defeating.

Take the *Quattrone* case, for example. After Credit Suisse First Boston received a federal subpoena investigating the firm's process of allocating initial public offering (IPO) shares among influential banking clients, Frank Quattrone, the mega superstar investment banker during the dot-com boom, sent e-mail to his colleagues, telling them to "clean up those files." Fear of personal loss related to being associated with the IPO process probably triggered the e-mail, but the e-mail unleashed even bigger losses. To the government, the e-mail was evidence of obstruction of justice. Quattrone was ultimately found guilty, fined, and sentenced to jail, as well as banned for life from the securities industry. He might have won the e-mail battle, but he lost the war. His brilliant Wall Street career was ruined. Had he framed the issues differently and known these costs up front, his actions might have been different.

The *Martha Stewart* case is also instructive. Her panicked cover-up of an Imclone stock sale was probably driven by a fear of loss resulting from the sale being connected to information about Imclone insiders' dumping large blocks of stock in advance of an announcement from the Food and Drug Administration about Imclone's cancer drug approval. As in the *Quattrone* case, the ultimate loss was substantially higher than the one she sought to avoid.

Convicted of obstruction of justice, Martha Stewart was fined and sentenced to jail. The drawn-out legal proceedings took a toll on the stock price of the company bearing her name, Martha Stewart Living Omnimedia Enterprises, and the reputation loss also made itself evident in the cancellation of her television show, the loss of advertisers, and the loss of her leadership position in the company she founded.

In a gutsy move to help stop the financial and emotional hemorrhage, Martha Stewart served her jail time while her appeal of the verdict was still pending. She realized that she needed to do the time in order to put the crime behind her and let the healing begin. The market response bore out her theory. Share values started to rebound and advertisers started to return almost immediately upon the news of her decision to accept incarceration. The market appreciated and valued Martha's accountability.

Obstruction of justice cases such as these are typically the result of actions that are panicked rather than planned. "It's done as a reflex," according to one former prosecutor. Thus it demonstrates how emotional reactions derail even smart decision makers.

Ironically, research has shown that when faced with uncertainty, we gravitate toward loss aversion *and* toward what we know

(Fox and Tversky, 1995). We prefer to deal with situations we feel knowledgeable about or competent in. As illustrated in Figure 2.2, this dual whammy isolates us further in our comfort zone. We stick with what we know because it's worked for us in the past. Yet staying stuck in our zone makes other relevant information unavailable and compounds our ignorance and overconfidence. The circular logic keeps us stuck in a closed loop, trapping us on a decision-making hamster wheel. As a result, we end up missing the big picture.

The Ford Pinto Lesson

Take, for example, the famous Ford Pinto case, *Grimshaw v. Ford Motor Company.* Designed to compete with lightweight, fuel-efficient Japanese imports that were flooding the U.S. car market in the early 1970s after the gasoline crisis, the Ford Pinto was stylish, competitive, and affordable. Unfortunately its gas tank design also left it vulnerable to explosion on rear-impact collisions, turning the vehicle into a Ford flambé and igniting a string of lawsuits.

Internal Ford documents revealed company estimates that the Pinto design could lead to 180 fatalities. Using cost-benefit analysis the company calculated that adding the necessary safety features to avoid such mishaps would cost $137 million. That number was

FIGURE 2.2. THE HAMSTER WHEEL: HOW LOSS AVERSION COMPOUNDS OVERCONFIDENCE AND IGNORANCE UNDER UNCERTAINTY.

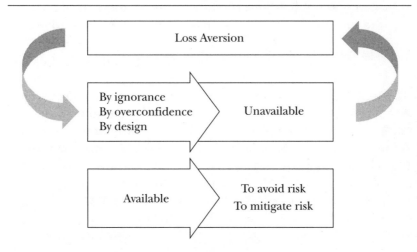

compared to the estimated cost of *not* making the safety changes. Using the National Highway Traffic and Safety Administration figure of $200,000 per death to calculate the liability associated with those fatalities, the company concluded that forgoing the safety features would only total $36 million. When framing the analysis in pure mathematical terms, living with the liability rather than incurring the higher cost for safety features amounted to a cost savings of over $100 million.

What at first glance appeared to be the cheapest solution, however, did not prove to be the least expensive. There's more to the equation than hard numbers. When the jury learned that the $137 million for additional safety features amounts to $11 per car, their frame of reference shifted radically. In the context of a single fatality it looked like the company would rather save $11 than a life. It transformed a human life into a trifling cost and an $11 cost saving into a coldhearted economic decision.

In the *Grimshaw* case the jury awarded punitive damages in the amount of $125 million. In its published opinion the Court took the extraordinary step of chastising the company for placing self-interest ahead of the public interest:

> Through the results of the crash tests, Ford knew that the Pinto's fuel tank and rear structure would expose consumers to serious injury or death in a 20- to 30-mile-per-hour collision. There was evidence that Ford could have corrected the hazardous design defects at minimal cost but decided to defer correction of the shortcomings by engaging in a cost-benefit analysis balancing human lives and limbs against corporate profits. Ford's institutional mentality was shown to be one of callous indifference to public safety. [119 Cal. App. 3d 757, 174 Cal. Rptr. 348, Cal. App. 1981.]

In 1999, General Motors was slapped with a similar verdict. Again, according to an internal memorandum, injuries resulting from car fuel tank fires were estimated to cost General Motors only $2.40 per vehicle while moving the fuel tank would have cost $8.59 per vehicle. The jury returned a punitive damage award of $4.9 billion. "We're telling [GM] that when they know that something . . . is going to injure people, then it's more important that they pay the money to make the car safe," said one of the jurors.

A better appreciation of punitive damages, jury perceptions, and the balance between public safety and profits could have led to better decisions in the Ford and GM cases. What initially appeared to be a smart cost savings lulled them into believing that only quantifiable costs are relevant. Behavioral economics artfully camouflaged latent legal costs until undesirable events and a jury exposed the emperor's new clothes for naked liability. For legal leverage purposes, hard numbers are where the analysis starts, not ends.

INSURANCE

"Mistakes happen," say managers, "that's why we have insurance."

Despite huge damage awards, many companies are remarkably willing to ignore and absorb latent legal risks in the belief that insurance is automatically available to pay their claims. While insurance certainly plays an important role in a company's overall risk management program, overreliance on insurance as a risk management tool is a flawed strategy.

Take employment practices insurance, for example. When it was first made available in the early 1990s it was a way for companies to protect themselves against unwanted sexual harassment claims and other types of employment claims. Rather than change the underlying behavior that could give rise to such a claim, companies turned to cheap insurance as an affordable Band-Aid.

As insurance companies developed more experience with claims made under these policies, they learned that harassment claims were more serious and more frequent than expected. The average jury verdict was over $1 million. As a result, some insurers stopped underwriting such policies altogether while the rest passed their costs through by doubling or tripling their premiums. As employment practices coverage became less affordable, companies were forced to reevaluate their internal compliance programs and address the root cause of these claims. They started to reduce or eliminate the risk instead of burying it as a cost of doing business.

On a broader scale, basic liability and property insurance in the United States has suffered a fate similar to employment practices insurance. The value of these policies has steadily eroded since the 1970s due to a flood of asbestos and environmental contamination claims. Overwhelmed with massive liabilities, insurers began trying to wiggle out of their responsibilities with self-serving policy interpretations. They contended in hindsight that certain types of losses were never contemplated by these policies. They often denied legitimate claims with a "sue me" attitude.

Health insurance fares little better. In 2000, Wellpoint Health Networks was among ten major health care providers named in a physicians' class action suit, accused of fraud for improperly rejecting claims and using computer software to automatically reduce payments to doctors for their medical services. In 2005, Wellpoint agreed to settle its portion of the case for $200 million. It thereby joins six other defendants who have already settled collectively in the neighborhood of close to $1 billion. Unfortunately, while these policy battles rage and wind their way through the court system, disgruntled policyholders and service providers who process these claims on behalf of policyholders, such as the physicians, are stuck in between the liability and a recalcitrant insurer.

Risk and the cost of insurance premiums go hand in hand. The higher the risk, the higher the premiums. As corporate scandals swept through the United States and Europe in the early 2000s, premiums for directors' and officers' insurance coverage increased proportionately to the market's perception of corporate governance and litigation risk. Unlike other goods and services, insurers do not offer volume discounts for policyholders with massive claims histories. Quite the contrary, in the United States they increase your premiums or drop coverage altogether.

When the Enron and WorldCom accounting fraud scandals made news, for example, their directors' and officers' insurance policies were nullified on the grounds that the insurance application referenced financial statements that were later proved to be false. As a result the officers and directors of these companies were *not* indemnified for shareholder claims made against them. Without company resources available to support them, their personal resources became at risk.

If you can't depend on insurance coverage to pay a claim when you need it most and you need to sue to recover a legitimate loss, your out-of-pocket costs can escalate quickly. On top of all that, insurance does *not* protect an organization against any and all losses. Some risks are simply uninsurable. Overreliance on insurance as a one-size-fits-all legal risk management tool is therefore a weak strategy.

According to Peter Drucker, good companies respond swiftly to problems while great companies anticipate them. The best insurance is therefore to avoid behavioral biases and poor decision-making practices that interfere with our ability to cultivate foresight and anticipate problems. Like black ice on a paved road, unavailability, overconfidence, and loss aversion cause decision making to lose traction, good judgment to slip, and legal risk to go up. When we slip and fall on our assets we lose leverage. But if we know where black ice is likely to crop up we can take precautions, tread more gingerly, and not allow our judgment to slip, or slip as badly. More traction leads to more effective legal risk management. Developing traction, however, requires a commitment to a solid framework of analysis and self-evaluation. It requires a process.

CHAPTER THREE

HOW LATENT LEGAL LIABILITIES ESCALATE THE COST OF DOING BUSINESS

There are three kinds of men. The one who learns by reading, the few who learn by observation, and the rest of them have to pee on the electric fence for themselves.
—WILL ROGERS (1879–1935)

Latent legal liabilities turn poor risk management into a high-voltage poker game. Just ask Warnaco Group. That company used to design and manufacture bras for Victoria's Secret, including the famous push-up Miracle Bra. It was business as usual until Victoria's Secret outsourced Warnaco's designs to other manufacturers. That's when the $90 million a year romance hit the rocks.

"They gave our bra styles to everyone else, and that's not fair— I'd rather not do it than share it with my competitors," Linda Wachner, Warnaco's then chairman and chief executive was reported as saying. Warnaco turned its back on the Victoria's Secret bra business and went back to the drawing board, determined to design something sexier than the Miracle Bra.

Although Victoria's Secret's outsourcing may not have been fair to Warnaco, it *was* legal. Had Warnaco done a better job of securing its legal rights early, it could have taken steps to stop the outsourcing, but it didn't. That error cost 8.5 percent of Warnaco's total annual revenue plus the time it took to ramp up new product development and the marketing costs associated with the replacement line, the Nothing But Curves bra.

This time around, rather than being overconfident about the strength of the business relationship with a customer, Warnaco got smarter about managing its legal interests. It took strategic steps early in the Nothing But Curves product development process to nail down and secure the intellectual property rights.

During the consumer-testing phase, a hundred women, who were asked to live with the garment, wear it, wash it, and give feedback, were asked to sign nondisclosure agreements to protect the confidentiality of all information relating to the new bra. Warnaco's experience illustrates how changing competitive alliances require more safeguards than the status quo or "business as usual." It also illustrates how small lapses in attention to the legal aspects of business can have a disproportional impact on the bottom line.

LEGAL WEAKNESS IN THE VALUE CHAIN: HIDDEN BUSINESS COST

Poor contract drafting and inattention to intellectual property rights were minor oversights, but it cost Warnaco a $90 million account and a host of new product development ramp-up costs just to climb back and compete with the business it had just lost. Little mistake. Big financial hit. And that was just one transaction. Imagine all the little cuts and nicks throughout the value chain—all quietly bleeding one drop at a time, silently hemorrhaging and dampening the profit picture.

We have already seen how small mistakes can have serious consequences. When Malden Mills failed to secure patent protection on its Polartec fleece manufacturing processes, the company lost its competitive advantage and allowed competitors to legally copy the technology and sell the same fabric under another name. When Huntsman Chemical compartmentalized engineering and manufacturing information into silos, the lack of internal coordination contributed to costly regulatory noncompliance. Similarly, when poor antitrust planning tanked the proposed GE-Honeywell deal structure, it plucked the crown jewel out of Jack Welch's storied reign.

An ounce of prevention can go a long way toward controlling latent legal costs. But it must be doled out consistently. It is not a one-time event; it's a process. Achieving legal leverage requires maintenance and periodic reassessment of the performance process portfolio. As my dentist says, "You only have to brush and floss the teeth you want to keep." The same holds true for your company's legal rights. How many teeth are you willing to lose? If you don't have time to secure your legal interests, you'll need to be prepared to have the bite taken out of your competitive edge.

The Yellow Pages telephone directory is a case in point. It was the sole occupant of the yellow page marketing platform until a competitor came along and used the same "yellow page" phrase to launch its own telephone directory. In their hearts the original publisher's leadership believed they had established a unique market niche that was being unfairly encroached by a competitor.

Legally, "The Yellow Pages" was a descriptive phrase that by itself was not inherently distinctive enough for trademark protection. (See the "Intellectual Property" section of Appendix B.) But over time, through extensive usage, the phrase had acquired secondary meaning that tied the product to a specific source of origin. The name had brand recognition. It was a marketing platform; it was an exclusive and unique space.

Secondary meanings *do* qualify for trademark protection, but in this case once secondary meaning was achieved the legal rights were still not secured. As a result, the yellow page franchise was left unprotected and vulnerable. A competitor was able to enter the same space with the same phrase. The new entrant in the field created the potential for confusion among advertisers whose advertising dollars the business model was based upon.

In a very real sense the failure to cultivate and maintain intellectual property rights left the revenue model unprotected. It touched the heart of the company's competitive advantage. The distinctiveness of the original directory's platform was shored up by the belated trademark registration of "The Real Yellow Pages" and "The Real White Pages," but the yellow page platform was no longer exclusive as a result of the initial failure to scope out the legal landscape and secure legal rights in a timely fashion.

INEFFECTIVE POLICIES

Business policies are a good way of managing the legal issues that permeate day-to-day transactional and operational issues. Indeed, businesses large and small routinely employ policies and guidelines to codify best practices and ensure consistency and quality in what they do and how they do it. Unfortunately, all too often employees treat policies as inconvenient restrictions, a business hindrance, rather than as tools for avoiding legal problems.

Such was the case for one of my executive MBA students, a mid-level manager at a Fortune 100 company, until one day in class—while we were discussing the subject of employment discrimination and sexual harassment—she had an epiphany. "*Now* I know why my company has the policies it does," she blurted out. Eureka! She suddenly realized that the purpose of these policies was to *help* her successfully navigate the intricacies of employment law and steer clear of potential legal problems. Sadly, not everyone makes the connection.

Policies that are viewed as speed bumps instead of speedways tend to be ignored and circumvented. One of the most annoying collection cases I ever worked on occurred when a salesman ignored the company policy requiring new customers to undergo a credit check. Not wanting to lose the sale, the salesman allowed personal loss aversion to trump the company's interest in loss aversion. He allowed millions of dollars in product to be shipped to a customer who couldn't afford to pay. When the customer subsequently filed for bankruptcy protection the company was among dozens of unsecured creditors looking to recoup a few cents on the dollar. Had that salesman reframed the loss potential from "me" to "we" the conflicting agendas could have been reconciled.

Unintended Consequences

In another case, a sales rep doing a favor for a customer ignored company policy and processed an order outside normal distribution channels. That single event set off a chain reaction that spanned two continents and ended with a bang.

Product was shipped from Belgium to the United States, where it was repackaged by a third party who failed to include highly specialized product warnings and safety instructions but nonetheless reshipped the goods across the Atlantic to The Netherlands, where the final customer attempted to further repackage the goods on his kitchen table. Unfortunately, without the proper warnings he did not know the product was highly reactive with oxygen. As he removed the product to repackage it, it made contact with air and promptly blew up in his face.

The explosion set off another chain reaction. The resulting fire damaged his thatched-roof duplex, including his neighbor's side, and the severity of the burns prompted him to ask for euthanasia as the ambulance sped him to the hospital. Although euthanasia is legal in The Netherlands, his request was denied. He lived through multiple reconstructive surgeries to pursue his claim.

For the company, the case turned into years of protracted litigation. Looking to cash in on favorable U.S. product liability laws, the customer brought suit in a U.S. federal court. But since the accident, the witnesses, and the evidence was all in The Netherlands, the company argued the suit should have been filed abroad. The court ultimately decided to let the case proceed in the United States, but ruled that the law of The Netherlands would apply.

The plaintiff did not take the news well. The ruling limited his chance of a handsome recovery and doubled his cost of litigation. He would need a U.S. lawyer to handle the procedural aspects and a Dutch lawyer to handle the substantive Dutch product liability aspects of the case. He was furious and fought the ruling, but not before making death threats to the judge, the company CEO, and the company's outside counsel. The case eventually settled, but it extracted a heavy financial and emotional cost from all parties involved.

These breaches of policy illustrate how casual risk management at critical junctures within the value chain can unleash severe unintended consequences. If left unchecked such negative chain reactions can engulf the entire company in scandal and send legal costs spiraling.

The Riggs Bank Lesson

Take, for example, the case of Riggs Bank, the venerable Washington, D.C., financial institution famous for being the bank of choice to foreign governments and diplomats, which held the personal accounts of more than twenty U.S. presidents during the course of its 160-year history. For years federal bank examiners had identified regulatory deficiencies regarding Riggs's ability to guard against money laundering by its customers, but they never fined or sanctioned the bank. Business continued as usual until 9/11 turned the smoldering compliance issue into a full-fledged crisis.

According to bank insiders and analysts, Riggs was slow to develop systems that could spot unusual or unexplained account behaviors designed to hide the origin or the destination of funds used for illegal activity. As a result, questionable transactions that should have been flagged went unreported. When the U.S. government stepped up its efforts to cut off potential sources of terrorist funding post-9/11, Riggs's casual practices put it squarely in the government's sights.

Within eighteen months Riggs became the focus of the biggest money laundering scandal in modern banking history. It's an intriguing tale that encompassed banking regulators, the Federal Bureau of Investigation, and three congressional committee investigations—and uncovered evidence that stunned Riggs's own board of directors.

There were allegations that Riggs accounts were being used to transfer bribes from U.S. oil companies to the dictator of Equatorial Guinea and that the Riggs Saudi Embassy account was linked to charitable donations that helped fund the 9/11 terrorists. The 9/11 finding would lead to a claim filed by survivors of the 9/11 attack and further increase the bank's legal headaches.

To make matters worse, evidence surfaced of possible *criminal* activities involving the Riggs accounts of former Chilean dictator Augusto Pinochet. References to Pinochet were reportedly communicated in code. Employees were instructed to use pseudonyms such as "Jose" and "Red Fox." Offshore shell companies were created to hide "Jose's" transactions from bank examiners while others were buried in suspense or concentration accounts that commingled the transfers with money from other customers.

These allegations led to *personal* liability exposure for senior management involved with the transactions. The former chairman and chief executive of Riggs, Joe L. Allbritton, his son Robert (who succeeded him as chairman in 2001), plus a Riggs board member who helped architect Riggs's international business, and the former account manager who handled the Pinochet accounts were added to a complaint by a Spanish judge who indicted Pinochet in 1996 for human rights violations of Spanish citizens. These victims of Pinochet's rule had been trying to seize his assets and extract reparations.

Riggs's stock price declined and short sellers lined up. Bank regulators designated Riggs a "troubled institution," and by May 2004 Riggs was fined $25 million in civil penalties for violating laws designed to prevent money laundering.

Aggravated by the growing financial pressure of mounting legal bills and a tarnished reputation, Riggs's financial performance continued to suffer. These troubles caused Riggs to seek a merger partner. In July 2004 PNC Financial Services Group made a $766 million offer to acquire the ailing institution, but by September the Pinochet allegations surfaced and criminal investigations were in full gear. For the third quarter of 2004 Riggs reported a loss of $10 million, most of which was attributable to the $13 million spent on lawyers and consultants since the legal nightmare began.

The criminal investigations put the merger in jeopardy. Under the terms of the merger agreement PNC could walk away in the event of a "material adverse change" in Riggs's financial or legal status. Such material adverse change language is a common provision in merger and acquisition agreements. It gives the buyer an insurance policy, helping to ensure that the buyer is getting a going business concern—a stable asset and not a deteriorating liability.

Hoping to clear the slate and salvage the PNC deal, Riggs agreed to plead guilty to federal criminal charges and pay a $16 million fine in January 2005. But PNC still sought to renegotiate the purchase price. By its calculation the $16 million fine was subject to approval by a federal judge and could be increased. All the while earnings continued to decline. Moreover, the growing number of legal problems assured that Riggs's armada of lawyers and consultants would keep the meters running and diminish future earnings forecasts.

PNC counteroffered a lower price plus a contingent security that could be valued up to 83 cents a share, thereby protecting PNC from the contingent liability represented by Riggs's legal woes. If the suits were quickly resolved Riggs would get a bonus; if not the liability was already factored into the purchase price. Riggs responded by rejecting the offer and filing suit to enforce the original merger agreement. More legal fees. *Ka-ching.*

The PNC deal eventually closed at a reduced purchase price of $650 million. But the Riggs experience points out how asymmetrical the cost of casual legal risk management can be. A single set of facts triggered multiple investigations and $41 million in civil and criminal penalties, shareholder and class action suits, claims from 9/11 survivors, and personal criminal liability exposure for individual officers. These added expenses detracted from earnings and created mounting financial pressure to find a merger partner. The continuing wave of scandal sank the stock price further, threatened to tank a merger, kept the bad news in the headlines for months, and damaged the reputation of a time-honored institution.

Even though the Riggs affair played itself out on a regulatory stage, cases that find their way into courts of law fair no better. Both avenues are fraught with latent risks that significantly increase the cost of doing business.

The Hostile Legal Landscape: More Hidden Business Costs

Once the whiff of a corporate problem makes news, high-speed communications networks ensure that the word spreads fast and that the plaintiff's bar will be in hot pursuit. When Merck announced the withdrawal of its Vioxx pain reliever in 2004 due to allegations linking the drug to an increased risk of heart attack, newspaper, TV, and Internet ads began to sprout like mushrooms after a rain. The news created a feeding frenzy among trial lawyers looking to cash in on the next big mass tort action. Some of the advertising was ethical, and some of it was not, but the consequences had to be dealt with either way. By November 2004 hundreds of plaintiff lawyers convened to lay the groundwork for a nationwide legal assault against Merck.

Large numbers of plaintiffs suing the same company can strain corporate resources to the breaking point. The silicone breast implant cases brought against Owens Corning illustrate the point. The massive number of tort claims paralyzed the company and forced it to seek bankruptcy protection.

The plaintiff's bar is highly organized and adept at cultivating litigation. Information and strategy is shared and settlements are used as war chests to fund bigger battles and extort even bigger settlements. There are even lawsuit tool kits available that make documents from prior litigation available on document Web sites. The practice assists other lawyers in suing the *same* company for *similar* claims by other parties.

Class Action Suits

When large numbers of plaintiffs with small individual claims that would not be worth bringing alone band together under the umbrella of a class action suit, they derive strength from their numbers. The class action phenomenon increases the likelihood that no corporate misdeed goes unpunished and exponentially increases the cost of minor missteps. That's what happened at Texaco when two employees filed a class action racial discrimination suit on behalf of all African American Texaco employees.

The case dragged on for nearly two and a half years, mired in class certification issues and discovery delays. Then in 1995 the class action plaintiffs found an unlikely ally in a white middle-aged senior personnel coordinator of the finance department, Richard Lundwall. It was the year Lundwall turned fifty-five.

Lundwall had heard Texaco managers say that employee productivity goes down when people reach fifty-five and he had also heard the company's chairman grumbling about Texaco having the oldest workforce in the industry. As a result, when Lundwall was asked to sit through a meeting about workforce reduction he thought it prudent to secretly tape it. His instincts later proved correct.

By December 1995 Lundwall was given his walking papers. He tried to use the tape recording to negotiate a better deal for himself since it included references to pushing out workers over fifty-five, but his pleas fell on deaf ears. That's when Lundwall decided to give the tape to the class action plaintiffs. Besides being dismissive of age, the tape made brazen and highly prejudicial references to black culture. It was a $176.1 million hand grenade. The plaintiffs turned the tape over to the media, which featured sensational excerpts on the evening news. It cracked the case wide open, leading to the landmark settlement.

Although class action suits and the debate about legislative steps to rein them in are largely a U.S. phenomenon, they have begun to migrate overseas. International business is therefore not immune to them. Great Britain and Sweden have recently permitted limited forms of class actions and Italy and France are considering them.

Civil and Criminal Liability

Some people are under the misconception that if there is a criminal conviction the legal principle of double jeopardy will protect them from additional liability arising from the same event. Not so. Double jeopardy only protects against the same *criminal* charge being brought. It doesn't immunize you or your company from civil liability—liability that can result from federal, state, or local laws, or all three simultaneously. One fact pattern can therefore trigger multiple hits.

In March 2005, for example, former WorldCom CEO Bernie Ebbers was found criminally liable on nine counts of securities fraud and other crimes related to the $11 billion accounting fraud that plunged the company into bankruptcy. In July the sixty-three-year-old Ebbers was sentenced to twenty-five years in prison. The *civil* portion of the suits relating to the collapsed company and Ebbers's hand in it, however, was another matter. To settle those class action claims, Ebbers was required to pay $5 million up front and to forfeit assets valued at approximately $40 million.

Diverted Attention

Curiosity over high-profile cases can capture the attention of investors, customers, business partners, and employees. When Microsoft found itself under antitrust scrutiny, its sales representatives discovered that customers wanted to discuss the pending litigation more than the latest product upgrades or new releases. The problem was so pervasive that it prompted Microsoft to create a booklet of frequently asked questions and answers to assist its sales force in addressing customer concerns.

Diverted Opportunity

When financial services giant Citigroup experienced a string of regulatory problems, the U.S. Federal Reserve Board barred the bank from making any major acquisitions until it put its regulatory affairs in order. The Board was fed up with Citigroup's woes, which ranged from the loss of its private-banking license in Japan to the European investigation into a bond-trading strategy (referred to as "Dr Evil") to the Italian investigation regarding potential securities laws violations in Citigroup's dealings with the failed dairy giant Parmalat. Tying the hands of a business known for its acquisition prowess diverted future business opportunity and was a huge slap in the face.

Even seemingly minor legal transgressions can derail future business opportunities. When the Cheesecake Factory Incorporated, for example, signaled it might miss the filing deadline for its restatement of financial results for the first three quarters of 2004 with the U.S. Securities and Exchange Commission, the NASDAQ stock market threatened the company with possible delisting of its shares. Even though the restatement had no significant impact other than to reflect adjustments to account for property leases, preserving the trust of the investing public through timely financial reporting is an important criterion for maintaining access to capital markets—hence NASDAQ's threat.

Unpredictable Juries

Headlines and TV shows have the potential to shape juror opinions and expectations. The conviction of the Media Vision Technologies chief financial officer in 2002 on five counts of corporate fraud led defense counsel to believe that jurors were unintentionally swayed by the impact of Enron-type headlines making news at the time. He felt it was the adverse publicity about corporate crime in general that was overwhelming. One of the jurors insisted the scandal-charged atmosphere had no bearing on the verdict, but did concede that the scandals raised "awareness that there could be wrong-doing in high-level corporate management."

Exactly how much people bring into the jury room with them and what effect it has on their decisions is difficult to prove. The facts of the *Media Vision* case may very well have led the jurors to the same conclusion regardless of breaking headlines, but their increased awareness no doubt heightened their distrust of corporate America. Whether such awareness is enough to bias or influence an outcome is uncertain. But the added layer of skepticism raises the bar proportionally for the defense and could make a difference in a case where the facts present a close call.

In the late 1980s and early 1990s it appeared that the image of jurors as out-of-control Robin Hoods who redistributed corporate wealth was overstated. Except for automobile accident cases the number of plaintiff victories had decreased and verdicts had moderated. But then along came movies like *The Insider* and *Erin Brockovich* and a string of scandals starting with Enron, and the antibusiness sentiment resurfaced. Some jury research skeptics, however, believe the antibusiness sentiment never really abated. The current climate merely deepened it.

According to one law firm partner, it's not that juries *dis*like corporations, it's just that juries hold companies—particularly big corporations—to a high standard because big corporations have a lot of power and jurors want to make sure that power is not abused. That may be true, but when jury expectations are high and company reputations are trampled in the court of public opinion even before jury selection begins, the legal risk factor goes up a notch, regardless of the merits of the case. The environment is simply less friendly.

The good news is that bad reputations are not illegal and that the layer of skepticism is not insurmountable. The bad news is that the effort required to jump the extra hurdle adds to the cost and increases the risk associated with litigation.

As if the antibusiness bias isn't enough, another potential jury hurdle is what some are calling the *CSI* effect: a phenomenon trial lawyers report as contributing to an increased incidence of juror misconduct. The term refers to the influence of popular television shows such as *CSI, Law and Order,* and *Court TV.* Hollywood-scripted investigations and evidentiary techniques are entertaining, but they raise juror expectations of what *should* be presented at trial. Some jurors go so far as to believe that they are qualified enough about the law to take matters into their own hands, even when doing so expressly violates the court's instructions.

Sometimes juror misconduct results in a mistrial, as it did in a California whistle-blower case where a juror conducted his own research instead of relying on the law and the facts presented in court. But in Virginia, when defense counsel spotted a juror leaving a convenience store with newspapers in hand, the judge denied the request for a mistrial after the juror denied the entire incident. Two hours later, the defendant was found guilty. It was not until the next day that the court finally granted a mistrial after defense counsel obtained the in-store video surveillance tape showing the juror buying two local newspapers and presented a copy of the receipt to the judge.

Defendants in a Philadelphia case were less fortunate. A juror was allowed to stay on the panel despite openly claiming to learn more about the case from the Internet than from the lawyers in court—and telling the judge so on the first day of trial.

Hardball Tactics

Once inside the courtroom, the risk can continue to multiply. If, for example, your opponents are recalcitrant or engage in a Stalingrad-type defense, filing motions and making objections because they *can,* not because they have any likelihood of success or any particular merit, the cost of litigation can skyrocket. Such motions do not advance the case to a fair resolution. Besides the added costs they only add unnecessary drama and can irritate the court.

"If the recent motion practice heralds what is to come, I predict that even with all the money and resources available to the parties at their fingertips, the victor will achieve something less than a Pyrrhic triumph. I urge the parties to reconsider whether a concede-nothing-take-no prisoners litigation strategy will advance their and their economic constituencies' best interest," advised Judge Jonathan N. Harris in *Bondi v. Citigroup* in response to the second application to dismiss claims after observing that the fifteen-minute oral argument was supported by the presence of at least fifteen lawyers associated with one side or the other.

The suit was filed by Enrico Bondi, the extraordinary commissioner appointed by the government of Italy to supervise the restructuring of the fallen Parmalat empire. He claims that misconduct at Citigroup contributed to the meltdown of Parmalat in 2003 and he's looking to recoup damages to the tune of more than $10 billion in Judge Harris's New Jersey courtroom. It is a high-stakes controversy that has erupted into a series of reciprocal Darth Vader–style death grips that is testing the court's patience.

"I have already issued a lengthy opinion adjudicating defendants' motions to dismiss. . . . In order to ease eyestrain, conserve ink, protect the Earth's dwindling forests, and avoid tedium, I will not repeat the background information," said Judge Harris. "While I generally appreciate a well-played match of hardball baseball, I cannot say the same for a campaign of hardball litigation that may have only limited utility in advancing the legitimate interests of the parties." He then expressly urged the parties to consider whether it's necessary to "churn the dispute."

Besides the procedural scorched-earth approach, another clever tactic is the use of professional actors to read into the court record the testimony of witnesses who are unavailable at trial. That's what happened in the class action lawsuit by former World-Com investors against WorldCom's auditing firm, Arthur Andersen. Former WorldCom chief financial officer Scott Sullivan took the Fifth Amendment, but an actor read into the record prior testimony wherein Sullivan pled guilty to the $11 billion accounting fraud. Typically, a lawyer, paralegal, or court reporter would have read the prior testimony into the record, but their flat line reading is no match for a professionally trained voice that brings life to the written word.

Professional actors have stage presence. They can project character and can color the testimony with nuances that would otherwise not exist. The actor standing in for Scott Sullivan, for example, reportedly improved on Sullivan's monotone speech and the tension betrayed in Sullivan's actual testimony by his hunched shoulders and squeezed diaphragm. While infinitely more entertaining and less likely to induce yawns or snores from the jury, the actor factor injects another element. In a close case the actor factor might make a difference. After all, if words were just words then roles in Hollywood would be fungible and anybody could read for a part.

Facing either form of drama, the procedural or the actor factor, feels like having your foot caught in the stirrup on a runaway horse. It's difficult and expensive to control and you get bloodied while figuring out what to do next. Eventually, making it stop becomes more important than making it right.

Electronic Discovery

Disorganized electronic files can send costs skyrocketing. When Lexar Media sued Toshiba America Electronic Components for alleged misappropriation of trade secrets, unfair competition, and breach of fiduciary duty, Lexar's discovery request included e-mail and electronic files for an eight-year period. Toshiba identified more than eight hundred computer backup tapes responsive to the discovery demand, but translating the data was estimated to cost between $1.5 million and $1.9 million.

As electronic communications and documents have become part of the business mainstream, such documents increasingly represent the bulk of document production in litigation. Historically, cheap data-storage solutions have made it easy to keep large quantities of data without organizing them in any meaningful way. But this unstructured data is difficult to review and costly to sort. The price of managing a hundred gigabytes of data in litigation, for example, which represents approximately 7.5 million printed pages, can exceed $1 million—and does *not* include the cost of attorney review.

The failure to properly maintain and produce electronic documents can be painful. When securities broker Laura Zubulake sued her employer UBS Warburg for sex discrimination, for example, she claimed the company failed to keep incriminating e-mail that would prove her case. The court agreed with her. When the company failed to produce the e-mail the court instructed the jury that it could make negative inferences from the lost documents. The jurors did. Then they returned with a $29 million verdict in favor of Zubulake.

Morgan Stanley, the investment bank, faced a similar unfortunate result. Electronic discovery was pivotal in its battle with financier Ronald Perelman over whether the bank had defrauded him when he sold the camping gear maker Coleman to Sunbeam in 1998. Perelman alleged he relied on the bank's representations in agreeing to the $1.5 billion deal and that the bank knew of Sunbeam's accounting fraud. According to Perelman the bank's failure to warn him misled him and Coleman into accepting the deal and caused them to sustain large financial losses when Sunbeam later went bankrupt.

When Morgan Stanley failed to produce the required electronic documents the court characterized the conduct as "bad faith." The judge then *shifted the burden of proof* in the case, saying the *bank* now had to prove it did not defraud Perelman. Shifting the burden of proof made the case easier for Perelman. The jury came back with a damage award of $604.3 million in his favor and sweetened the pot with another $850 million in punitive damages, making the grand total more than $1.45 billion.

Junk Science

Complex trials run the risk of jurors' being assaulted with junk science. Debunking those myths can run up the expert witness tab quickly. It can also raise legitimate fears that even with the best experts and lawyers the case is too complex for a jury to understand. The increased risk of an uncertain outcome creates pressure to settle out of court. It forces a comparison of the cost of settlement with the direct and indirect cost of taking the case to trial.

Unpredictable Results

Courtrooms are dangerous places. Even when the law is squarely in your corner you can never be certain of a verdict. The United States, for example, is notorious for its high damage awards. The potential for such awards has kept some foreign companies from entering the U.S. market and has sent some U.S. industries scurrying offshore.

Judges can be as unpredictable as juries. Their broad exercise of discretion sometimes approaches judicial activism, coming dangerously close to changing the law as opposed to merely interpreting it. Judicial activism steps on the separation of powers among the legislative, the judicial, and the executive branches of U.S. government and is illegal. However, in practice, judicial discretion is akin to a five-lane highway. It is extremely broad and, unless a judge swerves off into the shoulder, appellate courts are loath to use abuse of discretion as a basis for striking down a lower court decision.

You never quite know what lane a particular judge is in. Hugging the far right? Or the far left? Or safely motoring in the middle? As a result, some forums, such as Madison County in Illinois, are more hostile to business interests than others. Lower court decisions can be appealed, but again, favorable results are never guaranteed. Sometimes appeals can backfire, leaving the appellant worse off than before.

When CGB Occupational Therapy, for example, claimed a nursing home management company had tortiously interfered with its nursing home contracts by persuading two of the nursing homes to terminate their contract with CGB and then hired away five of its therapists, the jury awarded CGB $685,000 in compensatory damages and $1.3 million in punitive damages for a grand total of $1.985 million. The court of appeals overturned part of the verdict, reducing the compensatory damages to $109,000 and ordering a new trial on punitive damages. Unfortunately, the new jury came back with an award of *$30 million.*

The excessive damages were later slashed on appeal by $28 million, but do the math: the compensatory and punitive damage totals yo-yoed from $1.985 million after the first trial to $30.109 million after the second trial, and then back down to $2.109 million after the last appeal. The final tally of $2.109 million is more than the original $1.985 million awarded by the court, but the mere $24,000 price difference grossly understates the direct and indirect legal costs incurred to reach that final number.

Increased Enforcement

An ugly fact of corporate life is that the number of prosecutions by state regulators and attorneys general, such as New York's Elliot Spitzer, is going up and that prosecutors are increasingly hunting down executives at the highest levels of the organization. According to one law professor the point of all these high-profile trials is deterrence. The objective is to let CEOs know that even though the corporate governance system is broken and the likelihood of getting caught is slim, the consequences of discovery will crush you.

Increased enforcement sends the message that it is irrational to engage in fraud. Aggressive enforcement has also been used to expand the message to include even the *appearance* of impropriety. When Edison Schools, for example, took credit for certain monies that didn't actually flow through the organization, booking the sum as revenue *in accordance with Generally Accepted Accounting Principles (GAAP),* the U.S. Securities Exchange Commission stepped in. Apparently, violating the *spirit* of the GAAP was sufficient to provoke SEC action.

Deterrence may be the objective, but until the business community makes a *rational* connection between latent legal costs and the behaviors the law is trying to motivate, decisions will continue to be based on behavioral economics and the decision traps examined in Chapter Two. We continue to engage in denial, or, as Demosthenes instructed nearly two and a half millennia ago: "Nothing is easier than self-deceit. For what each man wishes, that he also believes to be true."

Until the connection is made, however, we will be forced to deal with more layers of law and regulation and will continue to read stories like that of Maurice "Hank" Greenberg, who led American International Group for thirty-seven years. Isolated in his palatial office suite, with private elevator, butler, and security guards, the seventy-nine-year-old Greenberg rarely heard a challenge from AIG employees or directors. People were afraid to test his authority, afraid of appearing ignorant, and afraid of losing face. When one director asked whether the company ought to consider reducing the ties between AIG and other companies controlled by Greenberg, Greenberg labeled the idea stupid, even though by then the Enron and WorldCom self-dealing scandals had been in the news for years. When faced with a government investigation about accounting improprieties involving these tight-knit entities, Greenberg reportedly railed against what he called a "McCarthy-istic" legal and regulatory environment.

Denial is a harsh mistress, and in Greenberg's case it detracted from an otherwise brilliant career. He retired in March 2005 in a humiliating ouster amid a brewing scandal when New York Attorney General Eliot Spitzer threatened to indict the company on criminal obstruction of justice charges after learning that records were being removed (and possibly destroyed) from Starr International, a privately held and controlled company run by current and former AIG executives, including Greenberg.

Trust is the currency of Wall Street, and no financial institution has ever survived such a criminal indictment. It would have been a death knell and destroyed the company Greenberg had spent nearly four decades building into a global powerhouse.

The indignity of retiring at age seventy-nine under these circumstances, however, is incalculable—a tragic ending to an otherwise brilliant career. What took nearly four decades to build was unseated in a few short weeks. Once Greenberg's retirement became a foregone conclusion, one AIG director recommended that he be named "director emeritus" in honor of the huge contribution he had made to the firm's development and to restore some vestige of dignity. The request fell on deaf ears.

High Personal Cost

The personal cost of being at the center of a corporate meltdown can be staggering. Take, for example, the case of former World-Com controller David Myers, the first of four WorldCom managers to plead guilty of securities fraud. His is the story of how one small decision turned into a personal hell.

The successful businessman and father of three led the good life through the late 1990s as WorldCom's stock continued to soar, inflating his stock options to more than $15 million. When the Internet bubble burst in 2000, however, price competition in the telecom sector began to squeeze WorldCom's profits and Myers was faced with a huge, life-altering ethical dilemma.

He testified that WorldCom's chief financial officer, Scott Sullivan, asked him to reclassify certain expenses. It was an accounting change that would materially alter the bottom line. He knew it was wrong at the time, but decided to follow orders. He initially believed Sullivan's explanation that the reclassification was a temporary Band-Aid and that business would improve. But business didn't improve. It got worse and the accounting hole got bigger, eventually turning into an $11 billion fraud.

When Myers saw no end in sight he began to spiral into a deep depression. Realizing that his Faustian deal would haunt his career, he even contemplated suicide. When confronted about the false entries by WorldCom's audit team, Myers confessed and the cleansing of his secret burden lifted his spirits temporarily. But his emotional roller coaster took a steep dive when he was advised to hire his own lawyer and stop confiding in WorldCom counsel.

Myers turned state's witness, but not before being fingerprinted and photographed by the FBI and led in handcuffs to the federal courthouse as cameras rolled and lights flashed. The waiting room for his court appearance was a jail cell. He counted the cinderblocks to pass the time.

To escape the paparazzi camped outside their door, his wife moved in with her parents in another part of town. The reverse in family fortune eventually caused the Myerses to downsize their lifestyle and move into a smaller home, but their five-year-old son doesn't understand what is going on and his mother hasn't figured out how to tell him why daddy might not be coming home for a while. What started out a small decision turned into a nightmare that created enough collateral damage to directly affect an entire family.

Disproportionate Costs

Indirect nonlegal costs are *at least three times higher* than direct legal costs. Uncontrolled legal risk is therefore an expensive land mine. The costs associated with those legal risks can be triggered when you least expect it and can least afford it. Once triggered, the legal process takes on a life of its own and costs are difficult if not impossible to rein in. Getting ahead of the legal risk curve is therefore a smart way to contain these risks that raise the cost of doing business. See Table 3.1.

Why does the legal environment of business keep getting more expensive and hostile year by year? When I first started practicing law, you couldn't go to jail for making an honest business mistake. Today you can. Has the system gone mad? What is going on?

Understanding the Rule of Law: Conquering Hidden Costs

The purpose of the rule of law is to drive behavior in conformance with the expectations of civilized society. In its most basic form the rule of law is a codification of ethics. When the rules get flouted, society responds with tighter rules or tighter enforcement, or both. In developed market economies it is the rule of law that provides stability and transparency, a vital component of commerce. It creates confidence. In 2005, for example, uncertainty surrounding the regulatory climate of China's telecommunications industry was a deterrent to foreign investment.

Things run smoother when everyone follows the same rules. It's as basic as the playground etiquette we learned in kindergarten. When a group of children gather to play a game, the first thing they do is establish the rules. In business the playing field is commerce and the rules are "The Law." The role of the rules is immutable. They set boundaries. They create expectations.

TABLE 3.1. LATENT LEGAL COSTS.

General Climate	Direct Cost of Mismanagement	Indirect Cost of Mismanagement
Expanded liability and new causes of action	Litigation lightning rod: • Multiple lawsuits, potential class action • Increased government scrutiny and multiple investigations	Diverts attention of clients, customers, business partners, employees
More laws and regulations in response to scandals and misdeeds	Court of public opinion influencing jury pool	Being implicated and named in your clients' or customers' lawsuits
Increased criminalization of civil offenses	Unpredictable juries and antibusiness biases	Drop in stock price and bond rating
Increased personal liability	Junk science	Reputation loss
Increased number of prosecutions and frivolous suits	Uncontrollable hardball tactics	Latent liability that jeopardizes pending deals
Organized plaintiff's bar	Business disruption	Tarnished personal careers
More media and faster communications channels	Damages, including punitive damages	Employee morale and exodus of top employees
	Government consent orders	Disrupted personal lives
	Judicial activism	Extradition
		Bankruptcy
		Increased risk aversion, erring too far on the side of caution
		Reputation rehabilitation

Most important, the rule of law is a dynamic force that evolves to meet the emerging needs of society. It is *reactive,* but it moves slowly, at a snail's pace. As economic needs grow in complexity, so too does the rule of law. In 1995, while in Beijing working on a joint venture project, I had the privilege of witnessing a local rule of law evolve firsthand.

Hungry for English-language news, I satisfied my craving by reading the local *China Daily.* One of the headlines that caught my eye involved elevator safety. The article went on to say that in 1994 approximately 30,000 elevators were produced in China, compared with 2,249 a decade earlier, that the country now had more than a hundred elevator manufacturers, and that the number of elevators in use had reached 150,000 (including some 10,000 imported elevators). Poor quality and maintenance had resulted in numerous accidents. Residents of high-rise buildings were regularly being trapped between floors, and one student at the Beijing Foreign Studies University was fatally injured when an elevator plummeted to the ground.

The *China Daily* reported that the Chinese government was implementing new regulations requiring elevator manufacturers to be held responsible for the quality of their products. The new law would also impose safety training and inspection requirements.

To those of us who ride elevators regularly, who take for granted the certificates of inspection that are prominently displayed, and whose legal system has a mature tort law, the perceived need for Chinese safety regulations may sound charmingly quaint. But from a legal perspective it is a glimpse into the evolution of product liability law. It demonstrates how the law keeps the emerging needs of a growing economy in synch with society's core values, in this case safety.

The law is designed to plug holes and fix problems. It is a quality control mechanism. When U.S. Internet users became plagued by spyware that infected and highjacked their computers without permission, the abuse of trust in online security slowed the growth of e-commerce and led to a new law that imposes fines and jail time to anyone who intentionally impairs a computer's security.

In crafting solutions, however, the law casts a wide net, micromanaging only when necessary. When the federal No Child Left Behind law went into effect in the United States, for example, it made available free of charge federally financed tutoring to families whose children attend failing schools. In the process it spawned a lucrative tutoring industry that education providers were eager to participate in.

Unfortunately, the law did not include any regulatory guidance regarding tutor qualifications or education standards to meet student needs. At one school on the West Side of Chicago, for example, six tutors failed to report to work one day, leaving seventy students to watch a "Garfield" movie instead of focusing on their reading and math skills. The uneven quality of tutoring services created an outcry for more regulation.

When quality slips to unacceptable levels the government can become your business partner through consent decrees that micromanage your organization (as in the *Denny's* case), through new laws and regulations, or through deferred prosecution agreements. Drug maker Bristol-Myers Squibb, for example, entered into a deferred prosecution agreement after it endured a three-year government investigation into a $2.5 billion fraud for inflating sales by getting wholesalers to overstock inventory, a practice called "channel stuffing." The deferred prosecution agreement allowed the company to avoid criminal prosecution if it could live up to the terms of the agreement for two years.

In the *Bristol-Myers* case those terms included the payment of $300 million into a shareholders' restitution fund, but more significantly, it provided for the appointment of an independent monitor who was empowered under the agreement "to take any steps he believes are necessary to comply with the terms of th[e] agreement." It gave the U.S. attorney the right to veto board members, thereby giving the prosecution an unprecedented ongoing say in company operations.

Whether we like it or not, when circumstances generate a public outcry the law steps in to fill the vacuum with new regulations and laws that clarify societal expectations and establish order. It's a quality control mechanism. See Figure 3.1.

GETTING AHEAD OF THE LEGAL RISK CURVE

From a practical perspective, the best way to avoid government intervention is not to give the government a reason to intervene. If

FIGURE 3.1. THE RULE OF LAW AS A QUALITY CONTROL MECHANISM.

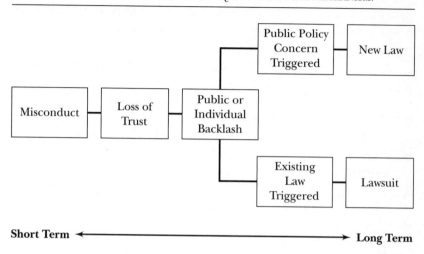

the elevator manufacturers in China had been more attentive to safety and after-sales maintenance, the industry would have been self-regulating. But they didn't, and instead the law did it for them—a regulatory smackdown.

In 2002, for example, when Enron's crown as the biggest bankruptcy filing in U.S. history was snatched by WorldCom, and both financial collapses were linked to financial engineering, the U.S. legislative response was the Sarbanes-Oxley Act (SOX), a law requiring greater financial transparency and accountability. SOX is a quality control mechanism designed to improve the accuracy of financial reporting and to restore the investing public's trust and confidence in capital markets.

When you stop and think about it, accurate financial statements are something companies *should* be doing anyway. It's how business keeps score on the real value it creates. But some companies are under the misguided impression that high-flying financial statements are ends unto themselves and that fluffed-up numbers create value. In reality, subverting the spirit of the accounting rules to fluff numbers is a fool's game. Eventually the market reality catches up to the fraud, and our old friend mathematical regression kicks the air out.

The DoubleClick Lesson

Compare the events surrounding the birth of SOX to the dilemma faced by DoubleClick, the Internet banner ad company. In 1999 DoubleClick purchased Abacus Direct, whose claim to fame was a database containing the household purchasing habits of 90 million households. The corporate marriage had the potential of taking direct advertising to new levels. The two powerhouses could add Web-surfing information to their database and use the combined data to personalize banner ads. The marketing potential excited many in the Internet community.

Unfortunately, privacy advocates got excited too. But for different reasons. They feared the marriage would lead to abuse of their personal information because now Web-surfing habits could be directly linked to a person's name and address and matched against offline purchasing patterns. The public flogging that ensued caught DoubleClick by surprise.

After attracting a lawsuit by the State of Michigan, a probe by the U.S. Federal Trade Commission (FTC), plus several civil suits, and watching its stock price slide in a few short months, DoubleClick decided to take action. It did an awesome about-face, announcing that until government standards were in place there would be no linking of anonymous Web surfing with people's names, addresses, or other personal information. Computer cookies would be tied to the computer, not individual users. Furthermore, the company would conduct a privacy audit and name a privacy officer to look after these issues.

"I made a mistake in moving ahead with these plans with no privacy standards in place," DoubleClick CEO Kevin O'Connor was reported as saying when the about-face was announced. His mea culpa combined with constructive steps to remedy the situation proved highly instructive.

The company recognized the need to *reframe* and communicate the decision to include public policy concerns. It decided to share information about how the databases were going to be used and not used. Best of all, it was able to address and manage the public's expectations without the government stepping in with onerous regulation or a consent decree. Admittedly, the suits and the government probe were motivational, but to DoubleClick's credit it took the hint. It didn't stay mired in overconfidence.

DoubleClick recognized the relationship between law, ethics, and public policy illustrated in Figure 3.2. Its leaders appreciated the fact that if they did not take appropriate action, the government's intervention would probably be more burdensome than their own self-restraint. Their strategy paid off. When the FTC report resulting from the probe was issued, the agency *endorsed industry self-regulation.*

Developing Foresight

Foresight is cheaper than hindsight when it comes to managing latent legal risks. Unless these risks are effectively hedged they're nothing more than land mines waiting to go off when you least expect it. Worst of all, you can compound the problem if you discover a land mine and do nothing about it. In that type of situation you or your company could later be accused of negligence or of a cover-up and charged with conspiracy to obstruct justice. The breach of any legal duty can be cost-prohibitive—and if it leads to a criminal conviction it can put you in a very uncomfortable position.

Sometimes it takes a crisis to jolt a company out of its complacency and improve its legal literacy. Hollinger International, for

FIGURE 3.2. THE INTEGRITY FLAME.

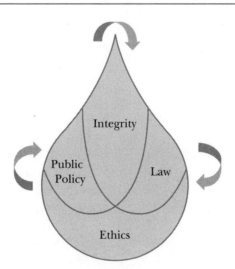

example, adopted a new code of conduct after its ousted chairman Conrad Black allegedly engaged in fiduciary abuses of the U.S. publishing group, using it as his personal piggy bank. And Mitsubishi Motor Manufacturing of America implemented a zero tolerance harassment and discrimination policy in the wake of a $34 million sexual harassment suit settlement in 1998, the largest settlement of its kind at the time. But some companies fail to survive the jolt long enough to rehabilitate themselves. It's a sad fact of corporate life that former employees of the now defunct yet formerly revered international accounting giant Arthur Andersen can attest to.

In sum, new markets, new customers, and new products are all terrific sources of revenue. But they yield little net gain if variable direct and indirect legal costs offset their profits. Legal risk sits like a third rail between sustainable business performance and good asset stewardship. Legal literacy and legal leverage, on the other hand, harness the risk and let you turn law into a business advantage.

CHAPTER FOUR

How Legal Leverage Creates Value and Competitive Advantage

Interdependence is a higher value than independence.
—STEPHEN R. COVEY (1932–)

Balancing and harmonizing competing business and legal interests to reduce the volatility of legal risk and its impact on your bottom line serves to manage the interdependencies between law and business. Such balance keeps you from being blindsided and creates a high-yielding state of operational business efficiency. It thereby lets you optimize the revenue streams and business opportunities you already have. It creates a business sweet spot.

Three key factors contribute to the achievement of legal leverage and the development of a business sweet spot: legal literacy, the ability to apply legal literacy, and an organization that lets you apply it consistently. See Table 4.1. The first step, developing legal literacy, involves building a working knowledge of the legal concepts and issues most relevant to your business and your specific job responsibilities. The availability of more information neutralizes the decision-making biases explored in Chapter Two. It makes employees more aware of the potential legal consequences associated with their actions.

TABLE 4.1. ELEMENTS OF LEGAL LEVERAGE PROCESS PORTFOLIO:
INDIVIDUAL EMPLOYEE AND ORGANIZATIONAL ASPECTS.

Information and Knowledge (employee focus)	Application (employee and organization focus)	Infrastructure (organization focus)
		Leadership commitment
	Manage document creation and retention	Healthy corporate culture
Neutralize decision biases	Manage expectations	Effective knowledge management
Legal literacy: human capital development	Translate legal obstacles into business opportunities	Effective communication systems
Effective communications	Effective communications	Business-savvy legal counsel

Legal literacy thereby sets the stage for the second factor necessary to exercise legal leverage: the ability to apply the legal knowledge responsibly. It's about utilizing the information to make smart decisions, to decide how much risk is appropriate for your organization. It's about developing knowledge, exercising good judgment, and making good choices. It lets you sidestep potential legal problems by managing expectations and influencing better outcomes. It thereby helps avoid misunderstandings and disappointments that later escalate legal risk into full-blown lawsuits and lets you leapfrog over the direct and indirect costs associated with latent legal risk—all those nasty costs discussed in Chapter Three.

Knowledge, however, and particularly the willingness to apply that knowledge, can flourish only in a supportive corporate environment. Hence the third factor necessary to achieve legal leverage: an empathetic organizational infrastructure and an encouraging corporate culture. When blended together, legal literacy, the ability to apply it, and a supportive environment form the foundation of a legal leverage process portfolio that generates positive tangible and intangible results.

Tangible cost savings associated with fewer lawsuits and lower compliance costs, for example, free up resources and can increase net revenue without the added expense of opening new markets, landing new customers, or developing new products or services. Freed resources can then be reallocated and invested in activities that facilitate growth, innovation, and improved competitive advantage. And that's just the stuff you can measure.

The Unmeasurable—and Immeasurable—Benefits of Legal Risk Management

Improving your company's legal risk management has the added benefit of building stronger business relationships and enhancing business reputations. Solid reputations and relationships create opportunities for competitive advantage that would otherwise not be available.

Enhancing Reputation

When Microsoft discovered that certain Xbox power cords had caused fires resulting in minor injury or property damage, for example, the latent legal liability caused the company to spring into action. Even though only thirty cases involved actual reports of damage and fewer than one in ten thousand consoles had experienced a failure, the company elected to close the window of liability in early 2005 by announcing an offer to replace the problematic power cords.

Given the rarity of a product failure, standard cost-benefit analysis could easily have led some companies to conclude that it would be cheaper to deal with the cost of occasional claims on an ad hoc basis than to replace power cords en masse. But the cheapest solution is not always the least expensive. What dedicated number crunchers miss, and what is difficult to quantify on a ledger sheet, is the domino effect intangible soft costs can have on overall business performance.

Keeping the old power cord in the market would not have been illegal, but it could have tarnished the reputation of the Xbox and Microsoft and cut into its competitive advantage. The Microsoft replacement offer came several months before the second-generation Xbox was unveiled in May 2005. Placing safety ahead of profits ensured that fiery mishaps stayed out of the headlines and would not detract from the new Xbox roll-out. Microsoft hedged the latent legal risk while simultaneously optimizing its chances of a successful product launch.

When the issue is reframed in competitive terms, the replacement program was a small price to pay for clearing an obstacle to a potential home run, particularly since the new Xbox was designed to allow Microsoft to go head to head with Sony for the leadership position in the video game market segment. The replacement offer was a way to generate customer goodwill at a sensitive time in the Xbox life cycle. The Xbox 360 was unveiled in mid-May 2005 and scheduled to go on sale at the end of 2005.

Juries, as we have seen, can be particularly unfriendly if they feel a company placed profits ahead of safety. By managing the product liability issue so effectively, Microsoft turned a reputation and product liability issue into a competitive business advantage. "Doing the right thing" was the fair thing and the smart thing to do.

FAIR DEALING

Perceptions of unfairness reflect poorly on business reputations. Yet when we look beneath the behaviors that bruise egos, hurt feelings, and cause finger-pointing, we typically find a legal issue. To live honestly, injure no one, and give everyone his due are precepts of the law, going back to the earliest written remnants of Roman law codified by Emperor Justinian in A.D. 533, known as the Institutes of Justinian or the Justinian Code. The notion of fairness is therefore one of the pillars of justice. It is a core principle upon which all legal systems throughout the world rest. Managing legal risk consistent with the teaching of the Justinian Code can thereby address one of the root causes of reputation risk.

In *The Transparent Leader* (2004), Dial Corporation CEO Herb Baum relates the story of how Reuben Mark, the CEO of archrival

Colgate Palmolive, called him one day to announce that he was sending Baum a computer disc containing secret Dial marketing plans that had fallen into Colgate's hands compliments of a defecting Dial salesman. Mark also said he was returning the disc to Dial unread. "It was the clearest case of leading with honor and transparency I've witnessed in my career," said Baum.

Mark's decisive action was also a preemptive legal strike. The disc was a hot potato. Being in possession of Dial's trade secrets without permission could have implicated Colgate in the theft. Accessing the information and acting on it to Dial's detriment could have made matters even worse by harming Dial and creating *actual* damages that could then lead to additional allegations of unfair competition. Not accessing the information but hanging on to it also could have backfired if Colgate's possession of the data later became public and one of its marketing strategies adversely affected Dial's market share. Therefore the best way to insulate Colgate from legal liability was to return the data immediately and not use it or access it. It was the honest and the right thing to do. The call from Ruben Mark was legal leverage in motion.

It took courage to make that phone call, but the risk of a cool reception was dwarfed by the latent legal risk associated with *not* making that call and the potential injury, alleged damages, and liability that might ensue. As evidenced by Baum's reaction, that act of integrity was appreciated and respected. Even archrivals must compete fairly. Ruben Mark honored the law's core ethical value of honesty with his act of integrity. In the process he averted a lawsuit and earned the respect of his rival.

INCREASING TRUST

Transparency is an important element of the trust-building process and is another essential building block of a good reputation. No one expects you or your organization to be perfect. But they do expect honesty and for organizations to tell the truth well. Honesty forges trust. It builds strong business relationships. When customers and shareholders believe in you and support you they are more likely to forgive minor transgressions that could otherwise lead to complaints and lawsuits. As a result, companies who do a great job of consistently conveying honesty and trust with the media have discovered they are better able to withstand and recover from business crises.

In 2000, when tire separation and roll-over problems plagued Ford Explorer utility vehicles fitted with Bridgestone-Firestone tires, Ford Motor Company spent more than $500 million on the recall. The crisis embroiled both companies for months, spilling over into the following year and spawning numerous lawsuits. At the heart of the matter was a safety issue. The incident rate raised questions about whether consumers could trust their tires and their vehicles. If consumer confidence got badly shaken it would damage both companies' reputations.

Reputations that take years to build can be tarnished in a mere matter of days or weeks and take years to rebuild. Some estimate it can take as long as four years to repair the damage of a bad reputation. Having an effective crisis management plan is therefore an investment. A survey of Ford's response to the roll-over crisis, however, showed that superior handling of the issue caused the company's reputation to bounce back almost immediately.

In the post-Enron environment more companies have become sensitive to issues of trust and reputation risk. These issues have risen to the top of corporate agendas—and rightfully so. "This is not a world in which you can sustain bad reputational impacts and balance them out by doing good elsewhere," according to one bank group vice chairman. "If you're to gain the benefit of the good you're seeking to do, you've got to prevent the banana skins from tripping you up."

He should know. Banking is one of the industries badly bruised by scandal. Ironically, in 2005, for the first time ever, bankers in fifty-four countries identified regulation as the number one perceived risk facing banks. Yet had they had a better understanding of the relationship between business and the rule of law and how their behaviors influence this delicate balance, they would have realized that their shameful behavior is what triggered the regulatory risk they now fear. They brought it upon themselves.

Had they been more astute in the past, they could have anticipated and mitigated the regulatory freight train—as DoubleClick did when faced with public outcry, a host of lawsuits, and the threat of regulation.

More Employee Satisfaction

Top-ranked college teams get their pick of top talent based on their reputations, a combination of excellent coaching, team skill development, high standards, and consistent results. Good reputations have a similar magnetic effect in corporate recruiting. People want to work for companies that are well managed and have terrific values and great corporate cultures. When corporate cultures are compromised by casual disrespect for the rule of law in compliance and decision-making practices, their business reputations suffer. This undermines the organization's ability to attract and retain star talent. When insurer Marsh & McLennan, for example, was charged with bid-rigging by Attorney General Eliot Spitzer in New York, the firm lost more than a dozen brokers in the weeks that immediately followed, including two employees known for their rainmaking skills.

Recognizing the career pressures a crisis environment can create, for example, Merck's board moved to adopt a golden parachute plan for its top 230 managers shortly after its stock dropped precipitously in the aftermath of its Vioxx pain reliever's being pulled from the market. The plan provided for enhanced one-time salary and bonus payments in the event Merck were taken over by another company. Although criticized by some as a sign of weakness on the part of Merck's directors, others recognized that the company had little choice. "I think they really felt they had to do this because otherwise people would start looking," one drug industry analyst was reported as saying.

Cumulative legal and regulatory setbacks prompted the investment banking firm Morgan Stanley to offer incentive packages in 2005 in an effort to keep key executives from being recruited by the competition. The incentive, however, failed to keep an eight-member stock trading team from defecting to rival Deutsche Bank and the co-head of the mergers and acquisitions division from joining Citigroup. The loss of the top dealmaker was reported as being part of an exodus of executives. Morgan Stanley's experience makes abundantly clear how employee retentions can't always be bought.

The best and the brightest members of the employee talent pool want jobs with "elbow room," a span of control over more than one business function, such as sales and marketing; and "headroom," the ability to make decisions independently without cumbersome layers of bureaucracy. Yet to make good decisions that keep reputations and employee résumés intact requires savvy management of business legal risks—it requires legal literacy and the ability to apply it consistently, a skill typically acquired through costly trial and error.

Legal literacy increases competency and performance levels that offset the effects of mathematical regression. Higher legal literacy rates thereby make it easier for companies to give high-performers the appropriate "headroom" they crave. Legal literacy also enables employees at all levels of the value chain to spot legal issues early enough to manage them while they are small and relatively inexpensive. As a result, it raises the bar on performance and makes excellence the new "average." It institutionalizes excellence.

Business decisions grounded in core values of honesty and fairness are ethical and also have the psychic value of allowing employees to feel good about their jobs. High employee satisfaction levels keep business reputations high, which in turn attracts other highly motivated and capable individuals. Morale soars. The benefit of good morale is more likely to lead to innovation and asset creation than bad morale. This is yet another way that legal leverage—a "soft" management issue—can generate hard returns.

THE FINANCIAL BENEFITS OF LEGAL RISK MANAGEMENT

Even though the law presumes a party is innocent until proven guilty, the market apparently prefers to hedge its legal bets. In a study of public attitudes toward corporations, for example, 65 percent said they would consider selling the stock of a company that is accused of wrongdoing in a lawsuit. Rather than depend on due process rights the market prefers to lock in accrued gains and hedge further losses by selling before the stock sinks lower. That's just the way it is.

There is a direct correlation between reputation, transparency, and financial performance. "If you underperform on regulatory, community, and social expectations, you destroy your own value," professor Robert S. Kaplan, the developer of the balanced scorecard, once told a lecture audience at Cornell University.

When Liz Claiborne, for example, sued closeout retailer Tuesday Morning for selling counterfeit Liz Claiborne jewelry at its stores, Tuesday Morning shares plunged more than 15 percent in the month after the allegations became public. Similarly, companies who sought to avoid the compliance costs of SOX, for example, and the financial transparency it affords, have seen their share price drop by more than 10 percent.

Investing is an act of faith. Investor support and trust depends on compliance and business prospects for growth, innovation, and profitability. The more publicity involved with an accusation and the bigger the scandal, the bigger the plunge in stock price. Worst of all, these costs are asymmetrical. What takes years to earn can be destroyed or diminished in a single act.

When concerns were raised about the liabilities involving fatal side effects linked to Bayer's cholesterol-lowering drug Baycol, for example, the news caused Bayer's share price to drop to a ten-year low. When Merck announced the withdrawal of its Vioxx pain reliever from the market in September 2004, its share price dropped 27 percent shortly after the announcement and drifted down nearly 40 percent by year-end. Paying attention to legal housekeeping issues protects capitalization. It's a smart business move.

Unfortunately, as Peter Senge, director of the Center for Organizational Learning at MIT's Sloan School of Management, says, "Company CEOs spend 90 percent of their lives making their companies look good for investors, not being good." Arthur Levitt, former chairman of the Securities and Exchange Commission, concurs. He has been reported as saying, "The business community tends to look at [financial reporting] in terms of what we can get away with, rather than what's right. Optics has replaced ethics."

Our innate penchant for loss aversion may explain why it's easy to be preoccupied with financial performance as an end unto itself, but it does not excuse the bias. Financial reporting is intended to *measure* performance, not *be* a performance. When financial transparency is obscured it means that real corporate value is out of synch with actual performance. At that point it's only a matter of time before the principle of mathematical regression lays bare that dirty little secret. The high-wire act loses its footing. The bubble bursts. The numbers fall and credibility, trust, and reputation fall with them.

Loss aversion is not an inherently bad concept. It serves a useful purpose. It makes us cautious. It conditions us to look both ways before crossing a busy street. But when loss aversion turns into a single-minded obsession, when we *have to hit the numbers,* and *have* to win at any cost, we lose our balance and trip into oncoming traffic. Obsessive behavior turns to unbridled greed, producing Enronesque results.

Fraud in any form is not a sustainable business model. Early Victorian advertisements are a case in point: the hucksters with their snake-oil-type promotions have all disappeared, but those who took pains not to overpromise, mislead, or deceive, such as Kellogg's and Campbell's Soup, have built sustainable businesses and real consumer value based on great, enduring brands.

Higher Return on Investment

Human capital is one of the few corporate assets that can appreciate over time. Studies have shown that when companies manage their human capital well, they can increase their market value by more than 10 percent. The average return on investment for every dollar spent on compliance training, as measured by reduced legal damages, settlements, and fines, is 37 percent. Furthermore, companies that at the beginning of the twenty-first century invested an above-average amount on training annually realized returns averaging 45 percent higher than the S&P 500 index.

"People make things happen," says Jac Fitz-enz, the father of human capital benchmarking. "Human capital leverages other capital to create value." Unfortunately, the downsizing, rightsizing, and outsourcing trends of businesses—driven purely by financial considerations—can have a chilling effect on human capital. They dehumanize the very human capital upon whose judgment and decision-making skills the organization must rely to navigate the shoals of legal risk.

Lots of companies say that employees are their greatest assets, yet few companies make the connection between well-managed legal risks, their corporate cultures, and their ability to retain top talent. Managing the employer-employee relationship can turbocharge an organization in multiple ways.

As competition for top talent increases over the next twenty years, so too will the need for legal literacy and legal leverage. A shrinking talent pool will develop as a result of shifting workforce demographics in the United States, according to a 2001 book titled *The War for Talent,* which is based on a report issued by the consulting firm of McKinsey & Company. McKinsey estimates that by 2017 there will be 15 percent fewer Americans in the thirty-five- to forty-five-year-old range while the 3–4 percent annual U.S. economic growth rate will increase the demand for labor by approximately 25 percent. The resulting gap between this shrinking labor supply and increased labor demand is expected to set the stage for a talent war.

To meet the growing need for qualified employees in the United States, companies will find themselves sandwiched between dual needs for legal leverage. On one hand, companies will need the benefit of an excellent reputation to give them a recruiting edge. On the other hand, the legal leverage process portfolio will provide the kind of best practices necessary to help new hires manage the company's legal exposures and protect its reputation.

When the shortfall in the U.S. labor pool causes more U.S. companies to rely on foreign labor, a labor pool that is even less familiar with the U.S. legal system and more likely to mismanage U.S. legal risk than their U.S. counterparts, legal literacy works to level the playing field and help protect the company. Indeed, the battle lines of the talent war are already starting to be drawn. China is already graduating four times as many engineers as the United States and Japan more than double. It is merely a matter of time before the need to innovate and stay in the forefront of innovation will require organizations to tap this rich reservoir of international talent.

Developing human capital with legal literacy and leveraging that knowledge is an effective hedge against an increasingly hostile legal environment. Research has shown that skills and knowledge are valuable when they are second nature and form an integral part of people's routines, like looking both ways before crossing a busy street. Making legal literacy second nature therefore provides unprecedented opportunity for leveraging the interdependence between law and business and developing the business sweet spot. Unfortunately, embedded skills are not easily bought. They must be developed.

As summarized in Table 4.2, the benefits of achieving legal leverage are many. It is a gateway to increased growth, innovation, competitive advantage, and organizational excellence. It strengthens business relationships, builds goodwill, and enhances reputation. In contrast, poor legal risk management is like swimming against a tide. It takes more sustained energy and resources to make incremental headway. A small error can have a disproportionate impact and can escalate into a legal surprise that drags you away from day-to-day responsibilities and forces you into damage control mode. In the worst case, an unfavorable verdict in a "bet the company" lawsuit can engulf the company in a tidal wave of debt, trapping it in a financial undertow that draws the organization with it into irretrievable bankruptcy.

WHY LEGAL LEVERAGE?

The costs associated with the consequences of poor legal risk management are higher than most managers realize. The legal leverage process portfolio offers a seamless method for reining in these costs and achieving compliance. Instead of sacrificing business performance, it actually enhances performance by anticipating and smoothing out the speed bumps and missteps that could slow you down. You maintain momentum.

More specifically, legal leverage is a pragmatic legal risk management process. It recognizes the dynamic relationship between law and business and offers insight on how to harmonize and harness the two. It lets you ride the tide instead of fighting it. It takes into account the various cause-and-effect flash points that naturally occur throughout the organization, how they touch third parties, and how they are touched by bureaucratic layers of management. It shows you what kinds of errors will lead to suits and what kinds won't.

Unlike traditional compliance programs that slap policies into place without cultivating the organization to make sure the policies will take root and thrive, legal leverage takes a holistic approach. It tackles legal risk from two directions. It looks at the organization from the top down as well as from the bottom up— and at the dynamic relationship between the two. See Figure 4.1.

TABLE 4.2. BENEFITS OF LEGAL LEVERAGE.

	Management Method	Results	Cost/Benefit
Legal Risk	Effective (with legal leverage)	Stronger business relationship	Save latent legal costs identified in Table 3.1
		More goodwill	More resources, including better talent pool, available for innovation, growth, and asset development
		More respect	Increased competitive advantage
		Enhanced reputation for: • Integrity • Fairness • Honesty • Trust • Transparency	Institutionalized excellence and enhanced performance
	Ineffective (without legal leverage)	Weaker business relationships	Subject to latent legal costs identified in Table 3.1
		More misunderstandings	Fewer resources, including diminished talent pool available for innovation, growth, and asset development
		More ill will	Decreased competitive advantage
		Escalating legal risk exposure: • Complaints • Claims • Lawsuits • Regulation	Institutionalized mediocrity and poorer performance
		Damaged reputation	

FIGURE 4.1. OVERVIEW OF LEGAL LEVERAGE PERFORMANCE PROCESS PORTFOLIO.

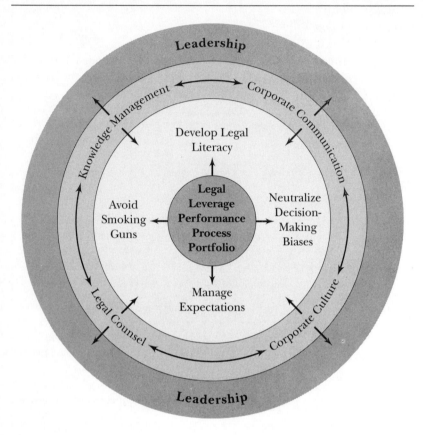

It squeezes out the unwanted legal risk resulting from behavioral bias and haphazard decision making as well as identifies the organizational infrastructure necessary to cultivate, build, and sustain a legally leveraged corporate culture—a culture that embeds the legal ethos into the corporate bedrock.

Legal leverage takes root by improving the legal literacy of the company's most powerful asset base, its employees. Once employees understand how the legal aspects of each job make a difference to the company as a whole, they can assume a greater role in the risk management process. Company policies make more sense.

Employees can take ownership of the issue in ways they previously couldn't. Their newfound sense of ownership creates a stake in the outcome and establishes buy-in.

The combination of know-how with *know-why* gives business policies context. It makes policies meaningful. When employees experience eureka moments like the MBA student I described in Chapter Three who suddenly realized the purpose behind her company's employment policies, the policies stop looking like inconvenient rules and become powerful tools that enable employees to perform consistently within the spirit and letter of the law.

Policies that are understood and respected as safeguards are more likely to be followed. They offer greater protection against corporate meltdowns. Establishing context thereby helps integrate policies into decision-making processes and leverages legal knowledge into asset creation and asset protection. Such behavior not only boosts the bottom line, it's a catalyst for enhancing reputations and achieving institutional excellence.

In the 1954 landmark work *The Practice of Management,* the first book to examine exactly what it is that managers really do, Peter Drucker described the purpose of business as creating value through the delivery of goods, services, and innovation: a value that is enjoyed by customers, shareholders, and society as a whole. In the more than half a century that has followed since Drucker's excellent work, the evolving rule of law and the slew of statutory and regulatory reforms, particularly the increased criminalization of corporate civil wrongs crowned by the Sarbanes-Oxley Act, suggests that the business community may have lost sight of its reason for being.

The purpose of legal leverage is to restore the equilibrium that is threatened by litigation and burdensome legislation and to avoid the legal headaches that divert resources and distract business from its primary mission. The chapters that follow examine how the legal leverage process portfolio can be applied to your job, your company, and your industry. I discuss how legal literacy can be used to avoid the creation of smoking gun evidence and how managing expectations can turn legal obstacles into business opportunities. I also explore the organizational infrastructure necessary to support and nurture legal literacy initiatives and applications and what it takes to incorporate legal risk management into the bedrock of corporate culture: the knowledge management issues, the role of lawyers, the role of effective communication, and the role of ethical leadership.

Legal leverage embodies the philosophy that the best defense is a good offense. It lets you get ahead of the legal risk management curve and make the law work for you instead of against you. It is the convergence of compliance and performance management that transforms the nexus between law and business into a business sweet spot.

PART TWO

HOW TO ACHIEVE LEGAL LEVERAGE

Developing Tools to Minimize Risk and Maximize Opportunity

HOW TO INTEGRATE LEGAL LITERACY INTO THE ENTERPRISE VALUE CHAIN
Who Needs to Know What

Being ignorant is not so much a Shame, as being unwilling to learn.
—BENJAMIN FRANKLIN (1706–1790)

Failing to cultivate legal literacy is like running down a football field or basketball court wearing a blindfold. The other team can steal the ball and you won't even see them coming. It's a strategic error that assists the competition. In business as in sports, the results can be disappointing, if not downright devastating.

You don't need to be a lawyer to manage your organization's legal risk. But you do need to understand the impact of your daily responsibilities on the legal health of your business. Being informed allows you to be more successful in what you do. It puts you ahead of the risk curve and makes you a more valuable team player. It lets you support the company vision more effectively. Sometimes being informed is as simple as reading the paperwork that crosses your desk. You may be surprised by what you discover.

Recognizing the Need for Legal Literacy

A customer account specialist who routinely signed order acknowledgments from customers thought she was merely signing receipts. She took the document's title literally and then aimed for the signature line. One day she actually read the words in between and was shocked to learn the document was more than a receipt. It was an acknowledgment of the *customer's* terms and conditions of purchase. Signing off on the form meant that the small gray print on the back of the *customer's* gray form would govern the transaction. The situation was a classic battle of the forms. (For more on this issue, see the "Contracts" section of Appendix B.)

Signing the acknowledgment might mean that the company was ceding territory on such important issues as warranties, indemnities, and even delivery. If, for example, the customer's terms stated that "time is of the essence," delivering the goods the day after the delivery date, even if it was only a stroke after midnight, would allow the customer to reject the order *legally*. If the item being delivered was custom-made and had no ready buyer, the company could be significantly disadvantaged.

Casual attention to the contract could mean the company was inadvertently promising more than it was prepared to deliver. It could set the stage for a future breach-of-contract claim *and* saddle the company with a difficult defense, because "a deal's a deal." The law assumes you will read the contract before you sign it, regardless of whether you actually do or not. Unlike consumer protections intended to protect ordinary Joes from the vagaries of commerce, the law treats businesses as sophisticated parties—hence the need to read. Unless you like surprises.

If the customer account specialist had been legally literate she could have recognized the potential problem and addressed the issue before it compromised the company's interests. She might, for example, have surgically removed the offending language with the stroke of a pen, added an addendum, or sought assistance from someone to help negotiate the issue.

Crossing out the unacceptable terms on the customer's acknowledgment and initialing the change would signify that the term was unacceptable to the company and reserve the company's legal rights until the issue could be properly addressed. The edit would not mean that the customer agreed to the change. The customer would also have to initial the page next to the change to make that happen. But it would at least indicate that the parties agreed to disagree on that one term.

Knowing and understanding what you're signing is prudent practice for *any* business document, particularly if your signature is a *certification, verification,* or *attestation* that vouches for the accuracy of the document's contents. Those are not fancy legal words for "sign here." They have precise legal meaning that can make you personally responsible and liable if there's a mistake.

The issue of personal accountability creates tension between the practicalities of being able to verify every detail the document is holding you accountable for and the ability to trust the employees preparing them. It's the same tension as between doing what's right and doing what's easy.

A chief financial officer of a publicly traded company, for example, once noted that for over a year he had been signing large numbers of signature sheets without reading or even knowing what was in the documents he was attesting. Apparently, he had such confidence in the person preparing bank agreements and SEC filings that attempting to review them would, in his words, have "hopelessly slowed things down, only to find that there were no problems." Nonetheless, even in a pre–Sarbanes-Oxley environment he realized that his habit was irresponsible, and he implemented a new system to balance expediency with prudence.

Legal literacy, knowing what you or your business can be liable for, is powerful information. Employees who understand the consequences of their decisions are able to make better choices. Better knowledge leads to better risk assessment. Better risk assessment leads to more efficiency, higher yields, and better overall performance.

Raising the bar on performance has the added advantage of neutralizing the negative impact of mathematical regression because the improvement creates a new and higher average. Behavior would therefore regress toward a higher, less risky mean. Legal literacy is thereby an antidote for the decision-making biases explored in Chapter Two.

DIAGNOSING BUSINESS HOT SPOTS

Organizations are studded with opportunities for small, highly targeted business changes that can make a huge legal difference. The challenge is finding them and determining which add the most value to your organization. Determining the organization's legal risk profile allows the company to target training and cultivate legal literacy where it's needed most. It helps you create a prioritized legal leverage agenda.

Targeted training is more practical and persuasive than a one-size-fits-all solution. Customization makes the law visible and relevant. The relevance factor reduces the risk that employees will tune out during training and increases the likelihood that they'll use what they've learned. Targeted training thereby hits the mark more effectively and maximizes the return on investment of training dollars.

LEGAL AUDITS

Legal audits offer a systematic way for companies to identify and diagnose business hot spots. The best legal audits, however, also look below the surface and connect the dots between the hot spots and the business functions and decision makers who create them. The added level of detail helps identify the organization's legal literacy requirements and creates a blueprint for customized training.

Traditionally, legal audits lack a well-defined identity, yet all involve some form of internal investigation. We could slice and dice them by subject matter (antitrust audit, environmental audit, contract audit, and so on), but for purposes of evaluating strategic advantage, it is more instructive to look at them from a business perspective, assessing the type of information they uncover and how the information can be used to advance business interests.

Legal audits fall in one of three loosely defined categories: *ad hoc internal investigations* (usually triggered by an urgent internal or external event such as a lawsuit, government subpoena, harassment complaint, or whistle-blower allegation), *regulatory compliance audits,* and *legal risk and opportunity assessments.* See Table 5.1.

How do we want to employ legal literacy? Do we want to be proactive or reactive in our legal risk management? Do we want to take advantage of legal opportunities and use the law offensively?

TABLE 5.1. SUMMARY OF LEGAL AUDITS: TYPES AND CHARACTERISTICS.

Audit Type	Ad Hoc Internal Investigation	Regulatory Compliance Audit	Legal Risk and Opportunity Assessment
Business objective	Compliance and cost avoidance	Compliance and cost avoidance	Compliance and cost avoidance
Nature of legal duty	Existing	Existing	Existing and future
Nature of legal tactic or strategy	Defensive	Defensive	Defensive and offensive
Behavior mode	Reactive	Proactive	Proactive

Or do we only want to use the law defensively? To cover ourselves in the event we're challenged? How we answer these questions influences what type of legal audit is best suited to meet our needs.

Unfortunately, compliance is often used too broadly: to mean too many things to too many people. As a result, the people involved head off in too many directions at once and are disappointed when they are unable to measure their progress. The objective of "being in compliance" or "using the law strategically" is a diffuse goal. The law's interface with business is too multifaceted for such simplistic treatment. That's why there is no one-size-fits-all plan or metric that satisfies all compliance interests and concerns. What's needed is a defined focus that takes into account the legal aspects unique to your industry as well as those unique to your company.

Keeping our objectives in mind frames expectations of what we expect an audit to achieve and thereby determines what level of legal leverage we can aspire to. We can then reverse engineer our goals to determine what behaviors, and subsequently what training, will be necessary to achieve those goals. Knowing where we're headed not only makes it easier to chart our course, it also makes it easier to chart our progress.

That's the beauty of keeping the end in mind. It keeps us from confusing the yardstick with what we're trying to measure. This is particularly important because much of the benefit derived from legal leverage is below the waterline. It is intangible and difficult to quantify.

Ad Hoc Internal Investigation

Ad hoc internal investigations are audits typically initiated in response to specific allegations. They are spur-of-the-moment and highly reactive. They occur, for example, after a company is threatened or served with a lawsuit. At that point the allegations can no longer be ignored and the organization must gear up to figure out what happened. Conducted under deadline pressure, the effort to get answers and find the truth takes on a sense of urgency as the company tries to extricate itself from the matter.

Government investigations and whistle-blowers can also trigger internal investigations. But unlike litigation, where rules of procedure govern the schedule and the pace of the process, the media attention and the near-crisis atmosphere of some government investigations and whistle-blower accusations create a fishbowl effect that magnifies the company's slightest move and intensifies the sense of urgency.

When New York Attorney General Eliot Spitzer, for example, filed suit against insurance broker Marsh & McLennan in 2004, accusing the firm of bid rigging and price fixing, the industry's open secret of contingent commission arrangements came under fire and quickly captured the media's attention. The spotlight caused Marsh to immediately halt the practice, which had yielded $845 million in 2003 and $420 million during the first six months of 2004, and to dismiss seven senior executives, including chairman and CEO Jeffrey W. Greenberg. The company was in damage control mode and was determined to keep a bad situation from getting worse.

Despite the fallout and drop in stock price, Marsh's swift action and clean sweep are credited with averting criminal charges against the company that some experts believed would have been fatal. As a result, the internal investigation was a huge success. The company's rapid response allowed Marsh to dodge a criminal bullet. But the ad hoc response was reactive—and reactive risk management carries its own special set of risks.

The Risk of Being Reactive

While I was waiting in line to drop off my car keys at the local tire dealer for a routine tire rotation, the man standing next to me asked what service I was having done that day. When I mentioned the tire rotation he was curious to know if I rotated them regularly.

"Yes," I said, "my job requires me to commute over a hundred miles each day. I need my wheels. Tires last longer when they're rotated regularly."

"I go as long as I can and only come in when something breaks," he replied. "I'm here for a flat tire."

If you don't have time to plan ahead, you need to be able to drop everything and make time for a flat tire at a moment's notice. You'll have no control over the matter. You're forced to operate on *its* timetable. Unfortunately, flat tires never happen at convenient times. That's the problem with reactive risk management.

Organizations that don't plan ahead and consistently expect to be bailed out cultivate a rescue culture. Making a habit out of waiting until something breaks increases the odds that multiple legal problems will happen at the same time. It's very risky to expect internal investigations to swoop down like a SWAT team and consistently rescue the company from itself. Overreliance on this method of risk management can lead to a system overload that traps you with insufficient resources just when you need them most.

That's what happened in the 1980s when the Prudential Insurance Company began selling limited partnerships through unlicensed individuals and promised high returns on investment. The marketing documents were sent to the legal department for review, but the lawyers there were too busy fixing another flat tire to spot their problems. They were jousting with an SEC investigation and were consumed with keeping the agency from filing formal charges against the company. As a result the marketing materials slipped through unnoticed until revelations of how investors had been bilked created a legal nightmare that ultimately cost the company more than $1 billion. The fiasco also caused Prudential's reputation to crash upon the very rock that for over a century had been its logo, its marketing platform, and its hallmark of trust.

Waiting for latent risks to blossom into full-fledged problems taxes limited resources. That's another problem with overreliance on the firefighting mode. It causes potential problems to be overlooked until they mushroom into bigger ones, at which point *they* become the fire du jour and the cycle continues. Meanwhile, over time—as bad habits are incubating into full-fledged problems—the bad habits are becoming accepted and commonplace. They are becoming embedded in the corporate culture. "This is the way we've always done it" is the corporate chorus.

Marsh's contingent commission practices, for example, were pioneered in the 1990s and were business as usual long before they appeared on Eliot Spitzer's radar screen. Had they been reviewed at the outset they might have been stopped. But once these commission practices became successful it is doubtful whether a subsequent proactive legal review could have weeded them out.

Doubtful? Yes, doubtful. Ironically, the more commercially successful the questionable behavior becomes, the more deeply rooted and more difficult it is to stop without strong leadership and objective decision-making processes (as discussed in Chapter Twelve). Who at Marsh would have wanted to explain the sudden loss of an annual $800+ million revenue stream? Loss aversion kicks in. It leads to denial over the severity of the problem and generates cover-ups. Not necessarily cover-ups in an obstruction of justice sense, of course, but still cover-ups in the "I don't want to deal with it" and "It's never been a problem before," "Don't rock the boat" sense.

Open secrets are prime examples of behaviors being held hostage by decision-making bias. Casual legal literacy protects these bad habits, entrenching them further and making it extremely difficult to exorcise them without outside intervention, typically intervention by a law enforcement agency. That's precisely what happened in the music industry when the common yet illegal practice of paying radio stations for air time to promote certain artists and records was revealed for the "payola" it was by New York Attorney General Eliot Spitzer's office.

Regulatory Compliance Audit

Regulations are the government's way of micromanaging your business. Regulatory compliance audits are therefore a more comprehensive means of avoiding predictable surprises than are ad hoc internal investigations. Similar to financial audits, regulatory audits are proactive and verify that the organization is following the appropriate rules.

What rules are appropriate is determined by various laws, such as those applicable to your particular industry, your organization's size, or its status as either a publicly held or private company, a nonprofit institution, and so on. Some employment laws, for example, only apply to businesses with more than a hundred employees.

Basically, regulatory compliance audits ask: Are you doing what you're supposed to be doing? If not, the business enterprise can be subject to fines and penalties and in some situations may even have a duty to report the noncompliance. When baby product manufacturer Graco, a unit of Newell Rubbermaid, failed for nearly a decade to report hundreds of injuries attributable to sixteen different products, the Consumer Product Safety Commission fined the company $4 million, the largest civil penalty of its kind.

The advantage of a regulatory compliance audit is that you get to find the problems and fix them before the government does. Doing it yourself is always preferable to letting the government do it for you. Fines and penalties can add up quickly.

Finding noncompliance issues on your own gives you the added bonus of retaining control over how to fix them. Consent decrees, like the one Denny's signed in the wake of its customer discrimination complaints, where the government becomes your partner and outlines *what* you have to do, *when* you have to do it, and *how* you have to do it, and then monitors your progress while you're doing it, are always more costly than an effective self-help program. Programs implemented in the wake of a scandal may be particularly heavy-handed if the government feels the need to set an example.

Government intervention can also lead to increased costs resulting from the efforts of inexperienced but well-meaning government employees. In one case a young environmental engineer, acting like a novice choosing a bottle of wine for an important dinner party, selected best available control technology based on price alone. As a result the company negotiating air permit compliance ended up paying significantly more for its technology than it would have if it had installed less expensive equipment earlier and avoided the noncompliance altogether.

Regulatory training is essentially a list of dos and don'ts with the dos being heavily punctuated with requirements of how the affirmative duties are to be performed. Compliance audits pinpoint regulatory nonconformance. They are therefore useful for identifying individual links in the value chain as well as interdependencies that create nonconformance and noncompliance. In the process they identify what training needs to be done to restore equilibrium. They identify where increased legal literacy will yield the greatest return on investment.

Chapter One details how Huntsman Chemical wrestled with an environmental permit Catch-22: manufacturing did not realize how production changes could cause manufacturing discharges to exceed permit limits while environmental engineers did not know about manufacturing changes early enough to apply for permit modifications. The source of the company's legal risk was multifaceted. It was a cross-functional issue. Once the company understood how and why the noncompliance occurred it was able to devise a better system of communication between the two departments.

The audit surfaced the problem, but a systems approach involving small yet timely changes is what remedied it. Now both departments could row in the same direction instead of working at cross-purposes.

Legal Risk and Opportunity Assessment

The legal risk and opportunity assessment audit is a three-dimensional top-line view of the organization's legal exposure. Instead of focusing on micro-legal issues, it deals with macro-legal issues: basic contract, product liability, and intellectual property issues, for example. It looks at past surprises to anticipate the likelihood of their recurrence and to learn from past mistakes. It also looks forward to anticipate changes in the current competitive and legislative climate in order to capitalize on the opportunities. Finally, it looks inward to evaluate how the law's business value can be mined and exploited for competitive advantage.

When a manufacturer, for example, saw damages, settlements, and fines related to product liability claims nearly double in a two-year period, the staggering legal bill demanded immediate attention. The company could have addressed the matter by merely dealing with the cost of legal counsel, perhaps negotiating a different fee schedule or changing counsel. But since the lawyers didn't cause the product to fail, that approach would have had limited value. It would have addressed a symptom, the high cost, and not the underlying cause of the product liability that generated the need for the increased legal services.

Instead, the company established a cross-functional team to isolate the source of the escalating liability. The team included research and development, purchasing, manufacturing, shipping and packaging, sales and marketing, plus the legal department.

The resulting evaluation revealed that multiple sources contributed to the company's product liability risk profile. The information was then used to target legal literacy training. Improving marketing's understanding of contract warranties, for example, allowed for better storage, shipping, and warning instructions as well as better sales training to manage customer expectations at the beginning of the product use cycle. Managing expectations up front helped reduce misplaced expectations that later turned into disappointments and escalated into claims (a point discussed further in Chapter Seven). Similarly, improving the purchasing department's understanding of product specifications and tolerances allowed for better vendor compliance with component specifications and less component failure downstream.

Improving the company's product liability profile also dovetailed with regulatory compliance. Providing a fresh perspective on nettlesome regulations gave research and development a better understanding of how the regulations affected product liability. The new information provided context and motivated R&D to build regulatory compliance *into* the product. Improving product quality in the invention process eliminated the need for Band-Aids later in the product's life cycle.

In sum, multiple functions making small changes had a huge impact and changed the course of the company's product liability history. Claims decreased by nearly 70 percent in the first year alone and reduced legal risks to more manageable levels. The legal risk assessment audit therefore laid the foundation for greater legal compliance and legal leverage going forward.

In addition to taming existing costs, legal risk assessment audits can be used to anticipate and control emerging legal risks. When Intel's then-CEO Andy Grove evaluated his company's growing market dominance in memory chips and microprocessors, he grew concerned that Intel could face the same competition and antitrust issues that led to the breakup of AT&T. Rather than sit back and wait for government action, the company devised a proactive strategy to ramp up employees' legal literacy of antitrust law.

Together, Grove and his general counsel, Tom Dunlap, established conservative internal compliance standards and launched an aggressive training program designed to galvanize the Intel value chain with antitrust. Although the program could not bulletproof the company from government scrutiny, it has been credited with reducing the risk exposure and keeping Intel from being as battle-scarred as Microsoft, AT&T, or IBM. As Grove says, "Since antitrust is embedded in everything we do, we can control our destiny."

Another way legal risk and opportunity assessments can be used is to ask: What legal tools and principles are available to help the business operate faster, quicker, easier, and smarter? How can the business enterprise leverage the law for long-term competitive advantage? How can the law's business value be tapped and integrated into a sustainable corporate strategy?

Astute contracting and the judicious use of trade secret, copyright, trademark, or patent law, for example, can add immeasurable value to your business. The Malden Mills example (in Chapter One) showed how the failure to patent the Polartec fleece manufacturing process put the company at a significant disadvantage in fending off competitors. The law does not require the use of intellectual property protection, but taking advantage of its provisions can certainly build assets and value.

McDonald's restaurants and their usage of the famous "Mc" brand prefix is an example of trademark law protection buttressing beautifully executed sales and marketing plans. Each trademark registration using the "Mc" prefix, from McChicken to McFlurry to McGriddles, adds to the McFamily and is another fence post cordoning off the "Mc" brand platform from competing uses. Consistent usage combined with aggressive enforcement makes the family of McDonald's trademarks among the most famous and valuable in the world. Those who try to use the same prefix without McDonald's permission will find themselves in McTrouble.

Trademark registration allows you to legally reserve and claim exclusive rights to certain words and phrases and create a near-monopoly on a brand name. It ensures that the distinctiveness of the name or phrase associated with your product is yours alone. It is a method for staking out market share and legally leveraging your marketing prowess—a valuable tool in any brand marketing arsenal.

Besides using intellectual property rights to protect brand recognition, you can also use them to generate income. In the early 1990s IBM, for example, realized its huge patent portfolio was an underutilized asset. Its staff began aggressively mining the portfolio for licensing opportunities. Within a decade it began generating more than a billion dollars in annual royalty revenue, which at the time represented approximately one-ninth of the company's annual pretax profit. Impressive returns, especially when you consider that much of that revenue came from licenses held by their competitors.

Licensing is a desirable strategy for any business, opening the door to piggybacking on competitors' sales. It lets *them* make money for you! Best of all, licensing requires very little overhead cost, making most of the royalty revenue flow straight to the bottom line. Now *that's* sweet.

Dolby Laboratories pursued a slightly different royalty revenue model. The makers of the Bolby B noise reduction system protected their invention with patents but licensed the technology in combination with the Dolby trademark for use on noise reduction buttons. Ironically, even though the patents eventually expired and could no longer generate royalties, consumers still wanted to see the Dolby name on their noise reduction buttons. The patent had set the stage for continuous trademark licensing of the name for use on the buttons.

When used and maintained properly, trademarks can last forever. Dolby's packaging of the two intellectual property rights served to leverage their legal horsepower in a creative yet highly effective way. It demonstrates a highly sophisticated use of legal leverage.

Employee Hot Lines and Ombudsman Programs

Legal audit results create a customized road map of legal strengths and weaknesses specific to your organization. Yet audits can often miss latent employment issues that are best ferreted out under the cloak of confidentiality and a veil of anonymity. To capture these potentially smoldering legal issues and keep them from erupting some companies supplement their legal audit program with hot lines and ombudsmen. These supplements allow employees to report suspected problems anonymously, without fear of retribution. When combined with the audit data the supplemental information helps fine-tune the contours of the organization's legal risk profile. However, international companies must always be mindful of foreign laws that may apply to anonymous hot lines. In the European Union, for example, the anonymous hot line obligations imposed by Sarbanes-Oxley may conflict with employment laws, human rights and data protection laws, and also run into the historical and cultural stigma attached to whistleblowers as informers. In Germany, for example, Wal-Mart encountered a problem when it established a whistle-blower hot line but failed to take consideration of the German workers' right of co-determination which is protected under the German Works Council Act.

FROM DIAGNOSIS TO IMPLEMENTATION

Regardless of what type of legal audit is pursued, it is important for the audit to identify the hot button business issues as well as their underlying causes. Without identification of these risky behaviors and the systems that support them, remedial action is nothing more than a superficial fix. The problem will recur. Zeroing in on the cause-and-effect relationship is the only way to seize strategic opportunities and manage the risk effectively.

According to organizational learning expert Peter Senge, "We learn best from experience but we never directly experience the consequences of many of our most important decisions." Unfor-tunately, in companies where decision making is highly specialized and fragmented, legal risk is often not evident until it evolves into a claim, a lawsuit, or a regulatory enforcement proceeding. At that point it is typically handed off to the legal or compliance depart-ment. Suddenly it's *their* problem. The decision makers who un-wittingly contributed to a company's liability are often unaware and remain isolated from the problem. Ironically, if they remain clue-less they are destined to make the same mistakes in the future.

Establishing minimal legal literacy requirements for decision makers minimizes cluelessness. It delegates responsibility for legal risk management where it belongs, to the people most likely to incur or avoid legal risks. It puts the employees, not the company lawyers, in the driver's seat of legal risk management. Over time, as employees become legally proficient, they will be able to inte-grate best practices into their daily routines and facilitate legal leverage by diminishing the overall risk exposure for the company.

Legal literacy thereby improves the quality of frontline decisions and allows organizations to identify potential problems early. It contributes to sustainable performance. In contrast, the ad hoc lessons supplied by the school of hard knocks—taught in a reactionary mode—are easily discounted as one-off surprises. At best the lessons that are derived are a loose collection of legal risk management tools with no overriding purpose other than to get the immediate crisis under control and resolved. "True proactiveness," says Senge, "comes from seeing how we contribute to our own problems."

It is not uncommon for job descriptions to omit legal competency requirements. Many years ago, for example, shortly before finishing my MBA degree, I was interviewing with various commercial banks; during one interview for a loan officer position I was told that it would be up to me to learn what documentation would be needed for a loan. Documentation was not important enough to be part of the bank's formal training program. It was left to trial and error.

Fast-track promotion policies in large organizations compound the legal illiteracy problem further. Promoted employees inherit their predecessor's problems. Rather than learn from someone else's mistakes, the tendency is to simply blame the predecessor. It's an endless cycle of easy explanations, but it perpetuates a learning deficit.

Although legal job requirements are unique to each company, the sample Legal Literacy Toolkit chart in Appendix A offers an example of how key job functions can be matched with corresponding legal competency requirements. As a practical matter, many job functions need only a few legal competencies to cover the legal aspects of their respective decision-making processes. But as employees move on in their careers, their legal literacy toolkits should expand commensurately to reflect the increased scope of their responsibilities.

Each substantive area of law has its own special language, and a working knowledge of these core competencies is necessary to avoid the creation or triggering of unwanted liabilities. Appendix B provides a legal primer that introduces legal ABCs relevant to day-to-day business decision making.

The purpose of the primer is to explain the principles and illustrate how they can cross your desk in day-to-day transactions. It helps you identify what legal skills need to be included in your legal literacy toolkit. It is designed to provide enough insight to help you spot potential problems and to assist you in asking the right questions sooner rather than later. It is not, however, intended to be a substitute for legal advice.

Legal literacy plays a central role in neutralizing decision-making biases. See Figure 5.1. Increasing the availability of information improves the organization's decision-making intelligence quotient and is critical to avoid running afoul of the law. It helps build peripheral vision and foresight.

Outstanding teams work together as part of a coherent system focused on a common set of goals. Their value chain is in synch and their individual roles compliment each other. As shown in Figure 5.2, legal literacy plays a key role in the legal leverage process portfolio. It galvanizes the value chain by keeping us inside the foul lines and keeping the ball moving forward. It is an investment in quality decision making.

FIGURE 5.1. CENTRAL ROLE OF LEGAL LITERACY
IN NEUTRALIZING DECISION-MAKING BIASES.

Legal Audits	Prioritized Legal Leverage Agenda	Neutralizing Decision-Making Biases			
		Legal Literacy Needs	Training Needs	Increased Availability of Information and Knowledge	Improved Decision-Making Quality

FIGURE 5.2. LEGAL LEVERAGE PROCESS PORTFOLIO:
HIGHLIGHTING LEGAL LITERACY.

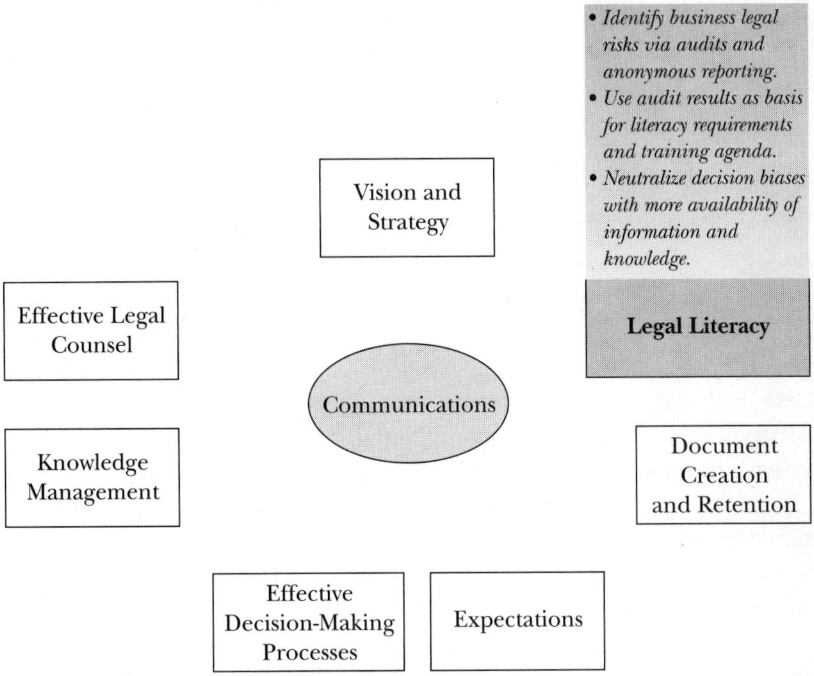

- *Identify business legal risks via audits and anonymous reporting.*
- *Use audit results as basis for literacy requirements and training agenda.*
- *Neutralize decision biases with more availability of information and knowledge.*

Vision and Strategy

Legal Literacy

Effective Legal Counsel

Communications

Knowledge Management

Document Creation and Retention

Effective Decision-Making Processes

Expectations

CHAPTER SIX

HOW MISCOMMUNICATIONS CREATE LIABILITIES
Avoiding Smoking Guns

Traffic cones on the highway slowly funnel cars into one lane. Up ahead, at the Delaware border, the first sign of trouble is a police car parked on the shoulder. Then the driver sees it: a sign with big black letters reading CLOSED right next to the "Welcome to the State of Delaware" sign. A man in uniform, clipboard in hand, walks slowly toward the car.

"What's going on here, officer?" the driver asks, rolling down the window.

"I'm sorry sir, but the State of Delaware is temporarily closed," the officer replies, pointing to the sign.

"Closed?"

"Yes sir. I'm afraid so," he says, emphasizing the sign again.

The driver stares incredulously at the sign, at the officer, and then back at the sign. "For how long?" He asks after a pregnant pause.

"We're not sure. A few hours. Maybe more. Could you come back?"

"Come back? What do you mean 'come back'? I've got family in there!" he says, trying not to let his voice betray frustration.

"I'm sorry sir, but the State is closed," the officer repeats in a measured bureaucratic tone polished by years of patient practice. The verbal volleys continue until the "officer," also known as Alan Funt, creator of the original TV reality show (which catches unsuspecting individuals in compromising situations), finally says, "Smile, you're on *Candid Camera!*"

This *Candid Camera* segment illustrates the power of the written word. When combined with the appearance of authority—in this case a man in uniform with a clipboard, a squad car, and a set of traffic cones—the word *closed* created expectations that brought cars to a standstill.

THE ROLE OF WRITING AND APPARENT AUTHORITY

Businesses cloak their employees with the appearance of authority in many ways. They give them business cards to identify their business affiliation. They let them use business letterhead to write correspondence. They program their fax machines to print the company name on the top line of every fax page sent. They assign e-mail addresses incorporating the company's name. Some even provide their employees with company cars or trucks to drive and expense accounts for business travel and entertainment. To outsiders, employees' trappings of authority confer credibility on their words and deeds. Indeed, this apparent authority literally transforms them *into* their employers.

In legal terms, employees are agents of their employer. They speak and act on behalf of their organization. As a result, everything they say and do in their job capacity reflects on their employer and can create legal liability for their organization. From a strategic perspective, the cause-and-effect relationship between employee actions and corporate consequences means that all employees are individual gatekeepers of their organization's legal liability. They can create liability, or they can mitigate it.

The business documents employees write have added legal significance. Unlike human memories that can fade, documents are tangible evidence that live in computer memories and conventional paper files. Once they are created they have a life of their own, one whose end is by no means certain. They can come back to haunt the company unless they are managed well during their life cycle. Unfortunately, most employees don't appreciate the pivotal role they play in a document's life cycle or the role documents play in protecting their company's legal health. This lack of awareness can turn business documents into wild cards.

We create more documents than we often realize. Sure, we write memos and reports, but we also write comments on the memos and reports we receive, and we underline, circle, highlight, and jot notes in the margins. We keep diaries, fill out forms, and respond to a slew of electronic messages. We might even scribble numbers or designs on a paper napkin or paper place mat while at lunch, a scrap of construction material while at a work site, on a sticky note, or any other portable writing surface that is later placed into the file. Over time, that adds up to a lot of words and a lot of evidence. Some of it is helpful; some of it is not.

The informality and the familiarity of routine writing create a comfort zone that causes us to lower our guard and be less careful about how we express ourselves. Stress, fatigue, and reflex reactions only exacerbate the problem, causing us to write things we may later regret. In the process, seemingly innocent documents get stored in hard files and hard drives only to resurface at a later date in a lawsuit, causing more heartburn than a bad burrito. As Intel's then-CEO Andy Grove put it, "It is entirely possible that when your actions and your heart are both in the right place, one document written in annoyance can outweigh mountains of evidence about your actions, principles and practices."

THE CARELESS SALESMAN LESSON

Take, for example, the situation involving a customer complaining to a salesman about poor product performance. The salesman fills out a standard customer complaint form, and in the section requiring *his* comments he writes: "PRODUCT IS NOT GOOD!" Why? Because that's what the customer told him. Later a credit memo issuing a refund to the customer identifies the reason for the refund as "out of spec—not working." Why? Because that's what the salesman told accounting. When the customer subsequently files a $5 million dollar suit for breach of a product warranty, the plaintiff uses both the customer complaint form and the credit memo as evidence to prove the contract violation. Essentially, the company's own words are used against it. The two documents become proverbial smoking guns.

The only hitch: the product delivered to the customer *could* perform as specified. Two years after the product shelf life expired, a sample was taken and tested. The product was still within specification. It should have worked. It didn't work because the customer didn't know how to use it properly in accordance with the instructions. As a result, it was doomed to fail.

Nonetheless, the words "PRODUCT IS NOT GOOD!" (in all capital letters and followed by an exclamation point) jumped off the complaint form like the sudden glare of a stop sign at midnight on a rain-slick highway. The person filling in the blanks was clearly annoyed. But annoyed about what? Another bad batch of product? *"Can't we get it right?"* Another complaint from the same customer? *"Why do I have to take the heat for manufacturing's mistake?"* Who knows what this agent of the company was thinking? What we do know, however, is what got put in the company file and that is what the company was bound by: a complaint form adopting the customer's statement as fact. It was the same blind acceptance that later cloned itself into a company credit memo saying "out of spec—not working."

Unfortunately, these two documents posed serious stumbling blocks in defending the lawsuit. In legal parlance, they were *admissions* by the company that the product was not good. Had the salesman written that the "customer *claims* the product is not good" or the credit memo stated that the "customer *claims* the product is out of specification," the analysis would have been different. It would have been more accurate. Similarly, qualifying the comment with reference to the need for further testing or inquiry about how the customer used the product, or acknowledging other factors that could contribute to the ultimate product performance would have made a difference. Instead, the exculpatory follow-up occurred only after a lawsuit was filed and long after the customer complaint form and credit memo accepting full blame were issued.

In this case it was unclear how a jury would weigh the subsequent in-spec test data. Would the data neutralize the smoking guns in the jurors' minds? Would they believe the customer misapplied the product? Or would it be too little too late? After evaluating the evidence the company reluctantly concluded that it was cheaper to settle the case than incur trial preparation expenses and take a chance on an unpredictable jury. The case settled for $200,000. It was considerably less than the $5 million originally demanded, but also considerably more than merited by the facts—

all because two little pieces of paper misstated the situation. It was a costly misunderstanding that was totally avoidable.

SMOKING GUNS

What exactly is a smoking gun? It is an instant replay of something that you'd rather forget. It is a documented problem with varying degrees of liability attached to it. It is a term that has been applied to records ranging from mildly embarrassing to hard-core criminal. See Table 6.1. From a business perspective it is evidence that tarnishes reputations, diminishes business opportunities, and drains finances. Even mildly embarrassing documents can morph into more unwanted baggage than would appear at first blush.

Take, for example, a company that had a history of grade inflation in its performance evaluations. Many evaluators gave good reviews even when they were not deserved. A female employee was therefore shocked to receive a pink slip instead of a raise at her annual review. Her boss cited performance issues she was not previously aware of, including a written reprimand he had placed in her personnel file behind her back.

She responded by filing a claim for sexual harassment. The company lawyer told the woman's lawyer the harassment claim was nothing more than her word against her boss's, and the company was going to back the supervisor. The company lawyer was happy with the position until the woman's lawyer faxed a copy of an old e-mail sent by the boss before he assumed supervisory responsibility over her. The note recounts plans for lunch. He suggested going to her house instead of a restaurant. She replied that she hadn't been grocery shopping recently and wasn't prepared to host lunch. "Well, we don't exactly have to eat!" he responded via e-mail.

TABLE 6.1. SMOKING GUNS: THE RANGE OF SEVERITY.

Embarrassment	Misunderstanding	Lawsuit	Lawsuit
	(complaint, claim, potential lawsuit)	(civil claims)	(criminal charges)

She had kept the e-mail for more than a year and now claimed the firing was in retaliation for not accepting his advances. It was sexual harassment.

A source close to the company lawyer was present when the fax of the e-mail arrived on his desk. It was a bombshell. It immediately changed the complexion of the case, forcing the stunned company to capitulate and settle.

According to quality expert Philip Crosby the largest cause of defects and problems in any organization relates to paperwork and communications systems. The legal environment of business is no different. Smoking guns fuel litigation. Memories can fade, but records have virtual immortality if not managed properly. They portray a sobering reality and are very powerful.

If we can reduce the number of smoking guns we create we can reduce the amount of ammunition that can be used against us and keep our files from turning into litigation lightning rods. Reducing legal problems downstream means more resources are available for other value-added activities. It leads to less legal risk and more business opportunity. Managing the process of how smoking gun documents get created and stored in hard files and hard drives is therefore a smart legal risk management tool and a good investment.

"I'll never put anything in writing again" is the first reaction I often hear when people are faced with the concept of smoking guns. Fearful of making a mistake, they take an overly cautious stance that is as impossible to maintain as a fad diet. The better and more sustainable course of action is to develop healthy habits that allow business records to showcase prudent business practices and thereby trim unwanted legal liability.

The following twelve legal leverage rules show you how to take control of your business documents and keep them from turning into a minefield. They show you how to avoid smoking guns and help you reshape your organization's risk profile.

Legal Leverage Rule #1: Stick to Company Business

When the Federal Energy Regulatory Commission gathered information from Enron as part of its investigation into Enron's alleged manipulation of the California energy market, it seized over a million documents, including e-mail messages that were later posted on a public Web site. For employees who blurred the lines between their personal and professional lives, it opened the door to affairs of the heart and gave the new Web site a salacious, voyeuristic quality. "So . . . you were looking for a one night stand after all . . . ?" read one e-mail. "I know you may or may not remember me, but I went to school with you," read another, whose writer added, "Never seemed to get your attention then, but I had the biggest freakin crush on you." For others, however, it opened the door to personal financial affairs, including Social Security numbers, credit card numbers, bank account information, and divorce details. These disclosures were potentially far more damaging.

Enron quickly petitioned the U.S. Court of Appeals and was granted the right to remove the most sensitive information. But for many the damage was already done. The incident left a feeling of being violated. Employees still working at Enron suddenly knew what their bosses privately thought of them, and everyone knew more about each other's personal lives than they wanted or needed to know. It was too much information. Retracting it helped stop further dissemination, but it could not erase the prior damage.

If you want to keep your personal affairs from turning into a public sporting event, stick to company business when writing on the job, regardless of whether you work in the office, on the road, or from home. Keep it separate and don't be lulled into a false sense of security if you access a personal e-mail account from work. Expectations of privacy are usually misplaced. You are still accessing your account through the company server and that leaves the e-mail and personal business you conduct open to view.

Blending work and play, for example, had a unique twist for one young bank analyst who sent an e-mail note about his latest sexploits shortly after joining the office of Carlyle Group in Seoul, Korea. "I know I was a stud in N.Y.C., but I pretty much get about, on average 5–8 phone numbers a night and at least 3 hot chicks that say that they want to go home with me every night I go out. I love the buy side." He also bragged about his job, saying bankers were showering him with opportunities and "pretty much cater to my every whim—you know (golfing events, lavish dinners, a night out clubbing)."

The e-mail was sent to eleven of his former colleagues at Merrill Lynch in New York but quickly ricocheted through global financial circles, eventually landing back on his boss's desk at Carlyle in Seoul. The macho musings about bankers catering to his every whim created the appearance of impropriety and a conflict of interest, making the e-mail and its author an unacceptable liability. Carlyle was smart and took appropriate action. The analyst was asked to resign his job three days after he started.

Damage from misguided e-mail missives is not necessarily limited to the people who write them. They can also backfire on the people who pass them around. When an employee at Royal & Sun Alliance Insurance sent around lewd pictures of cartoon characters on office e-mail, ten employees were terminated and seventy-seven more were suspended during the company's investigation.

Inappropriate e-mail sent over business servers implicates corporate assets and may confer responsibility on the company. In a class action racial discrimination case against R.R. Donnelley & Sons, for example, some 165 racial, ethnic, and sexual jokes sent through the company's e-mail network were used as evidence of the company's condoning a pattern of racial discrimination. These e-mail messages were offensive and disrespectful. Since employees are agents of the company, it was argued that not combating the dissemination of such material amounted to condoning it or ratifying it. It made the e-mail attributable to the company. This allegation not only reflected poorly on R.R. Donnelley, it also impacted the company's cash flow. The case was originally filed on November 26, 1994, and eight years later it continued to stay alive through various appeals, adding to the company's mounting defense costs.

Legal Leverage Rule #2: Keep It Respectful, Courteous, and Constructive

How would you feel if you knew your doctor was recording disparaging comments about you on your medical chart? According to Adam Fox, a doctor at London's St Mary's Hospital, doctors have used plenty of unflattering acronyms to insult their patients and colleagues. He has collected two hundred examples over the years, including GPO (good for parts only), UBI (unexplained beer injury), LOBNH (lights on but nobody home), and CTD (circling the drain)—the last one referring to a patient with limited life expectancy. Colleagues weren't immune to the barbs either. Anesthesiologists were referred to as "Gassers," surgeons as "Slashers," and psychiatrists are the "Freud Squad," to name a few.

Unfortunately, phrases such as "pumpkin positive," suggesting a patient whose brain is so small their whole head would light up if illuminated with a penlight, serve no useful diagnostic (that is, business) purpose. They are inflammatory and only diminish the individual's professionalism and reputation—and their organization's. From a liability perspective, they also make you wonder about the standard of care. They create negative inferences, suggesting perhaps that the patient had been "written off." Litigation has forced more doctors to explain their charts in court, and according to Dr. Fox the liability associated with being in the hot seat has contributed to the declining use of colorful language.

Maintaining a respectful and courteous tone avoids any subtext or connotations from which a negative inference can be made. It's just good business. Neal L. Patterson, the chief executive of Cerner Corporation, a software development company for health care, learned that lesson the hard way when he fired off the following memo to his employees:

> We are getting less than 40 hours of work from a large number of our K.C.-based EMPLOYEES. The parking lot is sparsely used at 8 a.m.; likewise at 5 p.m. As managers—you either do not know what your EMPLOYEES are doing; or you do not CARE. You have created expectations on the work effort which allowed this to happen inside Cerner, creating a very unhealthy environment. In either case, you have a problem and you will fix it or I will replace you.
>
> NEVER in my career have I allowed a team which worked for me to think they had a 40-hour job. I have allowed YOU to create a culture which is permitting this. NO LONGER.

The note included a list of potential punishments, including a 5 percent employee layoff in Kansas City, and indicated that Patterson would measure improvement by the number of cars parked in the parking lot. It needed to be "substantially full" Monday through Friday between 7:30 A.M. and 6:30 P.M., and half full on

Saturdays. Employees had two weeks to shape up. "Tick, tock," it said, as an added motivational touch.

Originally sent only to the Kansas City office, the e-mail was leaked and posted on a Yahoo message board a week after it was issued. Within three days of the memo's public debut, Cerner Corporation, which had been ranked by *Fortune* magazine in 1998 and 2000 among the 100 best companies to work for in America and had met analysts' earnings projections for the last five quarters, watched its $1.5 billion stock valuation drop 22 percent.

The e-mail created a major uproar, causing people to speculate about what was going on at the company internally to trigger such a shrill reaction. One financial analyst, who was among the first to post a warning about the stock, said the memo created the perception "that they have to work overtime to meet their quarter." Another said it raised the question of whether investors could be comfortable with a chief executive who reacted so harshly.

Essentially, the rough tone detracted from the underlying message. The problem wasn't what he said; it was how he said it. If left unchecked, however, persistent shrillness or lack of respect not only tarnishes reputations and depresses stock valuation, it can also contribute to legal problems.

Perceptions of disrespect trigger feelings of unfairness, victimization, and discrimination. Once triggered, those feelings often find expression in a legal action even though not everything that is unfair is necessarily illegal. For example, persistent shrillness can contribute to a hostile work environment, an illegal form of employee harassment. It can also contribute to illegal constructive discharge, a situation wherein a reasonable employee finds the working conditions so intolerable there is no choice but to quit. Or it can contribute to a discrimination case—as candy maker Mars discovered when it was taken to court over a sales manager's intimidating management style. (See the "Employment" section of Appendix B.)

Anyone can have a bad day, but persistent disrespect and the criticism it engenders means that disenfranchised employees will scrutinize every management action for further evidence of bad intent. It creates an emotionally charged climate and an incentive to sue. All that's needed is the right spark to set off the flames. For the employee who didn't want to entertain her future boss at home over lunch, the spark was a reprimand placed in a personnel folder behind her back coupled with a pink slip. For others, threats of employee layoffs that later come to fruition may spark age, race, sexual, or religious discrimination suits. Regardless of whether the accusations can later be proven in court, getting dragged through the process is expensive and time-consuming. E-mail messages such as Cerner's therefore carry ancillary and latent legal liability that can mushroom into legal headaches if not managed properly. (See Chapter Seven for further discussion.)

LEGAL LEVERAGE RULE #3: CHOOSE AND USE COMMUNICATIONS CHANNELS WISELY

Before the advent of e-mail, corporate chieftains would write out memoranda and correspondence in longhand or dictate to a stenographer, or into a Dictaphone. The item was typed, reviewed, edited, and often retyped. The built-in delay provided time to re-think the tone and content of the message. Tempers had time to cool and savvy secretaries would find tactful ways to get their bosses to smooth rough edges. In contrast, instantaneous screen edits and a "point, click, send" culture have squeezed out the cooling-off pe-riod and eliminated the sounding boards. We get an idea, start typ-ing, and boom—off it goes, faster than a bullet train.

Saving a document in draft form requires special care to avoid an oops-moment—when you "send" instead of "save," "reply" in-stead of "forward," or send something to the wrong distribution list. While troubleshooting a customer complaint, for example, a salesman engaged in detailed brainstorming with the company en-gineers and production personnel via e-mail. When they felt the need to include a third-party material supplier in the discussion, they did so by merely adding the supplier's address to the existing e-mail thread. As a result, all the prior discussions and speculation, including confidential attachments, were automatically forwarded outside the company. Afraid the supplier would share the rumi-nations with the company's customer, the salesman scrambled into damage control mode. "Getting trigger happy on e-mail is quite dangerous," he later reported insightfully.

In today's plugged-in world, we have more communications channels at our fingertips than ever before. Cyberspace, e-mail, pagers, text messaging, instant messaging, cell phones, Web logs, and other wireless technology offer immediate access and have dramatically increased interactive communications options when compared to the dark ages of carbon paper and manual typewriters.

Every keystroke, however, leaves an electronic fingerprint and some electronic marvels create records of transactions that used to be anonymous. Key card entries and security surveillance cameras record who comes and goes. Cell phones with global positioning systems can locate you wherever you are. Even tollbooth cameras take pictures that pinpoint when you were there—and with whom. There are more types of records to deal with than ever before, and they are increasingly finding their way into courtrooms in everything from divorce cases to kidnapping.

From a smoking gun perspective, e-mail is a particularly thorny medium. The proliferation of electronic messages has prompted more companies to engage in electronic monitoring and surveillance. Fast and convenient, its casual culture creates a false sense of security that lulls people into careless exchanges of statements that would never be uttered in a business meeting or put in writing on corporate letterhead. Web logs are another casual channel that invites gossip and confidences to be posted for the entire world to see. Hasty messages tapped out on handheld electronic devices suffer further from terse language encouraged by a small screen and an unfriendly keyboard. The economy of words can make messages sound abrupt, if not rude, and lead to misunderstandings and unintended consequences.

On one hand, e-mail may feel intimate—just you and the screen meeting over a keyboard for a little one-on-one time. But that's a cyber-illusion. E-mail winds its way through numerous networks—where it can be read like a postcard, unless an envelope of encryption protects it.

The Ping-Pong pace of e-mail further complicates matters. Its speed makes it fast and convenient, but it can also make conversations spontaneously combust, further escalating misunderstandings and shedding more heat than light. Take, for example, the situation involving a memorandum sent by a safety engineer wherein he discusses dust at the facility related to the use of a certain lead-containing alloy. The memorandum outlined dust control procedures and concluded, "Since lead poses a health risk to unborn babies, females in child-bearing age must be excluded from [the work] team."

A manager's e-mail response to the hard copy memo started by saying, "Your letter concerning lead . . . was very puzzling and alarming. We have been using [this material] . . . since the beginning of production and all the airborne tests that 'Safety' did showed no danger of exposure to lead. Besides, the percentage of lead appears to be under 1% in the alloy?! How about we study the true impact on our workforce of the dust before sending alarmist notes."

The safety engineer defended his memorandum and conclusion saying, "I am sorry that you choose to call me an alarmist when I am trying to bring up a serious problem for our employees. Lead exposure is a danger for our employees and the company's exposure to litigation is severe."

To which the manager replied, "I would sincerely have hoped that you'd spare me the self-righteous lecturing and simply do your job."

Ouch! Both parties were correct in their assessment to a certain degree—but the discussion would have better served the organization if the parties had also focused on the implications of what they said, how they said it, and the medium they chose to convey it in.

The liability exposure in this exchange relates to what was left undocumented. Both the employee and the manager shared a common interest in protecting employee health. But the exchange made it sound like the manager (that is, the company) didn't care about the problem. What the manager was really trying to say to the engineer was let's make sure the data supports your conclusion, while the engineer interpreted the message as a personal attack and the misunderstanding escalated from there. This conversation might have ended differently if it had occurred face-to-face instead of screen-to-screen.

We communicate messages on multiple levels. We carry on monologues as well as dialogues. We engage all five senses and these senses complement each other. I had one person tell me she couldn't hear when wearing her reading glasses. They apparently interfered with her ability to lip read.

No matter how hard we try, conversations on a computer screen will never have the same depth and texture as those spoken in a face-to-face meeting or over the telephone because we have no body language or verbal inflection to aid us in interpreting the words. Whenever we shortchange one or more of our data receptors we invariably shut out more than we shut in and are in danger of perpetuating the decision-making bias of overconfidence explored in Chapter Two.

The objective is to speak the same language. That challenge is large enough when we're trying to speak in the same tongue. It is further complicated when communicating with someone who speaks a foreign language. For hospitals in New York City, for example, addressing the health care needs of patients with limited English proficiency can lead to inadequate translations, misunderstanding, and unintended consequences.

One pregnant woman, for example, faced with life-threatening complications of an ectopic pregnancy (where the embryo grows in the Fallopian tube instead of the womb), was surprised to find herself sterilized after two emergency surgeries. Inadequate translation failed to communicate that one of her Fallopian tubes was removed during the first surgery. When a second ectopic pregnancy necessitated the same procedure she found herself sterile. She said she never knew they were going to remove her Fallopian tubes. Her lack of understanding raised questions about the adequacy of her consent to surgery. How could she give "knowing" consent if she didn't know what could happen?

In choosing and using a communication channel it is therefore vitally important to match the content of your message with the channel's strength while simultaneously guarding against its weaknesses, including poor translation and the human error associated with using technology improperly—as illustrated in Table 6.2. It takes very little to throw things off; for example, when a lawyer who had recently returned from paternity leave and was presumably functioning on less than a full night's sleep inserted a hundred-page pleading on behalf of the European Commission into the fax machine upside down, the European Court of First Instance in Luxembourg ended up receiving a bunch of blank pages and concluded there was no case. Luckily the Commission had a month to ask the Court to reconsider.

The London Stock Exchange, however, was less fortunate. In 2000 when it was engaged in merger talks with Deutsche Börse, a memo was inadvertently faxed to the press outlining a plan to blame the Germans for being stubborn if the discussions were unsuccessful. Unfortunately, the memo was faxed before the deal actually

TABLE 6.2. COMMUNICATIONS CHANNEL STRENGTHS AND WEAKNESSES.

Channel Type	Channels	Strengths	Weaknesses
CYBERSPACE	E-mail	• Fast • Convenient • Wired and wireless • Editable • Permanent record • Dialogue	• Security and confidentiality issues • Casual language usage • Casual culture • No visual or aural language cues • Misplaced expectations of privacy • Ease of distribution promotes distribution beyond those with a need to know
	Instant messaging	Same as e-mail, plus benefit of real-time chat	Same as e-mail, plus tendency for minimal editing, if any
	Web site	Wide audience reach	Confidentiality and security issues
	Chat room	See instant messaging and Web site	See instant messaging and Web site, plus heightened concern about inadvertent disclosure of confidential business information
	Web logs (blogs)	See e-mail and Web site	See e-mail and Web site—plus heightened concern about inadvertent disclosure of confidential business information
TELEPHONE	Land line	• Fast • Convenient • Not editable • Dialogue • Aural cues	• Not mobile • No permanent record of content unless recorded (legality of recording subject to State law) • Aural cues only • Casual language usage

TABLE 6.2. COMMUNICATIONS CHANNEL STRENGTHS AND WEAKNESSES, CONT'D.

Channel Type	Channels	Strengths	Weaknesses
	Cellular connection	See land line, plus wireless and mobile	See land line, plus wireless and mobile • Security and confidentiality issues
	Pager	• Quick access • Permanent record	• Limited character field • Monologue
	Text messaging	See pager, plus opportunity for dialogue • Editable	• Limited number of characters • No aural cues • Casual language usage
	Voice mail	• Fast • Convenient • Mobile • Wired and wireless • Usually editable • Repeatable	• Monologue • Casual language usage • No visual cues • Not suitable for lengthy messages
FAX	Land line	See telephone land line	See telephone land line and paper (below)
	E-mail	See cyberspace e-mail	See cyberspace e-mail
PAPER	Reports, letters, memos, and so on	• Editable • Permanent record • Limited distribution can protect confidentiality • Written word	• Slower distribution • No aural or visual cues • Written word

TABLE 6.2. COMMUNICATIONS CHANNEL STRENGTHS AND WEAKNESSES, CONT'D.

Channel Type	Channels	Strengths	Weaknesses
IN PERSON	Face-to-face	• Fast • Visual and aural cues • Confidentiality • Dialogue	• First impressions limit value of editing • Confidentiality • No record (unless recorded as audio or audiovisual, covert recording subject to State laws)
	Video conferencing	See land line telephone and face-to-face, plus visual cues	See face-to-face
	G-3 video phone	See cellular telephone and face-to-face, plus visual cues	See face-to-face and cellular telephone
	Computer camera	See e-mail, plus face-to-face	See face-to-face and e-mail

failed, and probably contributed to the outcome. Thus the failure to fully appreciate the pros and cons of various communication channels, including their operating manuals, risks creating misunderstandings that can turn a tropical depression–strength criticism into a hurricane-force lawsuit, or at the very least a major embarrassment.

LEGAL LEVERAGE RULE #4: KEEP IT CONFIDENTIAL

Confidentiality is a substantive issue as well as a procedural one. Procedurally, it relates to the security of the various communications channels and the possibility of having a message overheard and intercepted. Substantively, it relates to the contents of the message and how someone else's use of the information can harm you.

Murphy's Law intervened in 1996, when Speaker of the House Newt Gingrich participated in a conference call with Representative John Boehner and other House leaders to discuss the imminent ruling by the House Ethics Committee concerning Gingrich's ethics violations. Representative Boehner participated in the conversation via cell phone, thereby allowing a Florida couple to eavesdrop on the conversation with a scanner. The couple recorded the conversation and, according to court documents, forwarded the tape to Representative James McDermott, who recognized the voices and shared the tape with two reporters, who in turn made it into headline news.

Court documents? Yes, court documents. Representative Boehner sued the Florida couple. They later pleaded guilty to unlawfully intercepting the call and were fined $1000. He also sued Representative McDermott for leaking the tape in violation of federal wiretap laws, which prohibit disclosure of information that was illegally intercepted. It took six years and a deep pocket for the case against Representative McDermott to finally be resolved in Boehner's favor. But the collateral damage could not be undone.

If you want to keep your business private and confidential, you need to be sensitive to the security risks accompanying your chosen method of communication. What is the likelihood of a leak? How can it be plugged? Sometimes it's as easy as speaking in person instead of by e-mail, or waiting until you are out of earshot, or on a secure telephone line (that is, a land line) before making an important call.

In the *Boehner* case, protecting the contents of the phone call probably would not have affected the outcome of the House Ethics Committee inquiry into Representative Gingrich's conduct. Gingrich was ultimately reprimanded by the full House for using tax-exempt foundations for political purposes and fined $300,000. But not using a cell phone to conduct confidential conversations would have saved the time and effort necessary to deal with the collateral damage of unflattering publicity.

The lawsuits may have produced a moral victory, but litigation is rarely a cost-effective business transaction. Even those willing to take the battle to court find that the crushing weight of legal fees has a tendency to soften even the steeliest resolve, particularly when the case gets stuck in judicial gridlock. The financial hemorrhage of protracted litigation requires a very deep pocket that few can supply, particularly when the time and money could earn a better return on investment by advancing organizational goals instead of stepping backward to defend a black eye. In litigation, you can often win the battle and still lose the war.

When security leaks compromise the contents of the message and when that message contains sensitive proprietary information, the ante and the legal risk factor go up considerably. Slip-ups become major oops-moments, like the junior scientist described in Chapter One, whose bragging about an invention in a scientific chat room on the Internet irrevocably compromised his company's patent filing date and subsequent patent rights.

Proprietary information is anything that gives your organization a competitive edge, everything from customer lists and sales data to marketing plans, production methods, formulas, and employee information. Such things are your organization's crown jewels. They are assets and they deserve protection. Trade secret laws offer a ready-made solution, but only if the requirements set forth by law are followed. If you cut corners and discuss sensitive information in a megaphone voice on a cell phone in a crowded plane or restaurant, or with colleagues in crowded elevators or rest rooms, consider the information to be compromised. You never know who is within earshot and how they will use the data.

The best way to keep a secret is not to tell more people than absolutely necessary and to swear them to secrecy by creating a legal duty. Blurting out a secret in public has far-reaching effects. It destroys the secret and destroys the asset. That's why the Coca-Cola formula is locked in a vault and not plastered on the company Web site. That's also why the Catholic bishops in the Philippines have banned the use of fax, e-mail, and text messaging for communicating confessions and absolutions. These methods of communication too easily compromise the content of potentially embarrassing disclosures. The bishops understand the significance of confidentiality to their central mission.

LEGAL LEVERAGE RULE #5: APPLY LEGAL LITERACY

A group of volunteers were asked to view a short film of a basketball game and asked to count the number of passes made by the players. Partway through the film a man dressed in a gorilla suit walks into the room, tries to distract the volunteers by beating his chest, and then walks out. Half of the volunteers were so intent on the task of watching the basketball players and counting passes that they did not notice the gorilla in the room. According to professor Richard Wiseman, a psychologist at the University of Hertfordshire, the business lesson we can deduce from this famous Harvard psychology experiment is that companies can sometimes miss opportunities because they are too focused on what they are doing. The legal leverage lesson we can deduce is that companies can miss legal literacy opportunities because they are too focused on what they are doing—and that something does not include paying attention to the legal consequences of their business decisions.

Take, for example, Fleet Bank's $12.5 million construction loan to Berry Street Corporation. The focus was on making the deal, not on completing all the paperwork necessary to secure the bank's repayment rights. As a result a Notice of Lending was not filed. The omission allowed a subcontractor's lien to prevail under the applicable statutory priority provisions. The error cost Fleet Bank $1.9 million. Or how about the company seeking to compete against a competitor's new invention? Focus on the invention process instead of on avoiding patent infringement caused someone to write: "clone [the competitor's idea]." The handwritten note was found during discovery in a patent infringement lawsuit. It suggested the company was out to infringe rather than to improve or create a novel invention of its own.

Similarly, a consulting firm focused on meeting the needs of a new client stated in its meeting notes that the client "wants to get rid of [a contract] and needs backup documentation from us." Unfortunately, the consulting company didn't appreciate how manipulating financial data to justify the client's contract termination could land them in court as part of a commercial defamation and tortious interference of contract case. Had they had better legal literacy, they could have avoided the situation and applied that knowledge to enhance instead of detract from their value chain.

Legal Leverage Rule #6: Enhance the Value Chain

It pays to understand the laws that apply to your industry, your company, and your job. To manage legal risk effectively, legal literacy needs to be an intimate part of the job. It needs to be part of the process of counting those basketball passes, not a gorilla that only the lawyers see and wrestle with. Keeping the gorilla contained is everyone's job. Employees do not need to become lawyers, but they do need to know enough about law to recognize the gorilla in the room.

In applying legal literacy to the value chain it is also important to focus on the nexus between links as much as any single link, as illustrated by the experience of Huntsman Chemical Corporation described in Chapter One. Only by appreciating the cause and effect between the links in the Huntsman value chain and through better communication could the organization initiate change that ultimately led to more accountability, better compliance, and less liability exposure.

Galvanizing the value chain with legal literacy aligns the business and legal needs of the organization into a cohesive whole. It protects legal interests while simultaneously promoting business objectives. It also eliminates the inefficiencies created by unnecessary liabilities and contributes to effective resource allocation that improves the organization's return on investment.

LEGAL LEVERAGE RULE #7: STRIVE FOR CLARITY AND ACCURACY

Words create expectations that add to or detract from the value chain. The lead dust e-mail thread showed how misplaced expectations result from misused communication channels. Rule #7, on striving for clarity and accuracy, calls attention to the way misunderstandings are created through the careless use of language irrespective of the communication channel.

When a fine jewelry store interviewed candidates for a job vacancy, for example, the goal was to hire someone with prior fine jewelry experience. It was a perfectly reasonable requirement given the responsibilities of the job. Unfortunately, when one of the candidates did not meet the criterion, the interviewer demonstrated a lack of legal literacy by writing "no jew" in the margin of her résumé as a reason for rejecting the applicant.

In the interviewer's mind, this notation referred to the candidate's lack of fine jewelry experience. However, the candidate— who happened to be Jewish—read it as referring to her religious persuasion. Had the interviewer been legally literate enough to appreciate that it is illegal for hiring practices to discriminate based on religion and dangerous for them even to appear to do so, he could have avoided the misunderstanding—but he didn't. The case settled quietly out of court.

Words carry many meanings. They are the bullets we load into communications channels—and if we don't choose them carefully they not only miss their mark, they backfire.

Contracts are particularly prone to imprecise language that can lead to misplaced expectations and future conflict. Suppose a contract called for "bimonthly payments." Reasonable people can reasonably differ about what *bimonthly* means. Does it mean every two months? Or does it mean twice per month? Suppose a contract warrants the product for a "reasonable" period of time. How long is that? A month? A year? Longer? Suppose a product quality provision in a contract specifies that all products sold under the agreement "shall be equal to or better than the performance of other comparable [product] that is commercially available to [the customer]." What exactly is that supposed to mean? How is performance to be determined? Is it an objective or a subjective standard? If we are not sure what it means, how can the sellers possibly meet or exceed the customer's expectations? How can they make the customer happy if there is so much room for misinterpretation?

To achieve a true meeting of the minds between contracting parties it is essential that the parties attach the same meaning to the contract language. We should therefore always strive for clarity and accuracy in our business writing, to seek understanding and to be understood, or as Stephen Covey describes as part of a win-win strategy in *7 Habits of Highly Successful People,* to practice principles of "empathic communication."

Sometimes, however, in an effort to satisfy our customers and clients we stretch beyond our area of expertise and say things we are not qualified to say. In doing so we sacrifice accuracy and may incur liability for the organization. Remember the salesman who filled out a customer complaint form saying "PRODUCT IS NOT GOOD"? He had not tested the product himself and therefore had no personal, firsthand knowledge of the product's true quality.

In another case, a consultant also stretched beyond his qualifications when he wrote: "I was generally impressed with the quality of construction. Design review is not my domain per se but [my partner and I] both agree that the general . . . construction exceeded . . . standards and should be adequate for service employment."

To a lawyer this language represents the makings of a warranty. For the consultants it is the makings of a bottomless liability over a subject which they admittedly have no expertise.

Whenever I used this consultant example in my MBA classes it always generated a lively discussion. One student would inevitably raise a hand and say that the customer didn't have a right to rely on the construction opinion as a warranty because the consultant clearly admitted his ignorance when he said "design review is not my domain." The theory being that he can give an opinion but not be held accountable for it because he disclaimed it as an uninformed opinion from the start. That may be true. An argument can certainly be made for that point of view—and if the consultant is sued he will no doubt advocate that very point.

As a practical matter, however, if the construction later turns out to be faulty and leads to catastrophic financial loss, you can be sure that the losers will see themselves as victims and look to assign blame. They will say they relied on the consultant's letter and that because the consultant had seen dozens if not hundreds of these constructions before they were entitled to rely on his opinion.

The energy and passion that goes into the students' arguments about "who is right" goes to the very heart of legal leverage. If the consultant's letter had not opined on a subject outside his domain, there would be no opinion to rely on. There would be no litigation lightning rod and no need to debate who is right or wrong. It would have saved time and money, and therein lies the value of legal leverage: less misunderstanding, more customer satisfaction.

Mismanaged expectations divert resources. Once a problem has erupted, being "right" is a cost. Avoiding the problem before it erupts (at minimal or no cost) is always cheaper than winning in court. Besides the benefit of avoiding conflict, the beauty of communicating clearly and accurately within your area of expertise is that you can support your words with action. When you say what you mean and mean what you say, people can depend on you. They can trust you and they can respect you. It builds the foundation of a good reputation. It builds a valuable asset.

LEGAL LEVERAGE RULE #8: KEEP IT LEGAL

Illegal business practices are the antithesis of legal leverage. Legal leverage is about telling the truth well and documenting good business practices. It's about keeping communications clean in terms of clarity as well as legality. Legal leverage is not a loophole for hiding a set of poor business practices. A corrupt business model is fatally flawed and unsustainable. Such poor practices are fundamentally a leadership and business infrastructure issue. (More on this in Chapter Twelve.)

The importance of keeping business conduct and business practices legal may sound obvious. But in practice the combination of weak leadership, lack of legal literacy, and decision-making biases create pressures that can blind people to the gorilla in the room. At minimum, businesses and their employee agents need to understand the outside boundaries of the legal playing field on which their business operates.

Take, for instance, the case of the bookkeeper who sued a former employer for wrongful termination after being fired for refusing to continue filing false tax returns. A local district attorney read about the case in the newspaper and suspected that the business might still be engaged in an ongoing tax fraud scheme. The district attorney had a search warrant issued for the business and during the search found a to-do list with the following note: "fire employee who can spill the beans." The tax fraud scheme was not a sustainable long-term strategy; instead, it led to multiple and ultimately unconcealable violations of law. It was a fatally flawed business model.

The only way to make a bad situation worse is to do something illegal and then impeach your credibility, as with Frank Quattrone's misadventures described in Chapter One. The fatal e-mail urging the file purge was sent after a federal grand jury and the Securities and Exchange Commission had issued subpoenas to the company, including his banking group, in connection with the allocation of shares of initial public offerings made during the 1990s bull market. Initially Quattrone claimed he had no involvement in the share allocation process. But he later changed his mind, admitting he *might* have had something to do with it after all. Changing his perception about his involvement certainly didn't help his credibility, but involvement in share allocation is not what was ultimately found by the court to be illegal. It was more nuanced than that.

The involvement in share allocation is what made Quattrone's documents an essential part of the government probe and his subsequent order to clean up the files into an obstruction of justice. At issue was whether he knew he was breaking the law at the time he directed employees to tidy up the files. Quattrone denied having any knowledge of any illegality. But other correspondence and testimony led the federal judge and jury to conclude otherwise. Furthermore, the court held that Quattrone perjured himself—and increased his sentence to eighteen months in prison and fined him $90,000 as a result. Ignorance of the law is never a viable defense. Even if the case is later reversed on appeal and the actions vindicated, it cannot undo the impact this detour has had on a successful career.

LEGAL LEVERAGE RULE #9: KEEP IT ETHICAL

Ethical dilemmas, if left unchecked, can lead down a slippery slope of continuous rationalizations that deteriorate into illegal behavior. Indeed, situational ethics, the practice of rationalizing behavior to suit the circumstances at hand, can be hypnotic. The temptation to please shareholders, a customer, or a supervisor at any cost can be driven by a desire to stay employed and to continue providing our families with income, benefits, and a comfortable standard of living. Believing the ends justify the means, we rationalize our behavior in a host of different ways: *"Everyone else is doing it," "I'm just doing what the customer asked," "I have numbers to meet," "I'm just following orders."*

Situational ethics is also insidious. Over time it can lead us further and further from our core values. By the time we realize we've crossed the line and engaged in illegal or unethical behavior, it may be too late to reverse the damage. At that point the common tendency is to cover our tracks. Unfortunately, the cover-up can be more damaging than the underlying allegations.

As with Legal Leverage Rule #8 (Keeping It Legal), keeping it ethical is fundamentally a leadership and business infrastructure issue. It differs from Legal Leverage Rule #8, however, to the extent that ethical business issues deal with right-versus-right decisions *in addition* to the black-or-white, right-versus-wrong legal decisions.

A right-versus-right decision involves an ethical dilemma wherein two very different solutions can still be right. Take, for example, the case of a multinational apparel manufacturer who was looking to start a manufacturing joint venture in the People's Republic of China. After many months of negotiating concessions, both parties had gone as far as they could go. The one issue on which they could not reach agreement involved the one-child rule that was then in effect in China. The law was instituted in China for the purpose of balancing population size with the country's limited resource infrastructure. Large families were discouraged in all but the rural parts of the country. With minor exceptions, the rule for everyone else was one child per couple. The government, as a condition for approving the joint venture, was insisting that the multinational company test female employees for pregnancy and provide abortions if necessary.

Although not a customary practice in the rest of the world, the company could have accepted the policy mandate as a legal requirement of doing business in China—which indeed it was. By definition it was the legal thing to do in China. The abortion requirement, however, ran counter to the religious beliefs of the multinational's chief executive officer. To him it was a moral and ethical issue. To follow his conscience and not consummate the deal would also be the right thing to do. It was a right-versus-right decision. The company elected not to consummate the deal.

Situational ethics can seduce you in various ways. It can tug on your heartstrings and temporarily let right-versus-wrong decisions masquerade as right-versus-right decisions. For example, think about the consultant who in a letter offers to bring you a competitor's technology and formulations and tells you "I will not transfer this information in writing, [therefore] it can never be proved that this information is coming from me." Or consider the star employee who writes:

I'm really sorry about your . . . getting sucked into my divorce mess. . . . She got my cars, house, and even forged my tax return check. When I went to get my belongings she had burned my clothes and was using my favorite 3-iron for a fireplace poker.

I know [her lawyer] subpoenaed you for my income records so my wife can try to screw me for more money. What do you have to give them? Do you have to let them know about the bonus money since that is paid out on a monthly basis? What about my car? Since you gave me the car can that be left out and just kept between you and me? Please let me know what you can do to help me. I don't want you to lie for me but if you can just give them my base salary information and leave out the bonuses, car, and trips that would really help me.

To outsiders not involved with the transactions or the parties, the answer to these inviting requests is an obvious "no." But without strong leadership, it is easy for employees to get swept up in the vortex of self-serving reasoning and allow the undercurrent to blind them into bending the rules, thinking no one will ever find out. Unfortunately, we will know what happened after the situation escalates into a lawsuit because the lapse in judgment will inevitably come to light during the pretrial discovery phase of the case or during trial.

People unfamiliar with litigation in the United States often underestimate the depth and breadth of the litigation discovery process. Pretrial discovery allows the parties to gather and exchange information related to the cause of action on which the lawsuit is based. It is conducted in several ways, through written questions and answers (also known as interrogatories), oral questioning under oath outside the courtroom (depositions), requests to admit particular allegations (requests for admissions), written requests to produce and examine documents and other items, including medical examinations, site inspections, product testing, and exhumation (requests to produce), to name a few.

It is these document production requests that define "document" in broad, encompassing terms and make all records vulnerable to public scrutiny. Some people are shocked to learn that even documents stored at home or personal diaries are subject to discovery if their content relates to the subject of the lawsuit. It does not matter whether the information is stored in dusty file cabinets tucked away in dingy warehouses, in your basement or garage, or in a matrix of electronic immortality—where they sleep, waiting for a mouse click to resuscitate them. Everything reasonably calculated to lead to discoverable evidence is fair game. Its physical location or its format is irrelevant. The only exception to the rule is information that qualifies as privileged. That is why privilege is such a powerful tool and the confidentiality necessary to preserve it must be diligently guarded.

When situational ethics leads to bad behavior that offends traditional notions of fairness and justice, it can lead to more than just discoverable evidence; it can also lead to corrective measures in the form of new laws. The slew of business scandals at the turn of the twenty-first century is an example of how bad behavior led to the enactment of corporate governance legislation in the United States.

The resulting law, called the Sarbanes-Oxley Act, was enacted to deter financial conflicts of interest and to promote greater accountability for financial reporting of publicly traded companies. It has added to the compliance burden—and the operational costs— of publicly traded companies. Even if the individuals alleged to be at the center of all these scandals avoid penalty on a legal technicality, the added cost of Sarbanes-Oxley Act is in all likelihood permanent. If these scandal-ridden companies had only followed the spirit of law by doing more than the law requires and less than the law allows there would have been no perceived need for additional legislation.

Business records can showcase prudent business behavior as well as imprudent. The records simply are what they are. If we want them to reflect good corporate stewardship, we need to act accordingly.

Legal Leverage Rule #10: Listen and Respond to Warnings Responsibly

Legal leverage thrives on proactive behavior, on preventing and resolving problems while they are small, manageable, and relatively inexpensive to deal with. Warnings about problems are gifts. They let the company address a problem before it escalates out of control. Unfortunately, legal leverage suffers when decision makers treat warnings as problems to be wished away instead of part of the solution to be embraced. When that happens the organization's liability exposure increases.

When a big financial scam collapsed and the scammer's law firm was sued for aiding and abetting the fraud, one of the documents produced in discovery was a new client memorandum that had

been circulated among the partners when the scammer first asked
the firm to represent him. A handwritten note jotted by one of the
partners said: "Ponzi scheme. Would love the business, but want to
sleep at night." Too bad the failure to listen to the dissenting vote
embroiled the firm in an unflattering and costly lawsuit.

Similarly, when a young child was injured in the children's shoe
department after a glass display case collapsed on him and severely
cut his arm, the subsequent premises liability lawsuit showed that
the large retailer had ignored a safety bulletin received a year before the accident. The bulletin read: "Warning: Many of our display cases do not contain tempered glass. They can be attractive to
young children and if they were to collapse could result in injury.
Take steps to replace the glass as soon as possible."

In the case of Xerox's aggressive accounting practices in Mex-
ico, Assistant Treasurer James F. Bingham warned his management
about accounting irregularities, concluding that there was a "high
likelihood" of "misleading financial statements and public disclosures." Greg Tayler, Xerox's controller, claimed the warnings about
overstated revenues and profits were taken seriously but that the
company believed they were "factually without merit." Although
Bingham lost his job a few days after warning his bosses due to
what the company called "disruptive and insubordinate behavior,"
he was vindicated when the Securities and Exchange Commission
later imposed $22 million in fines on six former and current Xerox
employees, including Tayler. These were the largest fines ever
levied by the SEC against individuals and included disgorgement
of ill-gotten bonuses and stock proceeds based on the fraudulent
financial statements. The heaviest damage was sustained by former
CEO Paul Allaire. His personal share of the fine amounted to $8.6
million, and he was required to resign from his board of director
seats at Lucent Technologies and Priceline.com.

The failure to listen to warnings and act responsibly had much
more dire consequences for accounting giant Arthur Andersen
and energy titan Enron. Enron vice president Sherron Watkins's
no-nonsense letter to Enron's chief executive officer Kenneth Lay
in August 2001 outlining accounting irregularities involving certain off–balance sheet partnerships that could "implode in a wave
of accounting scandals" was met with lip service and a demotion.
By December 2001, however, the fragile financial construct collapsed and Enron filed the biggest bankruptcy in U.S. history.

Enron auditors from Arthur Andersen discussed the accounting issues that later were to form the basis of the criminal, civil, and congressional investigations in a client retention memorandum distributed in February 2001, nearly a year before Enron imploded, yet they failed to take appropriate action. When Sherron Watkins called Arthur Andersen energy specialist James Hecker to express concern about the Enron accounting practices and to act as a "sounding board," the firm's reaction was similarly reprehensible. It led to the destruction of Enron documents, a cover-up, and subsequent criminal conviction by a federal jury for obstructing the SEC's investigation of Enron. The venerable accounting firm did not survive the scandal and conviction. It is no longer in business.

Warnings can reflect a smoldering crisis. When the problems warned against come to fruition, the failure to act responsibly can take a heavy toll, including sullied reputations, injured children, personal fines, and business death sentences.

Legal Leverage Rule #11: Manage the Closure Process

If warnings are gifts in small packages, then managing the closure process represents the organization's opportunity to demonstrate integrity in action. For legal leverage purposes, the objective of managing the closure process is to tell the truth well, investigate honestly, act with integrity, and take responsibility for fixing the problem at hand without making things worse than they already are. Telling the truth well means there is less to remember. It also contributes to consistent documentation.

When Johnson & Johnson was faced with deaths resulting from the ingestion of cyanide-laced Tylenol capsules in 1982 and 1986—capsules made by the company's subsidiary McNeil Consumer Products Company—it did an exemplary job of tackling the problem responsibly. The company placed consumer health and safety over company profits and quickly recalled 31 million bottles at a cost of $100 million. It took responsibility for the problem and communicated openly with the public. Although its management of the closure process could not prevent the filing of wrongful death claims, it did help to mitigate some of the potential damage. When the last of the wrongful death suits settled in 1991, the plaintiffs agreed to a confidential, as opposed to a public, settlement. When asked why, plaintiff's counsel said, "Here all the harm was corrected at the out-set." McNeil was thereby spared additional negative publicity long after public memory had faded.

The Tylenol case is in stark contrast to the 2000 Ford Explorer tire separation and roll-over case involving Bridgestone-Firestone. One of the earliest warnings of a potential problem was an e-mail message sent by Sam Boyden, a State Farm Insurance researcher, in July 1998 to the National Highway Traffic Safety Administration (NHTSA) describing a pattern of tread separation he observed on certain Firestone tires in twenty-one different cases. Neither Ford's October 1998 experience in Venezuela nor its 1999 replacement of Explorer tires in Saudi Arabia due to tread separation were rec-ognized as warnings until it spawned a NHTSA investigation in May 2000 and a slew of unfavorable media stories. Another three months went by before Firestone finally recalled 6.5 million tires in August 2000. In hindsight, the company should have acted much sooner.

Foresight is an important tool for managing legal risk. Fire-stone's and Ford's delayed response to warnings added to their companies' risk profiles. While they were busy blaming each other for the unfolding crisis, citing vehicle weight, tire design, and tire pressure as factors contributing to the debacle, nearly 150 U.S. traf-fic deaths were said to be related to tread separations and roll-overs. By December 2000 the companies were facing class action suits that one headline estimated at $50 billion. In financial terms, fallout from the crisis cost Ford $500 million in recalls and caused its third-quarter 2000 earnings to fall by 7 percent. The Bridgestone-Firestone loss was far greater. Its consolidated net income dropped 80 percent from the preceding year. Damage control became job #1 for these companies, crowding out the basic duty of running their businesses.

Both large and small problems can impact the legal risk pro-file of the organization, depending on how events develop. Thus one of the first lines of defense is to develop the foresight neces-sary to recognize smoking guns for what they are, to tackle them head on, and to neutralize them by managing the closure process responsibly.

Achieving closure is not about spin control, wishing the prob-lem away, or inappropriate document shredding. It's about fixing problems and finding solutions. Organizations are quick to document problems but typically less diligent about documenting what they did to fix them.

Closure takes the potential for damage out of potential smoking guns. Take, for example, the following e-mail sent by a manager to an environmental engineer. It sounds like a smoking gun (in this case, the admission of a permit violation). The manager writes, "I've just been informed . . . that the . . . plant is in non-compliance with its air emissions permit and that we cannot put the [product] into production at this time."

The manager's observation was really a misunderstanding, causing the engineer to clarify the matter by replying: "I did not say we were currently in non-compliance with the air permit. I said that during our annual emission calculations it appeared we may have gone over our limits. . . . We *immediately* changed production procedures so we could operate within the requirements of our permits."

When read in conjunction with the original "admission" these additional documents take the bang out of the smoking gun. They match the documented problem with a documented solution. If challenged, the production changes can be independently verified to support the accuracy of the reply. It addresses the underlying the problem. It achieves closure.

In instances where fixing the problem requires more than clarifying a misunderstanding, managing closure will be an ongoing process. Take, for example, the following e-mail note sent to a senior manager raising a serious safety concern: "In reviewing our records for safety awareness I have come across some very disturbing findings that I believe you should be aware of. . . . If an inspector determines that this was a willful violation he could fine us up to $70,000 per incident. This is a $25.2 million liability. . . ."

The manager took the appropriate first step on the road to closure by taking responsibility for finding a solution, taking action, and responding: "Thank you for raising this concern. By a copy of this note . . . I am asking [our Steering Team] for specific action plans to be developed to correct all of these deficiencies immediately. Thanks again."

The next step in this example is to document the implementation of the Steering Team action plan. If certain recommendations will not be adopted, a proper explanation of the reasons why can help eliminate any negative inferences that would otherwise be drawn from not having an explanation.

Some people are under the mistaken belief that to avoid smoking guns it is necessary to avoid raising problems in writing. That approach is simply not practical. Dealing with problems is an inevitable fact of life. What is critical and what impacts the amount of liability ultimately incurred depends on the response to it and how we document that response. Managing the closure process is one method organizations can use to limit legal liability and keep problems from escalating into more liability than necessary.

LEGAL LEVERAGE RULE #12: MANAGE THE DOCUMENT RETENTION PROCESS DILIGENTLY

Business records serve the business needs of the organization. When they have outlived their usefulness they are typically discarded. However, business records also serve the *legal* needs of the organization, and if they are discarded too soon they create liability for the company in the form of civil charges for spoliation of evidence, criminal charges for obstruction of justice, sanctions, and negative publicity.

Various laws govern the document retention periods of certain types of business records. The Model Law on Electronic Commerce has been adopted in more than twenty countries and may require businesses operating in certain countries to maintain e-mail relating to commercial transactions for five or ten years, far longer than the typical "business need" for the document. The Sarbanes-Oxley Act, for example, imposes a fine of up to $5 million for anyone who "knowingly alters, destroys, mutilates, conceals, covers up, falsifies, or makes a false entry on any record . . . or document . . . with the intent to impede, obstruct, or influence the investigation or proper administration of [justice]." Having a sound document retention policy in place that meets both business and legal needs is therefore a wise step for avoiding unnecessary liability.

The proliferation of communications channels, however, adds a new dimension and challenge to the company's records retention obligations. The various channels, particularly the newer electronic media, provide a staggering amount of information in an unstructured format that complicates the task of sorting and analyzing information and drives up the cost of document production and litigation in general.

Instant messaging software, for example, can be freely downloaded from the Internet and may exist on corporate computers without the knowledge of the information technology department. Yet what many employees do not realize is that even though the software is external, these messages *can* be stored—and when created in the course of business are part of *company* records. To forestall some of the headaches of needing to retain unstructured documents, some companies are taking the aggressive approach of banning or severely restricting certain types of electronic communications altogether. Altria Group, for example, the parent company of Kraft Foods and cigarette maker Philip Morris, has banned the use of instant messaging technology across the entire corporation by blocking all commercial instant messaging portals.

An electronic network is a labyrinth with multiple nooks and crannies and multiple gatekeepers. It's easy for any one of them to alter or destroy documents and create a legal nightmare for the organization. The *Martha Stewart* case, with its altered computer records, highlights the problems companies can face in guaranteeing the integrity of their electronic records. Similarly, the *Arthur Andersen* case showed us that no document is as incriminating as the one that is destroyed. The very act of destruction invites negative inferences, and the inability to examine the phantom document makes it impossible to explain it. Moreover, the penalties for missing documents can be severe.

In the *Rambus* case, for example, the high-tech memory chip company was sanctioned for spoliation of evidence because it *should* have known that its documents would be relevant to some litigation in the future. The sanction took the form of a loss of the attorney-client privilege for those documents relating to the document retention policy's instructions on destruction.

In the *Philip Morris* case the court fined the company $2.75 million for routinely deleting e-mail more than sixty days old for a period of two years after the court ordered all documents that might be relevant to the lawsuit be retained by the company. In addition to the monetary fine, the court further punished Philip Morris by precluding it from calling as witness at trial any of the employees who violated the court's document retention policy by deleting their e-mail.

The sanctions in *Zubulake v. UBS Warburg LLC* were even stiffer. In this case the court initially held that the regular recycling of computer backup tapes caused the destruction of e-mail subject to the discovery requests in the plaintiff's unemployment discrimination suit and required the company to bear the cost of reconstructing the tapes. In the course of the reconstruction it was discovered that certain tapes were missing altogether. Delays in producing documents and the missing documents affected the deposition testimony of witnesses who had already been deposed and raised concerns about new witnesses that were identified by the new documents.

The court held that UBS had willfully destroyed the records and ordered UBS to pay the cost of any new depositions or depositions that need to be supplemented as a result of the untimely document production. It also required UBS to pay the plaintiff's additional cost for bringing the motion to compel production of documents that forced UBS to comply. To top it all off, this ugly pretrial discovery dispute had ramifications at trial. The court instructed the jury to draw adverse inferences from the missing documents. The jury later returned a damage verdict of $29.2 million, including $20.1 in punitive damages. The punitive damage award was meant to send a message—the courts really hate missing documents.

Investment bank Morgan Stanley's fight with financier Ronald Perelman about whether he was deceived in a business deal, discussed earlier in Chapter Three, also hinged on missing e-mail. In that case the court went even further than the *Zubulake* court. It was so outraged by Morgan Stanley's failure to produce the files that it shifted the burden of proof in the case from Perelman to Morgan Stanley. In meant, in effect, that Morgan Stanley had to prove it did not defraud Perelman. The e-discovery ruling contributed to a $1.45 billion judgment against Morgan Stanley.

Regardless of whether the *Zubulake* and *Morgan Stanley* decisions stand the test of time, they send a clear message about the importance of electronic document retention and highlight the value of legal literacy in the organization. It is necessary for all employees to draft and guard their documents carefully. Unlike traditional paper files, where a document's author and secretary with access to the file cabinet were the sole gatekeepers of the record, the multiplicity of gatekeepers means more people need to understand the central role business records play in litigation and the significance of document hold orders. They must be able to translate that understanding into action items. They need to recognize, for example, that recycling computer backup tapes may be inconsistent with the company's document retention obligations and to appreciate the ramifications of new computer technologies on the legal health of the organization.

Managing the document retention process diligently will help avoid the liabilities associated with poor document retention practices. Managing the document creation process will ensure that the retained documents tell a story of respectable conduct that the company can be proud of.

Conclusion

When practiced in concert, the twelve legal leverage rules for avoiding smoking guns will put the organization on the road to greater control over its legal health. These rules play a significant role in the legal leverage process portfolio. See Figure 6.1. They can lower the organization's risk profile and enhance the sustainability of the business enterprise by promoting accountability and encouraging documents that reflect sound judgment, and by managing expectations to avoid misunderstandings that can escalate into conflict.

Figure 6.1. Legal Leverage Process Portfolio: Highlighting Document Creation and Retention.

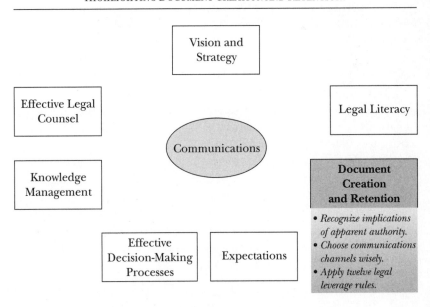

CHAPTER SEVEN

HOW TO KEEP THE WHEELS ON

Managing and Mediating Expectations

Two points of view in general regulate the conduct of men: honor and interest.
—FREDERICK THE GREAT (1712–1786)

After her permanent wave solution had processed, the matronly client of an upscale hair salon leaned back into the sink to have a neutralizing solution applied. Instead of hearing the familiar squishy gurgle of liquid being force-fed through a squeeze bottle, she heard pink plastic curlers bouncing in the sink. The stylist's jaw dropped. One stolen glance in the mirror confirmed the matron's worst fear. The rods had fallen off her head with the hair still tightly wrapped around them. The chemical processing had burnt her hair off at the roots. She was partially bald.

Panic-stricken and embarrassed, her eyes cried out for answers: "How did this happen? How can I go out in public? What am I going to say to my husband?"

Luckily the stylist was quick on her feet. She scrambled to locate a wig from another part of the salon. The color match was good, and with a few expert snips, a bit of styling, and a blast of hairspray the wig was magically transformed into a passable substitute. The immediate crisis was under control. With a sigh of relief, the matron turned to gather her things only to hear the stylist chirp, "You don't have to tip me today."

Outraged about paying anything, never mind a tip, the matron was irate. She was still irate over the stylist's misplaced expectation two days later when she visited her lawyer. Suit was filed against the stylist, the salon, and the manufacturer of the permanent wave solution. It resulted in money damages paid by the two businesses, a lost client, and the loss of client referrals—all because an ill-timed, insensitive comment pushed the woman over the edge.

THE FORCES THAT DRIVE LITIGATION

Lawsuits are triggered by the breach of duty, supporting evidence, *and* the incentive or motive to take action and sue. The first two items are the legal requirements necessary for a successful case; the third is the hidden catalyst that sets it all in motion. Put them all together and they converge into a perfect storm. Eliminate or reduce any one of these aggravating factors and the likelihood of successful litigation goes down.

If we were to graph these functions, with the merits of the case (that is, evidence and legal duty) on the X-axis and motive on the Y-axis, we would see latent legal risk fall into one of four quadrants, as shown in Figure 7.1. In the lower left-hand quadrant where the motivation to sue is low and the merits of the case are weak, the latent legal risk is the lowest. In the upper left- and the lower right-hand

FIGURE 7.1. MANAGING LATENT LEGAL RISK.

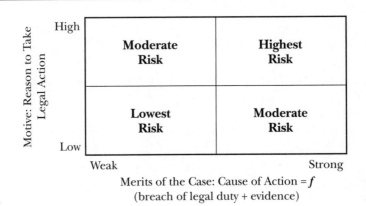

Motive: Reason to Take Legal Action

High	Moderate Risk	Highest Risk
	Lowest Risk	Moderate Risk
Low		

Weak · · · Strong

Merits of the Case: Cause of Action = f
(breach of legal duty + evidence)

quadrants, where either the motivation to sue is strong or the merits of the case are high but the other factor is low, the latent legal risk is moderate. In the upper right-hand quadrant, where both the motivation and merits are high, the risk is the highest.

Had that hairdresser been legally literate, she would have realized that she was partially responsible for denuding her client. Had she viewed the situation through her client's eyes, she could have also appreciated the sense of loss her client suffered: her humiliation and the inconvenience of having to deal with a wig, the lengthy process of waiting for her hair to grow back, and the social awkwardness. Had she listened from the heart and engaged in what Stephen Covey calls "empathic communication," she could have kept the legal liability pot from boiling over.

The hairdresser, for example, could have offered to inquire about the permanent solution with the manufacturer's representative. She could have communicated that she felt just as victimized as her client and would clear her inventory of the offending product so no one else would suffer the same fate. Or she could have apologized for the mishap and perhaps offered to make it up with future discounts on hairdressing services, a free perm, or special deals on other salon services. In short, she could have done any number of things to empathize with her client and align their interests.

If the hairdresser had done a better job of *managing* the emerging problem and *redirecting* her client's anger by reframing the situation to be more aligned with the solution instead of part of the problem, the scenario could have unfolded differently. It could have been transformed from a win-lose situation into a win-win. In the process she would have reduced the client's motivation to sue. The action would have collapsed the top tier of the legal risk chart to a relatively lower level of risk exposure, as illustrated in Figure 7.2. Who knows, had she been more empathetic and honored the client with more respect, her kindness might even have been rewarded with a tip.

But no. She focused instead on her own selfish interest. She just had to point out her willingness to forgo a tip. Let's see, when comparing the equities between the two women, we have forgoing a tip on the one hand balanced against partial baldness and the nuisance of wearing a wig on the other. Hmmm, is that an equi-

FIGURE 7.2. MANAGING THE MOTIVE TO SUE.

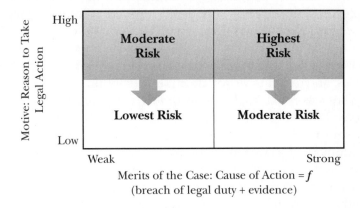

Merits of the Case: Cause of Action = f
(breach of legal duty + evidence)

table trade-off? Is it fair? Clearly the client didn't think so—and voted with her feet by marching straight to a lawyer and into court.

WHAT'S FAIR?

No one expects you to be perfect, but they do expect you to be fair. Fairness taps into our most basic concepts of ethics and of justice. It ties in to respect. It ties in to saving face. No one likes to be denigrated or taken advantage of. Fairness is so fundamental to human dignity that it is a core value recognized by cultures around the world, uniting all levels of society.

In a negotiation workshop I used to teach, "What's fair?" was one of my favorite questions. We'd explore the concept by negotiating the settlement of a family estate, the type of conflict that typically leads to bitter disputes. In the case study, the adult siblings each inherited an equal share of the estate. Selling the bulk of the estate would generate cash that was easily divided, but there were five items the heirs didn't want to sell: the family vacation cottage, an oil painting, an heirloom silver dinner service, some antique furniture, and the contents of the family library, including rare books. That's where the conflict lay. Each of the siblings had a favorite. The same item was often coveted by more than one person.

Each item had multiple values. There was the fair market value and the sentimental value. For some, the sentimental value exceeded the market value, but despite abundant valuations there was no self-evident mathematical solution for determining an equitable distribution. They were deeply divided over how to split the items. How much would they be willing to spend to buy out each other's share in the items that mattered? That was the question. The workshop participants were divided into teams, assigned family roles, and asked to negotiate a fair distribution.

What was remarkable about the exercise was how individual each team's solution was given the small number of facts. Team results were similar but never identical. The combinations and permutations were as varied as the participants. It made me realize that no matter how simple or straightforward the facts may appear, a fresh set of eyes will inevitably see them differently. Everyone brought their own frame of reference to bear on the issues. There was no single "right" answer.

One team, for example, had a particularly creative solution to the vacation cottage. They combined individual ownership with vacation timeshare rights to give the rest of the family an opportunity to create vacation memories with their own children. With respect to the diner service, another team gave one sibling "custody" with the understanding that others could borrow it for special occasions and when hosting the family during holidays. It assured the heirloom pieces would continue to play a continuing role in the family's traditions. Focusing on underlying interests created workable solutions and mutual satisfaction.

Each team felt it had reached a fair settlement even though the settlements were all different from one another. The results demonstrated how the art of listening could provide information about hidden issues that could be translated into sweeteners and deal closers. An antiseptic spreadsheet could not possibly identify or capture the intangible interests that ultimately made these deals happen.

SATISFACTION

The Rolling Stones may have topped the music charts with their hit song "(I Can't Get No) Satisfaction," but when the rest of us are dissatisfied the subject of our discontent is propelled to the top of an entirely different list. Conflicts are bound to happen even with the best legal risk management program. But whether someone feels dissatisfied enough to file suit depends on how the company responds. Attitude precedes behavior. One study that examined litigation patterns of terminated employees, for example, found that employees who felt they were treated unfairly by their former employer during the termination process were twenty times more likely to sue than those who thought they were treated fairly (Lind, 1998).

Business is about relationships: creating them, maintaining them, and if necessary, fixing them. Maintaining the equilibrium of what's "fair" requires the ability to read the warning signs early and translate those warnings into opportunities for joint problem solving. As shown in Figure 7.2, if we can redirect the motive to sue we can reduce our latent legal risk.

Similarly, as shown in Figure 7.3, if we can reduce the liability associated with the merits of the case, either by avoiding the faux pas in the first place or by clarifying how the evidence or the interpretation of the law is not as favorable as the opposing party believes, we can reposition ourselves to the lower end of the liability scale. If we can do both, we can effectively neutralize legal risk into a low-probability event, as in Figure 7.4. Thus, if we want to keep the wheels on the train and avoid a wreck, good negotiation and communication skills play an essential role in our legal leverage tool kit.

FIGURE 7.3. IMPACT OF MANAGING THE MERITS OF THE CASE.

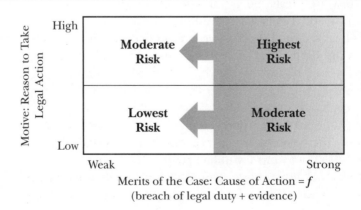

FIGURE 7.4 IMPACT OF MANAGING THE MOTIVE AND MERITS.

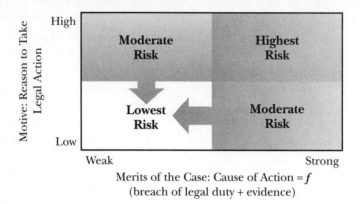

Merits of the Case: Cause of Action = f
(breach of legal duty + evidence)

MANAGING THE URGE TO SUE

Few people are so litigious they will file suit without first complaining and making their grievance known. Those complaints are opportunities; they give you a chance to address the concerns and reconcile differences of opinion. Negotiating and aligning interests is how you responsibly neutralize potential smoking guns and safely return them to the holster. It's an opportunity to address some of the issues explored in Chapter Six, particularly the smoking guns created by lack of clarity or accuracy (Legal Leverage Rule #7) and those created by a documented problem and the lack of responsiveness (Legal Leverage Rule #10).

All too often, however, we get entrenched in our positions. We focus on legal *rights* to the exclusion of all else. Unfortunately, when we dig ourselves a foxhole and shore it up with legal rights we set the stage for battle, not constructive negotiation.

Legal rights are certainly important. They establish a baseline of expectations and a protected zone of interests, one that is sanctioned by the rule of law. But even if you're right, hammering each other into the ground with legal rights comes at the expense of the relationship. It means you could win the battle and lose the war. If you don't mind being a battleaxe, including the reputation it earns, and prefer to have a judge pick a winner, I recommend you skip this chapter and the next. But if you feel that scorched-earth litigation practices only enrich trial lawyers, please read on.

For years software giant Microsoft refused to settle cases with anyone. But in 2002, with a new general counsel at the helm of its legal department, it reevaluated its litigation strategy and entered a less confrontational era. The uncertain nature of patent litigation hampered the company's long-term ability to innovate. A year later Microsoft settled approximately twenty-one cases, including some major ones: an antitrust and patent infringement case involving archrival Sun Microsystems, an antitrust case involving Time Warner, and a patent infringement case involving InterTrust Technologies.

Settlements, including cross-licensing arrangements and business collaborations, made more business sense than protracted litigation. Microsoft realized that it was easier to license patent technology than to design around it. The new philosophy was evident again in 2005. Microsoft settled an antitrust claim with Gateway for $150 million and agreed as part of the deal to collaborate on the marketing and development of Gateway products. Its new legal leadership focused on the future and recognized that there was more to be gained by making peace than war.

Does the new attitude mean that Microsoft has gone soft? Or that your company should adopt a diet of light litigation? Not so fast.

Some cases need to be litigated. What legal leverage does is filter out unnecessary litigation. Before sitting down to the negotiating table, legally leveraged companies determine which liability quadrant a case is in (see Figure 7.1)—and you should too.

Without knowing what the strengths and weakness of your case are, negotiation is nothing more than horse-trading. That's why before Microsoft will settle a patent infringement case, for example, its general counsel says he asks two questions: Is the patent valid? Is Microsoft really infringing it? If the answer is yes to both questions, he's prepared to talk.

DISTINGUISHING BETWEEN RIGHTS AND INTERESTS

Legal *rights* are nothing more than a collection of legally protected *interests*. Therefore rights and interests are not mutually exclusive.

An unbiased understanding of a case's legal merit establishes where the legal interests lie. *Why* someone sues determines the relationship interests that connect the dots between legal rights and mutual satisfaction. Relationship interests are sometimes referred to as hidden agendas. They're what drive behavior. For the estate heirs, the hidden agenda item was the importance of keeping the family intact and maintaining the continuity of family history. For Microsoft, it was the ability to innovate and develop future markets. For the matron at the hair salon it was the acknowledgment that something dreadfully wrong had happened.

Hidden agendas hold the key to conflict resolution. They are hidden treasures that turn negotiations into *Indiana Jones*–style adventures. Seasoned negotiators know that defusing or resolving adversarial situations begins with an understanding of each party's perspective, a focus on mutual gain, and attention to values such as fairness, compassion, accountability, and respect. Navigating these interests is a process—a journey.

If we dwell on rights to the exclusion of interests we overstay our welcome and slam the door on avenues of opportunity that can take us on that journey to a satisfactory solution. Rights-focus reduces the elasticity of the Y-axis in Figure 7.1 and severely limits our ability to influence the desire to sue. The sooner we realize this interrelationship, the sooner we are able to resolve litigation amicably or avoid it altogether.

Customer relations are what keep tourist gripes from turning into lawsuits, in the experience of Grand Circle, the largest travel agency for senior citizens in the United States. When fifty-four passengers died in the crash of an EgyptAir flight off Nantucket, Grand Circle went out of its way to be compassionate to the victims' families. It flew surviving family members to the scene at no charge, and its leaders believe that as a result people were predisposed not to sue. Helping the survivors cope with the sudden tragedy aligned Grand Circle's interests with the survivors'. It moved risk from the top tier of the latent risk chart and shifted it down, just as in Figure 7.2.

The airline industry recognized long ago that providing grief counseling to families whose loved ones died in plane crashes and assisting in them in making funeral arrangements helped reduce the number of wrongful death claims. The medical profession has similarly begun to appreciate the value of a heartfelt apology in reducing the number and size of medical malpractice claims.

"The hardest case for me to bring," said one attorney who represents medical malpractice victims, "is the case where the defense has admitted error. If you have no conflict, you have no story, no debate. And it doesn't play well."

What he really means is that, without the drama, he has no one to paint as the villain and thereby inflame the jury. Admitting error deflates the excess emotional baggage of unfairness attached to denials that don't stack up to the facts. No unfairness. No big punitive damage awards. At that point all that remains is a question of how much the injury itself is really worth, typically a smaller sum from which a personal injury lawyer is left with a smaller contingency fee. Net result: admitting error is cheaper than paying for the time and effort it takes to deny it and being proven wrong.

The Significance of an Apology

In some cases an apology can even eliminate the need for a plaintiff's lawyer altogether. That's what happened to a fifty-year-old former engineer who discovered two weeks after colorectal cancer surgery that he still had a sponge inside his abdomen. Instead of making excuses or denying the fact, the hospital administrator apologized. The surgeon said, "No matter how this happened, I was the surgeon in charge; I was the captain of the ship and I was responsible and I apologize for this." Instead of hiring a lawyer the patient settled the case directly with the hospital. He realized that it was probably for less than he'd have gotten if he'd gone to court, but he appreciated the hospital's honesty and sense of responsibility. "They honored me as a human being," he said.

Some people, however, are leery of apologizing. They may be concerned about saving face, the words "I'm sorry" may not be part of their vocabulary, or at some point in their life's experience they were advised never to admit liability. Early in my driving experience, for example, I was behind a car merging onto a highway from a post office parking lot. Watching the traffic on my left, I thought the car ahead of me pulled out in one of several openings. With my eye still on the traffic I pushed the diesel engine forward with a heavy foot on the accelerator only to discover the car ahead of me was still there. The dented bumper was clearly my fault and

I freely apologized, but when the officer arrived at the scene to write up the accident he admonished me never to say I was sorry at the scene of an accident again.

Granted, admitting a mistake saves the other side the time and trouble of proving liability, but if you're at fault, you're at fault— even if it's only partial fault. Admitting partial liability is easier if the other side to the dispute is similarly disposed, but all too often no one wants to go first. Some fear it is a sign of weakness. Ego and emotions enter into the process until the deadlines imposed by the judicial process force the parties to focus on the real merits of the case, or the assistance of a neutral mediator or arbitrator facilitates the communications process and helps broker a settlement.

A zealous defense is fine in cases with a genuine issue of fact, a gray area of the law, or both. But the rest of the time, zealous denial only serves to make the situation worse. It forces the other side to work harder to prove you wrong and drives up costs. One mother whose eleven-year-old son died when his heart stopped on the operating table was stonewalled by the hospital. They wouldn't tell her what went wrong. "I had to sue to get answers," she said. "You don't take someone's child into surgery and not be accountable when they die."

For the U.S. Navy, not owning up to a sexual harassment problem precipitated the Tailhook scandal in the early 1990s. Named for the Tailhook Association convention in 1991, where fifteen female Navy officers were groped and assaulted by naval aviators in the halls of their convention hotel in Las Vegas, the scandal broke when one of the women stepped forward to complain. Barbara Pope, the assistant secretary of the Navy at the time, who interviewed the whistle-blower, reported that what the woman really wanted was acknowledgment that something bad had happened. She did not want the naval aviators fired, only an admission that what had happened was wrong—an apology.

Instead, the Navy leadership did nothing. They shrugged it off with a "boys will be boys" attitude, they stonewalled, and then they tried to cover it up. The admiral who witnessed the misconduct, for example, was later accused of manipulating the Tailhook investigation for the purpose of avoiding personal liability. Pope is convinced that if the top brass had done *anything* when the allegations of harassment first surfaced, the ensuing scandal would never have happened. The matter would have been resolved quietly.

At the heart of sincere apologies is the notion of accountability, one of the cornerstones of justice. It says, "You're right, I made a mistake." Just because a lawsuit has been filed doesn't mean it's too late to identify and align mutual interests. Admitting responsibility and being accountable provides value in the form of vindication. A friend of mine, a mediator who has handled high-profile sexual harassment cases, recounts how most victims of harassment want an apology. They want an acknowledgment from their harassers that what occurred was wrong.

There is an art to a good apology. It's a delicate balance between accepting responsibility and exposing the company to additional civil or criminal liabilities. All too often, if the plaintiff can't hear those magic words from their tormentor, the next best thing is to hear them from the judge.

Vindication was the motivation, for example, behind a W.R. Grace toxic tort case. In the 1950s miners extracting vermiculite ore used to make asbestos inhaled mine dust for years. Gayla Benefield's father was one of those miners. The dust caused him to develop asbestosis, a thickening of the lung lining and shortness of breath that took his life at age sixty-two. Unfortunately, asbestosis also took the life of Gayla's mother.

Mrs. Benefield did not work at the mine but was exposed to the vermiculite dust through her husband. The company had no facilities at the time to allow employees to shower and change out of their contaminated work clothes, so every night he came home with the dust on his shoes, in his hair, and on his clothes. Clothing that Gayla's mother would launder. Her mother spent the last seventeen months of her life bedridden, cursing asbestos. She died an angry woman.

"You get the bastards, Gayla. Get the people who did this to me and your dad," she reportedly said with her dying breath. And that's exactly what Gayla did.

In the toxic tort exposure case that followed, Gayla refused W.R. Grace's pretrial settlement offer of $605,000 in favor of a $250,000 jury award. She said it was never about the money. The company had never apologized, she said in an interview, and that's why she let the jury decide. She wanted to hear them say the company was responsible, something the company would not admit to directly.

Dwight Golann, professor of law at Suffolk University School of Law, tells of another emotionally charged wrongful death action in his excellent book, *Mediating Legal Disputes* (1996). This case pitted the surviving family of a seventeen-year-old boy against a state trooper who was chasing a drunk driver. The drunk ran a stop sign and the squad car in hot pursuit crossed the intersection, hitting a third vehicle, the car driven by the seventeen-year-old. The teenager died instantly; the trooper survived unscratched. The boy's family sued, arguing that the trooper negligently ignored the stop sign and that their son had not been drinking or driving carelessly. Actually, the boy was a model student and salutatorian of his high school class with a bright future, just weeks away from graduation. But the trooper's defense team argued the officer was giving chase to a dangerous driver in the line of duty. It was a close case.

Two years after the accident, with a trial date fast approaching, the defense made a settlement offer. It was rejected, even though the family knew the trooper had a reasonable defense and that juries had recently viewed similar cases dimly. The family was adamant about not settling and instead wanted to meet with the trooper face to face. Suspicious, the defense counsel reluctantly agreed and a meeting was arranged. What happened next stunned everyone.

The victim's family talked about their lost son and brother, not the merits of the case. They talked about the hopes and dreams they had for him and how their future together was taken away from them. The trooper confided how awful he felt after the accident, how he could no longer do high-speed chases and had asked to be transferred to a desk job. He had three sons of his own and imagined how he'd feel if one of them suddenly died. As they walked out the door, a sibling turned to the trooper and said, "It's been three years since my brother died and now I feel he's finally had a funeral." The case settled two weeks later.

Each case, each plaintiff, and each defendant are different. I do not mean to suggest that an apology is the Mary Poppins equivalent of a spoonful of sugar that makes the medicine go down and everything is better. Poof, the legal problem disappears. But genuine apologies have been shown to help defuse the emotional depth charges that either start or keep the legal waters boiling.

Apologies are a sign of respect, respect for a loss and respect for the legal duty that was breached by the error. It honors the other party's rights *and interests.*

The Impact of Apologies on Remedies

Sometimes owning up to an error helps initiate a meaningful dialogue that starts the healing process and repairs damaged relationships that in turn contribute to a sense of satisfaction and closure, as it did in the trooper case. In some cases, that may be all that's necessary. The apology is enough of a remedy. When a friend of mine backed out of a parking space and hit the bumper of a very expensive car, the words "I'm sorry" poured out before he had a chance to even think about it. He knew the accident was his fault and freely admitted it, to which the other driver merely grunted and said, "Don't worry about it."

In a business setting an act of accountability can lead to leniency—and in certain situations amnesty. The DOJ Antitrust Division, for example, has an amnesty program for companies that report cartel activity that is not already under investigation. When co-conspirator Rhone Poulenc blew the lid off the international vitamin cartel and reported the activity to DOJ under its amnesty program, for example, the company's cooperation was rewarded: it paid zero fines. In contrast, its co-conspirators in the price fixing of nutritional food supplements, specifically vitamins A, B_2, B_5, C, E, and beta carotene, were zapped. They settled their case with DOJ in 1999 for $1.1 billion.

When a company comes forward and blows the whistle on illegal activity, it demonstrates a certain degree of remorse. In a way, remorse is a partial remedy. It cannot undo what happened, but it does convey the fact that the company has become more *mindful.* It's evidence of rehabilitation and offers hope that the problem won't happen again and that the interest of society has been advanced. See Figure 7.5. Such remorse is evidence that the lesson has been learned; it serves to mitigate harsh sentencing or additional prosecution. It influences the motivation to initiate suit as well as the incentive to press on to trial, the Y-axis in Figure 7.2.

Indeed, that's what international accounting giant KPMG was hoping for when a press release it issued in June 2005 did a commendable about-face from its previous scorched-earth litigation

FIGURE 7.5. SIGNIFICANCE OF AN APOLOGY.

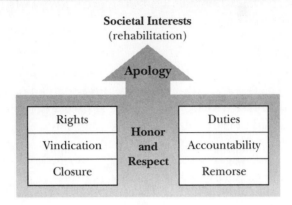

practices by stating the firm "takes full responsibility for the un-lawful conduct by former KPMG partners" for promoting improper tax shelters and "deeply regret[s] that it occurred." Unfortunately, KPMG learned its lesson the hard way.

The apology came two months after the firm paid $22.5 mil-lion to settle SEC charges in connection with Xerox's aggressive accounting practices in Mexico, which were discussed in Chapter Six. Fearing the tax shelter imbroglio could engulf the firm in more legal turmoil, the firm issued its apology in an effort to head off future problems.

Unfortunately, the apology was not enough to deter continued investigation by the SEC or lawsuits from clients. KPMG had a his-tory of being more scornful of government regulatory efforts and more overconfident than any of the other major accounting firms, and its past attitude no doubt played a role in its comeuppance. In August 2005 KPMG was brought to heel when it agreed to pay $456 million to head off a criminal indictment of the firm. The umbrella of protection, however, did not extend to former KPMG executives involved with the shelters—seventeen of whom were criminally in-dicted in October 2005.

Understandably, what holds many companies back from a KPMG-type apology is loss aversion—the fear that speaking out will open a floodgate of litigation. However, research has shown the exact opposite to be true. The Veterans Affairs Hospital in Lexington, Kentucky, for example, adopted a policy of extreme honesty in 1999 after losing two significant malpractice suits. The policy called for *every* medical error to be disclosed immediately and fully, with sincere apologies to the patients and their families as well as genuine proposals to avoid the recurrence of the mishap—a quality improvement initiative. The immediate acknowledgment of a problem minimized the opportunity for attitudes to develop and harden into reputations that inject another dynamic into negotiating process as in the KMPG example.

In a study published by the *Annals of Internal Medicine,* the 1999 edition, it was discovered that the Veterans Affairs Hospital's average cost of error-related payments ranked it not in the highest quartile of comparable VA hospitals as you might expect, but the *lowest,* with settlements and jury verdicts averaging just $15,622 per claim.

Maslow's Hierarchy of Human Needs

Skilled mediators and negotiators recognize that good relationships are built on shared interests and mutual gain. What companies like Grand Circle and many in the aviation industry and the medical community have discovered, whether they realize it consciously or not, is how to tap into Maslow's hierarchy of human needs (Figure 7.6) as a method of creative problem solving and for reframing conflict and aligning interests with customers, clients, or patients.

FIGURE 7.6. MASLOW'S HIERARCHY OF NEEDS.

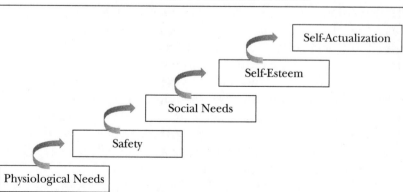

In the late 1960s, psychologist Abraham Maslow identified five instinctive human needs. The most fundamental need is physiological, the basic survival need for food, shelter, water, oxygen, and stimulation. According to Maslow, the basic needs at each level must be met before we can ascend to the next higher plane. Safety relates to the physical and psychological security of a home and family. Social needs have to do with the sense of love and belonging, the desire to be accepted by others. Self-esteem results from the self-respect derived from subject-matter competence or mastery of skills. It also derives from the respect, attention, and recognition provided by others. Finally, self-actualization is the state of achieving a true calling—of doing what one was born to do.

Apologies tap into the need for self-esteem. "They honored me as a human being," said the engineer who had the surgical sponge left inside him. The grief counseling of airlines and assistance with funeral arrangements immediately after an aviation disaster also taps into the survivors' self-esteem as well as their social needs. It reframes the relationship and makes it less adversarial, thereby reducing the incentive to sue. The customers and patients are fairly treated and the businesses avoid protracted litigation. It is a win-win.

Even in the trooper case, where suit had already been filed, communicating the trooper's own emotional turmoil over the fatality helped establish a community of interest with the family. In the mediation of sexual harassment cases it is often the acknowledgment of a wrong being committed by the harasser that achieves vindication and helps bring about a resolution without trial.

MANAGING THE MERITS OF THE CASE

Determining the magnitude of a problem and deciding where on the legal risk spectrum it stands requires objective information about the merits of the case: the applicable law and the facts. Often there is a misunderstanding on one or both of these fronts, and the problem can be resolved if information is made available to key decision makers—and they can focus on it long enough to recognize the implications and make a decision. As a result, resolving the merits of the case is a challenging knowledge management and communications issue. The hard part is getting *all* the key decision makers focused at the same time.

Remember the supervisor described in Chapter Six—the one who'd tried to set up a lunch date at a coworker's home, and replied, "well, we don't exactly have to eat" when she said she wasn't set up to entertain? The company viewed it as a he-said–she-said spitting contest until the legal department received a faxed copy of the e-mail. The company lawyer knew the applicable law. What he didn't know was whether the law when applied to the facts would demonstrate the breach of a legal duty (that is, a genuine problem). Once he saw the fax, the situation and the company's liability crystallized— as did his motivation to settle.

Clarifying the facts can be done the easy way or the hard way. In the e-mail example, suit had not yet been filed and sharing the smoking gun quickly got to the heart of the matter. Once the facts were clear the case was simple to resolve. On the other hand, for the mother of the eleven-year-old who died on the operating table, getting to the facts had to be done the hard way; she had to sue to get answers.

Recognizing the applicable law represents a separate communications challenge. Sometimes lack of legal literacy keeps people from appreciating that a legal duty has been breached. In those cases a choicely worded demand letter sent to your business counterpart will often prompt action. Even if the person you're addressing the letter to fails to see it your way, mentioning that you'll be evaluating your legal options usually routes the letter to your opponent's lawyers. If your position is solid, your opponent's lawyers (if they're competent) can serve as unwitting allies when they explain to their clients that they have more legal risk exposure than they first thought and more to lose than gain by ignoring or fighting your request.

Bridging the gap between conflict and collaboration is certainly easier when the parties are legally literate. But sometimes having a neutral third party facilitate the process makes the bad news easier to digest. In those instances alternative dispute resolution conducted by skilled mediators or arbitrators can be a winning ticket.

Mediators are neutral third parties whose role it is to resolve disputes. Arbitrators are also neutral third parties, but unlike mediators, they do interject their opinion. Their role is to evaluate the facts and the law and to render a decision. Whether the parties agree to be bound by the arbitrator's decision depends on whether they agreed beforehand to submit to binding or nonbinding arbitration. Mediators and arbitrators help cut through emotional and political power-play issues. They help manage legal risk by exposing raw liabilities. They thereby give the parties better information with which to achieve a resolution. Courts serve the same function, but the process is slower and more costly.

The use of alternative dispute resolution can cut the cost of litigation significantly. One company halved its legal costs and became less of a litigation lightning rod, reducing the number of suits filed against it from 263 in 1984 to 28 in 1993. Another company reported a 75 percent reduction in litigation costs.

A conflict management training company, for example, reported in 2001 that managers at Fortune 500 companies spend approximately one-fifth of their time on litigation-related matters. Thus saving even a small percentage of that time can add up to significant dollars.

Some cases deserve to be litigated and brought to court, but the vast majority don't. Nonetheless, that realization doesn't stop companies with weak or moderate legal claims from suing anyway.

Why do they sue if the case is anything other than strong? Plaintiffs often sue not because they want to take the case to a judgment but because it's the only way to get the other party to pay attention. It's how they manage *their* legal risk. That's why companies who ignore complaints do so at their peril.

In 2002, for example, Palm, the maker of the handheld personal digital assistant, faced a class action lawsuit over advertising that the m130 Palm could display more than 65,536 colors. In reality, the unit could only handle 58,621 colors, approximately 11 percent less than advertised. One m130 customer complaining would have had little clout and the economics of one person filing a suit would have been cost-prohibitive. But put a group of disgruntled m130 owners together and the cumulative impact of a class action forces the issue. The lawsuit is the equivalent of a baseball bat between the eyes. It says, "Hey, over here. Listen to me." Suddenly you notice.

Leveraging Litigation

At times *you* may need to be on the offense instead of the defense and will need to use litigation as part of your legal leverage tool kit. Sometimes an apology is not enough.

The advantage of litigation is that the process imposes an orderly method of conflict resolution. It compels accountability by imposing deadlines for discovery and trial and by interceding with a neutral decision maker to decide what's right and wrong and to impose relief. Deadlines and the threat of sanctions for not meeting them have a way of clearing decision-making cobwebs. They force both parties to focus on the issues and sort out their priorities. With a firm grasp of the case's strengths and weakness, revised expectations of what's fair, and the cost of trial looming, motivated parties can engage in constructive negotiations. That's why the majority of cases settle before trial.

Litigation, however, does have its drawbacks. It is costly and can quickly assume a life of its own. Filing suit is a serious decision that carries hidden consequences (see Chapter Three). It should not be undertaken lightly. It is *not* the best way to build relationships and achieve mutual satisfaction. But if *you're* the plaintiff and *your* legal rights are being abused, filing suit may be the only meaningful way to protect yourself.

MOVING TOWARD THE BUSINESS SWEET SPOT

To avoid being the target of the suit means paying close attention to trouble spots and then managing and mitigating the aggravating factors that contribute to a lawsuit (the breach of legal duty and evidence) and incentive to sue. See Table 7.1.

Managing expectations and aligning the parties' interests builds constructive relationships. It opens the door to better communications, more understanding, and increased opportunity for joint problem solving between the parties. It's good business.

Avoiding and managing conflict, however, is a process of continuous negotiation. It occurs before, during, and after a conflict arises. It is a process that is both nuanced and direct. The key to successful negotiation is preparation. We need a firm grip on the legal issues as well as the hidden issues. We need to know where we're heading and be sensitive to the foul lines. We start by asking ourselves the following questions:

- What is the nature of the relationship between the parties?
- Will you be working together again?

TABLE 7.1. SUMMARY OF THE FACTORS THAT DRIVE LITIGATION.

Aggravating Factors	Mitigating Factors	Navigation Guides	
		Goal	Method
Breach of a legal duty	Increase legal literacy and application of legal literacy to avoid unnecessary conflict	Identify relevant law	Communicate informally or formally
Evidence	Better document creation and retention practices	Establish the facts	Communicate informally or formally
Incentive to complain or sue	Proactive interest-based behaviors	Mutual gain	Communicate informally or formally

- What legal interests are at stake?
- What business interests are at stake?

We also need to be aware of negotiating chemistry:

- Are we listening to what the other party is saying? Or merely waiting for our turn to speak? Are we being respectful?
- Are we using legitimate standards that are persuasive? Or only self-serving standards? Are we being fair?
- Are we being creative in seeking solutions that achieve mutual benefit? Or inflexible? Are we meeting social or self-esteem issues?
- Are we engaged in joint problem solving and building a working relationship? Or are we engaged in a battle of wills?

Managing and mediating expectations relates to the powers of persuasion. (See Figure 7.7.) It refers to sales in the highest sense of the word. But before you can sell your ideas, you need to have something of value to sell. You need to be fair. Being fair requires

FIGURE 7.7. LEGAL LEVERAGE PROCESS PORTFOLIO: HIGHLIGHTING EXPECTATIONS.

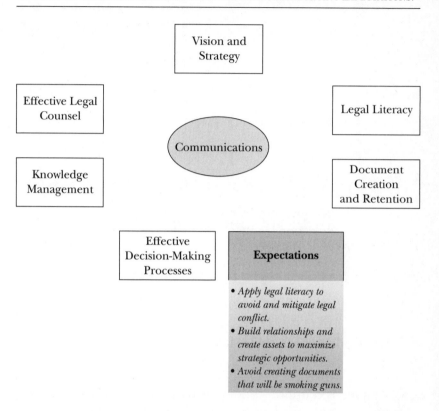

stretching beyond your comfort zone and neutralizing your decision-making biases. Once free of the straitjacket we begin to imagine the unimaginable and generate options that transform legal obstacles into strategic business gains. Managing expectations therefore plays a pivotal role in achieving legal leverage and customer satisfaction.

CHAPTER EIGHT

HOW TO TRANSFORM LEGAL OBSTACLES INTO STRATEGIC OPPORTUNITIES

The Role of Good Decision Making

*Opportunity is missed by most people because it is dressed
in overalls and looks like work.*
—THOMAS A. EDISON (1847–1931)

A corporate purchasing manager has just learned that, contrary to
the company's centralized purchasing policy, its consumer products division had negotiated its own deal with a supplier for components to be used in its newest product launch. Eager to be in on
the ground floor of a blockbuster product, the supplier had offered the component at a rock-bottom price.

"Purchasing is responsible for buying and negotiating all raw
materials," the purchasing manager hastily e-mails the head of consumer products. "Another division uses a million of these same
parts and is paying $2 more per piece than you are," he continues.
"This is one company and all divisions need to be treated equally.
When they find out about this pricing they'll want the same deal."

Purchasing now wants to contact the supplier and negotiate a
corporate-wide package to get the $2 per piece saving for every-
one. Unfortunately, the consumer products division has a confidentiality agreement in place with the supplier and the fact that

corporate purchasing even knows about the deal could signal a breach of the contract.

Circumventing the company's centralized purchasing policy got the division a better price, but it also created a potential lose-lose scenario for the company as a whole, particularly the purchasing department. If purchasing ignores the sweetheart deal, the rest of the company pays $2 more per piece and the department looks like it's not doing its job. Yet confronting the supplier could mire the company in a dispute over confidentiality negotiated with a division. If consumer products' employees had anticipated the problem they could have mitigated it. But developing such foresight and the ability to mobilize the law requires good decision-making processes. It requires noticing the legal implications of operational decisions.

Had consumer products reframed the issue as a company buying opportunity instead of a divisional buying opportunity and reframed the scope of the issue from "me" to "we," it would have been clear that purchasing had a legitimate corporate interest to protect. More specifically, consumer products should have asked, "Who else in the value chain can be affected by this decision?"

Reframing to include these stakeholders would have included other perspectives that needed to be part of the dialogue. It would have presented an opportunity for better intelligence gathering, or more "due diligence" as the lawyers like to call it. It would also have imbued the process with cross-functionality, providing more information from which to craft a mutually acceptable solution—one that satisfied a broader spectrum of the affected population. Instead, one constituency satisfied itself at the expense of another.

Loss aversion—the fear of being told no—is what stops many employees in their tracks and keeps them from investigating whether a particular course of action as originally envisioned optimizes the company's success. "It's easier to beg forgiveness than ask permission," they rationalize—while conveniently and over-confidently ignoring *why* permission might be denied. As a result, the lack of available information forecloses new data that could be inconsistent with their originally held beliefs and precludes the chance of a better solution.

Corporate purchasing, for example, might have offered a *larger* share of the company's component requirements in exchange for a bigger quantity discount. Such an arrangement would have benefited everyone. The company would have a lower unit cost. Consumer products would still be able to pursue their prototype project. Corporate purchasing would have generated a cost savings and the supplier would have increased the size of a profitable contract.

Reframing to include cross-functionality could have transformed a legal obstacle into a strategic opportunity. Best of all, it would have yielded a superior result from both a legal and a business perspective. It would have hit the sweet spot. Instead, poor processes left the supplier holding a breach-of-contract trump card.

THE ROLE OF LUCK IN DECISION MAKING

Skeptics might argue that whether an organization gets caught in a legal bind—whether it is called to task for upsetting a customer or vendor or held accountable to the government for violating a regulation—is merely a matter of luck. "If it's going to happen, it's going to happen anyway," the story goes.

In *Winning Decisions* (2002), authors Edward Russo and Paul Schoemaker acknowledge that decisions are a product of doing, deciding, and *chance*. They concede that luck plays a role when making decisions under uncertainty. According to the authors, the role of luck in decision making means that a good process can still lead to a bad result. See Figure 8.1. Thus to a certain degree the skeptics are absolutely right.

So is the time and effort necessary to establish good decision-making processes worthwhile? If good processes can't guarantee good results and bad results carry heavy legal consequences, why bother? *Wouldn't we be better off banking those resources and using them to pay the legal bills down the road? Is good decision making a smart investment?*

Yes, good decision making *is* a smart investment. Even if good processes unintentionally lead to criminal results, their consequences are mitigated in the United States through the U.S. Federal Organizational Sentencing Guidelines. These guidelines set forth strict formulas under which penalties are calculated. They determine how much an organization is to be punished for a "bad

FIGURE 8.1. VALUE OF GOOD DECISION-MAKING PROCESSES.

		Outcome	
		Good	Bad
Process Used to Make the Decision	Good	Deserved Success	Bad Break
	Bad	Dumb Luck	Poetic Justice

Source: Adapted from *Winning Decisions* by J. Edward Russo and Paul J. H. Schoemaker, copyright © 2002 by J. Edward Russo and Paul J. H. Schoemaker. Used by permission of Doubleday, a division of Random House, Inc.

result." When organizations have made an effort to avoid noncompliance through what the law calls an "effective" compliance and ethics program, the guidelines take these good intentions into account. Effective programs and cooperation with government law enforcement authorities generate credits that can be used to offset and mitigate the penalty calculations in criminal cases at the court's discretion.

The fact that noncompliance has occurred does not automatically mean that the program is ineffective. (See Appendix D for the parameters used to evaluate the effectiveness of compliance and ethics programs.) The law is practical enough to recognize that no compliance program is bulletproof. Yet having a good program does not guarantee safety or insulate an organization from sentencing liability under the guideline's penalty provisions. There is no free pass. It therefore still pays to take steps to avoid liability-triggering events, especially since the guidelines only apply to judgments in criminal cases, not in civil cases.

Just as good processes can lead to bad results, Russo and Paul also note that it is possible for bad processes to create a good result, as in the lower left-hand quadrant of Figure 8.1. Here we go again. We're back to the question of *why bother. Why work toward a good result when Lady Luck can make it happen using bad processes, and good processes can backfire?*

Mounting deadline pressures, increased multitasking, and information systems that provide a sensory overload twenty-four hours a day, seven days a week increase our need to cut through the clutter and follow the path of least resistance when making decisions. The bias is for action, not reflection. *Who has time for processes that slow things down? What good are they if "what will be will be"?* Maybe the skeptics are right again? Or maybe not.

THE VALUE OF DECISION-MAKING PROCESSES

Solid processes are valuable because the operative word in Russo and Schoemaker's hypothesis (that it is possible to get good results from bad processes) is *possible*. Given the increasingly hostile legal environment of business, as discussed in Chapter Two, it's *more probable* that a bad decision-making process will lead to a bad result—one that carries with it unacceptable consequences, perhaps at a catastrophic level—instead.

Bad processes combined with the mathematical principle of regression tempt the hand of fate. They pancake business decisions, stacking one legal risk on top of another, until the whole construct collapses. With bad decision-making processes it's not a question of *whether* latent legal liability will materialize, it's only a question of *when*.

In the 1990s—the high-tech heyday, when the entire stock market was climbing daily by leaps and bounds—the rising tide made everyone's boat float higher. Even losing stocks appeared to be winners. But years later when the bubble burst, traders who had ignored sound investment principles, and whose practices were more akin to gambling, were left with overweighted tech portfolios and valuations that were under water. Disciplined investors, however, who followed sound methods of investment in the face of get-rich-quick temptation, were less likely to be marooned by the imploding valuations. As a result, investments made pursuant to solid processes hedged portfolio risk and led to more sustainable and consistent returns.

The value of sound processes and methodology is similarly well established in the area of manufacturing, where repeatability is the hallmark of high quality. It's also key in science, where repeatability is essential to determining the merits and validity of any scientific breakthrough. After all, how do we know the miracle cancer drug is the real deal if the results can't be duplicated? Impressive results based on dumb luck do not create enduring brands. The marketplace values consistency and repeatability, the characteristics of long-term sustainability.

Besides, why should the decision making that supports the management of the business enterprise and steers the corporate ship of state, in small transactions and large, be any less rigorous than that used in other parts of the company? No reputable business would dream of running a haphazard manufacturing facility. Yet knowledge workers tend to chafe at process controls such as the Sarbanes-Oxley regulations that impose accountability. They're viewed as unnecessary straitjackets. So what if a few errors occur?

We justify and rationalize these errors as an inevitable side effect of working with uncertainty. They're a cost of doing business. Unfortunately, undisciplined thinking can harbor and feed decision-making biases that hamper our ability to manage legal risks proactively. This is precisely the decision-making hamster wheel we need to escape.

At first blush, the notion of disassembling and reconstructing decision-making processes sounds enormously inconvenient. But, as Russo and Schoemaker explain, the process of improving critical thinking skills and making winning decisions is similar to disassembling and reconstructing a golf swing. In the beginning it feels unnatural and awkward. But over time, with practice and persistence, it becomes altogether natural. Slight improvements can create significant results once you realize how these elements are interrelated. A minor one-degree course correction, when going the distance, can make the difference between landing on the green or in the rough, between quality results and extra strokes. Which would you prefer?

Developing Decision-Making Processes to Achieve Legal Leverage

Earlier chapters have introduced some of the individual building blocks used in the legal leverage decision-making process. Legal audits, legal literacy requirements, document creation and retention policies, and managing expectations all play a valuable role in managing legal risk and avoiding lawsuits. These building blocks work even better when they are joined together into a cohesive whole as part of a strategic decision-making framework. It's a framework that lets you identify *when* and *where* legal risk occurs in the value chain and lets you determine how much leverage you want to achieve. It's a process for figuring out how to take smart risks.

Lessons from a Research and Development Laboratory

Take, for example, the situation involving a manufacturing company whose research and development (R&D) efforts were largely dedicated to supporting the company's production and marketing efforts. The company's intellectual property strategy was very basic. Patents were trophies. Little thought was given to the strategic value of the patent, whether it related to core business objectives or not. If an invention was patentable, a patent was applied for. That's how far the analysis went. As a result the company found itself with a patent portfolio of marginal strategic use.

Changes in the competitive landscape, however, caused the company to change its thinking. Regulatory requirements forced R&D to collaborate more frequently with outside vendors to satisfy emerging technical needs. Competitors were aggressively patenting innovations that the company and others in the industry would need to use if they wanted to be in compliance with industry regulatory trends. When the company suddenly realized that it might end up paying royalties to competitors, the desire to develop its own inventions and be in the driver's seat on patent rights took on a new sense of urgency. Moreover, new leadership realized that savvy use of intellectual property could turn R&D from a company overhead expense into a profit center.

As the company looked at the strengths and weaknesses of its R&D practices, it realized that its nonchalant contracting practices with vendors, relying on little more than purchase orders and acceptances, might not offer enough protection for trade secrets. Since trade secrets are the backbone of patentability, their casual treatment meant that the ownership rights of any inventions created through collaboration could be at risk. Without better protection in place it would be possible for the vendor to claim ownership—at which point, with ownership rights in hand, the vendor would have nothing to stop it from offering a jointly developed innovation to the company's competition—a result that was totally unacceptable. Thus without good trade secret protection the company's long-term goal of staying in the driver's seat was in jeopardy.

Since the trade secret issue related directly to a strategic initiative, it was given a high priority by R&D. To remedy the problem the company began improving the legal literacy of key R&D staff. The legal principles of trade secrets and confidentiality were presented in an operational business context. Examples illustrating the relationship between trade secrets, patents, and the company's competitive advantage were supplemented with case histories from the company's own files. Looking at these interdependencies from the perspective of company files established the know-how and know-why that made the training relevant.

The program had people buzzing in the hallways for days. "Now I realize *how* what I do is important," said one of the participants afterward. As the lessons sank in the employees began to think more about the trade secrets they were entrusted with and the questions started pouring in.

Is the existing confidentiality agreement enough protection for the project I'm working on? When should I start thinking about a joint development agreement? What if I have already developed something with a vendor without a joint development agreement? Is it too late to protect the company's interests?

Individual projects were examined and fears allayed. Some documentation was sufficient in its existing form while other records needed to be supplemented to achieve the desired level of protection. The employees' timely response strengthened the value chain, averted future problems, and advanced the company's strategic patent agenda.

Five Steps to Leveraged Decision Making

Deconstructing the R&D example into the components of leveraged decision making reveals five distinct steps. See Figure 8.2. These steps systematically isolate the interdependencies between law and specific operational business issues in a way that prioritizes them for maximum return on investment.

FIGURE 8.2. LEVERAGING THE DECISION-MAKING PROCESS.

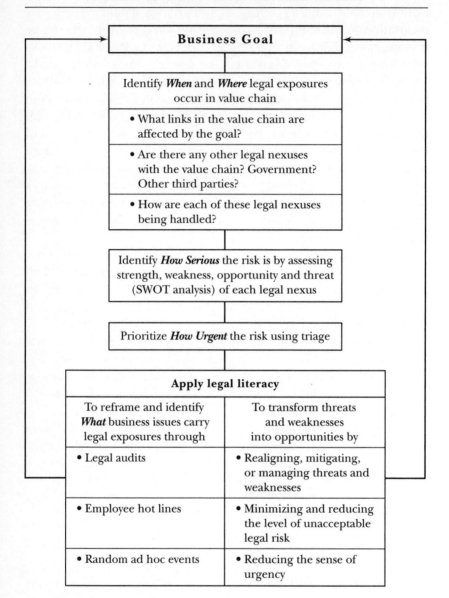

Identify the Strategic Business Objective

As illustrated in Figure 8.2, the process starts with the business objective. Keeping the end in mind keeps you focused. It makes sure that any legal steps taken will advance the business agenda. It allows for better integration and reconciliation of the two. In the R&D example, the business objective was to protect competitive advantage and profit margins by developing a stronger intellectual property portfolio that would protect the technology necessary to meet industry regulatory requirements.

Identify the Relevant Legal Issues

The second step of the process is to identify the legal ramifications of the business goal, and more particularly when and where these legal ramifications touch the value chain. The analysis showed that patentable trade secrets were concentrated in R&D and manufacturing operations. The increasing use of outside vendors presented another wrinkle. It was a third-party nexus that needed to be factored in. It required the company to broaden its span of control over trade secrets to include outsiders. This wrinkle heightened the importance of good contracts and business relationships.

Identify Strengths, Weaknesses, Opportunities, and Threats

The third step of the process is to assess the strengths, weaknesses, opportunities, and threats of each R&D-related trade secret nexus in the value chain for the purpose of determining the severity of the problem. This form of evaluation is also known by the shorthand name of SWOT analysis (strengths, weaknesses, opportunities, and threats). At this stage of the analysis you're noticing how these interdependencies work and how to exploit them.

The fact that a relatively small number of people were privy to patentable trade secrets was considered a strength. The small number made it easier to control access and keep the secrets secret. Casual past practices, however, were perceived to be a weakness, threatening the company's ability to secure its intellectual legal rights and protect its competitive advantage. The weakness, however, presented an opportunity for corrective action, for legal literacy training.

Prioritize the Legal Risk

The fourth step is to prioritize the legal risk and devise an action plan. In other words, how fast does the company need to act? Before turning loose an army of lawyers we need to determine how serious and how important a given legal risk is. Legal risks are not all created equal. Their severity and significance will influence the sense of urgency with which they need to be addressed. The urgency will in turn influence the amount of resources that can be justified and dedicated to the issue.

Some risks are larger than others. Some loom large because even a small risk has major strategic significance, such as the Microsoft Xbox power cord recall in advance of the new Xbox product launch. Others loom large because even a low probability of occurrence can lead to what is perceived to be unacceptable consequences—such as Intel's perception of antitrust risk and wanting to avoid the fate of AT&T and other monopolies that had been broken up through judicial intervention.

Using a process of triage, as shown in Table 8.1, we can prioritize legal risk by its level of severity. Level three is assigned to the most severe and serious cases—those that are crisis oriented. These pit decision makers against a ticking clock and leave little room for error. Time is of the essence. The objective of risk management

TABLE 8.1. LEGAL LEVERAGE TRIAGE CHARACTERISTICS.

Level	One	Two	Three
Leverage opportunity	Win-win	Win-lose	Lose less
Behavior mode	Preventive	Preventive or reactive	Reactive
Characteristics	Creating and managing expectation mode	Mediation mode	Crisis mode
Key questions	Is it possible to eliminate or avoid the problem?	Is it possible to mitigate or contain the result?	Is it possible to minimize the damage?

level three is damage control: to stop the bleeding, to stabilize the situation, and quell the immediate crisis-lowering the risk to level two where more time and management options are available. Level two seeks to mitigate or contain a liability, while level one tries to nip it in the bud. Level one is what we typically refer to as preventive law or medicine.

In the R&D example, the situation did not rise to crisis-level proportions requiring level-three treatment. But some of the subsequent questions and contract issues raised by the employees did pose containment and mediation issues. It would have been fair to characterize them as at level two. As a result, steps were taken immediately to amend certain agreements and renegotiate others. Given the strategic importance of these issues, remedial action was not delayed.

Apply Legal Literacy

Finally, the last step of the leveraged decision-making process involves legal literacy. In the R&D scenario, increasing R&D's legal literacy allowed employees to apply the information to their current projects, reframing the trade secret issues in more tangible and more specific terms. Reframing raised a set of subsidiary issues that were project and contract specific.

Each of these subsidiary issues was similarly analyzed through the leveraged decision-making lens. The specific trade secret issues surrounding each project were identified, a SWOT analysis was done, their severity was prioritized, and an action plan was created. All concerns were clarified with contract modifications. Legal literacy was thereby a catalyst for achieving targeted remedial action.

As illustrated in Figure 8.2, the legal literacy step was pivotal. It allowed employees to notice the legal aspects of their work. In the first pass through the legal literacy filter, for example, when the issue was framed in terms of building a strategic intellectual property portfolio, legal literacy helped identify the issue of trade secret protection and prompted a call for training. Those results led to a reiteration of the process, but the second time it had a more refined and tightly focused objective.

The first pass led to more due diligence and better availability of information. The second pass led to specific action items. Reframed and refined, the issues reloaded the decision-making process and squeezed unwanted legal risk out of the value chain with each iteration. In highly complex matters several iterations of the process may be necessary before the risk is reined in to acceptable levels.

Engaging managers in the process of critically thinking through the legal ramifications of their business objective created an ownership interest in the solutions they developed. The shared effort improved the odds for lasting success far beyond those of any policy or procedure imposed from above. Thus the legal leverage decision-making process fosters lasting solutions that keep performance tightly focused on achieving legitimate business goals.

LESSONS FROM THE SCHOOL OF HARD KNOCKS

Good decision making and just-in-time legal literacy work. They helped save DoubleClick from strangling regulation. Early miscalculation about information privacy initially placed DoubleClick in the hot seat. But as privacy issues, lawsuits, and investigations began making headlines, the company realized it was better to address those issues quickly than to let them fester and become a rallying cry for regulation. Quick action in the face of an escalating conflict transformed a level-three event into a level-two event. When DoubleClick's decisive self-regulation convinced the government there was no need for legislative intervention, the level-two risk exposure was further reduced to level one.

Every mistake has a halfway moment, a split second where you can pull back and remedy the situation or when you decide to dig your bunker and fight it out. Compare the DoubleClick experience to that of United Airlines.

In 1971 two United employees doggedly pursued a great idea. They suggested that the airline fill unused seats by offering discounts to airline employees. United eventually implemented the idea and it soon began generating an additional $3 million in annual profits. There's nothing illegal about that.

Where United ran afoul of the law, however, was in how it managed the expectations of the employees with the brainstorm. The employees thought they had submitted their idea as part of United's suggestion plan, which included a provision for awards based on 10 percent of the estimated first or typical year's savings, whichever is greater. But instead of receiving 10 percent of the profits as they expected, they were rewarded with a prize of $1,000 that they *split*. Feeling shortchanged, they sued.

United, however, alleged that some suggestions are not eligible for awards, such as ideas that were previously submitted, or were initiated by United before receipt of the suggestion. The record showed that United had indeed received the same suggestion from others and had been working on the discount seat idea on its own. As a result, United's management characterized the $1,000 payment as an impetus award, that is, a discretionary gratuity separate and apart from the suggestion program.

The case dragged on for nearly twenty years, until 1992, when the California Supreme Court upheld damages of $479,000 and set aside a lower court judgment awarding $2.5 million in punitive damages. Ineffective implementation of processes, rules, and standards for evaluating and compensating suggestion box ideas contributed to misunderstanding and a slew of unwanted costs.

Such examples of flawed decision making are not uncommon. Malden Mills's decision to forgo patent rights on its proprietary fleece manufacturing process left it defenseless against competitors. Similarly, delaying the investigation of European antitrust issues surrounding merger approvals scuttled the proposed General Electric–Honeywell merger, and narrow cost-benefit analysis in the Ford Pinto case placed profits ahead of consumer safety and led to unfavorable legal rulings.

At the same time, it's also possible to see the results of good decision-making processes and legal leverage in action: Colgate's return of unread Dial trade secrets preempted future legal liability and earned respect; Intel's antitrust training protected the legitimacy of its competitive position; Microsoft's Xbox power cord replacement paved the way for a trouble-free new Xbox generation that could go head to head with Sony, and Huntsman Chemical's use of past experience to implement better communications between manufacturing and environmental compliance functions avoided future environmental permit violations.

STRIKING A BALANCE BETWEEN HEALTHY AND UNHEALTHY RISK

The leveraged decision-making process eliminates business blind spots. It lets you systematically identify, evaluate, and prioritize legal risk. If a legal risk is then discounted for business reasons, the discount is a result of critical thinking and a conscious decision based on solid, unbiased information, not decision-making bias. When such risk is embraced it is a knowing and a calculated risk. It's not a surprise. No more "oops" factor.

The objective of legal leverage is to strike a healthy balance between manageable and unmanageable risk taking, a balance that requires careful examination of the severity of the legal risk, its likelihood of occurrence, and its consequences in relation to the organization's goals and objectives. The goal is to avoid unmanageable legal risk exposure and to reduce existing risk exposures to more manageable levels.

The real size of a legal risk must always be determined by the *business consequences* of the risk. Sometimes even a "small" risk can have a huge impact—the same way a single flea can drive even a large dog crazy. Discounting legal risk because a liability-triggering event is *possible* but not *probable* can nonetheless create massive problems if the consequences created by the risk are unacceptable, if they are catastrophic.

One hospital, for example, found itself in a horrible legal jam after a young heart transplant patient died when her body rejected a donor heart. The organ was rejected because the organ's blood type did not match the patient's. The mismatch should never have occurred. It was a possibility, not a probability. Yet it happened. Even though it was unlikely to happen again, the legal liability and reputation risk associated with even a statistically small chance of recurrence was too large to take. The hospital built redundancies into its procedures, little safety nets designed as backup systems to catch and eliminate any future mistakes. These procedural changes were designed to ensure that such a tragic error would never happen again.

To avoid corporate tragedies resulting from financial engineering, a consequence deemed unacceptable as a matter of public policy, the U.S. Congress imposed its own set of safety net procedures. The Sarbanes-Oxley Act, for example, is a legislative response to a statistically small risk that carried catastrophic consequences.

RISK TOLERANCE AND EXCELLENCE

While some businesses are content to shrug their corporate shoulders and believe legal risk is an inevitable side effect of uncertainty that can't be controlled, other organizations—like hospitals and nuclear power plants—realize that operational excellence is not optional but rather something that must continuously be strived for. They can't afford to make mistakes. They *must* function reliably, yet like everyone else, they are forced to operate in an uncertain world. How do they do it?

In *Managing the Unexpected* (2001), authors Karl E. Weick and Kathleen M. Sutcliffe examine what they call "high reliability organizations" and look at how these top-performing entities keep passing problems from turning into pressing problems. Their fascinating research reveals that the key to success is the organization's attitude about risk: a state of mindfulness.

Mindfulness is a combination of aptitude and attitude. It's a state of alertness that continuously assimilates information, recognizes the significance of small changes early, and mitigates potentially negative consequences. More specifically, the organizations studied by Weick and Sutcliffe took pride in looking for interdependencies and noticing new things. Generally speaking, they were all

- More preoccupied with failures than with successes. They appreciated that achieving strategic goals is as much about knowing what mistakes to avoid as it is about knowing what you want to achieve.
- Reluctant to oversimplify. They preferred to reconcile interdisciplinary perspectives without sacrificing important nuances.
- Sensitive to operations and relationships within the value chain. They were particularly alert to the risk associated with latent failures.
- Committed to resilience. They bounced back from past errors by learning from past mistakes and developing knowledge.
- Deferential to expertise.

Research on mindfulness significantly dents the "no risk, no gain" mentality that encourages aggressive risk taking. Indeed, it proves that the only sustainable and *reliable* gain is based on sound decision-making processes and a commitment to preserving the integrity of those processes.

Conducting business in a legally leveraged and compliant manner means flying straight, not necessarily narrow. It is not the same thing as zero risk tolerance. When we add mindfulness to leveraged decision making we get a higher commitment to legal compliance and to legal leverage. See Table 8.2. It's a process of continuous awareness that bridges law and business. By building bridges instead of walls, it systematically embeds better risk management throughout the value chain and forges customer satisfaction.

Mindfulness preserves the integrity of the decision-making process. The goal is to leave you in a position to choose wisely between the battles and the wars, to advance and protect legitimate business interests and avoid a corporate Waterloo. The ability to use such decision-making processes to transform legal hot spots into business sweet spots has unprecedented strategic value. The return on investment of such disciplined integrity is sustainable quality, productivity, and reliability—in short, institutionalized excellence. See Figure 8.3.

TABLE 8.2. HOW APTITUDE AND ATTITUDE CONTRIBUTE
TO BETTER DECISION MAKING.

Leveraged Decision Making (Aptitude)	Mindful Decision Making (Attitude)	Enhanced Commitment to Legal Compliance and Legal Leverage
Identify business objectives	Recognition of failures	Anticipate potential problems and neutralize overconfidence bias
Identify relevant legal issues	Reluctance to simplify	Neutralize availability bias
SWOT analysis	Sensitivity to operations	Optimize performance of the value chain
Prioritize risk	Commitment to resilience	Commit to excellence by systematically reducing risk
Apply legal literacy	Deference to expertise	Neutralize overconfidence and availability bias

FIGURE 8.3. LEGAL LEVERAGE PROCESS PORTFOLIO:
HIGHLIGHTING EFFECTIVE DECISION MAKING.

Vision and
Strategy

Effective Legal
Counsel

Legal Literacy

Communications

Knowledge
Management

Document
Creation
and Retention

**Effective
Decision-Making
Processes**

Expectations

- *Reframe issues.*
- *Increase the availability
  of information by using
  cross-functional teams.*
- *Neutralize overconfidence
  by utilizing processes.*
- *Prioritize issues using
  triage and SWOT analysis.*
- *Be mindful of
  interdependencies.*

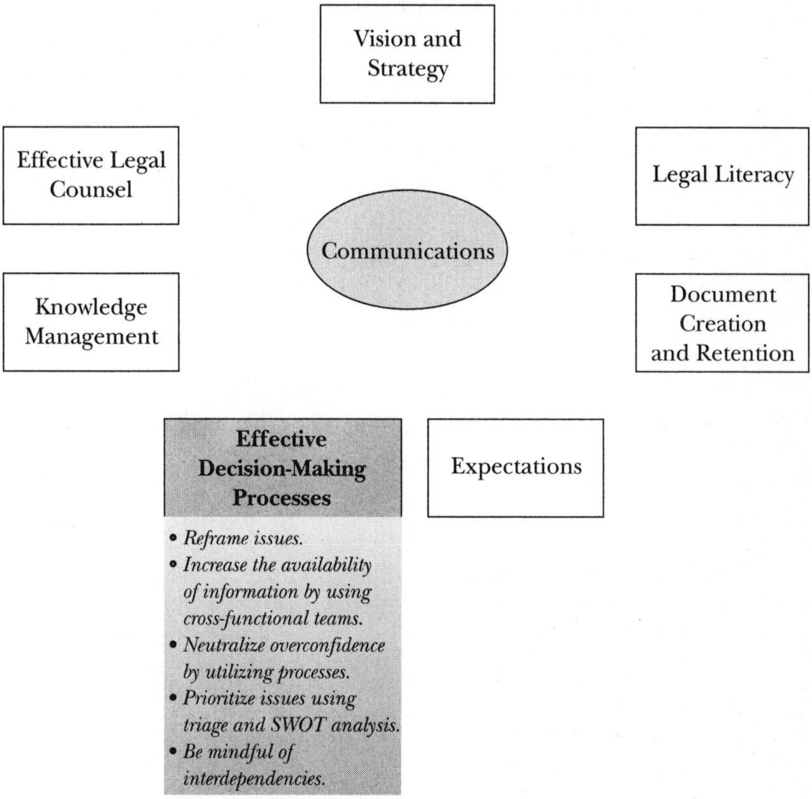

PART THREE

HOW TO MAINTAIN LEGAL LEVERAGE

*Developing a Supportive
Corporate Culture*

HOW TO STAY ON COURSE
The Role of Continuous Learning and Knowledge Management

Integrity without knowledge is weak and useless, and knowledge without integrity is dangerous and dreadful.
—SAMUEL JOHNSON (1709–1784)

In March 2002 international accounting giant Arthur Andersen was indicted for obstruction of justice in connection with shredding documents related to the collapse of Enron Corporation. The indictment specifically alleged that Andersen "did knowingly, intentionally and corruptly persuade . . . other persons, to wit: [Andersen] employees, with intent to cause" them to withhold documents from, and alter documents for use in "official proceedings, namely: regulatory and criminal proceedings and investigations." The case was tried before a jury, and on June 15, 2002, Andersen was found guilty.

While Andersen spent the next three years appealing the criminal conviction all the way to the U.S. Supreme Court, its reputation lay in ruins. "Ladies and gentlemen, I have good news and bad news," quipped President George W. Bush in an after-dinner speech. "First, Saddam Hussein has agreed that we can count his weapons of mass destruction. But he wants Andersen to count them."

In May 2005 the high court held that the jury instructions leading to Andersen's criminal conviction were "flawed in important respects" because they failed to communicate the proper statutory elements necessary to establish "corrupt persuasion." More specifically, the court said the jury instructions diluted the meaning of the word "corruptly" to the point where even innocent conduct could trigger a violation. Furthermore, the instruction misled the jury into believing that there didn't need be a connection, or nexus, between the "persuasion" to destroy documents and a particular legal proceeding. As a result the case was reversed and remanded.

The reversal meant there was a misinterpretation of the law. It meant that without the proper legal standard to evaluate Andersen's behavior, the jury's decision-making *process* was flawed and therefore its conclusion is suspect. As a result, Andersen was innocent—for now. Casual observers of the court system often miss this subtle but important distinction. They confuse the ruling on the issue of law with a ruling on the merits, thereby inferring more from appellate ruling than is warranted.

It is the role of appellate courts to decide issues of law as opposed to issues of fact. It is up to the trial courts to determine the facts and apply the law to the facts. If the lower court's reading of the law is flawed, the defective information affects the decision-making process and the verdict it produces. The appellate process is the cure for such errors. Each rung on the appellate ladder is a check for the rung beneath it. It is a quality control mechanism that makes available accurate and consistent interpretations of the law. It is this *availability* that protects the integrity of the decision-making process and the end product: justice.

Thus, in the *Andersen* case it is up to a properly instructed jury to determine whether the facts are sufficient evidence to meet the burden of proof and establish a violation of the law. The high court's remand is therefore the equivalent of a "do over." But for Arthur Andersen, the decision is too little too late.

The criminal conviction in 2002 was a de facto corporate death sentence. Andersen's license to conduct financial audits was revoked after the conviction. Then its business dried up. The meltdown interrupted the careers of twenty-eight thousand employees. The few who are left are merely mopping up legal matters before they turn off the lights for the last time. It is a sad requiem for a respected firm.

Significance of Knowledge Management

Knowledge management is how the business enterprise makes information available to the organization and how it develops employee judgment that consistently converts the information into results the organization wants. Without the ability to convert information into action, learning is nothing more than the acquisition of information and data. Unfortunately, we can easily find ourselves caught in the learning paradox experienced by students. They take a course, master the material sufficiently to pass an exam, and graduate. But once the course is over they remember very little.

Organizations cannot afford to be stuck in a learning paradox. In an increasingly hostile legal environment they have too much at stake. Having the right information is essential to good decision making, whether in the jury room, the boardroom, or elsewhere. Achieving a quality output requires quality input.

The process of knowledge management determines *what* we know about our organization's legal risk and influences *how* we can apply that information. An effective system therefore adds muscle to decision making and helps align business practices with the law.

As illustrated in Figure 9.1, business objectives are supported by company policies that establish standard operating procedures and govern the value chain. Meeting targets is determined by the ability to implement these operating procedures and implement them hassle-free. The success of such implementation is in turn determined by legal literacy.

The Arthur Andersen Lesson

The *Andersen* case is a cautionary tale that highlights the role of effective knowledge management in keeping business and legal interests aligned. One of Andersen's business objectives, as with all businesses, was to maintain business records in accordance with business and legal requirements. To achieve this goal, Andersen adopted a document retention policy that allowed for document destruction. Again, nothing earthshaking or illegal about spelling

FIGURE 9.1. ALIGNMENT OF BUSINESS OBJECTIVES,
POLICIES, AND POLICY IMPLEMENTATION.

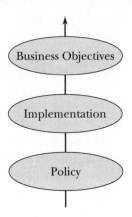

out how and when to clean out files that no longer serve a useful business or legal purpose.

When the Andersen jury, however, was given broad instructions and convicted Andersen for shredding documents related to the Enron, some people began to wonder whether *any* document destruction could subject them to a similar fate. Luckily, the Supreme Court laid that concern to rest when it said, "It is, of course, not wrongful for a manager to instruct his employees to comply with a valid document retention policy under ordinary circumstances." Thus, *valid* document retention policies providing for document destruction are not illegal per se. Andersen's methodology and business objective were squarely aligned.

What was potentially misaligned, however, was the *implementation* of its document retention policy. If a policy is not implemented properly it will miss its intended business objective. The gap between good and bad implementation represents an opportunity cost. See Figure 9.2. If improper implementation also violates a legal duty, as alleged in the *Andersen* case, it can also creates a *legal* liability. See Figure 9.3.

Although the *Andersen* court blessed retention policies in general, the court qualified its statement, saying that compliance with

FIGURE 9.2. COMPARISON OF ALIGNMENT AND MISALIGNMENT OF
BUSINESS OBJECTIVES, POLICIES, AND POLICY IMPLEMENTATION.

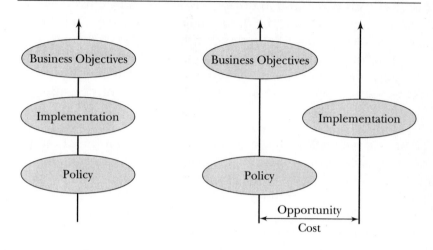

FIGURE 9.3. HOW LEGAL LIABILITY IS CREATED WHEN BUSINESS OBJECTIVES,
POLICIES, AND POLICY IMPLEMENTATION ARE MISALIGNED.

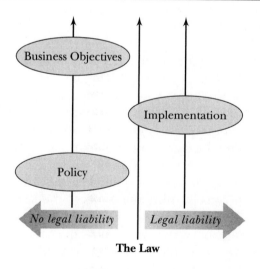

such policies was not illegal under *ordinary* circumstances. It therefore left open the issue of compliance under *extraordinary* circumstances. Was shredding in the shadow of the Enron investigation
extraordinary? That is the question. Thus the issue after the reversal and remand is whether Andersen *knew* it was "corruptly persuading" its employees to shred documents for the purpose of
keeping them from being discovered in the Enron case. Was there
a connection between reminders and the SEC's investigation of
Enron investigation?

If we look at the Enron-Andersen time line (Exhibit 9.1) we see
that Andersen's Enron engagement team was reminded on numerous occasions to follow the company's document retention policy after the Enron scandal broke. Yet in looking at the court
record, we see misunderstanding among Andersen employees
about *how* to follow the policy and what exactly was meant when
they were repeatedly instructed to comply with it.

One of Andersen's Enron engagement partners, David Duncan, interpreted compliance to mean he could keep shredding
documents until Andersen was officially subpoenaed for Enron
records. The subpoena was served on Anderson on November 9,
2002, and the next day Duncan's secretary sent e-mail saying: "Per
Dave—No more shredding. . . . We have been officially served for
our documents."

As early as October 26, 2002, however, one of Duncan's partners saw him shredding documents and said, "This wouldn't be the
best time in the world for you guys to be shredding a bunch of
stuff." *He* clearly had a different opinion on what compliance
meant. And then there was Andersen's forensics investigator. On
October 31, 2002, he saw Duncan pick up a document marked
"smoking gun" and toss it into a shredder, saying: "We don't need
this." The investigator warned against it, but it was too late. Did
Duncan *know* he was pushing the limits of the law? Was "compliance" with the document retention policy done intentionally and
corruptly? That's what a remand would answer.

For legal leverage purposes, the real question to ask is whether
Duncan would have continued his shredding if he had any clue
about its lethal aftershocks and their impact on the firm and his
career. The inconsistent understanding among Andersen employees about what it meant to comply with the policy was the result of

Exhibit 9.1. Arthur Andersen–Enron Time Line.

2000	Enron's financial performance begins to suffer.
August 2001	Enron Vice President Sherron Watkins warns newly appointed Enron CEO Kenneth Lay that the company could "implode in a wave of accounting scandals." She also informs the partners responsible for the Enron account at Arthur Andersen, David Duncan and Michael Odom, of her concerns.
August 14, 2001	Enron CEO Jeffrey Skilling resigns unexpectedly.
August 28, 2001	A *Wall Street Journal* article suggests accounting improprieties at Enron.
September 2001	Arthur Andersen forms an Enron "crisis-response" team including Andersen in-house counsel Nancy Temple.
October 8, 2001	Arthur Andersen retains counsel to represent it in any litigation arising from the Enron matter.
October 9, 2001	Nancy Temple discusses the Enron situation with other Andersen in-house counsel and her notes from that meeting reveal she thought "some SEC investigation" was "highly probable."
October 10, 2001	Andersen partner Michael Odom speaks at an Andersen general training meeting that includes ten members of Andersen's Enron engagement team and urges everyone to comply with the firm's document retention policy, which called for a single central engagement file that should contain only the information relevant to supporting the work.
October 12, 2001	In-house counsel Nancy Temple enters the Enron matter into her computer, designating the "Type of Potential Claim" as "Professional Practice–Government/Regulatory Inv[estigation]"; she also sends a memo to Michael Odom, saying, "It might be useful to consider reminding the engagement team of our document retention policy."
October 16, 2001	Enron announces its financial results for the third quarter of 2001.
October 17, 2001	The SEC notifies Enron by letter that an investigation commenced in August; it requests certain information and documents.

EXHIBIT 9.1. ARTHUR ANDERSEN–ENRON TIME LINE, CONT'D.

October 19, 2001	Enron forwards the SEC letter to Arthur Andersen, and Nancy Temple e-mails another copy of Andersen's document retention policy to internal team members.
October 20, 2001	Andersen's Enron crisis-response team holds a conference call and Nancy Temple instructs everyone to follow the document retention policy.
October 23, 2001	Enron CEO Kenneth Lay declines to answer questions from analysts because of "potential lawsuits, as well as the SEC inquiry." After the call Andersen partner David Duncan meets with other partners on the Enron engagement team, telling them to ensure team members are complying with the firm's document retention policies. Duncan repeats this process with other members of the team and distributes copies of the document retention policy.
October 26, 2001	A senior Andersen partner circulates a *New York Times* article discussing the SEC's Enron investigation and comments in e-mail: "The problems are just beginning and we will be in the cross hairs." Another Andersen partner sees David Duncan shredding documents and suggests this might not be the best time to do that.
October 31, 2001	An Andersen forensics investigator cautions David Duncan about document retention after seeing him shredding documents and watching him toss a document labeled "smoking gun" into the shredder, saying, "We don't need this."
November 8, 2001	Andersen is served with an SEC subpoena seeking Andersen records about Enron.
November 9, 2001	Duncan's secretary sends e-mail to the engagement team saying "Per Dave – No more shredding. . . . We have been officially served for our records."
December 2001	Enron files for bankruptcy protection.

Source: Excerpted from *Arthur Andersen LLP v. United States,* 125 S.Ct. 2129 (2005).

poor legal literacy. It's unlikely Duncan would have done what he did had he known how it all would end.

Cynics might argue that since criminal cases require criminal intent and proof "beyond a reasonable doubt," you are better off *not* knowing what is going on because you can't "intend" what you don't "know." No intent, no crime. In *Andersen,* it would be like saying if they didn't *know* they were corruptly persuading employees to shred documents there would be no crime. It's an interesting theory. But before you get too attached to this loophole, remember that actions speak louder than words.

It reminds me of the story about the technician and the salesman. They were both told to stand at one end of the room opposite their "significant other" and told to walk toward their respective beloved—but only halfway. The exercise was repeated several times and after each iteration they were told to close the distance some more—but only halfway. Whoever reached their partner first could kiss.

The salesman immediately began walking, halfway, halfway, and so forth. In the meantime, the technician was frozen in place but visibly shaken. When asked why, the technician replied despondently, "Mathematically, under the rules of this game, I'll never get there." The salesman, however, knew that after a certain point the baby steps and the "distance" didn't matter. And so it is with juries and the concept of intent. The words may say one thing, but the footprints and fingerprints may well point to a different conclusion.

Historically, juries have proven to be adept at seeing through defendants' feigned ignorance. A defendant's willful blindness and selective memory often offend the jurors' sense of fairness. To them, being responsible in your job means you're *expected* to know what is going on. Not knowing therefore means you *should have known.* In civil cases that's negligence! In criminal cases, where the burden of proof is higher, it's a bigger lift—but it is not impossible with the right set of facts.

Ignorance does not make you bulletproof. It makes you vulnerable. The head-in-the-sand approach to legal literacy and knowledge management creates a false sense of security that leaves other portions of the anatomy grievously exposed, particularly after Sarbanes-Oxley. The Act changed the definition of "obstruction" by removing the requirement that a proceeding be pending at the time the destruction occurs. It's now broader and includes within the scope of obstruction of justice the destruction or falsification of records "in relation to or contemplation of any matter or case."

The new definition raises the importance of "collective knowledge," the idea that the business "knows" everything its agents know and can connect the dots between these pieces of information. As a practical matter it means that the organization can be held liable even though no single person within the company has complete knowledge. The legal doctrine of collective knowledge therefore raises the importance of knowledge management. When combined with solid leadership it's these knowledge management systems that let you keep your head out of the sand and held high.

COMPONENTS OF KNOWLEDGE MANAGEMENT

When people think of knowledge management they often envision databases and technology solutions that put information at their fingertips. At one level, they are absolutely correct. But there is more to knowledge management than that. To appreciate the breadth and scope of the knowledge management playing field it is helpful to distinguish between data, information, and knowledge.

Data represent raw facts. They have little meaning until they are given context. Legal data, for example, would consist of a laundry list of laws and case holdings, or check lists. This type of data can be gleaned from the Internet or a library, but without more instruction or guidance, a collection of data is difficult to use. It's hard to know what all that stuff is supposed to mean.

Data enriched with relevance and purpose has more value. It's information. Legal information explains why the data collection is relevant to your business. Some companies use intranets to make legal information available to the organization. Some, for example, make standard form contracts available. These standardized agreements are tailored to reflect the products and services unique to the industry and the company. They are often accompanied by instructions that permit certain preapproved changes to the agreement. If someone tries to go beyond those parameters—say, by cutting and pasting provisions together from different agreements—it can lead to problems.

When a salesman eager to make a big sale offered the customer a conveyor belt as part of the deal to make it easier to off-load the product from a truck and commit to larger orders down the road, the customer readily agreed. The cost of the conveyor belt was amortized over the course of a year by surcharging the product by a few cents per pound.

The salesman handled the contract paperwork himself, using a standard form contract from another deal. He simply changed the name and added a paragraph setting forth the agreed payment schedule. He even added a sentence saying title to the conveyor would not pass to the customer until the final payment was made. He thought this would ensure the sales volume necessary to fully recover the cost of the conveyor.

Unfortunately, he did not know that a standard part of the form agreement already addressed the issue of title. It provided that title passed when the equipment was fully installed. Because of this oversight the contract contained conflicting terms. Furthermore, the salesman was unaware that a standard rule of contract interpretation requires contracts to be construed strictly against the drafter of the agreement, in this case, in favor of the customer. As a result, title passed at installation, regardless of whether the final payment was received. As you've probably guessed by now, this boo-boo didn't come to light until the customer stopped buying product, leaving the company stuck with an unpaid conveyor balance.

The salesman's contract modifications created unintended consequences because he lacked the knowledge necessary to know *how* to amend the contract beyond the preapproved changes without running into trouble. Thus knowledge has an even higher value position in the knowledge management hierarchy. It connects *knowing why* these contract provisions are important with *knowing how* to use them and leverage them for business advantage. Knowledge is therefore both an end result and a process. See Table 9.1.

Developing Data and Information

Prior chapters have offered a sneak preview of knowledge management. Chapter Five, for example, examined legal audits and their role in isolating legal risk in the value chain and creating legal literacy requirements. Chapter Seven examined the importance of knowledge in setting and managing expectations. But now I take the subject to another level by looking at *how* companies develop

Table 9.1. The Role of Knowledge Hierarchy
in Achieving Legal Leverage.

Building Block	Characteristic	Role in Identifying Risk	Role in Managing Risk	Role in Creating Knowledge
DATA	Raw facts	Legal audit work product	Availability for identifying strengths and weaknesses, opportunities, and threats (SWOT analysis)	Databases
INFORMATION	Data enriched by context	Legal audit conclusions	Availability for SWOT analysis	Training designed to communicate context
KNOWLEDGE	Information imbued with wisdom	Applying the law strategically to create legal leverage agenda	Knowing how to address strengths and weaknesses	Training designed to provide practice opportunities for developing good decision-making skills and exercising judgment

information and *how* they use knowledge management systems to manage expectations and performance of employees and customers.

When new management took control of The Scotts Company in 1996, after accounting irregularities caused restatement of 1995 earnings, the company (maker of Miracle-Gro and other popular lawn care and garden products) decided to use the negative event and turn it into a positive learning experience. Once the financial fires were under control, Scotts undertook a company-wide internal risk assessment. It focused on nine key areas: antitrust, business ethics, financial reporting, environmental law, human resources, product liability, safety, intellectual property, and international issues.

Cross-functional business-legal teams were assigned to each area and tasked to evaluate the company's current practices, policies, and procedures. The information they gathered provided a snapshot of the company's legal profile. One of the teams, for example, examined the sales team's tactics and developed new procedures to enable the company to avoid repeating the kind of mistakes that had led to the meltdown. The information they gathered allowed them to reformulate their operating standards and procedures.

The real benefit, however, resulted from the *quality* of the change. Engaging managers in the grassroots risk assessment process not only garnered more information than if the lawyers had done it by themselves, it also generated ownership in the process and the end result. It helped establish interest in brainstorming sessions and in the subsequent training agenda, which provided personal employee tutoring. It sowed the seeds of compliance and let a culture of compliance take root.

Honeywell International, a conglomerate whose businesses range from aerospace products to thermostats, took a slightly different approach with its knowledge management system: the Honeywell Law Web. Described as a near-encyclopedic legal services intranet, it was designed for the purpose of removing lawyers from routine transactions and making the delivery of legal services more efficient. It allows employees to access online standardized form contracts, includes answers to frequently asked questions, and includes access to the company's entire patent and trademark portfolio.

It was created using the Six Sigma efficiency and quality control method championed by former General Electric CEO Jack Welch and was built in conjunction with advice solicited from managers and employees. Using surveys, Honeywell's legal department identified the most frequently requested bits of legal information. It then placed as much content online as it could to anticipate and satisfy those requests.

The project took approximately four years to complete, but the company reports that the effort has been well worth it. More than one-fifth of Honeywell's employees visited the Web site within the first eight months of its roll-out and 80 percent of its visitors returned.

The program has been credited with making managers more self-sufficient and has reportedly had a positive effect on the company's productivity.

BUILDING KNOWLEDGE

Training is a pivotal element in the knowledge management system. It facilitates the learning process and helps build the judgment necessary to consistently convert information into performance. Training is conducted in various ways. At Honeywell, for example, online compliance training is part of the Law Web. The benefit of online training is that the program can be accessed at any time from anywhere, thereby linking far-flung offices together. The convenience provides flexibility that adapts well to busy schedules. A uniform online format also assures consistency between training sessions and maintenance of records of who has successfully completed the various online programs.

Face-to-face training, however, has its benefits too, particularly if it includes hands-on learning. When Intel, for example, made the decision to embed antitrust compliance into the corporate psyche, then-CEO Andrew Grove recognized that perfunctory rules and training would not be enough. Being a dominant player, even a monopoly, within your industry is not illegal *if* your market power is earned fairly. But even when it's fairly earned, market dominance can still subject you to scrutiny. Grove had seen what it did to AT&T and was determined to avoid a similar fate.

Developing a knowledge management system devoted to improving the organization's literacy of antitrust was an investment in keeping its competitive edge. Intel's aggressive approach to antitrust compliance helped ensure that Intel has a solid story to tell, one that honors both the spirit and the letter of the law.

Partnering with his general counsel, Tom Dunlap, Grove created and adopted a conservative set of corporate antitrust compliance standards. The two breathed life into the dusty concepts with live simulations. The way other companies would practice fire drills, Intel practiced antitrust compliance, conducting random audits and collecting the kind of documents the Department of Justice or the Federal Trade Commission might demand in a subpoena. There was zero tolerance for any noncompliance the documents revealed. Even the smallest irregularities would be scrutinized, investigated, and remedied. The high compliance threshold was due to the fact that even a small error could have disproportionately high, and potentially devastating, impact on the company's future.

Mock depositions were conducted as part of the simulation to duplicate the experience of what it's like to be grilled by a hostile lawyer. This was reported to be among Intel's most powerful tools. Grove called the process fascinating. "A memo is introduced into evidence and you shrug," he says. "You fully understand how that memo could be written. Moreover, you could have written it yourself. And then you see that memo turned into a tool and a weapon against you, in front of your eyes. . . . You start shivering, 'There but for the grace of God go I. I could have written that memo.'"

My own experience with clients is consistent with Intel's. First-hand experience is a powerful teacher. Once clients have watched opposing counsel lob a grappling hook into their documents, they are much more cautious about what they say and how they say it in the future. Being in the witness hot seat, whether actual or simulated, is a defining moment. It forges the link between cause and effect. It clarifies *how* a particular document leads to an invitation to testify and helps managers understand why lawyers think the way they do.

Raising awareness with live simulations and showing employees how to avoid liability in the future helps manage risk by jump-starting proactive thinking. The experience helps integrate legal literacy into the decision-making processes, letting employees become more mindful about the potential legal consequences of little things, and motivates employees to manage expectations more precisely. They can then act in ways to protect the company more in the future.

To consistently convert information into high performance the organization must link each decision with the ultimate result. Intel's simulations, for example, linked the documents collected during the subpoena fire drills to a specific type of liability: antitrust. It showed *how* those documents make a difference in a liability analysis. The exercise lets you reverse engineer the liability and take steps to avoid it in the future. It shows how to prevent smoking guns—the kind of smoking gun documents that may not be appear to be all that dangerous on their face.

As Grove accurately observed, when you see the kind of business documents that get entered into evidence you understand why and how they got written the way they did. What is not readily apparent is the latent legal risk these memoranda carry. The liability in each document is often nuanced. But when a number of such documents reach a tipping point their critical mass can trigger cascading legal liability. This cumulative effect is good news and bad. It's good because once these small errors are identified they are usually easily corrected. It's bad news because the cause-and-effect relationship between these small gestures and the difference they can make far down the value chain is not readily apparent. It must be communicated effectively. Otherwise, employees will think what they do doesn't matter.

Using Knowledge to Manage Expectations

For Intel, embedding antitrust principles into the corporate culture provides a baseline and a standard by which employees can evaluate their decisions and actions. It helps manage their expectations by drawing a bright line that clarifies what works and what doesn't work.

The movie and recording industries in the United States have used knowledge management to educate consumers and manage their expectations. Faced with so-called customers who download unauthorized copies of films and music over the Internet, the industries have fought back. They are using television ads and other media to show how piracy is harming the industry and the individuals who work in it. They are also educating their customers about copyright law. The objective is to communicate how digital piracy is illegal and that it is not a faceless, victimless crime.

The goal is to revise expectations of the Internet culture that believes everything on the Web is free. The training thereby eliminates the surprise of subsequent legal enforcement proceedings. To lend credibility to the program and give it teeth, the two industries have backed up their education programs by aggressively enforcing their legal rights and suing thousands of downloaders to stop the freeloading and unauthorized distribution of their intellectual property.

Value of Continuous Learning

Learning improves your competencies—that cluster of related knowledge, attitudes, and skills that affect your job and correlate with performance (Parry, 1998). It makes people better at what they do. Increased competency therefore leverages human capital and improves one of the strategic resources used in business strategy: employees.

The strategic value of knowledge management systems is their ability to provide access to unbiased information. Accessible information facilitates the learning process. It also helps neutralize organizational decision-making biases and provides a foundation for sound decision making.

People who stop learning stop improving. Building an effective knowledge management system and a reservoir of intellectual capital is therefore an investment in building human capital. It establishes institutional memory and contributes to institutional excellence.

Quantifying the Value of Knowledge Management

Metrics add discipline to the compliance and legal leverage process. However, finding an accurate way to measure a sophisticated process is a challenge. Anyone can collect numbers for the sake of numbers. But are they meaningful? Do they accurately reflect progress? Or do they merely measure the appearance of progress. Tracking the number of training hours, for example, doesn't tell you much about the value of learning: what was absorbed or how it was applied.

Just as legal risk is managed (or mismanaged) through a series of cause-and-effect relationships that start with a small ripple and gradually cascade through the value chain, measuring the organization's success or failure in achieving compliance or legal leverage must take a similar path—otherwise you won't know whether you are measuring a change in operating procedure and culture, or merely a symptom. Legal audits can provide a baseline of the organization's legal risk profile, and successive audits can help map before-and-after changes. Together, these interrelated events create a complex matrix. There is no one-size-fits-all metric that adequately captures progress and improvement in all of its nooks and crannies.

There is certainly nothing wrong with measuring the number of training hours, or the number of lawsuits filed. Exhibit 9.2, for instance, provides a sampling of commonly collected legal risk

EXHIBIT 9.2. SAMPLING OF LEGAL RISK MEASURES.

1. Litigation-related metrics
   a. Number of lawsuits filed and type
   b. Duration of case
   c. Damages, settlements, and fines
   d. Outside counsel fees and expenses
   e. Impact on insurance premiums

2. Legal audit–related metrics
   a. Number of audits conducted and type
   b. Number of compliance deficiencies discovered
   c. Cost of addressing compliance deficiencies
   d. Average time and cost to conduct audit
   e. Impact on insurance premiums

3. Regulatory-related metrics
   a. Number of reportable compliance failures
   b. Number of government investigations
   c. Number of government notices issued
   d. Total costs related to regulatory noncompliance
   e. Impact on sales (for example, late delivery, lost sales, product defect)

4. Contract-related metrics
   a. Number of new contracts executed (by type)
   b. Number of expiring or terminated contracts (by type)
   c. Average time from start of deal to execution of contract
   d. Number of contract nonperformance issues
   e. Type of nonperformance and cost

5. Patent-related metrics
   a. Number of new concepts
   b. Average time from concept to filing of application
   c. Average time from filing of application to patent issuance

6. Training-related metrics
   a. Number of employees trained
   b. Average total number of training hours per employee, for the company as a whole
   c. Average regulatory employee training hours (industry specific)
   d. Average scores on training comprehension tests and trends of commonly missed answers
   e. Training costs

Exhibit 9.2. Sampling of Legal Risk Measures, cont'd.

7. Employee reporting metrics
   a. Number of calls to employee hot lines
   b. Number of compliance failures identified
   c. Percentage of employees reporting alleged misconduct
   d. Type and nature of compliance failures or alleged misconduct
   e. Impact on employee morale

measures. But meaningful metrics, like the portfolio of risk they seek to monitor, are multifaceted and must ultimately link legal literacy and learning to company objectives and the bottom line. They must be performance *and* process oriented.

Process control technology in manufacturing measures and monitors quality at key points during production to ensure that the goods being delivered consistently meet specifications, and good risk management metrics do the same for legal compliance. It's the only way to verify whether the end result is a function of luck or reflects instead a fundamental change in the way things are done.

Tapping into the value chain at key decision nodes monitors the course of compliance. It can verify whether compliance is on track or not. It provides better information than any reports from managers, who might exaggerate their department's compliance performance, and is the only way to determine whether a culture of compliance or legal leverage has taken root.

General Electric uses Six Sigma methodology to help manage its legal compliance and drive defects from the value chain. By looking at customer complaints, for example, GE has been able to identify problems early and avoid potential class action suits. Similarly, looking at the number of new sales representatives assigned overseas can alert the company to the fact there could be an increased exposure to the Foreign Corrupt Practices Act (discussed in the "International Law" section of Appendix B). Identifying the exposure early allows for increased training to avoid potential noncompliance with the Act.

Sales representative head count and customer complaints are not typically identified as legal risk metrics. Yet if we look at a compliance objective, say reducing the number of class action product liability suits, and we deconstruct the dynamics that lead to such suits, we recognize that the incentive to take legal action starts with a customer complaint (see Chapter Seven, Figure 7.1), not a legal Complaint. Managing expectations well when dealing with complaints keeps them from growing into Complaints. Thus, when we consider the effect customer complaints have on litigation, monitoring them from a legal risk management perspective in addition to the traditional customer satisfaction perspective makes a lot of sense.

Some companies are afraid to document deficiencies. They believe the effort provides a road map for plaintiffs' lawyers. That may be partly true, but there is more to gain than to lose by tracking compliance. Deficiencies are what they are and will surface during discovery by plaintiffs' lawyers regardless of whether they have been compiled in metric form. Moreover, the reward may well outweigh the risk. There's evidence to suggest that companies who are aggressive about monitoring and remedying legal noncompliance experience higher motivation and satisfaction levels among employees, which improves both their performance and the company's bottom line.

In sum, knowledge management systems are assets. They enrich decision making. They bring best practices to life and they help to gradually diminish the level of unwanted legal risk within the organization. They help organizations leverage human capital.

As a result, knowledge management plays a significant role in the legal leverage process portfolio. It creates a reservoir of institutional memory that neutralizes decision-making biases. It establishes the foundation for an understanding of legal rights that assists in managing expectations, and it leverages institutional wisdom to reduce risk and increase competitive advantage. See Figure 9.4.

FIGURE 9.4. LEGAL LEVERAGE PROCESS PORTFOLIO:
HIGHLIGHTING KNOWLEDGE MANAGEMENT.

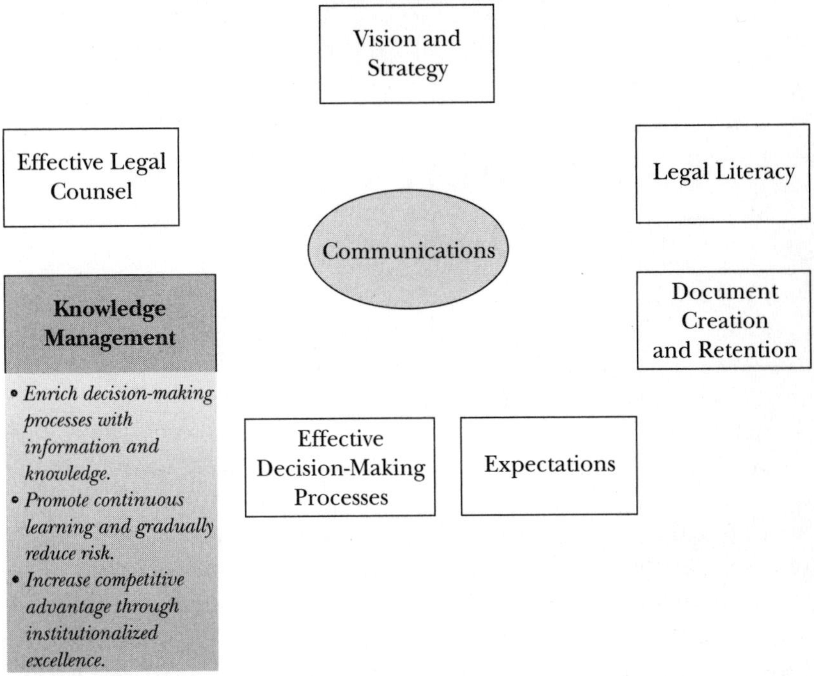

Vision and
Strategy

Effective Legal
Counsel

Legal Literacy

Communications

Knowledge
Management

Document
Creation
and Retention

- Enrich decision-making processes with information and knowledge.
- Promote continuous learning and gradually reduce risk.
- Increase competitive advantage through institutionalized excellence.

Effective
Decision-Making
Processes

Expectations

CHAPTER TEN

HOW TO STAY IN SYNCH
The Role of Lawyers

A principal source of erroneous judgement [is] viewing things partially and only on one side.
–SAMUEL JOHNSON (1709–1784)

While legal literacy can go a long way in helping an organization manage routine legal risk, it is no substitute for the legal fluency a licensed attorney can bring to the management team. Some issues are more complicated than they appear at first blush, and sometimes the law is just plain counterintuitive.

When Salesforce.com decided to take its stock public in 2004, the San Francisco–based software company didn't realize that co-operating with the *New York Times* on an article profiling the company prior to its IPO would violate a U.S. Securities and Exchange Commission (SEC) rule. When the *Times* trumpeted the Salesforce.com IPO (in a headline that read: "It's not Google, it's that other big IPO"), the SEC construed the *Times* story in combination with other media coverage of the event as crossing the line of permissible company disclosures.

SEC rules require investor information for initial public offerings to be exclusively communicated through official registration statements. It's a provision of the law that is vague and seldom used because it is so heavily dependent on context. But in this case the SEC concluded the company went too far and mandated a quiet period. As its name suggests, the quiet period prohibits managers from engaging in communications that could be interpreted as influencing investors. It's a management muzzle.

For managers and entrepreneurs who build businesses on their ability to promote, such behavior is counterintuitive and requires expert guidance. Having access to a trusted legal professional either in-house or through a law firm can therefore provide a valuable reality check. Advice from a licensed professional also carries with it the benefit of attorney-client privilege, a special form of confidentiality that allows communications to remain within the confines of the relationship.

Having legal literacy makes it easier to have that dialogue. It gives you a head start on the issues and lets you use legal resources more efficiently. Finding the right lawyer and establishing a constructive relationship, however, can present a special set of challenges. Lawyers and managers view the business world through different lenses, and the sides are each partial to their own view. In *The Clash of Cultures* (1985), Joseph A. Raelin attributes these differences to a unique set of educational backgrounds, work habits, and professional social cultures. For the legal profession, these differences have sadly evolved into caricatures and lawyer jokes that have earned the profession an unflattering stereotype.

Some years ago, when my best friend from high school gave birth to her first child, I asked whether there would be high expectations placed on the baby's future academic achievement since both parents were accomplished professionals with doctorates. "My daughter can be anything she wants as long as it's not a lawyer," my friend replied in a dead-serious tone. I was speechless.

Clearly the respect, honor, and admiration associated with lawyers like Atticus Finch in the 1962 film version of *To Kill a Mockingbird* and the *Perry Mason* television series, which inspired a generation of young men and women to become members of the legal bar, has all but evaporated in the intervening years. Today, lawyers are mocked and ridiculed on shows like the television drama *Boston Legal,* launched in 2004, whose characters try to bribe opponents with "a bottle of scotch and some money to buy some bus bench ads." Words you would never have heard from Perry Mason or Atticus Finch.

I'll be the first to admit that I've met many lawyers I don't care for either. Every industry and profession has its share of opportunistic rogues, and the legal profession is no exception. Nonetheless, it is sad that an unscrupulous or overzealous few bring down the rest. Sadder still is when the malignancy metastasizes into stereotyping and causes managers to shun legal advice until a business situation has gotten too hot to handle.

"When you talk to lawyers you want to minimize the problem," one such manager advised his underlings. "You don't want the lawyers to overreact. That's what they get paid for, you know—to find problems and blow things out of proportion." Regrettably, these are the same managers who don't attend company training sessions—and when they do go, they sit with their arms folded.

As discussed in Chapter Two, pooh-poohing risk eventually leads to being knee-deep in it. Overconfident behavior limits the availability of information and perpetuates decision-making biases that reduce decision-making quality. Over time the mathematical principle of regression reveals persistently flawed decisions and what starts out as one person's fear of an overreaction is ultimately exposed as someone else's underreaction.

The only way to reach these folks is to tangibly tie legal literacy to their performance requirements or to let their bad habits catch up with them. But learning the hard way can be expensive, particularly if the decision maker sits high up in the value chain and has a large span of control.

Good corporate governance demands that risky behaviors be addressed before they jeopardize the sustainability of the organization. Selective recall, minimization, or outright denial of facts allows latent legal problems to fester below the skin until BA-boom: they reach a tipping point and develop faster than a digital photograph. Such behavior patterns do not advance the company's best interests. They rob the company of the opportunity to resolve the problem early.

CULTIVATING UNSELFISHNESS

It takes unselfish teamwork to break the self-defeating politics of discriminatory stereotypes—and that includes stereotypes held by managers and lawyers *about each other.* Yes, it's sad but true. You may be shocked to know that some lawyers hold unflattering opinions of their clients. Unfortunately, disparaging others only detracts from the relationship. It builds walls, not bridges.

Unlocking the value of legal literacy and legal leverage requires managers and lawyers to learn to work together. It means passing the ball and clearing the way to the goal. It requires trust. In *Five-Point Play* (2001), Duke University basketball coach Mike Krzyzewski, who holds the record for the most wins in collegiate basketball history, identifies trust as an attribute of high-performance teams.

Trust allows us to let go of the ball long enough to let someone else run with it a distance. It allows us to bounce ideas back and forth. If there's no respect, there's no real trust and no basis for collective responsibility. Negative stereotypes short-circuit trust. They're mental shortcuts for how we *expect* people to behave. They blind us to reality.

Trust means opening yourself up to being part of the solution instead of the problem. Taking advantage of each other's strengths and forgiving weaknesses creates a better result. It also cements team spirit and fosters collective responsibility. It lets participants be part of something bigger than themselves. It's a springboard for making the leap from good to great and separates the real champions from the pretenders.

Organizations that want to get legal costs under control and reap the benefits of legal leverage therefore owe it to themselves to reevaluate their game plan and the role of lawyers in it. With the cost of poor legal risk management being prohibitive (Chapter Three) and getting worse from year to year, the ability to efficiently tap legal resources has strategic value. It opens the door to competencies that add value to the knowledge management process (Chapter Nine).

Breaking stereotypes and building trust takes time. Moreover, it requires a good-faith effort by managers *and* lawyers to engage in transparent communications. To get the process rolling, we need to take a collective time-out. Better yet, we need to take a cold hard look at some popular lawyer jokes to see what they tell us about each other.

What's wrong with lawyer jokes? Lawyers don't think they're funny and nobody else thinks they're jokes. Yet they can be highly instructive for discussing perceptions that divide the two camps. They can show managers and lawyers how to identify and advance each other's mutual interests. As a result we can build a more productive relationship—one characterized by more insight, better judgment, and better long-term business results.

So what can lawyer jokes tell us about ourselves? Let's examine a few and see.

WHY WON'T SHARKS ATTACK LAWYERS?
Answer: Professional courtesy.

So lawyers are sharks. They're predators. They're out to kill. *Right?*

If we take a closer look at sharks we learn that they have remarkably keen sensory perceptions. Humans have five senses; sharks have six. Special sensory organs let sharks detect vibrations and electrical fields—usually put out by their next meal. In addition, the sense of smell, the shark's sharpest sense, is enabled and supported by two-thirds of the shark's brainpower, and its excellent vision is attributable to a mirror-like layer in each eyeball that penetrates murky water. Moreover, not all sharks are carnivores. Some of the biggest, the basking shark and the whale shark, prefer plankton to people.

What makes sharks successful hunters is their ability to quickly and efficiently gather and assimilate data through their six senses, make decisions, and execute successfully. Wait, isn't that what *managers* do too? Gather and assimilate data? Make decisions and execute? If we tune out the *Jaws* music in the background long enough for our fear factor to subside, we see that employing these killer lawyer skills and putting them work *for* us could be a powerful advantage. The lesson for management: *Unselfishness means recognizing that "sharks" have assets worth harnessing.*

Intellectually, this may make sense, but emotionally you may still be less than reassured. After all, lawyers are so, well, *annoying*. OK, then let's dig a little deeper. Developing a better understanding of what shapes and drives a lawyer's legal instincts can explain why these annoying behaviors exist and offer suggestions for how to deal with them.

The Source of Legal DNA

A lawyer's legal senses are sharpened and honed in law school through the rigorous study of appellate case law. Using the Socratic teaching method, professors interrogate future lawyers, pelting them with endless questions about case law: which facts are significant, how slight variations in the facts can lead to different results, and so on. Law students quickly learn the relevance of factual distinctions and the role of legal definitions in applying the law to the facts.

The movie *Paper Chase,* starring John Houseman as the incorrigible Professor Kingsfield, illustrates the Socratic method in action. The story chronicles the travails of a first-year student at an Ivy League law school as he wrestles with the daily grind in Kingsfield's course on contracts. On the first day of class, in a memorable monologue, Kingsfield tells the students that their brains are "mush" but that with some luck and hard work they'll be able to "think like lawyers" at the end of the term. Our hero struggles with arcane pedagogy but by the end of the movie his transformation is complete. He earns an A from Kingsfield.

The kind of performance that wins kudos in the classroom or courtroom, however, can wreak havoc in a corporate boardroom. Thinking like a lawyer drives a need to examine and nail down as many contingencies and distinctions you can think of. It's done for the purpose of assuring a winning outcome. Unfortunately, it also translates into a tendency toward perfectionism, low risk tolerance, and a combative negotiating style.

The intense desire to win in court activates the desire to build an airtight case that then manifests itself in an "I know better than you" kind of arrogance that says no to any proposed activity not aligned with the winning agenda. Sadly, law schools' laser-like focus on appellate cases and the study of rules of civil and criminal procedure, as well as the rules of evidence, puts litigation on a pedestal and leaves little room for the client's business perspective and the role of preventive law.

The Storage Tank Manual Lesson

When a business client sent a proposed storage tank installation manual to its law firm for review, it expected to receive a marked-up manuscript revising the language with an eye toward *reducing* legal liability. What the firm sent instead was a well-researched memorandum of law explaining rudimentary product liability and the risk exposure that would result from distributing such a manual. The memorandum ended with a recommendation to *eliminate* liability: don't issue the manual. Publishing equaled liability and liability was bad. The memorandum was accompanied by a four-page cover letter echoing the same sentiment.

The firm's advice was ultimately useless, not because it was wrong but because it was inappropriate. The question posed was not "How do we make sure we can win a lawsuit?" It was "How do we minimize the risk of being sued?" Therefore, from the client's perspective, the firm delivered the wrong product. The client already knew there was some legal risk involved in issuing the manual. The decision being made was not *whether* a manual would be published, but *how* to do it with the least amount of exposure. To the company, the manual was a value-added service for its customers. The overall business advantage outweighed the legal risk, *provided* the legal risk was managed properly.

Even though in-house counsel explained the company's objective to the firm when the assignment was issued, outside counsel chose to ignore the client's direction. *They* knew better and *they* were going to make sure the company was well protected. Unfortunately, in the process *they* answered the wrong question and the real work necessary to prepare the manual for publication was left undone. In-house counsel eventually completed it, but not without missed deadlines and frustrated business objectives.

Overzealous lawyers inserting themselves into the client's decision making created more problems than they solved. It's the kind of scenario that contributes to management's perception of lawyers as being insensitive and obstructionist. The lesson for lawyers: *Being unselfish means redefining winning to include achieving the client's legitimate business objectives.*

Most lawyers are specialists. When you couple specialization with a penchant for risk aversion, its easy to see why cases are generously staffed and how costs quickly escalate. When the owner of a small business, for example, engaged a law firm to represent him in a routine acquisition, his lawyers refused to revise existing documents

---

HOW MANY LAWYERS DOES IT TAKE TO SCREW IN A
LIGHT BULB?
Answer: Six:
- One to research the bulb wattage and write a memorandum
- One to consult with the bulb manufacturer
- One to hold the ladder and observe the process
- One to actually climb the ladder and exchange the bulb
- One to organize the bulb and pass it up the ladder, and
- One to supervise the process and explain it to the client

---

prepared by other lawyers in similar deals for the same company. Instead they drafted their own. The tab: a cool $27,000. The business owner was upset at the price tag for what he viewed as a straightforward deal.

Was that much legal work really necessary? Was the redraft a "got to have" or a "nice to have" document? It's hard to know. What is clear, however, is that the owner characterized the transaction as "straightforward" and didn't understand the need for the huge rewrite. The bottom line: the firm did a poor job in managing client expectations.

If the deal wasn't straightforward, it was incumbent on the firm to explain why special issues required additional research or redrafting and why the current documents were inadequate. Pointing these issues out ahead of time and providing an estimate of how much it would cost would have avoided the $27,000 surprise and a disappointed client. Ironically, the expenses associated with thorough preparation are typically incurred in the name of quality, but a client who doesn't recognize the quality will be reluctant to pay for it. The lesson for lawyers: *Unselfishness means delivering value and being mindful that client satisfaction depends on properly managing client expectations.*

DELIVERING VALUE

When I first started practicing law in the 1980s it was not uncommon for legal invoices to read: "For services rendered in the month of June" and an invoice amount—a *big* amount. There was no itemization or explanation of what services were included. Opaque invoices made it tough for managers to understand or challenge what they got for their money.

In no other area of business was so much money being spent with so few controls or so little attention to cost efficiency. That development ultimately paved the way for growth of the in-house bar. Suddenly management had someone on their team who was a legal insider, who could weed out the issues deserving royal treatment from those that didn't, someone who could handle certain legal tasks more economically, and who was in a better position to manage law firms than any nonlawyer could. The new segment of the bar made a lot of economic sense to clients.

As companies downsized and rightsized throughout the 1980s and 1990s, cost-cutting pressures spread to legal departments and outside counsel bills. Clients began placing more emphasis on value-added services. Companies adopted outside counsel guidelines as rules of engagement to rein in excesses. Itemized billing and computer software were used to analyze legal bills to assure billing compliance and ferret out inefficiencies.

Today, the mounting cost pressure has even led big business to start using plaintiffs' firms to do their defense work. Shunned for years because they represented plaintiffs who sued big business, these firms have now become increasingly attractive because of their historical willingness to embrace alternative billing arrangements, including contingent fee arrangements (where they get paid only if they win). Nonetheless, the concept of value-added billing is still misunderstood by many traditional lawyers.

The value-added dance consists of three steps. First is identifying the scope of the work and determining what really needs to be done. If lawyers sorted their recommendations into two lists, the "got to have" list and the "nice to have" list, they'd realize that the "got to have" list is fairly short. Prioritizing zeros in on the most pressing issues and the steps that really need to be taken. Addressing those issues first moves the ball closer to the goal. It adds the most value. It also streamlines the process and minimizes unnecessary detours.

Explaining the logic behind the two lists to the client provides the client with information and knowledge. It allows people to compare the lawyer's priorities to their own and participate in a constructive dialogue. The client may see a business opportunity in the "nice to have" list of legal issues and suddenly elevate it to the "got to have" category. Together you begin to shape the future and create solutions that make business sense as well as legal sense. The joint brainstorming builds bridges. It clarifies misunderstanding and helps develop a cohesive business strategy.

The second step in the value-added process is to allocate resources effectively. It means staffing the project with individuals whose contributions are cost-effective. Here again, drawing a distinction between "got to have" and "nice to have" staffing is important. Efficient staffing must balance competence and experience against project requirements.

Senior lawyers' participation, for example, may be more cost-effective if their unique competency or experience is required to complete the task, or allows them to complete the task faster and more economically than someone else. But more experience is not always necessarily better. Sometimes, installing a light bulb is just that. Twenty years of experience doesn't make it faster or better. Someone more junior can take care of it and do it just as well. Failure to realize this creates top-heavy staffing that inflates costs.

The third and final step in the value-added dance is managing the process efficiently. It's about deploying resources in a timely manner, about anticipating deadlines and avoiding last-minute expenses that result from failure to plan ahead, such as expedited transcript charges, overnight delivery services, or staff overtime. It's about setting clear parameters and managing each step on the time line against the client's expectations and against the client's budget. It does not mean, for example, dismissing a case from the court docket before settlement agreements are signed and then spending more of the client's money to reinstate the case when the settlement collapses. Such case management is inefficient and adds unnecessary expenses.

The quality of legal services is an extremely sensitive subject. It raises concerns about professional autonomy and brings us full circle to the lawyers' penchant for risk aversion and the education that trains them to accept nothing less than total victory. Indeed, some law firm cultures treat settling a case as a defeat. It touches the heart of the firm's own self-image and perception of its reputation—the main currency in the legal profession and deciding factor in determining what fees the firm can command. It is therefore fiercely guarded. Nonetheless, there's still a lesson for such lawyers: *Unselfishness means respecting the client's decision to take calculated legal risks and control costs by managing processes and staffing efficiently.*

Unfortunately, the lesson is a difficult pill for some lawyers to swallow. "[Clients] pushing for cut-rate, slapdash work butt right up against judges with overburdened dockets with little patience for screw-up by trial counsel," one law firm partner laments. "[It] tempt[s] sanctions from the court for handling cases improperly and wasting the court's time—not to mention the sting of losing because the case was not properly prepared."

These lawyers have difficulty reconciling the concept of efficient case management with quality. They feel constrained by the client's effort to exert control and fear loss of control threatens the quality of their work product and compromises their professional independence or their credibility with the court. The lesson for these lawyers: *Unselfishness means remembering that the cause you are advocating or protecting is the* client's *and not yours, and that entitles the* client *to direct the battle plan.*

THE SOURCE OF BUSINESS DNA

Whether lawyers like it or not, managers are wired differently when it comes to risk. Buying low and selling high is how businesses generate profit. The economics of capitalism and private enterprise therefore favor risk taking. Indeed, the entire profit-making process is fraught with risk. But it's a calculated risk. To make an informed decision about legal risk it is therefore essential that management have enough legal literacy to recognize it and understand how it relates to their business.

Unfortunately, management's formal business training is unlikely to include the study of business law. Of the top business schools, the Wharton School of Business at the University of Pennsylvania is the only program that includes law as one of its five required core disciplines. Other schools may offer business law in the form of an occasional elective course, but the trend post-Enron is to focus on ethics instead of law. Interestingly, these ethics courses are usually taught by someone with a political science or economics background, or perhaps an executive in residence or retired dean, and are unlikely to include much real law at all.

It is estimated that CEOs spend approximately 20 percent of their time on legal issues, yet their only glimpse of legal issues in business school is from faculty members who often treat the law as an obstacle. Robert Prentice, who teaches business law at the McCombs School of Business at the University of Texas at Austin, reports that he has heard finance professors tell him that insider trading rules and other SEC requirements undermine market efficiency. He's also had accounting professors tell him that accounting rules discouraging accountants from preparing the books they would later audit are "pointless" because no firm would stake their reputation by acting improperly and risking a conflict of interest.

Regrettably, such academic attitudes create the impression that law and regulations are inconvenient roadblocks that can and should be manipulated and evaded at will. They promote an "ends justify the means" business attitude measured solely by the bottom line. The classroom message is further reinforced by the curriculum as a whole, with its dearth of interdisciplinary offerings. The lesson for management: *Unselfishness means opening yourself up to different points of view and being willing to listen even if the news conflicts with short-term goals. Appreciate that a lawyer's loyal opposition arises from a passion for excellence and an independent professional duty. It's nothing personal.*

In the aftermath of Enron and its progeny, Richard Schmalensee, dean and professor of management and economics at the MIT Sloan School of Management, implicitly recognized the shortcomings of traditional business education when he conceded that the system had produced managers who were more focused on short-term gains that beat the market than they were on building sustainable value. To address the problem, he said, MIT would immerse its students into more real-life situations requiring interdisciplinary skills.

In 2003, for example, the students were asked by a Fortune 100 company to develop strategies for markets in which intellectual property played an important role. Schmalensee writes, "Rather than coming up with clever ways to dodge accounting rules, we want students to stay focused on broader questions. Is what I'm doing about trying to create lasting value, or is it just tricking the market? What do I want to see when I look back over my career, or when my grandchildren ask me what I've accomplished?"

The lesson for management: *Unselfishness means being mindful of a wider array of costs, both tangible and intangible, and interdependencies that are triggered by issues outside your traditional area of expertise.* Reframing the business objective allows decision makers to notice more risks and the costs associated with them. Such mindfulness lets them turn obstacles into opportunities (as discussed in Chapter Eight).

WHAT DO YOU GET WHEN YOU CROSS *THE GODFATHER* WITH A LAWYER?
Answer: An offer you can't understand.

All too often legalese is confusing and intimidating. Although legal literacy can provide a functional vocabulary, it is still incumbent on lawyers to explain the law in easy-to-understand terms. When it comes to communicating clearly and concisely, lawyers' training as problem spotters can be a mixed blessing. It's good because they can spot legal risk early. But it's bad when the kaleidoscope of converging and diverging legal issues creates an information overload and leads to vague recommendations and indecision. "On the one hand we can do xyz, but on the other hand . . . " and so forth is the kind of waffling that drives managers nuts. The observations may be technically accurate, but without more, they are also confusing and frustrating.

At one company, for example, the general counsel had an unnerving habit of cornering the CEO to advise him about the latest "legal risk" he had just read about. After discharging his advisory duty the lawyer would stride down the hall, leaving the CEO standing there like a wet fire hydrant. It was always a hit-and-run exercise—the general counsel never followed up by providing a suggestion for how to address the issue.

After a while the general counsel's showers of wisdom were ignored. His tenure with the company was also short, because management needed problem solvers and not just problem spotters. The lesson for lawyers: *In a business team environment, it's necessary to tie legal issues to business objectives and solutions and make the law vis-*

ible in a constructive and meaningful way. If you're not part of the solution you're part of the problem, and you won't last long.

Law firms often commit the same error when their marketing communications fail to identify a nexus to the client's business. Sending copies of a recent court ruling to brag about a case they won, or reporting on a new piece of legislation that they like or dislike, doesn't add any real value to the client relationship unless the communication also includes an explanation of why the information is relevant to the *client's* business. It's not always obvious from the face of these communications, and the client doesn't always have the time to figure it out. If you have a point to make—make it. Don't turn it into a treasure hunt.

Is it a "need to know" item as opposed to a "nice to know" piece of information? Will the new law change the way the client does business? Answers to these questions are a few examples of ways that information becomes more interesting and useful. By itself, the news is just information—or maybe even just data. But when it's reframed in the context of the client's business, it creates knowledge—and knowledge adds value.

Creating such relevance and knowledge, however, requires understanding the client's business. The lesson for management: *Unselfishness means helping counsel understand the nature of your business, including the major challenges you face in achieving legitimate business goals.* Without understanding what drives your bottom line, counsel will find it difficult to bridge your world and theirs.

LEARNING TO BUILD A BETTER TEAM

We can't change the way we've been hardwired, but we *can* modify our circuitry with new learning that adds circuit breakers and surge protection to keep relationships from overheating. The more we know about each other the easier it is to understand each other's motivations, strengths, and weaknesses, and the easier it is to identify common interests that can be used as a foundation for joint problem solving. Understanding leads to respect. Respect fosters trust. Trust opens the door to terrific relationships.

As illustrated in Figure 10.1, counsel can play an important role in the legal leverage process portfolio. They can facilitate the other portfolio components. They can help create legal literacy and assist

FIGURE 10.1. LEGAL LEVERAGE PROCESS PORTFOLIO:
HIGHLIGHTING EFFECTIVE COUNSEL.

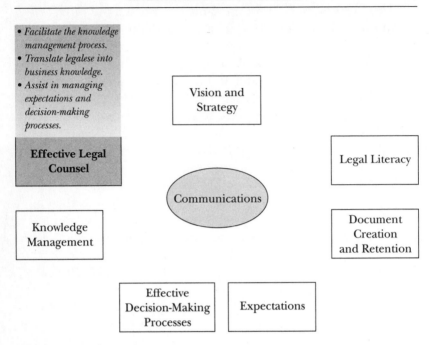

with document creation and retention. They can help management's decision-making processes by translating legalese into business knowledge. They can help manage expectations, and they can facilitate the knowledge management process. Using these resources on a transactional rather than a remedial basis will stretch your business budget further. There is more to be gained by including effective counsel than excluding them. *But* they can only help you and the organization attain business goals to the extent that *you let them.* The lesson for management: *Unselfishness means letting counsel play ball. Respect the organization's need to benefit from counsel's skill set.*

Lawyers can make it easier for clients to ask questions sooner if they start thinking of themselves more as healers than as advocates. They need to be mindful of the limits of their role as advisers and of the *client's* role as the final decision maker. They need to recognize that there will never be a risk-free deal or optimal solution and that aiming for an airtight defense is unrealistic. Being reasonable makes lawyers more approachable. Similarly, managers can assist the process by becoming legally literate and overcoming their hesitation to ask questions and seek counsel. See Table 10.1.

Better Formal Education

Schools help shape opinions. They provide the foundation of learning and play an important role in building professional competencies and toolkits. More interdisciplinary courses at institutions of higher education would help bridge the gap between law

Table 10.1. Ten Steps to Building a Better Relationship.

Lawyers	Managers
Respect client's legitimate business objectives and redefine winning to include the achievement of those objectives.	Respect lawyers' unique skill set and its value to the organization.
Respect client's limited resources by delivering value and being mindful that client satisfaction depends on properly managing expectations.	Respect different points of view even if they appear to conflict with short-term goals by listening and by recognizing that loyal opposition arises from a passion for excellence and a professional duty.
Respect the client's decision to take calculated legal risks and control costs by managing processes and staffing efficiently.	Respect the fact that tangible and intangible business costs can be triggered by legal issues outside your area of expertise.
Respect the fact that the cause you are advocating or protecting is the client's, not yours, and that it entitles the client to direct the battle plan.	Respect counsel's need to understand the nature of your business by explaining the major challenges you face in your business and industry.
Respect the need to make legal issues visible by tying them to legitimate business objectives and solutions in a constructive and meaningful way.	Respect the organization's need to benefit from counsel's talents by finding more proactive rather than reactive ways to make use of them.

and business by teaching tolerance and promoting mindfulness of strategic interdependencies between the two disciplines.

I've already touched on how the leading business schools have been largely remiss in addressing this vital area. Unfortunately, the score is not much better with law schools. Even though the concept of "preventive law" has been around since the 1950s, starting with the early work of Louis Brown, it has not been adopted as part of the mainstream legal curriculum. Preventive law is a body of scholarly work that draws on case law as well as the knowledge of experienced lawyers who practice principles of prevention, having developed them instinctively through years of practice experience. Functionally, preventive law restores the meaning of the word *counselor* to the phrase "counselor at law."

Most law schools, however, prefer to take a narrow approach to legal education. They prefer to let law firms and local bar associations deal with knowledge transfer associated with practice. It took years before law school clinic programs were included as part of the curriculum. Similar to medical internships, clinic programs put budding young lawyers in face-to-face contact with real live clients who have real live legal problems. But unlike medicine, where such programs are important rites of passage, the legal profession treats them as optional.

The failure of many law schools to adequately lay the foundation for preventive law, particularly the elite schools that feed the prestigious law firms that serve the largest corporations, means that every year yet more law students graduate and take bar exams with only half the foundation necessary to properly meet their clients' real needs. Academia thereby places a greater burden on business to compensate for these oversights and fill the knowledge gaps.

When properly aligned, the partnership of law and business is unbeatable. Yet to reap the full benefit of the unparalleled partnership requires good communications and a healthy respect for each other's unique talents and boundaries. The goal of the partnership is to achieve legitimate business objectives by being vigilant and mindful of corresponding legal consequences, because when the telephone rings late on Friday afternoon and management urgently ask counsel, "Does our contract cover us?" We *all* want the answer to be yes.

CHAPTER ELEVEN

HOW TO STAY ON MESSAGE
The Role of Communications

Every man hears only what he understands.
—GOETHE (1749–1832)

What do you fear more? Contracting West Nile virus from a mosquito bite? Or having a bout of food poisoning? For many of us, the threat of West Nile virus sounds scarier than common food poisoning. It's no wonder. In 2002 the major American newspapers carried no less than 2,240 articles on the subject of West Nile virus between the end of May and early September. Yet during the same time period only 257 articles addressed the subject of food poisoning—even though food poisoning killed an estimated five thousand Americans that year, while West Nile virus was only responsible for three hundred deaths.

What we hear influences what we know. It affects our thoughts and our actions. I've already discussed the way skillful communication plays a central role in the legal leverage process in some detail—how it operates as a vehicle for teaching legal literacy as well as providing the means for applying it, how it is the heartbeat of knowledge management, the genesis of reasonable expectations, the smoking gun neutralizer, and the antidote for decision-making biases. In short, it activates the corporate immune system by keeping legal problems from turning into full-scale meltdowns. Now I turn to the big-picture messages, because the strength of this corporate immune system and the ability of these elements to function well together is directly proportional to the overarching message management sends about the law.

Communications are intensely powerful, that's why they figure prominently in product marketing strategies. Yet when it comes to selling employees on policies and new management initiatives, few businesses use the same degree of sophistication as when communicating their product or service message to customers. Internal selling seems, well, . . . unseemly. *We don't have to* is the commonly held attitude. *If they want to work here, employees have no choice but to accept our corporate edicts with unwavering loyalty.*

"Adopt that policy! Check off another brilliant initiative completed on the to-do list! Discuss? Why? What for? We're done here." *Or are we?*

Exactly what kind of compliance message does your organization send? How often is it sent? Compare that answer to how often the sales and cost-saving message is sent. Which message is louder? Are you focusing on West Nile virus more than food poisoning? Does the policy say "no-no" while a wink and a nod says "just don't get caught"? Does that mean employees are more likely to swat at flies at the company picnic while chowing down on the glassy-looking potato salad?

Sometimes a company inadvertently drowns out its compliance message. Bottom-line pressures are interpreted as an endorsement for major risk taking. *Everybody does it. Nothing ventured, nothing gained.* It leaves the impression that making money, particularly racking up short-term gains, takes precedence over everything else.

By now, however, it should be clear how unmanaged legal risks can quickly eclipse those gains and in the worst-case scenario plunge the business enterprise into a death spiral. If employees are expected to know where to draw the line, it is incumbent on the business enterprise to broadcast the message loud and clear in both word and deed that good legal risk management *is* good business.

DEMONSTRATING COMMITMENT

Commitment is the glue that makes corporate codes of conduct stick. It galvanizes the value chain with awareness and it makes organizations more mindful of the law's far-reaching value to the business. It infuses understanding—the kind of understanding that embeds legal leverage into the bedrock of corporate culture. Commitment thereby breathes life into codes of conduct, policies, and guidelines. It is the essence of mindfulness.

Words, however, are not enough. The most beautifully crafted words can be neutralized by contradictory actions that undermine their plain meaning and effectiveness. The former Soviet Union, for example, had word for word a more liberal Constitution than the United States does. But in practice, the narrow interpretation of those Soviet rights was repressive and the citizenry were left with less freedom than their American counterparts.

Similarly, before its fall, Enron's ethics policy was heralded as a model for industry. Yet in reality it was subverted with an intoxicating mix of money and misguided moxie. No executive would openly endorse flouting the law, yet some unwittingly sent that message by their actions and by the incentives they created for bending the rules. As a result they silently endorsed a corporate culture of casual compliance or noncompliance that ultimately drove the company into bankruptcy.

The actions in both examples betrayed evidence of limited commitment to the written word and the constituents responded accordingly. They got the message. The decision-making bias of loss aversion motivated people to "go along to get along." Most were afraid to speak up.

The resources devoted to compliance and the level of management involvement, for example, can speak volumes about management commitment. The U.S. Federal Sentencing Guidelines for Organizations, the law that offers sentencing leniency if organizations have an effective compliance program, specifically acknowledges the relationship between management involvement and compliance program efficacy. It's even one of the factors used to gauge a program's effectiveness. More specifically, the Guidelines urge that "high-level personnel . . . [be] assigned overall responsibility to oversee compliance." The role of senior management is therefore intended to give the program teeth and credibility. (See Appendix D.)

As a practical matter, such leadership must be more than symbolic. It must inspire action. The belief patterns and decision-making biases explored in Chapter Two change slowly even when faced with overwhelming evidence to the contrary; therefore, keeping bottom-line pressures from being interpreted as endorsing unreasonably risky behaviors therefore takes planning and persistence. Otherwise employees follow their old habits. They will stay in their safety zone.

Expanding employees' safety zones requires steering clear of misunderstandings and creating a community of joint interest. Special attention must be paid to the elements of communication—the who, what, when, where, why, and how. Applying these elements to our goal of improved legal literacy, compliance, and leverage means looking at points like these:

- *Who* communicates: Are they credible? Do they have authority? Do they know what they are talking about?
- *What* is being said: Is it consistent? Is it appropriate? Is it serious?
- *When* it is being said: How often is the message sent? Is the timing appropriate? Why now?
- *Where* it is being said: Is it being whispered in the hallway? Or posted on the company intranet?
- *Why* it is being said: What's really going on? What are the consequences for the employees? Is there a hidden agenda?
- *How* it is being said: Does the message make sense? Can it be taken at face value or is there more between the lines? Is it likely to be misinterpreted and misunderstood? How loud is the message? What kind of resources are behind it?

Another way to vet corporate communications is to evaluate them on the basis of whether they are constant, clear, consistent, correct, and convincing:

- *Constant:* Is the message repeated often enough?
- *Clear:* Is the message understandable?
- *Consistent:* Do different editions of the message agree with one another?
- *Correct:* Is it the right message? Right time? Right place? Can the audience understand it?
- *Convincing:* Is the messenger credible? Is the content persuasive? Is the timing correct? What resources are being devoted to it? How important is it?

These two lists complement each other by capturing slightly different nuances. Together they expand our thinking and understanding of what creates a compelling message and what factors affect the audience's comprehension and understanding. Ignoring them or treating them superficially can compromise your message. If left unchecked, those compromises can leave you worse off than before.

When management issued a memorandum to announce the implementation of an anonymous employee hotline to report regulatory noncompliance at a manufacturing plant, the union employees called for a walkout. They labeled the hotline the "snitch line." They weren't *convinced* that it was only aimed at identifying regulatory noncompliance and fixing it. They believed someone would get blamed for the noncompliance. The compliance angle was not *consistent* with prior messages from management. They were suspicious of management's intent. It was not *clear* to them that they wouldn't be retaliated against for using the hotline.

In a nutshell, they simply didn't understand. Loss aversion kicked in and the new hotline got trashed. As a result the employees' acceptance of the new compliance tool was exactly the opposite of what management had hoped for.

Given these circumstances, popping a policy into place with a mere memo was not the *correct* message. It was an incomplete message. Management had some explaining to do about *why* the policy was being implemented before the compliance message could be heard. There was too much static that needed to be cleared up first. Until that question was satisfactorily answered the rest of the compliance message fell on deaf ears.

The Role of Listening to Employees

Communication is a two-way street. Unfortunately, listening is often underused when management implements new policies and programs. That is not to say that management can't direct change, it is merely to say that management is typically better off by first *cultivating* change.

You can't throw seeds on a sidewalk and expect them to grow well. A few sprouting up between the cracks is not much of a success story, particularly if those seeds are expensive. The rule of thumb in gardening is that a $5 tree should be planted in a $50 hole, not the other way around. A $50 tree in a $5 hole can look good for a few weeks or months, but eventually poor drainage, poor soil, or a boxed-up root system will cause it to die. Poor preparation leads to poor results, and so do poor communications. They do not support sustainable change.

Confronting employees' misconceptions and preconceptions and breaking down those barriers of entry would have been a more appropriate and correct communication in the hotline case. Explaining why the hotline was being proposed, how regulatory noncompliance was hurting the business, how customers were leery of committing to large orders for fear that the plant's noncompliance could lead to a shutdown and how interfering with product delivery would hurt the customers—all that would explain why the policy was being proposed now and how it was in everyone's interest to make the program a success.

Recognizing Social Networks

Instead of merely hoping the employees would understand the purpose of the hotline, management could have *planned* for better understanding. They could have found out how the workers at the plant might react by tapping into the informal social networks. It's similar to the focus groups conducted by marketing but with a twist.

Social networks represent who talks to whom and who is plugged into the information pipeline by virtue of *respect,* as opposed to job title. These are the opinion leaders and opinion makers within the organization. They represent the real horsepower behind the corporate engine. They get the work done. Because they know what's going on at the grassroots level they can act as powerful change agents. Enlisting their aid enhances the credibility of the compliance message and plays an invaluable role in reinforcing the company's commitment.

People issues can make or break a program. Nonetheless, some skeptical managers might counter that they have neither the time nor the inclination to stroke employee egos. It's counterintuitive and offends their sense of positional power. These are the folks who are more comfortable with managing relationships up the chain of command instead of down and prefer to execute change through executive fiat rather than finesse.

Sure, you might get by with a command-and-control approach for a little while; but research and experience both show that such methodology does not create sustainable change. When, for example, the business process reengineering (BPR) movement, made popular by Michael Hammer and James Champy's book *Reengineering the Corporation* (1993), first gained popularity the hot new tool was pitched by its authors with strong, take-charge, macho language. Companies were urged to "nuke" their organizations or "take an axe and a machine gun" to them. They were told to "carry the wounded and shoot the dissenters."

Unfortunately, BPR's success rate was less robust than its sales pitch. By the authors' own admission up to 70 percent of the organizations adopting BPR initiatives failed to achieve their intended goals. It was later conceded that inattention to people issues contributed to the poor results and *The Reengineering Revolution Handbook* (1995) was published to supplement the original manifesto. Suddenly, everyone realized there's more success when everyone is rowing in the same direction.

The Role of Management Listening to Itself

In 2001 accounting giant Arthur Andersen dismissed as an isolated incident the fact that it paid $7 million to settle SEC charges of filing false and misleading audits on behalf of client Waste Management, the Houston-based waste services company, overstating income by more than $1 billion. The SEC had unfortunately found that Andersen was too eager to please its client and compromised its objectivity by failing to stand up to improper accounting practices. This went on for years and it caused the SEC to conclude in an Order that "Andersen knew or was reckless in not knowing that the unqualified audit reports . . . were materially false and misleading."

As part of the settlement Andersen neither admitted nor denied the allegations. While it is understandable how for legal reasons the company would publicly deny the charges, it is less clear why denial was perpetuated inside the Andersen family. To an outsider it would appear that $7 million and words such as "knowing and reckless" and "materially false and misleading work product" would make a professional certified public accountant sit up and take serious notice, particularly since the penalty was the first anti-fraud injunction by the SEC in twenty years. But the senior leadership at Andersen didn't do so, and the tacit message to the firm was carry on: it's business as usual.

A valuable window of learning was wasted. Later that same year Andersen's client objectivity was once again headline news. At the center of the storm: Enron.

When the unexpected happens—and particularly when it carries a seven-figure legal liability—a company would be wise to step back and do a legal autopsy to determine what if anything can be learned. Such an assessment requires objectivity. But it also requires recognition that *not* learning from a past mistake means it's doomed to happen again.

Compare the *Andersen* case to that of international chemical giant DuPont, which *publicizes* its compliance missteps to its employees. Using its own files to create mini case studies, DuPont produces one-page bulletins that demonstrate that the company means business when it comes to compliance. Designed to instruct, not embarrass, the bulletins outline the facts of the case and the policy or law being violated, and then they offer lessons that can be directly applied to the workplace.

Taking examples from company files makes the compliance message accessible. It shows that noncompliance is not an abstract concept. It can happen here. It therefore makes employees more mindful of potential missteps. DuPont has also discovered that employees are particularly curious to know the results in each case. They want to know what discipline was meted out. Fortunately, even-handed accountability and disciplinary fairness has made these bulletins popular with employees.

The beauty of the DuPont bulletin policy is its constancy. It not only lends credibility to the compliance message, it keeps the message alive and fresh while helping to build best practices within the corporate culture. Best of all, enforcing their policies fairly helps build trust throughout the organization.

BUILDING TRUST

Trust goes hand in hand with commitment in establishing legal literacy and legal leverage. Trust regulates the white space between the boxes on the organizational chart. It influences credibility and whether a message is convincing or not. It also adds stability to relationships by creating the freedom and confidence necessary to try new things and apply past lessons. Trust can thereby seal the deal on change by providing a platform that lets us flex our new-found legal muscle. It lets new risk management processes grow into old habits.

There is a chicken-egg relationship between trust and understanding. When we trust we are more willing to listen. When we genuinely listen we hear more. When we hear more we understand more. When we understand more we learn more. Trust thereby makes information accessible and more available. It lowers our defensiveness and skepticism. It allows messages to get through and take hold.

When trust follows a positive spiral it inspires more trust, making it easier to convey commitment and increase your span of influence. Trust spiraling in a negative direction is demotivating and reduces your span of control.

It's tough to get anything accomplished without trust. Employees may grudgingly accede to a limited amount of influence by virtue of someone's authority, but their hearts and minds won't really follow. Trust is that leap of faith that leads us to believe that the organization is being true. It inspires us to follow and lets great leaders accomplish great things. See Figure 11.1.

Trust, however, starts to evaporate the minute the organization behaves inconsistently or without clarity, or both. It's replaced by

FIGURE 11.1. THE RELATIONSHIP BETWEEN TRUST AND SPHERE OF INFLUENCE.

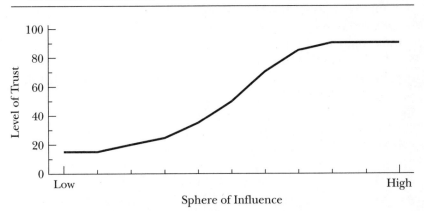

loss aversion. The bad part about fear is that "frightened people play office politics," writes former ITT CEO Harold Geneen in *Managing* (1984). "They won't come forward and admit there's a problem early enough to be solved."

Fear is the antithesis of trust and it dampens legal leverage. The less trust the more legal trouble your organization could be in because politics creates a chokehold on information and high-jacks the decision-making process. Employees abstain from straight talk because sharing information represents a loss of power. Their loss aversion sparks defensive behavior that makes them adept at hiding the serious issues. It breeds what one study calls "skilled incompetence," the ability to camouflage and sidestep real problems (Argyris, 1986).

What are the symptoms of a highly political organization? Political organizations are often highly autocratic in nature. What you know in political organizations is less important than who you are and whom you know. As a result, those who are not part of the inner circle lose their sense of satisfaction and ownership in their work. They stop taking extra responsibility or putting forth extra effort—it's just not worth it. The tolerance of generous incentive packages that are un-related to performance further exacerbates the disenfranchisement of the rank and file. These organizations tend to adopt unclear and unmeasurable goals that hamper any effort to introduce merit-based pay. They perpetuate a highly discretionary reward system.

Politically charged organizations also tend to shoot the messenger who brings bad news. As a result no one is willing to tell the emperor he has no clothes. The objective is to make the boss look good at any cost, so information gets suppressed, sanitized, and minimized on its way up the chain. Open secrets are not discussed, but everyone knows there is an elephant in the room. As a result, these organizations are crisis oriented.

As a practical matter, most corporate cultures are touched to one degree or another by office politics. But politics will not sub-vert sound decision making if the organization is unequivocal in its commitment to legal compliance.

How do you build trust about the organization's commitment to compliance? How are employees to know such commitment is true?

You build trust the same way you clear out a weed-choked gar-den. You need a clear vision of what stays and what goes. You then systematically start eliminating weedy messages in the areas that are most important to you. Weeding sounds harsh, but weeds distract the eye and rob the more important plants and trees of valuable nutrients and resources.

Legal audits, for instance, can help identify the high-value hot buttons that need immediate attention. But don't do an audit unless you plan to fix what you find in a reasonable period of time. Employees will understand that everything can't be done at once. But they won't understand the company's so-called commitment if there's a lack of genuine progress. Integrity can't be faked.

Where you encounter gnarled roots or bottlenecks you need to ask why—and not be satisfied with superficial answers. Keep asking why until you hit pay dirt—the truth. It typically requires asking the question five times before you strip away all of the defense layers and reach the real bone of contention. The more politics, the more layers of defensiveness need to be peeled back and the more patience, persistence, planning, and time it will take to grow genuine trust. Oh, and persistence. Did I mention persistence? Yes, *lots* of persistence.

Recognize that the full compliance message may not be heard or understood the first time. Be prepared to repeat yourself a lot. Multiple messages periodically sent in different formats add consistency. Multiplicity also addresses idiosyncratic learning styles of employees and increases the likelihood that everyone will actually hear and understand one or more of the messages.

Retrace your steps periodically to make sure the cleaned-up areas are properly maintained and new weeds haven't sprouted. Employees will be testing the organization to see if the change is real and trust is merited. Yank any resulting misconceptions while they're small, before they spread.

Constancy requires surround sound. The organization's voice must ring true throughout its formal and informal networks. Be prepared to show you mean business; don't just talk about it. The organizations that have the most success with reining in their legal risks are the ones that demonstrate commitment through various forms of participatory management.

PARTICIPATORY MANAGEMENT

Just as focus groups aid in product development, employee input in the change management process can help craft better policy implementation. Hands-on experience helps employees point out practical considerations that could detract from a policy's effectiveness. Best of all, when employees are part of the process instead of being merely subject to it there's less shock to the system. Employees see how their contribution makes a difference. The effort creates a sense of satisfaction and ownership that embeds the experience into the corporate culture and contributes to lasting change. It renders the integration of new ideas and processes more effective and seamless.

In Chapter Five, for example, I described a company that successfully implemented policy changes and reduced spiraling product liability claims that had more than doubled in the previous two-year period. A cross-functional team isolated the problem and recommended changes. The team included research and development, purchasing, manufacturing, shipping and packaging, sales and marketing, plus the legal department. Together they parsed out the interdependencies that contributed to the product liability exposure. Together they improved quality and lowered the company's risk profile.

Better understanding of contract warranties, for example, led to better storage, shipping, and warning instructions as well as better sales training to manage customer expectations at the beginning of the product use cycle. Better understanding of product specifications and tolerances allowed for better purchasing practices and less component failure downstream. Better understanding of regulatory requirements created a better understanding of how product regulations impact product liability and motivated R&D to build regulatory compliance *into* the product, reducing the need for Band-Aids later in the product's life cycle.

If the company had short-circuited the teamwork and through a stroke of brilliance distilled the same conclusions into procedures and practices, the net result would not have been the same. The participants would not have experienced the sense of discovery or the sense of ownership that comes from reaching personal conclusions and hands-on learning. The lesson for other companies is clear: no matter how good someone else's solution looks, it's worth working through the process to some degree to make it your own—to validate it. The investment of time unlocks the creativity of a team that really knows your business and enhances the policy's effectiveness because key stakeholders were actively involved in its development.

Research has shown that most adults learn best by doing. That's why the highest-ranked executive education programs include a healthy dose of live simulations and team case studies as part of their learning experience.

The Teledyne Lesson

Government defense contractor Teledyne already had a formal ethics program in place, blessed by senior management and backed by training dollars, in the late 1980s when one of its subsidiaries was put in the awkward position of pleading guilty to falsifying tests on a government contract. When another subsidiary was convicted in a fraud case, the company realized that something was dreadfully wrong.

Determined to make the program better, Teledyne benchmarked its program against other companies and conducted one-on-one interviews with employees. Its leaders wanted to understand what the company's ethics and compliance program looked like from the trenches. In thousands of employee interviews they asked about what level of awareness the program created, perceptions of management commitment, and about how the program could be improved to make the message more relevant.

What the company discovered was very insightful. For starters, Teledyne discovered pockets of inconsistency with respect to training. The ethics and compliance message was not homogeneous between operating units. Some units simply did a better job of reinforcing the message than others.

In examining where the message went off track Teledyne came to the realization that the policy established values but that it was silent on *how* those values were to be achieved. To fix the problem the company developed a more comprehensive set of training tools and dedicated more personnel to supervising their implementation. The change provided more clarity across the board, more constancy, and more consistency in the training message. Among the tools used to keep the message alive are "paycheck stuffers." These little notices are used to remind employees of the availability of the company hot line and ethics officer.

Another piece of valuable feedback related to the policy itself—it wasn't user-friendly. There was too much legalese. It was hard to understand. So the company rewrote it with an eye toward making it a reference tool, not just something that was read once and then put on the shelf or framed on the wall. The code is now easier to navigate and includes frequently asked questions and answers. The plain language and ease of use makes the policy more accessible, relevant, and meaningful.

As a defense contractor, the company knows that contract compliance is vitally important. When Teledyne Relays pled guilty to falsifying test results, for example, the subsidiary was barred from bidding on government contracts for a period of one year. Contract compliance is therefore more than legal mumbo jumbo for Teledyne. It's a hot button issue that is directly tied to the basic revenue model. To make sure that contract requirements were consistently being met Teledyne launched what it called a "contract compliance matrix" process whereby all contracts were systematically reviewed. Processes were examined, and if necessary put in place, to ensure that contract requirements were faithfully met. Reminiscent of Sarbanes-Oxley's process controls, the Teledyne contract compliance matrix is another example of compliance being employed as a quality assurance program.

As a measure of the program's success, Teledyne looks to the number of calls it receives from its employees on the company's ethics and compliance "helpline." The company believes that employees would not pick up the telephone if they risked retaliation. The steady use of the helpline is therefore seen as a measure of trust. It validates the policy and verifies that the employees and the company are in this together.

The Teledyne experience shows how commitment and trust go hand in hand in making compliance programs more effective. Without the cooperation of employees, policies and codes of conduct are nothing more than "mission impossible." Commitment and trust form the backbone that supports the legal muscle developed in the preceding chapters. They give employees the freedom and support necessary to flex their legal literacy and achieve legal leverage.

The role of corporate-wide communications in the legal leverage process portfolio is to create a community of common interest through commitment and trust. See Figure 11.2. Participatory management styles contribute to the trust-building process and open the door to trust and transparency. In contrast, autocratic management styles have a chilling effect on information. As a prac-

FIGURE 11.2. LEGAL LEVERAGE PROCESS PORTFOLIO:
HIGHLIGHTING COMMUNICATIONS.

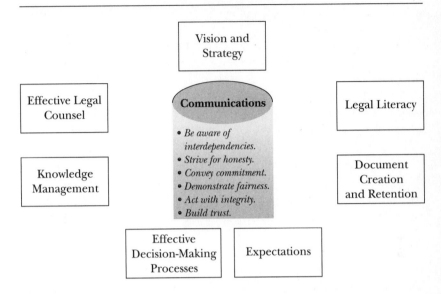

tical matter, however, real-life corporate cultures represent a blend of both styles and corporate policies will therefore always be viewed a bit like foreign film subtitles. Employees will always wonder whether something is being lost in translation.

In the movies, we look to the action on the screen to fill in the blanks, the picture being worth a thousand words. In business, we look to our leaders for clues about the unwritten rules of the organization and what is really expected of us. Therefore unwavering commitment requires more than the flawless execution of corporate communications. It requires genuine leadership.

CHAPTER TWELVE

HOW TO STAY CENTERED
The Role of Ethical Leadership

*Leaders are people who do the right thing; managers are
people who do things right.*
—WARREN BENNIS (1925–)

Meet Betty Vinson. In 1996 she began a midlevel accounting job
at a small long distance telephone company. The telecom boom
was in its infancy, and as the company grew, so too did Vinson's job
duties. She was eventually promoted to senior manager, responsible for compiling quarterly reports. By all accounts the company
was doing well, but one day she was asked to make some questionable accounting entries, the kind that would generate false profit.

Outraged, she initially refused to engage in the scheme and even
threatened to quit. But the reality of a family dependent on her income, insurance benefits, and the prospect of being a middle-aged
job seeker made her reconsider. Finding another job would be difficult. Being unemployed would create family hardship. But staying would mean compromising her principles. How could she do
that? She was teetering on an ethical tightrope.

When the company's chief financial officer assured her that
nothing was illegal and that he would assume full responsibility,
Vinson saw her way clear. The assurance gave her the confidence
necessary to muzzle her fears. She further rationalized it as a one-
time event. Sales would catch up the next quarter. The entries
would be offset. It would be a wash. She was just helping out the
company.

Unfortunately, doing it once was the first step down the proverbial slippery slope. She ended up "helping" for more than eighteen months. Each time she thought would be the last, until the illegal entries totaled over $3.7 billion and her employer, WorldCom, fell off its Wall Street pedestal. When the criminal indictments were handed down Vinson's name appeared among the unindicted co-conspirators. The company and the chief financial officer who promised to "assume full responsibility" were too busy fighting their own battles to make good on their promise.

At first glance, accounting scandals such as WorldCom's look like a twisted Greek tragedy—a fatal leadership flaw leading to the corruption of power, unbridled greed, fraud, and the accumulation of great wealth for a select few. When the lie is ultimately revealed there is a great struggle between the betrayed and the betrayers. At the end, regulators assume the godlike *deus ex machina* role and solve the problem with Sarbanes-Oxley legislation. Curtain.

The leadership message of WorldCom and other accounting frauds is often couched as a right-versus-wrong decision, and at one level of analysis that characterization is spot on. Steering due north with unflinching determination and being legally literate enough to know right from wrong when pursuing the best interests of the company is a course of conduct few would dare disagree with.

But saying the right words and living up to them are two different things. Good intentions, press releases, and mission statements are not enough. An uncharted gray area lies between legal and illegal, a seeming void between the letter of the law and spirit of the law that many companies are trying to fill with ethics training. But such training is not enough. "The best of us can be tempted," says one white-collar criminal serving time in federal prison. "If you think a good set of ethics will keep you out of prison, you are mistaken."

What's a company to do?

The major accounting frauds prompted an outcry for more oversight and "corporate governance," a fancy phrase that covers everything from more nuts-and-bolts compliance to coaxing boards of directors to be watchdogs instead of lapdogs. But as the bravos and applause die down the audience shuffling out the door is grumbling about the onerous requirements of Sarbanes-Oxley and how a few selfish individuals have ruined it for everyone. *What does it have to do with my company and me? It's not fair. It's gone too far.*

Sadly, the whining drowns out the bigger message—the story *behind* the story of WorldCom. It's the one told by the chorus in this Greek tragedy and it's the one applicable to those of us who want our organizations to resist temptation.

ARCHITECTING MORAL AUTHORITY

Establishing moral authority within the business enterprise starts with a clear understanding of what's legally right or wrong. It starts with a baseline of legal literacy that is supplemented with knowledge of the laws that apply to your business. It also includes implementing the tools and processes discussed in earlier chapters as a system of checks and balances to encourage and enforce ethical behavior. See Exhibit 12.1. But the leadership challenge in architecting moral authority within the business enterprise is in creating enough freedom to allow employees to *use* these risk management tools.

EXHIBIT 12.1. SUMMARY OF BEST PRACTICE TOOLS
AND PROCEDURES FOR MANAGING LEGAL RISK.

- Establish legal literacy job requirements and a tailored curriculum to enhance relevance and improve training effectiveness.
- Develop and implement good document creation and retention policies to guide the responsible application of legal literacy and the avoidance of unnecessary smoking gun liabilities.
- Use legal audits and triage methods to prioritize the legal leverage agenda and break risk management down into bite-sized pieces.
- Increase mindfulness by reframing issues and identifying interdependencies using cross-functional teams.
- Build knowledge management systems that put vital legal information at employees' fingertips.
- Draw on professional legal expertise to supplement employees' legal literacy.
- Use communications tools wisely to demonstrate commitment and leadership integrity and to build trust.

Betty Vinson, for example, knew that making the false accounting entries was wrong, but she did it anyway. She justified her decision as helping the company and protecting her family. Actually, the conspiracy of silence was so strong within WorldCom's corporate culture that employees who disapproved of the accounting methods were unwilling to speak up because they were afraid of not being "team players." They even resisted the efforts of colleagues who ultimately blew the whistle.

There were no huge stock option packages or personal piggy bank privileges for these lower-ranked employees. They just wanted to keep their jobs, feed their families, and keep a roof over their heads. The decision to look the other way was driven by loss aversion. These employees were protecting their physiological needs, the needs identified at the lowest rung of Maslow's hierarchy of human needs, the set of standards first discussed in Chapter Seven and shown in Figure 7.6.

The perceived threat to these fundamental human needs created an incentive to maintain the status quo and look the other way. It had a chilling effect on the availability of information to the organization. Employee loss aversion conflicted with organizational needs. It created a negative incentive.

For outsiders looking in, it's easy to be judgmental about the failure of these employees to step forward and report the fraud. It would have been the "right" thing to do. Yet outsiders who make such judgments do so in the relative safety of their reading chairs. The employees' view from the corporate trenches looks quite different. When you feel trapped you go into survival mode. Emotions overrule logic. Situational ethics takes over and can lead to major rule bending and breaking. Such dynamics explain the behavior—but they don't excuse it.

Building Incentives

Leaders have a moral responsibility to not put employees into such ethical dilemmas. They must be mindful of their role in creating incentives and how those incentives shape expectations and drive behavior. The power of incentives is important to note because if negative incentives can push good people to suspend their judgment and engage in criminal acts, how likely is it for such pressures to cause employees to engage in lesser infractions where lesser corporate liabilities are at stake? Exactly, it's very easy.

It's *too* easy—and therein lies the bigger lesson of WorldCom and all the other outlaw enterprises that crashed and burned around the same time. They illustrate how incentives can be used to mislead and trump core values.

"Shine the light on someone—it's funny how numbers improve," boasted one fallen CEO. Some employees compared the corporate culture to being in a cult. Harsh criticism and intimidation tactics were used to discourage naysayers. Delivering on numbers was paramount and the pressure was enormous.

Overconfidence turned into a false sense of invincibility and in the end it biased decision making to the point where it not only pushed the limits of the law but ignored them altogether. Once the behavior was ingrained as corporate culture it spread out of control and derailed corporate governance. Only someone with nothing to lose, like the boy in "The Emperor's New Clothes," would dare to stand up and tell the king he is naked—and that's where Maslow's hierarchy fits in.

Maslow's hierarchy lays out five instinctive human needs that when threatened create "situations." The basic needs at each level must be met before we can ascend to the next higher plane. Had Vinson, for example, had an independent source of income or felt more confident about her job prospects she would have been better able to hold fast to the principles that ignited her initial outrage. Instead, she felt she had no choice. She looked for a decision-making loophole—a way to rationalize her behavior and compromise her personal values.

No legitimate business enterprise would openly encourage its employees to break the law, nor would it exploit their vulnerabilities to achieve the same end. But it is nonetheless possible for incentives operating behind the scenes to have the same effect. Such incentives threaten a loss of position on Maslow's hierarchy.

Company leadership may not always be cognizant of the incentives created by organizational politics. Leaders often live and work in a different world from that of their typical employee. As a result, they function on a different plane within Maslow's hierarchy. It's easy for them to underestimate and misunderstand these powerful forces.

The Betty Vinson subplot of the WorldCom saga is therefore a cautionary tale of how incentives *enable or disable* legal risk management. At WorldCom the willingness of employees to tolerate criminal activity and stymie the efforts of whistle-blowers was highly destructive. It *also* meant that the pot of risky activity had been simmering for some time before the lid blew off.

Inadequate information detracts from decision quality and creates higher levels of legal risk. Such hoarding of information hampers mindfulness and creates a reservoir of unmanaged legal risk. The size of the reservoir is directly proportional to the degree of employee inertia and the severity of the misconduct. As illustrated in Figure 12.1, the less transparent communications are, the more severe the misconduct and the bigger the reservoir of risk.

The curve in Figure 12.1 turns sharply upward because trust wanes as communications shut down. Distrust causes risk to pile up and go off the chart when the fear of retribution is high. Poor communications and lack of transparency thereby dam up what is otherwise readily available information and create a reservoir of unmanaged legal risks.

Figure 12.1. Legal Risk as a Function of Misconduct and Level of Open Communication.

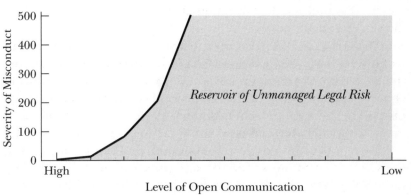

Better incentives would make employees more willing to step forward and raise potential problems while they are small and relatively inexpensive to handle. They would encourage the mindfulness that improves the decision making process and would let companies drain the liability swamp, thereby *enhancing* the effectiveness of risk management and unlocking the benefits of legal leverage.

Incentives create expectations and exist at each level of the value chain. They are shaped by leadership that is spelled with a capital "L" as well as a lowercase "l" and shouldn't be assumed or taken for granted. All positional power carries with it an element of leadership authority and establishes its own microclimate. It can be within a division, a department, or even a small team. You might be surprised about what is automatically inferred from positional power and how it can lead to unexpected results.

The Final Exam Lesson

"Negotiate a fair deal," I told my MBA students, as I handed out their final exam—a mergers and acquisitions (M&A) case study simulation. "That's your assignment."

The class was divided into transaction teams and given a fact pattern that included an unfolding due diligence process. Some of the new information was accurate and relevant and some of it was not. Some of it was communicated to everyone and some of it was not. Would the team openly share information or would individuals hoard it? What kind of corporate culture would each team embrace? How would they factor the legal risk into their analysis? How would they determine the right thing to do?

On the last day of class, after all the reports were handed in, we would debrief the case together as a class. Despite the occasional jaw that would drop in betrayal over some piece of information that had been withheld by a teammate, or in awe over the stellar valuations another team seemed to extract from the buyer, almost everyone thought they had struck a fair deal. Less than 5 percent of the students reached a stalemate in their deliberations due to irreconcilable differences.

I gave this exam nearly a dozen times, and every time I asked how many would have walked away from the deal if their own money were on the table, at least 95 percent of the hands would fly into the air. "If we found this many problems now," one student volunteered, "there'll only be more later."

"OK. Then why would you spend the company's money faster than your own when you know it's a bad deal?" I asked. "Why accept these liabilities?"

"It was expected," most of them chimed in. "It's what you told us to do." *Well, not exactly.* But it *is* how they interpreted my instructions. It's the expectation they inferred, and of course the incentive was passing the course and moving a step closer to graduation and a coveted MBA.

What the students didn't know at the time was that the simulation was cobbled together from assorted real deals, including some deals that *weren't* consummated because of unacceptable legal risks. It was literally a combination of the best of the worst. (Of course, the real names and places were changed to protect confidentiality.) Yet even with the facts stacked against a good deal, very few were willing to stand up and say it wasn't good at any price when wearing their assigned team hats. The prevailing thinking was that the price just needed to be low enough. They were looking at the hard costs. Yet when speaking in a personal capacity they were more than aware of the soft costs and would have been unwilling to risk their own capital.

"In this case the optimal ethical solution and the best business solution happen to be one and the same," said one of the students. "Unfortunately in today's business climate this has become increasingly rare."

The perception that the ethical solution and the best business solution are divorced from each other is troubling. It illustrates how incentives and the expectations they create are subtle yet fragile, and it underscores the important role of corporate leadership in structuring incentives to keep these two properly aligned.

Also interesting is how easily "doing the right thing" can be highjacked by a desire to please. It wouldn't be the first time that the desire to please senior management caused legal liability to be discounted to the point of buyers' remorse and burdened the organization with a legal albatross. In architecting moral authority and keeping the company ethically centered, the risk of retribution should never outweigh the value of open and transparent communications. There should always be enough trust to allow employees to take a leap of faith and risk displeasing their bosses. As the great leader Mahatma Gandhi once said: "Honest disagreement is often a good sign of progress."

Neutralizing Blind Spots

The relationship between incentives and their ability to motivate ethical behavior and marshal resources that drive business performance empowers leadership. Unfortunately, leaders are subject to the same decision-making blinders of overconfidence and loss aversion as everyone else. They are not infallible. As a result there is a *greater* imperative for leaders to neutralize their own biases when compared to the rest of the organization. See Table 12.1.

Leaders are in a pivotal position. If they inadvertently tip the balance toward negative incentives it can seriously hamper the company's efforts to manage legal risk. On the other hand, respecting and capitalizing on these relationships to encourage open dialogue, mindfulness, and honest feedback can drive extraordinary performance. The only way leaders will be able to benefit from all the intellectual horsepower in the organization is to be cognizant and humble enough to appreciate their own limits and encourage constructive dialogue.

In *Only the Paranoid Survive* (1996), Intel founder Andy Grove warns against managerial complacency—a form of overconfidence. Written in the aftermath of the half-billion-dollar Pentium chip product recall, he warns that companies face a never-ending challenge in distinguishing valuable information from background noise. He cautions that the only way to know which is which is to engage in rigorous debate and analysis, as well as information sharing and brainstorming. In other words, information needs to be made available—and leaders and managers must be willing to *listen*.

Leaders can take steps to neutralize their own decision-making biases by adopting the best practices and implementing the tools discussed in preceding chapters. See Exhibit 12.1. Creating these structures points the corporate compass due north and communicates what is expected. But making these constructs come alive requires commitment—and commitment requires integrity.

TABLE 12.1. ROLE OF INCENTIVES IN MANAGING LEGAL RISK.

Factors Influencing Incentives	Type of Incentive Created	Impact on Maslow's Hierarchy	Impact on Resource Mobilization	Impact on Knowledge Management	Impact on Legal Risk Management
• Positional power • Overconfidence • Direct or indirect threats and intimidation • Desire to please	Negative	Threatens position and is a potential step down	Low	Disabling	Disabling
• Empathic communications • Respect • Mutual interest • Joint problem solving • Desire to please	Positive	Enhances position and is a potential step up	High	Enabling	Enabling

Demonstrating Integrity

Listening is integrity in action. I have already discussed the importance of listening from the perspective of its content value. But when it comes to establishing moral authority, the act of listening does more than gather information. It demonstrates commitment by showing respect for employees. It shows a willingness to engage in mutual discussion and joint problem solving. It demonstrates the company's resolve to do the right thing.

Listening shows you care. It helps guide employees when they feel torn between competing goals. It injects sincerity into best practices standards by adding another layer of commitment to established tools and procedures that further embeds them into the corporate bedrock. It's another way to express and reinforce expectations and precisely the kind of management commitment the Federal Sentencing Guidelines (excerpted in Appendix D) seek to encourage, one that energizes legal risk management tools and strengthens their effectiveness.

Listening must be genuine. It must be part of what Stephen Covey calls "empathic communication." It requires hearing and making a good-faith effort to understand what the other person is saying. It means connecting with the other person's point of view. It is not about politely going through the motions and waiting for your turn to speak. It is also not about cherry-picking information and parsing it out piecemeal, as Enron's CEO Kenneth Lay did after whistle-blower Sherron Watkins sent him a memorandum warning that the company could "implode in a wave of accounting scandals" when he asked Enron's outside counsel to review the situation, but not challenge Arthur Andersen's work. It's about genuine understanding and finding solutions, not about addressing concerns without answering them.

Leaders are the moral compass and the ethics teachers of their organization. If they are unwilling to listen with an open heart and act responsibly, it is impossible for the organization to consistently do the right thing. In its most basic form, doing the right thing means complying with the law. But doing what's right isn't always easy.

The role of compliance functions, for example, is to look for *non*compliance. These folks typically deliver the unpopular news, the kind of news that runs against the grain of our desire to please.

It takes courage to deliver such news. How these communications are listened to and ultimately handled by the organization's leadership sends an important message that creates incentives.

Is the messenger shot—demoted as Sherron Watkins was? Or is she heralded as a hero who saves the company from unwanted fines and liabilities? Does leadership's response enable or disable effective legal risk management? Are they doing what's right—or what's easy?

The whistle-blower protections of the Sarbanes-Oxley Act may enable employees like Sherron Watkins to step forward and for future Betty Vinsons to vote their conscience instead of their paychecks. But in all likelihood the misconduct they allege would need to reach a certain critical mass before a whistle-blower rips open the corporate trench coat and bares all. That time delay represents a missed risk management opportunity and a gradual accumulation of unmanaged risk.

It also leaves the company open to the possibility that the whistle-blowing employee will reach out to law enforcement officials instead of management. Such a move preempts the company's ability to address the problem on its own terms. It lets law enforcement set the agenda. Thus relying on whistle-blower protections is a suboptimal strategy and considerably less effective than developing incentives that motivate effective knowledge management.

The power of incentives is that employees will only achieve within the business enterprise what they think their leadership *allows* them to achieve. How well leaders manage this process makes the difference between performance that has the gravel-stirring traction and the power of "we" or a ho-hum corporate yawn that defaults to the safety of Maslow's hierarchy and the power of "me." It largely depends on leadership's ability to provide unbiased guidance, to provide resources and processes, and to let others make wise decisions.

Active listening without having employees fear retribution is a test of leadership strength. It tests the organization's ability to continue doing the right when faced with information it would rather not hear. Fearing an information overload or a difficult decision, some leaders are reluctant to open the door too wide. A distinction, however, needs to be made between listening to issues that facilitate healthy debate and making someone else's decision for them. Effective leaders coach their employees through decisions they are responsible for, but they don't make decisions for them. They know when to step in and when to step out of the process. It's part of the art of being a leader. "To lead the people," Gandhi once said, "walk behind them."

Listening is part of the incentive matrix that operates, as I've said, in the white space on the organization chart—in between the various levels of leadership and management throughout the value chain. It empowers the organization. It invigorates the processes, procedures, incentives, and expectations that operate within the white space. It also bridges and mediates the relationship between leadership and management. See Figure 12.2.

How we align these layers within the value chain and how we manage that white space establishes our corporate culture. It determines how much legal risk is avoided, transferred, shared, reduced, or mitigated. As tempting as it is to brush aside thorny legal and ethical leadership responsibilities in favor of straightforward cost-benefit analysis, it must be remembered that traditional cost-benefit analysis does not capture the nuanced cost of misaligned incentives.

FIGURE 12.2. RELATIONSHIP OF THE LEGAL LEVERAGE
PROCESS PORTFOLIO TO MANAGEMENT AND LEADERSHIP.

The Space Shuttle Lesson

Take, for example, the 2003 *Columbia* space shuttle disaster. During liftoff a piece of foam insulation from an external fuel tank broke loose, hitting the leading edge of the shuttle's left wing. The damage contributed to lethal heat buildup, ultimately causing the shuttle to disintegrate during reentry into the earth's atmosphere, killing all aboard.

In the investigation that followed it came to light that NASA rarely conducted actual experiments or physical testing on parts used in flight. The agency relied instead on mere analysis. That strategy appeared to work for decades as the shuttle fleet flew one successful mission after another. The lack of serious negative consequences perpetuated confidence in the data. But the catastrophic loss of the *Columbia* challenged the status quo.

An independent board of inquiry characterized the situation as a broken safety culture. It recommended that nondestructive testing and analysis could have made better information available that would avoid shuttle catastrophes in the future. Such testing would replace hindsight with foresight. But at a press briefing shortly after these recommendations were announced, the head of the board of inquiry defensively noted that the prior level of testing should not be interpreted as indicating fault on the part of the agency: "Testing to understand things will always compete with real-world realities and will almost always lose." His observation is deeply rooted in a cost-benefit analysis mindset.

In the final minutes of the doomed *Columbia* flight temperatures shot up erratically in the left wing, causing sensors to fail. Landing gear sensors reported irregularities. Four tire pressure and tire temperature sensors melted. The vulnerability of the tires under those conditions and the risk of what could happen if they exploded was well known, according to a former NASA engineer who had worked on the program from 1986 to 1994. Two days before the *Columbia* was lost a NASA safety engineer sent an e-mail warning about those very consequences. But the NASA mission team had already concluded the foam had caused no serious damage. As a result, no one listened enough to take any action. The risk of foam damage had already been discounted.

Fast forward two and a half years. The agency worked on the board's recommendation of eliminating foam and ice debris during launch, strengthening the orbiter's outer layer, and developing procedures to allow in-orbit repairs to damage incurred during liftoff. Overall, the loss of the *Columbia* made NASA more mindful about the quality of its decision making. Knowledge management improved. More effort was made to gather and evaluate relevant information pertaining to the shuttle's safety.

Nonetheless, as the space shuttle *Discovery* became the first shuttlecraft to resume space travel since the *Columbia,* close examination of launch video showed debris falling and raised concern about the integrity of the spacecraft's outer skin. Happily, the *Discovery* was the beneficiary of a host of new inspection techniques.

Cameras and lasers were used to examine every inch of the vehicle during the mission. These instruments gathered information of cracks or gaps in the delicate thermal shield that could give cause for alarm. Before docking with the International Space Station the shuttle orbiter did a back flip maneuver to provide the opportunity for a thorough vehicle inspection. An unprecedented space walk was conducted to remove two pieces of tile filler material that were protruding too far and might create turbulence and unnecessary heat buildup during reentry. Even a torn thermal blanket near the cockpit window that might otherwise have gone unnoticed was evaluated. The mission managers' decision process examined all the options, including whether they should order the astronauts to board the space station until a rescue shuttle could reach them, before unanimously deciding the *Discovery* was safe to return to Earth.

"We put the orbiter under a microscope," said the deputy shuttle program manager during a news conference. "I mean, we're out there with every little spot, scuff, ding, you name it. It's not ignored. It's not brushed off. It's evaluated by a large team of engineers who are very knowledgeable about the orbiter."

The availability of information was increased and the process for handling liabilities associated with product failure improved. The margin for error decreased. The agency's traditional cost-benefit analysis has been supplemented in an ethically responsible way and changed behaviors that contributed to the safe return of the shuttle crew. The inherent risk of space travel is still there, but it is being managed better. But is it enough?

In the minority report issued after the *Discovery*'s safe return to earth, officials blasted the agency for failing to eliminate debris during liftoff. They cited schedule pressures that caused corner-cutting and short-changed goals. They also criticized the agency for not being able to have any objective data to indicate whether the tank modification was merely "safer" than before or truly "fixed." The report vividly illustrates the inherent clash between hard costs and soft costs.

The report's assertion that the agency "must break this cycle of smugness substituting for knowledge" further highlights the importance of managing expectations by communicating which goals can't be compromised and the importance of communicating unambiguously to what degree these goals are achieved. It also demonstrates the inherent difficulty of transforming a culture and how intractable decision-making biases can be.

Measuring Progress

Some leadership activities simply defy easy quantification. When it comes to measuring ethics and the organization's willingness to follow the spirit of the law, looking for a single killer app is ultimately frustrating and futile. It's too complex a phenomenon to be oversimplified or trivialized by metrics. That's not to say it's impossible to weigh or gauge progress in this area, or to unambiguously communicate what actions are acceptable and what are not. It's merely to say that traditional tools are inadequate. Placing too much stock in them discounts qualitative norms and can cause someone to draw disappointing and inaccurate conclusions.

Most attempts to quantify legal and ethical concerns suffer from trying to apply measurement techniques that are appropriate for manufacturing to nonmanufacturing environments. Compared to manufacturing mishaps, the direct cause of a legal or an ethical lapse is more difficult to isolate and is less subject to precise repeatability. It typically involves multiple decisions, some of which contribute only indirectly to the problem, that are made by decision makers whose legal and business acumen vary. This combination of dependent variables makes it difficult to apply any one-size-fits-all metric.

Nonetheless, when looking for signs of progress, it is necessary to figure out what success looks like. It needs to be framed in terms of the organization's business objectives. What are we trying to accomplish? How do we know when we're there? Once we can clearly articulate the objective, we can reverse engineer it to identify what to measure and how to measure it. If instead we fixate on measurements first and try to cram the objective into the metric, we will probably be disappointed. The metrics could be met and show progress on paper. But if our expectations are left unfulfilled because they weren't articulated properly we can still be left feeling as frustrated as if we had wallpapered the wrong room.

Finding the right metrics requires a combination of quantitative and qualitative judgments:

- Did improved legal literacy reduce the company's liability exposure? How do we know that? Fewer lawsuits and better regulatory compliance? Or better processes that eliminate the cause of lawsuits and regulatory noncompliance?
- Did it eliminate a lawsuit? Or keep a claim from escalating into one? What factors contributed? Was it something within the company's control, such as better dispute resolution techniques? Or outside the company's control, such as limited law enforcement funding causing an agency to focus on a bigger fish?
- Did it lead to better contract negotiation or a more constructive business relationship and customer satisfaction?
- Did securing intellectual property rights generate revenue or competitive advantage?
- Did the spirit of compliance generate customer goodwill? Enhance the company's reputation? Or boost employee morale?

If the answers point to a fundamental improvement in processes and increased mindfulness, or to sustainable cost savings or asset creation, then legal literacy generated genuine business value.

Some people may decry what they feel is a soft and imprecise measure of progress. Granted, it's less verifiable than tidy test data, but the lack of laboratory repeatability does not impeach its legitimacy. Ironically, ethics and following the letter and spirit of the law is a lot like pornography—you know it when you see it. No thermometer can accurately measure the legal heat. That doesn't mean it's not there. Core values speak to the gut. They speak to our notions of fairness and justice. We know when it's there and when it's not.

Directing Progress

Consistent enforcement of company policies and continuous improvement of best practices are two methods for directing progress and keeping legal leverage on track and proceeding toward the business sweet spot. But, systems that provide checks and balances can only go so far, even if they include redundancies as fail-safe mechanisms. Why? Because systems are only as good as the employees who actually follow them.

A review of past banking disasters, for example, reveals that they could have all been detected sooner if senior management had kept a closer eye on what was going on. These scandals all demonstrate a pattern of bypassed controls and unenforced rules that created a window of opportunity for unscrupulous employees.

For example, a rogue trader who is familiar with the ins and outs of company procedures and is motivated to scam the system to compensate for heavy losses or misaligned incentives will go ahead with the scam. The only way to mitigate the problem is by monitoring and enforcing company rules and procedures. Such monitoring and enforcement would flag low-probability–high-impact events (for instance, the rogue trading of Nick Leeson) before they lead to catastrophic meltdowns (the demise of Barings).

Poor oversight and poor internal enforcement are the soft underbelly of commitment. They encourage casual compliance and situational ethics that mock risk management structures and procedures. They create a swamp of latent legal liability that puts the company at risk. Good oversight and enforcement or better corporate governance and responsibility, on the other hand, create a leadership mandate that says, "We mean what we say."

Leadership wake-up calls typically occur after one or more scandals have created enough legal quicksand to mire the company's reputation. In one year, for example, banking behemoth Citigroup agreed to settle $2.6 billion in securities claims in connection with the WorldCom fraud, two of its investment banking executives in China were suspended by the bank for falsifying financial information, Britain's security regulators announced an investigation into a $13.5 billion bond trade, *and* Japanese regulators shut down Citibank's private banking operations. The disappointing legal picture prompted Citigroup's new chief executive officer, during his quarterly conference call to industry analysts announcing the 2004 third-quarter results, to acknowledge that the bank's reputation had been sullied.

"When things happen that cause that legacy and history to be tarnished a little bit, it hurts all of us," he said, stepping up to the plate. He further noted that the bank would take strong action to resolve these "cultural problems." Taking such action would coincidently preclude the need to add billions of dollars to an already large legal reserve-an action representing yet another of the many hidden costs associated with casual legal risk management.

Unfortunately, when organizations tighten up their alignment between the letter and spirit of the law it is sometimes difficult for employees to appreciate the shift in expectations—and they sometimes get caught amid the changing gears. At American International Group (AIG), for example, when Martin Sullivan took over the reins of the embattled insurer after his autocratic predecessor, Hank Greenberg, was ousted, Sullivan tried to scrap some of the company's old ways. Unlike Greenberg, who disdained regulatory meddling, Sullivan urged full disclosure and cooperation with regulatory probes. But old habits die hard. When one of AIG's senior executives, a Greenberg confidant, refused to cooperate, Sullivan had no choice but to fire him. He needed to enforce the new rules.

In the end, cooperating was the right thing to do. AIG's about-face on cooperation prompted New York Attorney General Eliot Spitzer's office to issue a public statement indicating that a civil resolution was within reach. The statement lifted the cloud of a possible criminal indictment and AIG's stock rose nearly 5 percent in response.

LETTER OF THE LAW VERSUS SPIRIT OF THE LAW

Legal compliance is about meeting the letter of the law—the minimal requirements—whereas meeting the spirit of the law speaks more to corporate responsibility and higher ethical concerns. Most companies want to be good corporate citizens but secretly wonder how good they really need to be. Some fear that the Sarbanes-Oxley backlash has created an unnecessary moral Puritanism among businesses.

Perhaps the best way to address that concern is to look to sports. The spirit of fair competition demands that players play by the rules. That's the baseline from which the best are judged. Being the best also requires *mastering* the competency needed to consistently meet those rules in full. However, it's the extra effort necessary to precisely line up a putt, slam-dunk a basketball, or run *past* the finish line that separates the truly outstanding from the merely good. More specifically, excellence requires a deep understanding of how all the pieces fit together, how the extra concentration or momentum ensures the victory.

When it comes to the law, a healthy respect for how the letter of the law and the spirit of the law meld can work the same way. Take, for example, the case involving the involuntary termination of two senior investment bankers at Bank of America. The separation occurred after the two men followed up on a confidential tip about a pending merger, which had been provided to them by a rival banker who had just accepted an offer to join Bank of America. The termination took them by surprise because they hadn't broken a regulation or engaged in insider trading. It sounded draconian.

What these gentlemen failed to appreciate was the legal duty associated with *confidential* information. The whole purpose of confidentiality is that the owner of the information gets to control its dissemination. Confidential information is an asset and taking it or using it without permission is stealing. *Technically* the rival banker had no business disclosing the information. *He* is the one who breached a legal duty owed to the owner of the information. The two recipients didn't have such legal duty to the owner of the information, but to suggest that it made their use of the confidential information legal is morally unsatisfying. Their action did violate the spirit of the law—the owner's ability to control the asset. It was an exercise of questionable judgment.

Enron similarly alleged that *hundreds* of off-balance-sheet entities it created to shelter debt were perfectly legal. Even if it's true that the off-balance-sheet entities were allowed under the accounting rules and *technically legal,* their sheer number raises the question of whether the law ever contemplated such heavy-handed use of these finance vehicles. Given the role of these entities in Enron's collapse, the technical answer rings hollow and sounds incomplete.

There is a dynamic relationship between ethics, public policy, and the development of the rule of law. Ethics represents society's expectations and public policy, the embodiment of those expectations, is ultimately expressed as law—the incentive and enforcement mechanism for driving the right behavior. The common denominator that unites them all is integrity. When integrity is compromised the equilibrium is violated and the disparity eventually surfaces. That's why stretching the law and exploiting perceived loopholes only begets more laws. In the long run it doesn't fool anyone and only causes harm in the process.

Leadership carries with it a heavy mantle of responsibility. It ultimately sets the tone for the organization's corporate culture. It also creates incentives that heavily influence the organization's legal risk profile. Therefore, steering an ethical course by establishing moral authority and respecting the rule of law is a leadership challenge of the highest order. It determines the level of legal leverage that is attainable.

EPILOGUE
Winning from the Beginning

If your business can't afford a legal meltdown, it pays to develop an understanding of how the company's moving parts touch the law—how they trigger liability and how they don't. Once you know how the pieces fit together and what makes them tick, you are in a better position to anticipate them in advance and control them. Such knowledge eliminates decision-making blind spots and promotes good habits and performance that let you start winning from the beginning.

You can't win if you don't play by the rules and you can't play by the rules if you don't know what they are. A gut-level sense of right or wrong is a good start, but in today's complex business world it is not enough. Business champions know how to keep themselves and their companies out of legal trouble.

Champions embody a special blend of talent, training, and attitude. They know the rules and they play by them. They combine these traits into a winning formula for continuous learning and improvement. Their disciplined habits promote excellence.

Legal understanding comes in three levels. The first is a glib grasp of the issues and a devil-may-care approach to their consequences. Legal risk at this stage of understanding is pretty much "no problem." Decision-making biases run rife and it's a fertile ground for the mathematical principle of regression to expose bad habits for what they are. It's an operations danger zone.

The second level of legal understanding is the white-knuckled stage. Here, the light goes on. As one of my students once said, "It's

like going to the eye doctor and getting a new pair of glasses—
suddenly you see things differently." Managers at this stage recognize the issues and start to realize how vulnerable their organizations really are. Their blood pressure rises as the weight of this
responsibility sinks in and they feel overwhelmed and not in control. They are out of their comfort zone. *Not* out of control, but not
in control.

Some managers react to this second stage by quickly retreating
to their former state of ignorant bliss, adopting an *if it isn't broken,
don't fix it* attitude. Others rail against the system instead, adopting
a scofflaw approach. *They can't seriously expect us to comply with all
these laws.* The rest, however, are unwilling to leave the legal force
field surrounding their bottom line to chance, so they soldier on.

Those reaching the third level of legal understanding are still
overwhelmed about the magnitude of the legal risk surrounding
business, but unlike their second-stage counterparts, they know
how to find solutions. They mobilize the resources necessary to
capture the legal anaconda that is curled up in the corporate chandelier. They recognize that not having a systematic approach to
business legal problems *is part of the problem.* Moreover, they recognize that replacing *ad hoc* risk management practices with a system
reduces errors of discretion and builds habits that protect profits
and provide peace of mind.

When it comes to the law, what you don't know really can hurt
you. There is no way to operate in the business world without coming into contact with legal issues. How you handle that contact will
make a profound impact on the habits you develop, and on the organization's corporate culture and its legal risk profile. It could
make or break a transaction, a business relationship, or a court
case and alter a company's legacy.

Developing a foundation of legal literacy, a deeper understanding of what legal issues to think about, helps managers recognize the avoidable opportunity costs the law can impose on
them. It lets them make better decisions and choose wisely about
what kind of risk and how much risk to take. When that happens,
risk becomes a conscious choice, a calculated risk, and the window
for surprises shrinks. There might still be shock if you miscalculate,
but that's not the same as not calculating. One is a function of
poor judgment or misjudgment, the other of ignorance. They are
worlds apart.

As a practical matter, the tug of war between legal risk and the cost associated with reducing or eliminating it will never end. The struggle is particularly acute when risk management projects are forced to compete with revenue-generating projects for the same limited resources. Some margin of error is bound to result from the trade-offs that inevitably get made when determining how much legal literacy or legal leverage a particular business enterprise needs.

Increasing sales and the size of the pie often looks sexier than protecting it. Yet the net effect on the bottom line is the same. A sustainable business requires a healthy dose of both to be successful. What you get to keep is as important as how much you make. Companies that pursue the bottom line to the exclusion of all else eventually hemorrhage financially from legal liabilities. It's like driving until the engine overheats. One day the car catches fire, and there's no fixing it.

AT WHAT PRICE EXCELLENCE?

The goal of legal literacy is to build bridges between law and business, to point out interdependencies and relevancies. The heightened awareness can then drive improved performance. Legal leverage is the *amount* of strategic value derived from applying legal literacy. It can be as simple and straightforward as being in compliance with the law. Or it can be as sophisticated as applying legal literacy tactically and strategically for the purpose of building new assets and protecting old ones.

Legal literacy and legal leverage are not a prescription for corporate sainthood, but they *do* reduce the organization's vulnerability to unethical or illegal behavior. Infusing the corporate culture with the tools and foresight necessary to leapfrog legal liabilities has the effect of turning problems into opportunities. It also creates reliability, dependability, trust, and customer satisfaction.

The legal leverage process portfolio is a series of incremental steps designed to align business decision making with the organization's essential purpose and the rules of the legal playing field. The portfolio process is grounded in the timeless core values of integrity, fairness, honesty, trust, and transparency—the equitable principles embedded in the rule of law.

Unfortunately, the intense focus placed on revenue leads many employees to believe that the sole purpose of business is to make money. While sales and profits are as important to business as oxygen is to life, it would be a mistake to lose sight of the heart. From a public policy perspective, the higher purpose of business is to provide goods and services. Money is merely a result of how well we perform that function. It's how we keep score.

The value chain gets compromised when the single-minded pursuit of money clouds decision making. Goods and services get shortchanged, creating assorted legal liabilities ranging from civil negligence to criminal fraud. These hiccups occur as a result of decision-making biases and misaligned priorities. Over time these habits get woven into the corporate fabric.

When we accept these misalignments as a "cost of doing business" we are in effect ratifying these deviances and normalizing them. In the process we begin to lose touch with the moral significance of the deviance. We start disrespecting our values. The strain anesthetizes us to the importance of these values and their relationship to business practices. Typically it takes some act of misfeasance or malfeasance to reach a crisis point and snap us out of the complacent stupor.

Given the vast number of interdependencies between law and business, even a small realignment—an ounce of prevention—can often go a long way toward controlling latent legal costs. Thus legal literacy and legal leverage offer a highly effective way for the business to keep more of its hard-earned money. After all, generating revenue is nice, but being able to keep more of it to reinvest in new products and services or to provide a return on investment to shareholders is even nicer.

The ultimate therapeutic value of that ounce of prevention, however, is directly proportional to its seamless integration with business. Seamlessness is important because managing legal risk requires consistency. It is not a one-time event; it's a process, one that requires maintenance and periodic assessment. The smoother the practice blends into the business routine the easier it is to sustain. Seamless integration is a function of how accessible and how relevant the law is made to decision makers, the incentives that drive their acceptance, and the corporate commitment that supports the whole shebang. Compliance processes that are intrusive, obstructive, or disruptive are the corporate equivalent of a fad diet—and have the same success rate.

As small changes and baby steps in the way we think about business and legal risk give way to bigger strides, the changes of habit and attitude cultivate a corporate culture of consistent legal compliance. This allows the business to move from hindsight to foresight and to look for opportunities. It enriches the decision-making process and unlocks the value of legal leverage.

Nothing worth doing is ever easy. You can't change the legal risk profile of your organization without better decision-making processes. You can't improve the decision-making processes without improving legal literacy. Aligning business practices with core values makes it easier to follow the law and is emotionally far more satisfying than the turmoil, confrontation, liability, and missed opportunities provoked by misalignment.

In sum, developing legal literacy helps you navigate the three levels of legal understanding and puts you in the driver's seat and on the road to greater competitive advantage. It provides a path for promoting better understanding and tolerance of legal rights and duties. It's up to you to decide how far down that path you ultimately wish to go in developing a business sweet spot—a set of winning habits that maximize competitive advantage and promote sustainable excellence.

LEGAL LITERACY TOOLKIT CHART

Sample: Employee Competency Requirements

Competency Requirements*	Sales Representative	Sales Manager	Research Chemist	Director of Research and Development
Core knowledge				
Ethics	x	x	x	x
Contracts	x	x	x	x
Unfair trade practices, including antitrust	x	x	x	x
Document creation and retention	x	x	x	x
Confidentiality	x	x	x	x
Workplace harassment	x	x	x	x
Advanced employment issues		x		x
Intellectual property	x	x	x	x

Competency Requirements*	Sales Representative	Sales Manager	Research Chemist	Director of Research and Development
Industry-specific knowledge				
Foreign Corrupt Practices Act	x	x		
Sarbanes-Oxley Act				
Safety			x	x
Environmental			x	x
Securities				
Industry-specific laws and regulations				

* Literacy training to be tailored with job-specific examples of the issues to highlight relevance and enhance understanding.

APPENDIX B

THE ABCS OF LEGAL LITERACY

This legal primer is intended as a quick reference guide to assist you in connecting the dots between core legal concepts and their business applications. *It is not intended to be legal advice or a substitute for competent counsel who represents you or your business.* It is offered instead to provide a baseline of information to help you develop awareness of the most common legal issues to cross a manager's desk. Industry-specific regulations are not addressed.

The pages that follow introduce six core legal disciplines. Each section surveys and highlights important concepts in one legal discipline, explains their business relevance in general terms, and offers a list of questions for you to think about that will help you translate the legal concepts to your own work environment.

Please note that what follows are only the ABCs. To do the whole topic justice would require an encyclopedia. The law is a nuanced endeavor. What follows is intended as a quick acid test to help you see if you are heading in the right direction and to provide a good starting point for gathering your thoughts before seeking expert counsel. Together with your counsel you can develop the foresight and peripheral vision necessary to manage your organization's legal risk effectively.

1. INTERNATIONAL LAW

When we refer to international law we are loosely referring to four things:

- International treaties and conventions
- The law of sovereign foreign countries
- Foreign custom and religious law
- Private contracts between parties in different countries

This collection of rules and agreements establishes the norms of acceptable behavior, providing the certainty and stability necessary for commerce and healthy economic development. A weak or volatile rule of law increases the level of risk of doing business in a particular country. Such risk is often referred to as *political risk,* as distinguished from the more routine cost or difficulty associated with enforcing or defending legal rights abroad that can be attributed to unfamiliarity with the forum or sheer distance.

Cultures throughout the world recognize the legal concept of *justice* as a combination of integrity, fairness, honesty, trust, and transparency. If we look at the rule of law country by country we see that there is a degree of consistency regarding *what kinds* of issues are recognized. What can vary significantly from country to country is *how* the issues are dealt with.

At first glance it may look like treaties have very little to do with private business enterprise. After all, international treaties and conventions are international agreements entered into by recognized governments of sovereign nations. Their purpose is to harmonize substantive differences between jurisdictions and articulate a common set of rules and standards on subject matter that is of greatest common concern. These agreements lend consistency and certainty to world affairs. As a result, we typically associate such laws with public policy concerns such as the Geneva Conventions, a set of public international laws that limit the barbarity of war.

Yet a great many treaties do affect trade and commerce. The Hague Convention, for example, deals with private international law and issues of commerce such as the international sale of goods, product liability, and procedural issues for the filing of suit, among others. The World Trade Organization is itself a creation of the treaty and convention process. It was established after World War II to spell out rules of trade between nations that govern goods, services, and intellectual property.

When domestic legislatures ratify treaties and conventions signed by their diplomats, the countries are agreeing to conform their domestic law to the treaty standard. It is in this way that international law trickles down and has an effect on private domestic commerce—even businesses that may not be selling their goods or services in international markets.

Each sovereign nation state determines the law within its territory. Treaties and conventions play a role in harmonizing laws from jurisdiction to jurisdiction, but such harmonization is not comprehensive or complete. It still leaves room for a substantial amount of nationalism.

What is significant to note when dealing with foreign law is that various levels and subdivisions of government may have simultaneous jurisdiction over your business operations or transactions. These political subdivisions go by different names in different countries. They may be called states, provinces, cantons, or shires, to name a few. Certain countries may also include territories that are subject to tribal laws as well.

To calculate your legal risk exposure, you need to find out how many sets of rules govern your activities and know what those rules are. This effort can also help you prioritize compliance risks. If, for example, a chemical spill triggers federal law subjecting a company to fines and remediation, and the same event can trigger separate state and municipal fines, the trebling effect of fines increases the cost of noncompliance and simultaneously creates the opportunity for an increased return on investment of spill prevention or spill containment practices.

Identifying the legal risk exposure associated with your international business operations sounds straightforward, but sometimes it's not so simple. Events touching multiple jurisdictions invites forum shopping. Chapter Three discussed a case that involved a volatile compound shipped from Belgium to a distributor in the U.S. who repackaged it and resold it to a customer in The Netherlands who blew himself up while repackaging it on his kitchen table. Even though the product was just passing through the United States on its way back to Europe, it had sufficient contact with the forum to allow a U.S. court to exercise jurisdiction. Managing distribution channels and operations can therefore help minimize the risk associated with multiple jurisdictions, particularly unfavorable jurisdictions.

Where transactions make it impossible to avoid a foreign jurisdiction, doing your homework in advance helps avoid ugly surprises. In Europe, for example, antitrust laws have been interpreted to protect competitors, not just the concept of competition per se as in the United States. That distinction allowed the proposed merger of General Electric and Honeywell to sail through U.S. pre-merger approval, only to run aground in Europe.

With respect to product development and intellectual property, some countries do not allow inventors to assign their rights to companies, while others allow it but require compensation to the inventor, and still others peg the amount of compensation to the commercial success of the invention. If you don't find out about these quirks ahead of time, you might suddenly find yourself with a business partner you hadn't planned on.

Part of the problem is that it is so easy to assume that foreign commercial law is like your own. Such assumptions are decision-making blind spots and can be costly. In one deal, for example, a U.S. company acquiring Canadian operations planned on consolidating the two and terminating Canadian employees. After the deal closed, the U.S. executives learned that Canadian employment laws operate differently from those in the United States and that their proposed shutdown needed to meet certain regulatory requirements. The prospective cost savings wound up being significantly delayed.

A maze of regulatory requirements can create some counterintuitive results. When the discount store Wal-Mart entered the German market the German antitrust authorities ordered the company to raise its prices, alleging that Wal-Mart exploited its market power to sell products below cost on a continuous basis in violation of German trade laws. While such underselling benefits consumers in the short term, the government reasoned, the price squeeze forces medium and smaller competitors that can't match the low prices out of business and therefore concentrates market power in the long term.

Jurisdiction management is both a substantive issue and an operational issue, and the failure to be sensitive to such issues can have dire personal consequences. Take, for example, the case involving a U.S. executive attending a trade show in India. Unrelated to the trade show, the company was in the middle of a civil lawsuit in India, and in connection with that case the executive was arrested and detained to answer questions upon his arrival in India. Had he known about the welcoming committee he might have thought twice before boarding a plane and subjecting himself to personal jurisdiction on Indian soil.

DIFFERENCES IN LEGAL TRADITION

Domestic legal systems are a product of different legal traditions, culture, and sometimes religion. How they developed and spread throughout the world is largely an accident of history and economic development, but there are some common traditions that help make sense of the tangled maze. Every substantive area of law, from tax to employment to intellectual property to real estate, takes on different legal dimensions once you cross a national border. *Why are the legal practices so different from country to country?*

The basic concepts and institutions of modern Western commercial law, for example, were formed in the eleventh and twelfth centuries and are rooted in Roman law, specifically the Texts of Justinian. They are manifest in the civil code tradition represented by countries such as France, Spain, and Portugal and the common law tradition represented by countries such as England. These European legal traditions were then exported to the New World through colonial conquests. Most of the United States, for example, was originally colonized by England. But the state of Louisiana, which has French roots, still retains traces of its civil code heritage.

Most of the world follows a civil law model. It is based primarily on a systematic compendium of laws, rules, and regulations—"the code." In comparison, the common law tradition also relies on code, or statute, but supplements it with a large body of case law that has significant precedent value. The role of case law is what makes the common law highly contextual and fact-specific.

As a practical matter, the globalization of world commerce and the Internet's acceleration of globalization have quickened the pace of harmonization between the civil law and common law legal traditions. Yet important procedural differences remain with respect to the amount of discovery that may be conducted before trial, the type of evidence that is admissible at trial, the role of witnesses, and the role of juries.

In contrast, Asia has no single unifying legal tradition. East Asia is geographically and culturally very diverse. Before the expansion of Islam into central, south, and southeast Asia between the eleventh and fifteenth centuries and the arrival of the Portuguese in the late fifteenth century, east Asia was generally dominated by two traditions: the Indian Hindu Buddhist tradition and the Chinese Confucian tradition. These traditions differ fundamentally from their Western counterparts by the lack of private rights and duties typically associated with democratic forms of government. Rules relating to property, contracts, commercial transactions, and familial relations are addressed by these traditions only to the extent necessary to protect or promote state interests. It is essentially a penal law designed to perpetuate the existing political and social order.

The United States as Litigation Lightning Rod

The United States is an attractive forum for lawsuits because of its supersized damage awards, including punitive damages and the general lack of liability caps. Civil law countries generally do not recognize the concept of punitive damages and often cap product liability awards, resulting in lower damage awards. As a result, lawsuits offer less financial gain, so fewer are filed.

The fee structure for attorneys in the United States and the use of contingency fee arrangements is another reason the United States is more litigious than other countries. The theory behind contingency fees is to provide injured parties who have legitimate legal claims access to counsel if they can't afford one. A contingency fee is dependent on the outcome of the case. If the plaintiff wins, counsel receives a percentage of the proceeds. If the plaintiff loses, counsel receives nothing. In some countries, a lawyer's receiving a percentage of the client's recovery is viewed as an unethical conflict of interest. These countries prefer to address the fee issue by requiring the losing party to pay the winner's attorney's fees. The prospect of paying the winner's fee increases the cost of losing. With more to lose, plaintiffs evaluate their cases more carefully, and fewer suits of marginal merit are filed.

Contingency fees, typically offered by the plaintiff's bar in product liability cases, can lead to extremely high awards in class action suits. The concept behind class actions is that the amount of damage sustained by an individual is too small to merit the filing of the case on its own. But there is strength in numbers and if enough people are similarly situated and can be certified as a "class," then the cost-benefit analysis weighs in favor of proceeding.

Although class action suits and the debate about legislative steps to rein them in are largely a U.S. phenomenon, the class action suit concept seems to have migrated overseas. International business is therefore not immune. Great Britain and Sweden have recently permitted limited forms of class actions and Italy and France are considering them.

Favorable procedural practices are another factor that contributes to the U.S. legal system's reputation as a litigation lightning rod. Smoking gun documents, for example, are bad in any language. But in the United States, generous pretrial discovery rules provide the opportunity to find more smoking guns and other damaging evidence. Civil law jurisdictions often decide the merits of the case based on the pleadings and the plaintiff's existing files. They sharply curtail pretrial discovery or even the use of witnesses during trial. Furthermore, a judge, not a jury, may often decide the case.

Different Latitude, Different Attitude

Ethnic cultures, religion, and legal traditions combine to create differing frames of reference and perceptions that influence business conduct. Understanding these nuances is important because they play a significant role in our ability to manage expectations and legal risk. As summarized in Table B.1, those of us steeped in the traditions of Western countries tend to view relationships more legalistically and approach negotiations as equals with mutual rights. Those of us steeped in Eastern traditions tend to view relationships more paternalistically and approach negotiations hierarchically, expecting decisions to be guided by more unilateral duty than by legal rights.

These differing worldviews affect perceptions and the ability to manage expectations. If they are not managed appropriately they can also set the stage for a culture clash. Understanding these nuances thereby helps you develop more effective communication strategies that build good business relationships and lead to more mutually satisfactory solutions.

When operating in a foreign country it is essential to respect the local laws. However, where local business practices are rife with bribery, do you go along to get along?

TABLE B.1. COMPARISON OF EASTERN AND WESTERN LEGAL SYSTEMS.

	Adjudicative ("Legal")	Disciplinary ("Parental")
Essential character	Confrontation between parties on equal footing	Confrontation between unequals
Role of rules	Central and indispensable	Peripheral, dispensable
Most commonly observed	Western countries and sports	Asian and Middle Eastern countries and military
Society classifications	Individualistic and egalitarian ("contract oriented")	Hierarchical ("status oriented")
Societal links	Mutual rights	Unilateral duty
Behavioral guides	Please yourself but don't break rules. Laws set standards.	Please your group leaders at any cost. Leaders set standards.
Essential theory	Jurisprudence	Unsystematic

Source: Reprinted by permission of the University of Washington Press. T. Stephens, *Order and Discipline in China: The Shanghi Mixed Court* (1992).

EXTRATERRITORIAL LAWS

Even if local custom condones corruption and bribery, engaging in such practices while you're away from home does not necessarily make them legal. Under U.S. law, for example, the Foreign Corrupt Practices Act (FCPA) makes it a criminal offense for U.S. businesses to bribe foreign officials to obtain a favorable advantage when bidding on government contracts. It is one of several laws that governs the conduct of U.S. companies abroad and has extraterritorial effect.

Pressure to remove any hint of impropriety involving international business dealings has been further increased with the post-9/11 adoption of USA Patriot Act that mandates tighter scrutiny of cross-border dealings. As a result FCPA enforcement has been rising.

Bribes are distinguishable from "facilitating payments," which are legal under the Act. But before you conclude that such definitions are nothing more than buzzword bingo, it is wise to seek expert counsel regarding the activities or payments your company may be contemplating. The price of erring is high.

In the early 1990s, for example, General Electric ultimately paid an $8 million fine and another $52 million in restitution for its involvement in bribing Israeli military officials to obtain a defense contract. Similarly, the Baxter International health care group paid $6.5 million in civil and criminal fines after it admitted to bribing Arab officials in an effort to have Baxter's name removed from a blacklist of companies doing business with Israel. But the pain for Baxter did not stop there. When New York City Comptroller Elizabeth Holtzman heard the news, she banned Baxter from bidding on the City's contracts.

The FCPA, enacted in 1977, finds its origins in the 1974 post-Watergate era of heightened scrutiny and suspicion and the SEC's discovery of numerous questionable payments to foreign government officials as part of company filings. Twenty years later, in 1997, the International Convention on Combating Bribery of Foreign Public Officials in International Business Transactions, a multilateral treaty modeled on the FCPA, was adopted by the international community. It entered into force in February 1999. The ratification status of signatories to the convention is set forth in Table B.2. Thus depending on where you are doing business, engaging in local customs of bribery may be more illegal than you think.

Between 1981 and 1986, only one indictment was brought under the FCPA. The low enforcement rate was largely attributed to poorly drafted record-keeping requirements in the original law, which made proving a case difficult. Those accounting rules have since been changed. Furthermore, we now have the transparency and accountability requirements demanded by Sarbanes-Oxley. As a result, during the first eight months of 2005 alone, three deferred or nonprosecution agreements were entered into between the Department of Justice and three different companies who admitted to making illegal payments in violation of the Act.

Other U.S. laws with extraterritorial reach include antitrust, employment, and re-export laws. Price fixing conducted outside U.S. borders can still be subject to U.S. price-fixing laws *if* the price fixing affects U.S. commerce. Similarly, U.S. workers working for U.S. companies abroad are protected by U.S. employment laws.

U.S. re-export laws, for example, don't permit you to do indirectly what you can't do directly. When dual-use products (those that have peaceful as well as weapons use) are sent to unfriendly nations, it can cause legal problems. A European company was fined $800,000 for re-exporting U.S. origin nuclear-related metals to countries such as North Korea. Similarly, when a U.S. company purchased a German manufacturer of truck treads, the merger didn't raise an export eyebrow until it was realized that the truck treads could also be used on tanks—and that the company did a brisk business with Libya. Even though German export laws did not prohibit the shipment of such products to Libya, the U.S. export laws did; the change in ownership suddenly turned an asset into a potential liability.

TABLE B.2. OECD CONVENTION ON COMBATING BRIBERY OF FOREIGN PUBLIC
OFFICIALS IN INTERNATIONAL BUSINESS TRANSACTIONS:
RATIFICATION STATUS AS OF JANUARY 25, 2005.

Country	Deposit of Instrument of Ratification and Acceptance	Entry into Force of the Convention	Entry into Force of Implementing Legislation
Argentina	February 8, 2001	April 9, 2001	November 10, 1999
Australia	October 18, 1999	December 17, 1999	December 17, 1999
Austria	May 20, 1999	July 19, 1999	October 1, 1998
Belgium	July 27, 1999	September 25, 1999	April 3, 1999
Brazil	August 24, 2000	October 25, 2000	June 11, 2002
Bulgaria	December 22, 1998	February 20, 1999	January 29, 1999
Canada	December 17, 1998	February 15, 1999	February 14, 1999
Chile	April 18, 2001	June 17, 2001	October 2002
Czech Republic	January 21, 2000	March 21, 2000	June 9, 1999
Denmark	September 5, 2000	November 4, 2000	May 1, 2000
Estonia	November 23, 2004 (accession instrument)	January 22, 2005	
Finland	December 10, 1998	February 15, 1999	January 1, 1999
France	July 31, 2000	September 29, 2000	September 29, 2000
Germany	November 10, 1998	February 15, 1999	February 15, 1999
Greece	February 5, 1999	April 6, 1999	December 1, 1998
Hungary	December 4, 1998	February 15, 1999	March 1, 1999
Iceland	August 17, 1998	February 15, 1999	December 30, 1998
Ireland	September 22, 2003	November 21, 2003	November 26, 2001
Italy	December 15, 2000	February 13, 1999	October 26, 2000
Japan	October 13, 1998	February 15, 1999	February 15, 1999
Korea	January 4, 1999	March 5, 1999	February 15, 1999
Luxembourg	March 21, 2001	May 20, 2001	February 11, 2001
Mexico	May 27, 1999	July 26, 1999	May 18, 1999
Netherlands	January 12, 2001	March 13, 2001	February 1, 2001
New Zealand	June 25, 2001	August 24, 2001	May 3, 2001
Norway	December 18, 1998	February 16, 1999	January 1, 1999
Poland	September 8, 2000	November 7, 2000	February 4, 2001
Portugal	November 23, 2000	January 22, 2001	June 9, 2001
Slovak Republic	September 24, 1999	November 23, 1999	November 1, 1999

TABLE B.2. OECD CONVENTION ON COMBATING BRIBERY OF FOREIGN PUBLIC OFFICIALS IN INTERNATIONAL BUSINESS TRANSACTIONS: RATIFICATION STATUS AS OF JANUARY 25, 2005, CONT'D.

Country	Deposit of Instrument of Ratification and Acceptance	Entry into Force of the Convention	Entry into Force of Implementing Legislation
Slovenia	September 6, 2001 (accession instrument)	November 5, 2001	January 23, 1999
Spain	January 4, 2000	March 4, 2000	February 2, 2000
Sweden	June 8, 1999	August 7, 1999	July 1, 1999
Switzerland	May 31, 2000	July 30, 2000	May 1, 2000
Turkey	July 26, 2000	September 24, 2000	January 11, 2003
United Kingdom	December 14, 1998	February 15, 1999	February 14, 2002
United States	December 8, 1998	February 15, 1999	November 10, 1998

International Questions to Think About

- Where are your business operations physically located? Where are you doing business? Are they the same geographic territory? Or does your product or service extend beyond its point of origin?
- What laws affect your business? Are any of them extraterritorial?
- How can you limit contact with unfavorable jurisdictions?
- If contact can't be limited, what steps can be taken to ensure compliance and avoid unnecessary legal liabilities?
- How are you managing expectations in international business relationships to avoid a clash of cultures?
- Is your business engaged in local practices abroad that are in conflict with the laws of your home country? If so, what implications would these activities have for the company's legal risk exposure and reputation should they be brought to light?

2. CONTRACTS

Deal making is the lifeblood of commerce. Merchant trade law, the law of contracts, was therefore one of the earliest laws to evolve. The need for stability and trust in transactions demands that the law of contracts be predictable.

Essentially, a contract is a promise or set of promises that when breached give rise to a remedy and the performance of which creates a duty. Unlike consumer agreements that are subject to legal protections designed to save unwary consumers from harm, business agreements are deemed to be between sophisticated equals even if the size of the companies varies. As a result, if you sign a contract on behalf of your employer you are deemed to have read it, even if you really didn't.

Contract issues fall into three broad categories:

- *Contract formation and enforceability:* If there's no contract, there's nothing to enforce. The basic requirements of a contract must be fully met, without loopholes.
- *Contract interpretation and performance:* Having established the existence of a valid, binding contract we now need to know what it says and what it means. Who is responsible for doing what? When? Where? And how?
- *Contract breach and remedies:* Having determined the rights and duties of the parties to the agreement we then need to ask whether the performance of the parties measures up or falls short and, if the contract is breached, what remedies are appropriate.

CONTRACT FORMATION

Contract formation requires the existence of an offer, an acceptance of the offer, and some form of consideration or inducement for entering into the agreement, typically some form of payment. In the United States the three elements of offer, acceptance, and consideration are sufficient to create a valid contract. International contracts require a fourth element: price.

The contract formation process is often characterized by a series of offers and counteroffers. *What is the legal effect of a counteroffer?* It serves as a rejection of the offer. Once rejected the offer is legally dead. In the course of testing boundaries during negotiations, however, a party may initially reject an offer only to want it back later on in the process. *What happens then?* It all depends on whether both parties want the deal. The rejecting party *can* offer the rejected terms as a counteroffer and hope the original offeror accepts. Or the original offeror could reissue the offer.

What's important to note is that a rejection creates no *legal* duty or contract. The parties are free to walk away. Contract formation happens only when there has been a true meeting of the minds. As a practical matter, however, the parties may feel a moral duty to resurrect a prior offer—but that's a different story.

Enforceability

Just because a valid contract has been created does not necessarily mean it is enforceable. Factors that interfere with the parties' state of mind such as mistake, fraud, duress or undue influence, or lack of competency can make a contract voidable. Impossibility can have the same effect. Impossibility occurs, for example, in service contracts when the incapacity or death of a performer, such as an actor or singer, makes it impossible for the show to go on. A natural disaster can have the same impact on the delivery of goods, say if a manufacturing plant is destroyed by a tsunami. That's one reason purchase agreements typically include a *force majeure* provision. It excuses nonperformance for events beyond the seller's control without invalidating or jeopardizing the enforceability of the entire agreement.

Public policy concerns can also affect the enforceability of private contracts by making them void right from the start. A contract to engage in an unlawful act, to deal in stolen goods and other contraband, or to commit a crime is unenforceable as a matter of public policy. Contracts that are unconscionable, that shock the public conscience and offend our notion of fairness and ethics, are also unenforceable.

Do contracts have to be in writing? It depends on the type of agreement you're talking about. Some transactions are too important to be left to verbal agreements and may be voidable if not commemorated in writing. The purpose of a written document is to reduce the potential for fraud by providing tangible proof of the deal. Indeed, the Statute of Frauds specifically sets forth what type of contracts must be in writing to be enforceable. It can vary from state to state, but typically includes real estate transactions, service agreements that cannot be performed in less than a year, and the sale of goods valued at more than $500.

The classic handshake, or verbal gentlemen's agreement, involving subject matter not falling into the above categories *would* be enforceable. But as a practical matter, establishing the exact terms of the contract presents evidentiary problems. What exactly *are* the terms of the verbal agreement? Transactions are often dynamic. They evolve over time along with the expectations and recollections of the parties. If these processes are not managed well there is plenty of room for disappointment and disagreement. At that point the gloves come off and gentlemen often stop being gentlemen.

A written document helps avoid such misunderstandings. It commemorates the understanding and gently refreshes faded memories. Having a written document makes the evidentiary burden of proof much easier when compared to a verbal agreement. It also helps manage the moving target of evolving expectations and evolving transactions with what is called an "integration clause."

An integration clause is typically found at the end of the agreement where miscellaneous legalese is lumped together. The purpose of the clause is to recognize that the written contract represents the full and complete embodiment of the deal. It's all the prior understandings rolled up into one. If at a later date the parties choose to renegotiate, that's fine. But until there is a new meeting of the minds, the existing contract terms as written are the promises the parties have agreed to live by. It establishes a baseline.

Some people deride contracts, saying they're not worth the paper they are printed on. Someone who is determined to break a promise, the theory goes, will do so whether or not it's written down. That may be true, but if that happens the real problem lies with the contracting party, not the contract or the contracting process.

Contracts are not a substitute for integrity. It therefore behooves us to conduct the appropriate due diligence beforehand to know who we're dealing with and whether they have the wherewithal to keep their promises. Otherwise, you may be in for a surprise.

Besides memorializing the intent of the parties, the written contract benefits from the negotiation process necessary to create the document. Working through the detail helps clarify expectations, build relationships, develop trust, and open lines of communication that are invaluable when unexpected events later require some deal mending.

The best contracts are the ones that are thoroughly negotiated, signed, put in a drawer, and never looked at again—not because they're forgotten but because the relationship of the parties is so strong that resorting to the contract terms is not necessary. The parties understand the rules, respect each other, and negotiate in good faith to find mutually acceptable solutions to problems. If they *do* need to refer to the contract, a good agreement sets forth the rights and duties of the parties in clear and unambiguous language. It operates as a reminder, not a baseball bat.

Someone who has no prior knowledge of the deal should be able to pick up the document and be able to read it and understand it. Clarity is essential. It is particularly crucial for avoiding misunderstandings in conditional contracts. These are contracts that shift the burden of who does what before a corresponding duty of performance is owned. A condition can precede acceptance, called a condition precedent, such as when a retailer requires the presenter of a promotional coupon, for example, to buy a certain quantity of the specified product before paying the coupon amount.

Conditions can also occur after contract formation. Insurance policies fall into this category. You buy a policy and pay a premium. You have a binding contract. But before you can receive the full benefit of the contract you must submit a claim in a timely fashion. The claim can be disallowed and coverage denied if it is filed late. The underlying insurance policy, the contract, is still intact, but the full benefit is not received.

Similarly, a confidentiality agreement that requires information exchanged under the agreement to be reduced to writing and marked "CONFIDENTIAL" must meet those requirements before the information is legally protected under the agreement. The failure to meet these requirements has the net effect of making the information public. *Why?* A secret stops being a secret if you tell someone and they don't have a duty to keep it quiet. If a contract defines "secret" as only those pieces of information that are written and marked confidential, then everything else is not secret. The contract establishes a black-and-white dichotomy between what's protected and what's not. That's not a loophole. That's merely understanding the substance of the contract terms.

Obtaining the full benefit of a contract requires discipline and good procedures to ensure that conditions subsequent are properly met. Discipline can be particularly challenging in long-term contracts where the relationship of the parties creates a comfort level and makes legal formalities feel out of place. Don't be hypnotized. The relationship is only as good as the person filling the position. If your counterpart moves on and leaves the company, your business relationship must be rebuilt.

What if you don't get along as well with the successor? Contracts hedge the risk associated with changing the guard by providing a baseline performance standard that binds *the company*. That's why contracts are a good legal risk management tool.

The enforceability of a contract can also be affected by how long you wait before trying to enforce it. You can't wait forever. It wouldn't be fair. There has to be a point where if a problem exists and nothing happens it's over. It's not right to keep dragging up past wrongs. The law determines that point in time with a mechanism called the statute of limitations. If you haven't brought a claim in x amount of time you lose your right to do so.

The statute of limitations for a breach of contract may vary slightly from jurisdiction to jurisdiction, but what's important to note is that the time frame is measured in *years*. Some contracts, however, may seek to limit the statutory rights you already have.

Can they do that? Yes, you can give up existing rights as long as the purpose for doing so isn't illegal—that would come under the illegality exception to contract formation discussed earlier. The way the statute of limitations is modified is through language found at the end of the agreement and often dismissed as *boilerplate*—standardized material used over and over and alleged to be insignificant. It might, for example, say, "All court actions or proceedings with respect to this agreement must be filed *within one year.*"

Wow! In large organizations you might still be trading telephone calls and trying to negotiate the problem after one year. Not being aware of a shorter contractual time frame can prematurely cut off your legal rights and increase the amount of risk you absorb.

Interpretation—Battle of the Forms

The most common contract issues involve "standard" form agreements. A standard preprinted form with terms and conditions on the back and a few fill-in-the-blank fields on the front make it easy to focus on the variables: the name and item being ordered, the quantity, price, and delivery date. They simplify the order placement and acceptance process.

Sellers have their terms and conditions of sale. Buyers have their terms and conditions of purchase. But if you put them side by side, the legal language is rarely a perfect match. Some terms are mutually consistent and others don't match at all. Ironically, what's "standard" isn't too standard. This situation is commonly referred to as the battle of the forms.

Many managers dismiss the fine print of a contract as legal boilerplate, believing there is little if anything they can be done about it. That may be true for consumer purchases. A consumer's lack of bargaining power is why legislatures step in and enact consumer protection laws. Business-to-business transactions are different. You're expected to stand up for your business rights—to negotiate. If you don't negotiate, you may get stuck with more risk than you want or need.

How do you know what the real terms of an allegedly standard deal are? To answer that question requires looking at all the terms on both the buyer's and seller's preprinted forms. The common law operates under a "last in time rule." In other words, what happened last, the offer or the acceptance? The party who had the last say is the party whose terms and conditions rule. It may be the buyer's *or* it may be the seller's.

How can that be? It all depends on how the events are characterized and how the transaction is initiated. Is the seller making an offer to sell? Or is the buyer making an offer to buy? It can get confusing. If one set of terms specifically disallows inconsistent terms or the parties exchange "order acknowledgments" that trump the last set of terms and conditions, it gets even more confusing. All the twists and turns of the contracting process need to be looked at before you can identify the exact dimensions of a particular contract. It is a very fact-specific exercise.

Luckily, common law contract doctrines limit the interpretation of the contract to the "four corners of the document." In other words, all the contract clauses are read together, not out of context, to determine the party's intent. If multiple preprinted forms or acknowledgments are involved in the duel, all of those documents are within the "four corners" and examined in total to determine the real deal.

Limiting interpretation to the four corners is a good thing because if a particular risk is not addressed in the agreement a common law court is most likely to conclude that the parties would have included it if they wanted to. In contrast, a civil law court would be more inclined to *rewrite* the agreement and that could lead to unintended results. That is why most international commercial contracts include a common law jurisdiction as the choice of law.

What do you do if you don't have time to scrutinize or negotiate every so-called standard transaction? What can you do to minimize risk exposure in a common law jurisdiction?

Procedurally, you can look at your processes and maximize your opportunities for being the last to present your terms and conditions in the contract formation dance. You can also be mindful of the other party's order acknowledgments that try to negate your terms.

Substantively, you can strive for reasonable terms and conditions in standard form agreements rather than lopsided ones that invite comment and controversy. Overreaching by one party forces the other side to push back. Egregiously lopsided terms are unfair. They also cast a shadow on trustworthiness and integrity. Besides, negotiating the same issues over and over again chews up your time and is tiresome. If negotiations keep smoothing over the same rough edge, why keep it? Reasonable language is more likely to match up with the other side's standard form, less likely to be challenged, provides more consistency from contract to contract, and presents less of an administrative burden.

Administratively, you can examine the terms and conditions of the most important standard contracts. That's one way to manage the risk associated with the battle of the forms.

How do you prioritize standard form transactions? Orders can be prioritized in several ways. The size of an order, for example, may merit a closer look at the deal terms. Most businesses are unwilling to subject a large chunk of their total sales to unfavorable contract terms. Similarly, the importance of the customer is another factor meriting a closer look. Even though a single order may not be particularly large, if the aggregate number of orders represents a sizable amount of total sales, unfavorable contract terms can be the equivalent of death by a thousand cuts.

What your product is being used for and where it's being shipped to might also deserve a closer look. Special product usage, for example, might trigger warranty issues that need further discussion. Similarly, shipments abroad are prime candidates for standardized language that could inject a *foreign* choice of law provision, or a foreign conflict resolution provision. Such changes can represent hidden costs that change the value of the deal.

A top-line review of any contract should scan the terms and conditions with an eye toward seven hot buttons. First, does the agreement accurately capture and describe the business deal, how it's supposed to work, and who does what, when they do it, how they do it, and where they do it? What does it say about the transfer of title and the risk of loss while the product is en route to the customer? What about the delivery date?

If a contract includes language that *time is of the essence,* beware! Those five little words have a very precise legal meaning in the common law tradition.

Reasonableness generally governs the interpretation of contracts. It would probably be reasonable, for example, to deliver a turnkey manufacturing project two weeks late given the size and complexity of such a task. However, if the installation contract specified that "time is of the essence," the due date is etched in stone and delivering even a stroke past midnight gives the buyer the legal right to walk away.

Second, what are the termination provisions and what are the conflict resolution provisions? If things aren't going well you'll want to know how to cut your losses and move on. Termination provisions can be quite creative. Some agreements only allow termination for "cause," such as a material breach of the agreement. Some contracts are "evergreen," automatically renewing from year to year unless notice is given pursuant to the termination clause. Some may allow for termination only during narrow windows of time. For example, a clause may say: "Notice of termination may only be given within ninety (90) days of the contract anniversary date and absent such notice will automatically renew for a successive twelve (12) month period."

Make sure you understand how you can terminate, or can get terminated, and what the hidden costs associated with it are. Some of these costs may be pure business issues, such as midproject termination and work-in-process costs. Other costs may be statutory. In some jurisdictions, for example, terminating a distributor, as opposed to letting a contract expire, can trigger the payment of money damages by operation of law!

Conflict resolution may also harbor hidden costs. If the contract provides that suit can only be filed overseas, the cost of bringing a claim or defending one away from home just went up exponentially. The speed, convenience, and out-of-pocket costs associated with conflict resolution should be considered in evaluating what kind of conflict resolution makes the most sense for the contract at hand. Is it a court of law? Is it some form of alternative dispute resolution? Arbitration? Mediation? Should it be binding or nonbinding? How will it work? Who bears the costs? No one likes to think about conflict when negotiating a deal. But prudent risk managers recognize the value of planning ahead and establishing procedures to manage those costs effectively.

Third, is there any intellectual property involved in the transaction? Intellectual property is an asset. Often in our zeal to please a customer, by customizing an application, for example, it's easy to lose sight of the "thing" that is being created and its transferability to other industries. Who owns the "thing"? The customer may want the exclusive right to use "it" in their industry, or they may want to own it outright. If "it" has widespread commercial value, the failure to spell out past, present, and future ownership rights and license rights is a legal nightmare waiting to happen.

Fourth, what warranties are being made? A warranty is an assurance of quality. It's important to know what you're promising because if something bad happens, the warranty standard is what your business will be held to. Warranties are express and implied. Express warranties typically refer to the specifications and the scope of service performance criteria set forth in the agreement. Yet you may not realize that the sale of goods in the United States automatically carries with it two *implied warranties:* the warranty of merchantability, which provides that goods be fit for the ordinary purposes such goods are used for, and the warranty for fitness for a particular purpose, which applies if the seller knows or has reason to know that the buyer wants the goods for a particular purpose and is relying on the seller's skill or knowledge to select them. If you don't wish to make these implied quality assurances your contract terms must conspicuously disclaim the warranties.

Fifth, what do the indemnity provisions call for in the agreement? Indemnities address to what extent you agree to be accountable if something goes wrong. This is a form of liability limitation. Will damages be limited to the value of the contract? Or all damages sustained by the injured party? Will it include their attorney's fees too? The answers to these questions go to the heart of the liability and the risk embodied in the contract-and conversely your profit margin.

Sixth, what is the choice of law? Whose laws will govern the interpretation of the contract? Parties whose contract is silent on the choice of law issue will have it decided for them by a court based on which jurisdiction has more contacts with the subject matter. When contacts cross state lines or sovereign borders it can get very complicated very quickly. Sorting it out is time-consuming and expensive.

Besides making the question subject to judicial interpretation, not specifying the choice of law subjects the business to the risk of substantive differences in the law between jurisdictions. If, for example, in a technology development agreement the inventor's rights can't be assigned to the company, the choice of law can frustrate the essential business purpose of the agreement. Thus the provision is more than legalese. It can have serious substantive implications for business operations.

Finally, the assignability of the contract is an important term to be familiar and comfortable with. Assignability refers to a party's ability to let someone else stand in their shoes with respect to contract performance. A contract is assignable unless its wording specifies otherwise. If, for example, the contract is a confidentiality agreement you may want notice of any intent to assign the agreement and the right to terminate the agreement if the assignee is not to your liking. Otherwise you could have your trade secrets assigned to your competitor.

Here is a summary of the seven hot button issues.

1. Are the key deal points accurately described? Including delivery? The passing of title and the risk of loss during the title transfer process?
2. What are the contract termination and conflict resolution provisions? Are there any hidden costs associated with either event?
3. How are intellectual property rights addressed? Are they adequately protected?
4. What express or implied warranties are being made?
5. What do the indemnity provisions provide? What other limitation of liability provisions are included?
6. What choice of law has been selected? How does it affect the substantive business terms of the agreement?
7. How is assignability handled? Does the assignor require prior written consent of the other party to the agreement?

CONTRACT DRAFTING CONSIDERATIONS

"It's only a contract; what's the big deal?" Plenty. A well-written contract that's plain on its face doesn't leave much room for interpretation. A party who breaches the agreement will have a legal problem. As the finder of fact a court can exercise some discretion. But unless the court abuses its discretion or misinterprets the law there's not much to appeal to a higher authority. That means you will be stuck with the contract terms you negotiated. It therefore makes sense to understand and manage contract risk and the jurisdiction risk associated with it.

What about drafting control? Can't I save money by letting the other side do the first draft? Contracts are construed strictly against the drafter. That means inconsistent terms will be interpreted in favor of the nondrafting party and may initially lead you to believe that letting someone else create the document is a brilliant cost saving. But ceding drafting control has its downside. It's the difference between building a house and renovating an existing one. When you build a house you determine the footprint and establish the parameters. When you renovate, additions don't always flow smoothly with the existing floor plan. It may require knocking down a wall or two. If that wall is a load-bearing wall you'll have a problem.

In one merger agreement I reviewed, the drafter had a penchant for carving out exceptions and would nest multiple exceptions into exceptions all within one paragraph. It was very convoluted and confusing. No one could read the indemnity provision just once and have a clear understanding of what was going on. After the fourth layer of exceptions you reached for a pen to diagram it. The same substance could have been stated more clearly and more elegantly in positive terms. But after hammering the language and living with it a few weeks the parties thought they knew what it meant. Besides, fixing the problem would have entailed a major rewrite of that particular section and some other sections that were interdependent. It would also have delayed the talks and jeopardized the momentum of the discussions. No one wanted to take that chance. The deal was finalized with the horrible language in place. It was a target-rich environment for multiple interpretations that haunted the business for several years.

REMEDIES

Money damages are often the first thing that comes to mind when we think of contract remedies. The goods were delivered, but the customer didn't pay—a collection issue. But sometimes disputes arise as to what remedies are appropriate. Money doesn't always solve everything. Sometimes resolving the problem requires an equitable remedy.

Specific performance is one remedy used where money damages would be inadequate compensation. In the battle to enforce a child custody agreement, for example, the failure to allow visitation with a child is an issue more appropriately remedied with an order for specific performance rather than money damages. The destruction of counterfeit goods is another example where monetary damages alone would not be a sufficient. Only destruction would ensure that the offending product could never reenter the stream of commerce to disenfranchise and defraud customers who think they're buying a genuine product.

Injunctive relief, a court order prohibiting someone from doing a specified act, would be appropriate if a trademark licensee, for example, abuses the license privileges and sells product into nonlicensed territories. Besides seeking to recoup lost sales, you would want to force the licensee to stop selling beyond the territory set forth in the license.

Quantum meruit is an equitable remedy derived from the Latin, meaning "as much as deserved." It is a measure of recovery used in implied contracts. Finally, the remedy of *rescission* is used to cancel a contract for a material default by a party, and *reformation* is used to fix legal errors in an agreement to reform it and align it with the original intent of the parties.

Contracts are fabulous tools for managing legal risk. When artfully employed, contingencies, indemnities, and warranties are vehicles for shifting, reducing, or eliminating legal risk. Key contract principles are summarized in Table B.3. Contracts, however, are also living documents. The dynamic nature of contracts means we must be mindful of legal risks at the formation stage as well as during the life cycle of the deal. It's a three-dimensional process. The failure to meet contract obligations entitles the other party to remedies that increase the cost of doing business.

Contract Questions to Think About

- What is your contract, or deal, trying to accomplish? Do the contract terms accurately reflect the business transaction?
- Do you understand the terms of your most important contracts?
- What are the hidden costs? How are they managed?

TABLE B.3. CONTRACT OVERVIEW.

Basic Building Blocks	Basic Stumbling Blocks	Remedies
Offer	Mistake	Damages
• condition precedent	Fraud	Specific performance
Acceptance	Duress	Quantum meruit
• condition subsequent	Undue influence	Rescission
Consideration	Competency	Injunction
Price	Impossibility	Reformation
	Illegality	
	Unconscionability	
	Statute of frauds	
	Statute of limitations	

- What is the business on the hook for? What did it promise to deliver, warrant, indemnify?
- What systems or procedures are in place to ensure the performance of contract contingencies? How do we minimize potential loss due to nonperformance?
- What happens if the transaction outgrows the contract? What mechanisms are in place to keep the contracts in synch with business realities and amend contract provisions if necessary?
- How is the contract going to be amended? Can one party do it unilaterally? Or does it require mutual consent? Is there room for surprise?
- How do you unwind or terminate the agreement? Does it automatically renew?

3. PRODUCT LIABILITY

Product liability is an obligation incurred by manufacturers and sellers that occurs when damages or injuries result from defective or unreasonably dangerous goods. The term is an umbrella that encompasses a range of defects under three legal theories: breach of contract warranty, negligence, and strict liability. The United States has no single product liability law. Instead, it is a creature of state law. It has a reputation for generating high damage awards, including punitive damages, and is the poster child for U.S. litigiousness. Its reputation therefore makes it one of the scarier areas of U.S. law. However, if we peel back the legal layers and examine how products turn into ticking liabilities we can develop processes and procedures to defuse them sooner rather than later.

BREACH OF CONTRACT WARRANTY

When the breach of a contract warranty—those express or implied warranties discussed earlier—involves a product, it can create product liability. This latent liability raises the importance of managing customer expectations well through clear, concise contract language and not promising more than can reasonably be delivered. Whenever a breach of warranty occurs the natural inclination is to ask *why? What happened?*

NEGLIGENCE

If the mishap was due to the failure to exercise a reasonable standard of care, the company may find itself defending against a charge of negligence. Negligence is a private or civil wrong that is *independent* of a contract claim that results from a breach of a legal duty. A business is negligent if it "knew or should have known" that its product could cause injury. The famous case of the McDonald's coffee involving a woman who scalded herself after a cup of coffee purchased at a drive-through window spilled in her lap is a case based on negligence that made headlines, with McDonald's getting slammed with a $2.9 million damage award that included a $2.7 punitive damage award.

How could that be? Yes, the woman contributed to her injuries by balancing hot coffee precariously in her lap as the passenger of a moving vehicle. But the evidence also showed that the company knew for more than ten years that it sold its coffee at significantly hotter temperatures than its competitors did. Yet it didn't turn down the heat. The few extra degrees of heat made the difference between third-degree burns and second-degree burns during the time it would take to wipe up a spill.

The jury realized that coffee can be hot without being scalding and damaging skin. The punitive damages were in response to what the court perceived was a callous company attitude. McDonald's had enough information to know that someone could get badly burned. Not doing anything about it made the company negligent. The damage award represented two days worth of McDonald's coffee sales at the time. It was later reduced to six figures on appeal.

What some managers fail to realize is that a misbehaving product that causes injury or damage can generate two causes of action: a contract claim and a tort claim. Avoiding the problem in the first place therefore has a multiplier effect on risk reduction.

STRICT LIABILITY

Besides negligence, a manufacturer of a defective product can be liable for damage caused by the defect under the tort theory of strict liability. Unlike negligence, whose standard involves a shred of knowledge and intent—the *knowing* disregard of a risk—strict liability has no such intent requirement. It's liability without fault.

At first glance, liability without fault sounds incredibly unfair. But a look behind the curtain shows that it applies to product defects that *only the manufacturer can control*. The purpose of law is to drive responsible behavior: the theory behind strict liability says *society doesn't care about excuses, make sure your product is right before it goes out the door.* Recognizing what product defects trigger strict liability and managing them effectively thereby puts the business in charge of managing its own product liability risk.

What about contracts? Can't we limit the amount of damages we're exposed to through warranty and indemnification provisions? It might help in some circumstances, but not all. Contract disclaimers typically do not prevent third parties who do not have a contractual relationship with the manufacturer, such as consumers, from recovering for personal injury. Furthermore, the adoption of strict liability laws makes breach of contract theories less important in product liability claims than they used to be, because strict liability claims are easier to prove.

Types of Strict Liability

Three types of defects trigger strict liability. The first is defective design. This assertion requires the plaintiff to prove that a particular design defect was the proximate cause of the damage or injury. The methods of proof include expert testimony and reports, government and industry standards and studies, the defendant's own employees and records, and the frequency of similar incidents. To successfully defend against such accusations, or to be proactive about avoiding them, it is a good idea to document sound decision-making practices. If the best information available at the time was used, and it was reasonably relied upon to make a decision, it will be difficult to prove a defective design.

Demonstrating good decision making requires evidence of objectivity, such as supportable test data by an independent or certified testing facility. If the company engages in its own testing, the test standards and methods must be able to withstand scrutiny and be comparable to those used by an independent or certified facility. Potential smoking guns must be responsibly addressed and the loop closed with documentation explaining why a particular course of action was taken and why that decision was prudent. The public policy concern—for example, not unnecessarily compromising safety in exchange for profit—is another factor to keep in mind.

The second type of defect that can trigger strict liability is defective manufacture. Here again the plaintiff bears the burden of proof and uses expert testimony and reports, government and industry standards and studies, and the defendant's own employees and records, as well as similar incidents to make the case. This is one reason quality control in manufacturing is so important.

If the evidence shows that the company repeatedly allowed product that did not meet its own quality standards to get out the door, a strict liability claim will be coupled with a negligence claim on the grounds that the manufacturer knew or should have known that a product not meeting its own quality standards would fail. This is one of the issues that hounded Firestone in the tread separation recall connected with Ford Explorer roll-over accidents.

The evidence showed that tire quality waned at certain Firestone plants, particularly during labor strikes when replacement workers operated the production line. Given the facts, it's easy to understand how quality got compromised. But such understanding does not excuse the downstream consequences—particularly the lives lost in subsequent Explorer roll-over accidents if the tires were the proximate cause of the accident.

What looked like a straightforward labor issue evolved into a quality issue and a huge product liability issue. The case illustrates how management's responsibility for operational issues goes hand in hand with responsibility for legal issues too.

The third type of product defect relates to defective warnings. Warnings can be defective in a number of ways. They can be misplaced on the product and hard to see. They can miscommunicate their message and be hard to read or comprehend. Warnings can also be defective if they mislead and deceive. If the nature of the defect is such that you knew or should have known that the warning was inadequate, the strict liability claim will be coupled with negligence claim. Plaintiffs' lawyers will mix and match.

Proper warning labels represent a delicate balance between giving customers the information they need to use the product safely and scaring the sauce out of them. The objective is to tell the truth well—fully and accurately, but not overdramatically. Unfortunately, business is increasingly burdened by a growing victim mentality among plaintiffs that at times suspends common sense and caters to the lowest common denominator of society. The litigation lottery mentality forces manufacturers to idiot-proof their products as much as possible. As a result, getting customers to understand product use instructions and warning labels may at times feel like a near-impossible task.

The Michigan Lawsuit Abuse Watch (M-Law), a nonprofit organization devoted to exposing frivolous lawsuits, keeps track of such suits and the crazy-sounding warning labels that result. Since 1997 M-Law has held a Wacky Warning Label Contest to highlight the absurdity. Past winners include a label on a baby stroller: "Remove child before folding," a carpenter's electric drill: "This product not intended for use as a dental drill," and a massage chair: "Do not use massage chair without clothing . . . and, never force any body part into the backrest area while the rollers are moving." See http://mlaw.org for more on this project.

Ultra-Hazardous and Abnormally Dangerous Products

Besides design, manufacturing, and warning defects, some business categories are subject to strict liability by virtue of their ultra-hazardous and abnormally dangerous nature. Hazardous waste disposal, pyrotechnics, and radioactive anything are examples that would fall into this category.

JOINT AND SEVERAL LIABILITY

When the plaintiff's injury is caused by two or more companies, the concept of joint and several liability means everyone who contributed to the problem is responsible for it and any one of them can be liable for *the entire amount*. The public policy theory behind it is that a little guy who is injured can't afford to sue everyone. People can therefore recover the entire amount of their injury from any one tortfeasor. In practice, however, it motivates plaintiffs to sue the deepest pocket associated with an injury. That practice certainly makes things easier for the plaintiff but it also makes it tougher for the defendant because it places the burden on the manufacturer to seek contribution from others whose actions contributed to the plaintiff's injury or damages.

The unfairness associated with this burden has made joint and several liability a popular target of tort reform. But until reform happens, joint and several liability provides an extra incentive for avoiding product liability claims. The potential for contribution also heightens the value of contract indemnity provisions in supplier agreements. Such indemnities won't keep a third party from suing for injury, but they provide an extra layer of protection when seeking recourse for contribution and make sure that the ultimate liability is in proportion to the proximate cause of the injury.

POST-SALE DUTY TO WARN

Managing potential product liability is a dynamic process. The duty does not stop once the product is out the door. Many states have laws requiring a post-sale duty to warn if a new safety issue is discovered or it is later learned that product warnings are inadequate.

The types of information that could lead you to conclude your product may have a problem include product service histories. *Are a significant number of people having the same problems?* Patterns of tire tread separation in several countries tied to Ford Explorer accidents, for example, eventually led Firestone to reexamine its tires and issue a product recall.

Information about problems experienced by manufacturers of similar products are also a valuable source of information. When the prescription pain medication Vioxx was withdrawn from the market after news of deaths related to its use made headlines, it prompted other manufacturers of cox-2 inhibitors, the generic class of drugs to which Vioxx belongs, to reevaluate their product liability exposure.

Depending on the nature of the product and the post-sale information that becomes available, it may be necessary to consider a product recall. In other cases a design improvement may be accomplished with a retrofit kit. Post-sale duties apply even if you are no longer manufacturing the particular item.

One of the biggest challenges businesses face in carrying out their post-sale duties is knowing where all their products are. Having procedures in place to gather this information and managing this data properly is extremely useful. These measures facilitate the exercise of post-sale duties and allow for targeted notices as opposed to broadcast messages that reach a wider audience than necessary.

TORT LIABILITY EXPOSURE IN THE SERVICE SECTOR

Product liability is an umbrella term limited to products. However, as summarized in Table B.4, many of the same legal liabilities apply to the service sector as well. Service contracts are subject to the same warranty and indemnity concerns as product sales. Often the sale of products and services are mixed in one transaction. Because services are less tangible than goods, objective and measurable performance criteria are harder to come by. It thereby increases the importance of managing expectations well.

Besides contract warranty claims, services can also be subject to claims for negligence. In some industries or professions the failure to use certain standards of care rises to the level of malpractice. The concept of strict liability is less transferable to the service sector because the triggers of design, manufacture, and product warning don't apply. However, a comparable concept is embodied in the notion of fiduciary duty.

The concept of fiduciary duty received a significant amount of attention during the era of Enron-style business scandals. People in positions of trust and responsibility, such as corporate directors and senior management, have *fiduciary duties*—that is, they are required to place someone else's interests (generally the shareholders')—ahead of their own. The conflicts of interest resulting from self-dealing in these various

TABLE B.4. COMPARISON OF PRODUCT LIABILITY
CLAIMS TO SERVICE LIABILITY CLAIMS.

Products	*Services*
Contract warranty	Contract warranty
Negligence	Negligence and in some industries malpractice
Strict liability: • Design • Manufacture • Warning	Fiduciary duty (certain job functions)
Joint and several liability	Classic professional partnerships

accounting scandals represented a breach of the boards' fiduciary duty to shareholders. Boards had become lapdogs instead of watchdogs. The flap led to a heightened awareness of the role of corporate governance.

To summarize, product liability does not need to be a financial abyss. It largely relates to quality control in the form of product design, manufacture, and product warning, and how we manage expectations surrounding those parameters and expectations of product performance.

Product Liability Questions to Think About

- Are product warranties clear and accurate?
- How are decisions about product design, manufacture, or warnings made? Does the company opt for the easy way out? Or does it pursue what's morally and ethically right?
- How are problems addressed? Are they buried or dismissed? Are good decision-making processes used to evaluate the situation and reach a solidly defensible conclusion?
- How are decision-making processes documented?
- What procedures or systems are in place for gathering information about product performance problems? How is that information being used?
- If the product includes ingredients or components supplied by other vendors, what steps are being taken to ensure the quality of the incorporated materials?

4. Employment

Unless you work by yourself, you have employees and have potential employment law exposures. As managers rise through the organizational ranks, the number of employees reporting to them increases and they find more and more of their time being consumed by employment matters.

One employee is chronically late to work. Another spends inordinate amounts of company time surfing the Internet. The ones with children are more likely than their childless fellows to be called away from work to attend to family matters such as doctor's appointments and school events. Still others have poor grooming habits or are territorial about sharing information and don't play well on teams. Managing it all often feels like mediating a fight in the backseat of your car while keeping your eyes glued to the road and one hand on the wheel.

What we do is often a big part of who we are. Earning a decent living, being able to support a family and pay the bills, goes straight to the heart of the needs identified in Maslow's hierarchy. Coupled with our natural predisposition toward loss aversion, those needs mean that employment issues tend to be more emotionally charged and exhausting than any other business legal issue crossing your desk.

"Any idiot can manage a crisis," the great playwright Anton Chekov once wrote. "It's the daily routine that's stressful." Employment issues are symptomatic of that daily stress. We often spend more time with coworkers than with our spouses or families, and the wear and tear of that human interaction can take its toll. Successfully navigating these sensitive waters requires consistency and an even keel, because at the heart of 99 percent of all employment disputes are perceptions of unfairness. If you can do a good job of managing each employee's expectations of what's fair, aiming for the spirit of the law and avoiding double standards, you will avoid a lot of headaches.

EMPLOYMENT AT WILL DOCTRINE

The common law doctrine of employment at will has defined the foundation of the employee-employer relationship in the United States since the late 1800s. As its name suggests, it means that people work at the "will" of their employers. In its early incarnation it allowed employers to reject applicants on whim, set arbitrary rules, compensate inequitably, and terminate employment without notice or reason. The economic laws of supply and demand tempered certain abuses, but the cyclical nature of supply and demand often meant that power was largely held by the employers.

Over time public policy concerns injected a degree of fairness and smoothed over some of the doctrine's rough edges. During the Industrial Revolution at the turn of the nineteenth century, for example, grave working conditions gave rise to child labor laws. Working conditions also spawned the organized labor movement, whose collective bargaining power helped level the playing field and diffused the concentration of power between employers and employees.

Then individual employee rights came of age. In the 1960s, the principles of implied contract were applied to the employer-employee relationship, imposing a duty of good faith and fair dealing. The tort theory of trespass was applied and anti-harassment laws were born. The "trespass" was upon the person in the form of unwanted touching. Changing political sensitivities and the Civil Rights movement contributed antidiscrimination laws, and so the rule of law continues to evolve in response to industrialization and emerging economic needs.

The at-will doctrine, albeit modified, still governs the employment relationship in many states. While that leaves the employer in charge, employers still have plenty of reasons to take employment issues to heart. Managing these relationships successfully can unlock hidden talents and motivate employees to reach higher levels of performance. That's good for business. Managing them poorly can lead to lawsuits—and not just lawsuits by employees against employers for alleged transgressions but lawsuits by third parties against the employer.

BASIS FOR THIRD-PARTY SUITS

How can an employer be held responsible by a third party for the acts of its employees? And why? Employees are agents of the company. As such they act on behalf of the company. To the outside world they *are* the company. When employees behave badly in their employment capacity it reflects poorly on the business and can put the company on the hook for their misbehavior. An employee maligning a competitor, for example, could subject the company to defamation or libel claims. A new employee transferring confidential information from a prior employer could subject the new employer to intellectual property infringement claims.

If the company does not take the proper steps to discipline such rogue employees for violating company policy or otherwise distance itself from its rogues, it is viewed as *endorsing* or *ratifying* the behavior. It will be held accountable under the legal doctrine of *respondeat superior*—a Latin phrase meaning "let the master answer." That is why having clearly articulated policies and enforcing them consistently is essential to maintaining a level playing field of employee expectations.

If the company knew or should have known about an employee's penchant for trouble (say, for example, it hires a driver without discovering that the applicant's license was suspended for driving while under the influence of alcohol), the company may find itself facing a negligence claim if the driver hits a school bus with the company truck. Hiring without running the appropriate background checks is negligence, something the parents of the injured children are sure to mention in their lawsuit.

BASIS FOR EMPLOYEE SUITS

Employers may find themselves at the receiving end of lawsuits from employees too. The most frequent causes of action used to base such suits are discrimination, harassment, and wrongful or constructive discharge.

Discrimination

When employees feel they have been treated unfairly some are quick to say they have been discriminated against. Common usage of the word *discriminate* means to differentiate. *Discrimination,* however, is a legal term of art. It has a precise meaning. Not every "discrimination" rises to the level of an actionable offense. The law in the United States protects employees against only certain types of discrimination—those based on race and color, national origin, gender, religion, age, disability, and equal pay—and even these aren't necessarily ironclad.

It is permissible, for example, to set gender-based requirements if the requirement is *reasonably* related to the job. The business model of Hooters restaurants is based on waitresses flaunting their assets, similar to the Playboy bunnies in their heyday. A man would simply not be able to fill out the wait staff uniform the same way. The difference would dramatically change the appeal of the restaurant. Therefore discrimination based on gender was upheld in that particular case even though gender is a protected class.

When Kohler Company, the manufacturer of bathroom fixtures, imposed a height minimum of 5'4" for all employees working on the manufacturing line, the restriction appeared to be reasonably related to the job. The policy objective was to make sure that employees could handle the required lifting and other physical labor. Unfortunately, the height restriction had a disproportionate impact on women, making them ineligible for the higher-paying production line jobs. In fact, more than two thousand women were turned down for jobs in 1994 and 1995 due to the height restriction policy.

The disparity was discovered in a routine compliance review by the Office of Federal Contract Compliance Programs. Since Kohler had $27 million in government contracts it was motivated to settle to avoid any further breach of contract or a cancellation of the same. It ended up paying $886,500 in compensation to the two thousand–plus women who had been discriminated against.

The Kohler case illustrates how job requirements can't arbitrarily shut out qualified employees. The weight-lifting requirement was reasonable. But height was the wrong way to measure it. It threw a wider net than necessary to achieve its goal and in the process amplified the discriminatory impact to include those who *could* meet the lifting requirements. That disparity is what made the requirement arbitrary and unsustainable under the law.

The Kohler case also points out how discrimination against protected classes is often subtle and indirect. Care must be taken when evaluating the consequences of reorganizations or reductions in force to see if illegal discrimination is a side effect. Look at the demographics. Are protected groups being disproportionately affected? Sometimes you don't even have to discriminate actively to be liable. It happens indirectly.

The Americans with Disabilities Act, for example, makes it illegal to fire or discriminate against someone because of a disability. But it also requires employers to make "reasonable accommodation" to compensate for employees' disability so they may be able to do their jobs. What constitutes a reasonable accommodation is sometimes a tough judgment call. It's those nuances again.

When an employee suffering from multiple sclerosis in Florida complained to her boss about the uncovered company parking lot, asking for a covered space close to the building next to the ones reserved for management, it looked like she was angling for a perk. Her request was denied even though a doctor's note explained that climbing into an overheated car advanced the progression of her disease. Management thought they were being fair by treating all employees the same. The jury decided they needed to make a reasonable accommodation and returned a verdict that totaled more than $600,000, including attorneys' fees, damages, and compensation.

Sexual Harassment

Sexual harassment is a touchy area of the law and represents yet another potential theory of liability for which employers can be held accountable. It has serious exposure potential because employers can be liable even if they didn't know about the harassment. It's called *vicarious liability*. That's why employers must take harassment claims seriously and investigate them.

Harassment typically evokes images of executives chasing secretaries around the desk or kisses stolen in the copier room. It includes quid pro quo arrangements wherein sexual favors are unwillingly being traded for career advancement. But the law governing harassment is more sophisticated than that. It also includes a range of behaviors, not all of which are sexually charged, that contribute to a "hostile environment." *Any* unwelcome behavior that is *severe* and *pervasive* and *unreasonably interferes* with a person's work creates a hostile environment.

Hostile environment claims fall into three categories: third-party claims, sexual favoritism claims, and sex-based claims. Sexual conduct that is *welcomed* and reciprocated, for example, can create a hostile environment for coworkers. The happy couple's exclusionary behavior, for example, can place coworkers in the uncomfortable position of watching the cooing and cuddling. Welcomed sexual conduct between consenting adults can also result in unfair treatment of others if the romance causes favoritism between the partners and disqualifies otherwise qualified candidates for promotions or job assignments. If the romance cools and one of the employees is in a supervisory capacity with a direct reporting line to the other, the soured relationship can quickly morph into a *quid pro quo claim*.

Some companies seeking to eliminate this risk have a zero tolerance policy regarding employee fraternization. Others appreciate that the business environment represents a fertile meeting ground and that Cupid's arrow will strike where it may. Rather than trying to prohibit nature's call and lose valuable employees in the name of love, these companies coach such couples to be mindful and respectful of their coworkers. If direct supervisory reporting lines are involved, one of the partners is reassigned to reduce the risk of a *quid pro quo* claim. The risk exposure is managed, not entirely eliminated.

The third form of harassment constituting a hostile environment relates to any harassing conduct that is based on gender—behavior that is often dismissed as teasing. The first female millwright working at the plant that manufactures the Jeep Grand Cherokee sport utility vehicle, for example, was the recipient of lewd poems, cartoons, pornographic Polaroid pictures, and lascivious missives all sent to her anonymously. One coworker even urinated on the clothes in her locker after she complained to human resources. Management shrugged it off. Firing all forty-two hundred workers at the plant would have been overkill and a union violation. Boys will be boys.

When the woman recounted more than fifteen thousand incidents of harassment to the jury, they awarded her $20 million *retroactively*—with interest, the total amounted to $45 million. Regrettably, plant management failed to appreciate that what conduct is "reasonable" is viewed from the eyes of the victim. There is both a reasonable man standard and a reasonable woman standard. They are not identical.

Mitsubishi experienced a similar hostile environment situation at one of its plants. Groping and lewd photographs created an out-of-control culture and led 350 female factory works to receive a $34 million settlement. Ignoring the behavior was viewed as ratifying it. Maintaining the proper discipline is therefore an important risk management tool.

Wrongful or Constructive Discharge

The termination of employees can also be riddled with liability land mines. It can result in either a constructive discharge or a wrongful discharge claim. *Constructive discharge* occurs when the employment conditions would force a reasonable person to leave the job. Harassment, for example, could lead to a constructive discharge claim if a reasonable person believed it was the only way to escape their tormentors. The employee initiates the termination.

In contrast, in a *wrongful discharge* claim the employer initiates the termination. If the employee was terminated unfairly, contrary to existing company policy or guidelines or contrary to an existing legal right, it may result in an added claim for wrongful discharge.

Take for example the Allied Universal Corporation case involving a chemical engineer who was overcome by chlorine gas while on the job.

In an effort to get some air he stood on his desk to open an air conditioning vent but got lightheaded and passed out from the gas. The next thing he remembers is waking up in a pool of blood and the commotion of coworkers. His fall caused serious injury to his teeth, face, neck, and back.

Unfortunately, he had difficulty identifying dentists who were willing to do the work under the meager compensation reimbursement rate schedule. His extensive dental injuries were not all covered by workers' compensation insurance. With medical bills mounting the engineer hired a lawyer to help him with the workers' compensation claim. Two days later he was called by the compensation carrier and then into his boss's office and fired. The pretext for terminating the employment was allegedly the engineer's failure to obtain a professional engineer's license and failing to meet job requirements in a timely fashion. But during the termination process his boss said, "Hiring an attorney is the worst mistake you made in your life."

The engineer's subsequent job search was fruitless for two years. He blamed Allied for tarnishing his reputation. It didn't help that they filed a police report the day after he was fired claiming he stole company property even though they knew it wasn't true. The jury returned a verdict of $750,000 for emotional distress plus lost wages, accrued vacation time, and his 401(K) retirement account. The total tab was over $900,000. Poorly handled terminations can be expensive.

ROLE OF POLICIES

Policies are road maps that help you steer clear of the legal obstacles summarized in the following list. These types of issues can occur in all phases of the employment process, from hiring to managing and disciplining to terminating.

Theories of Employment Law Liability

1. Respondeat Superior
2. Negligence
3. Ratification
4. Discrimination: Race, color, national origin, gender, religion, age, disability, equal pay
5. Sexual Harassment:
   a. Quid Pro Quo
   b. Hostile Environment:
      - Third-party claims
      - Sexual favoritism claims
      - Sex-based claims

6. Wrongful or Constructive Discharge

Policies and guidelines provide checklists and tools designed to help make the job of managing employees easier and more consistent. Use them. They facilitate fairness. They manage expectation in employment relationships. The key to success is using them consistently. Too many exceptions to the rules create double standards. If an added layer of distinction is merited, that's fine, but it is important to *communicate* how others can become eligible for the same treatment.

What objective criteria are being used to establish "fairness"? If employees understand how and why distinctions are being made and why these distinctions make sense they are less likely to feel they've been singled out unfairly. Ask yourself: "Am I treating my least favorite employee the same as my favorite employee?" If the answer is no you may want to examine how the two are being treated differently and whether the reason for the disparate treatment has been clearly communicated, along with concrete recommendations for improvement.

INTERNATIONAL ISSUES

The growth of international commerce has made it imperative to be aware of labor idiosyncrasies in other countries. Some trading partners exploit these quirks. Japanese and Korean steel companies, for example, have been known to monitor employment situations in Australian mining and maritime industries and have used those bits of industrial intelligence to their advantage when negotiating purchases of coal and other raw materials. Employment issues are therefore more than an internal management matter. They can position a company for competitive advantage or disadvantage, and they can open the company to product liability as in the Firestone tire example.

A comparison of foreign employment laws shows that management's ability to manage employee expectations may be dampened by statutory or union constraints in other countries. The employment at-will doctrine does not reign supreme.

Industrialization, market forces, and political preferences shape the legal infrastructure of employment. As a result some countries take a more socialized approach to employment law and employee rights. Unions are industry-wide as opposed to divided by occupation and often more vertically integrated in industries and in management decision-making processes. The institutionalized cooperation between labor and management in these integrated union structures centralizes decision making.

Employment Questions to Think About

- Are the company's employment policies regarding hiring, disciplinary, and termination practices understood by all employees? Are they being consistently followed?
- Is there favoritism, an insider's club? If so, is it arbitrary? Or are standards and eligibility requirements clearly communicated and equal opportunity afforded to all, regardless of race, color, national origin, gender, religion, age, or disability?
- Are employment decisions being clearly communicated to employees? How are expectations of fairness being managed?
- What procedures are in place to evaluate latent employment liabilities?
- How are harassment claims handled? Are they all investigated? Or are the victims' requests to "not tell anyone" honored?
- What processes are in place to train managers regarding the structural difference in foreign labor markets and how it can affect their day-to-day decision making?

5. UNFAIR COMPETITION

Unfair competition is an umbrella term that encompasses antitrust laws, the tortious interference with contract, disparagement of another company's products or services, employee raiding, intellectual property infringement, unfair import competition, and gray market, also known as parallel market, goods. It is a blend of law and economics and based on the premise that economic development and social welfare are both enhanced when competitors compete fairly.

What's considered fair can be highly contextual. Some industries are more protected than others in certain countries. Some countries even tolerate anticompetitive cartel behavior, for example, the OPEC oil cartel or the diamond cartel. Yet more than a hundred countries, representing close to 95 percent of world trade, have some form of unfair trade laws. In the United States, for example, antitrust laws (statutes designed to protect commerce from unlawful restraints of trade, price discrimination, price fixing, and monopolies) can be summed up in a series of horizontal and vertical restraints that together broadly define the framework and fabric of antitrust.

HORIZONTAL RESTRAINTS

Horizontal restraints refer to agreements made between you and your competitors. These types of agreements are the most closely scrutinized and most likely to be illegal on their face. Price fixing, dividing markets, allocating customers, suppressing quality competition (such as jointly restricting research and development), and refusals to deal that amount to boycotts are examples of activities that are illegal per se. In other words they are illegal by definition—no exceptions, no excuses. Don't do it!

VERTICAL RESTRAINTS

Vertical restraints refer to the relationship between you, your suppliers, and your customers. Resale price maintenance, requiring the goods to be resold at a certain price as opposed to merely recommending a resale price, is illegal per se, as is the refusal to deal. But other restraints, such as territory or customer allocations, exclusive dealing, requirements or output contracts, tying or reciprocity, price discrimination, promotional allowances, predatory pricing, and termination are subject to interpretation under a "rule of reason" analysis. The law recognizes that such restraints *may* have an anticompetitive effect, but that such restraint might also be reasonable under certain circumstances. Therefore a rule of reason was adopted to evaluate situations based on the merits rather than impose a blanket rule of illegality.

When it comes to avoiding antitrust entanglements in vertical relationships, contracts with clear performance criteria serve a valuable role. They establish and manage expectations that keep transactions within the realm of the rule of reason. Contract expiration and renewal provisions, for example, are a terrific way of addressing termination. A contract expiring under its own terms avoids claims of wrongful termination—and so do clearly defined termination provisions.

Price discrimination is a topic that generates much discussion and requires careful analysis. Just as with employment discrimination, not every differentiation is illegal. To be illegal it must meet the legal definition of price discrimination *and* there must be no valid defense to justify the discrimination.

Definition of Price Discrimination

In the United States price discrimination is governed by the Clayton Act and requires *differentiated pricing* in at least *two contemporaneous, consummated sales* of goods that are of *like grade and quality* to *two different purchasers* with at least *one sale crossing state lines*, where the goods are for *use, consumption, or resale within the United States* and there is an *injurious effect on competition*. All the italicized elements must be met for price discrimination to exist.

Defenses Against Charges of Price Discrimination

Even though a price differential meets the legal criteria for discrimination set forth here, not every discrimination is illegal. It may be legal if there is a valid defense. Cost justification due to differences in manufacturing, sale, or delivery cost can legitimize price discrimination. The cost justification, however, must relate to the class of purchasers, not an individual order. The objective is to treat similarly situated customers similarly. For example, if a plant that is running at 100 percent capacity on an eight-hour shift receives additional product orders, the subsequent orders would push production into an overtime mode. Passing on the overtime costs would be reasonable, provided all subsequent orders are subject to the same overtime charges. Price differentials due to sales and distribution networks made up of agents who add commission to the price of goods or differences in delivery charges that change the total cost of goods can also legitimize price discrimination.

Meeting the competition in good faith is another legitimate defense to price discrimination. As a practical matter prudent business practice demands that an effort be made to investigate and document the existence of a lower competing price before meeting it, lest it be a negotiating bluff. It should be noted, however, that *meeting* the competition does not mean *beating* it. *That* would be illegal price discrimination. It makes no legal sense or business sense: the extra reduction in price nullifies a perfectly valid legal defense, the drop in price cuts deeper into your profit margin, and undercutting the competition creates a margin of injury and actionable damages for the competitor whose bid you've undercut. *Why hand them a lawsuit?*

Does that mean I can never underbid my competitor? No. If your cost structure and the price you normally charge is genuinely lower than your competitor's, it doesn't rise to the level of an unfair trade practice, provided such cost structure represents fair market value and is not the result of a government subsidy or goods being sold at less than fair market value. Because in that case you would be making the same low price available to everyone similarly situated. The scenario in the preceding paragraph is distinguishable. In that case a special, lower price was established solely for the purpose of clinching the business. That's permissible, but only if the competitive price is met, not beaten.

Changing conditions resulting from perishable or seasonal goods, or bona fide going-out-of-business sales, are also legitimate defenses to price discrimination. Similarly, the limited availability of goods and the natural forces of supply and demand can be a legitimate cause of price discrimination.

COMPLEXITY

Although the principles of unfair trade competition laws, including anti-trust, are straightforward and make sense when explained in isolation, the challenge with these laws is in applying them to commerce. It's those tricky nuances again that complicate the analysis.

Sophisticated partnering, joint ventures, and strategic alliances sometimes make it difficult to know who is a competitor and who is a customer. Even a no more than moderately complex distribution system—say, the one diagramed in Figure B.1—where the company's goods can reach the customer through an agent, a distributor, and direct purchase from the company, can create hidden antitrust issues.

As summarized in Table B.5, the horizontal restraints on trade between competitors are more stringent than the vertical restraints in terms of what is illegal by definition. Pricing discussions between competitors are *verboten.* Yet in the vertical value chain price discussions are permitted. Resale prices may be recommended if made within the rule of reason. The law stops short, however, of allowing a company to mandate a particular resale price. In practice, however, there can often be a fine line between coercion and persuasion—and therein lies the challenge.

It turns out that by selling directly to customers the company may indeed be *competing* with its distributors for certain accounts on the same tier of the distribution chain. It is not uncommon for companies to allow distributors to develop a customer, and then, after the account grows to

FIGURE B.1. COMPLEX DISTRIBUTION SYSTEM.

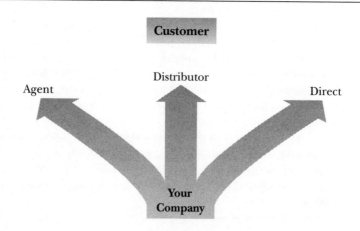

TABLE B.5. COMPARISON OF HORIZONTAL AND VERTICAL TRADE RESTRAINTS.

Horizontal Restraints *(between competitors)*		*Vertical Restraints* *(between suppliers and customers)*	
Per Se Illegal	*Rule of Reason*	*Per Se Illegal*	*Rule of Reason*
Price fixing or bid-rigging		Resale price maintenance	Predatory pricing
Dividing markets			Dividing markets
Allocating customers			Allocating customers
Refusal to deal (boycott)		Refusal to deal	Exclusive dealing
Suppressing quality competition			
			Requirements or output contracts
			Tying or reciprocity
			Price discrimination
			Promotional allowances
			Terminations

a certain size, to designate it a "house account" and bring it in-house to be supplied directly by the manufacturer.

To avoid antitrust complications, watch out for the distinctions imposed by horizontal and vertical restraints and how they apply to the transaction at hand. Good knowledge management is required to keep vertical price discussions from evolving into horizontal discussions. Or requests from a subdistributor to the manufacturer to put pressure on the distributor to offer the subdistributor a better price from turning into resale price maintenance claims.

It is these subtleties, when coupled with the desire to please, that create blind spots and put the company at risk for anticompetitive-practice claims. One issue should be top of mind when entertaining requests for a special deal: *How does this pricing impact my customer's competitors? Will it put them at a competitive disadvantage?* If the answer is yes and there is no legitimate defense you may be setting in motion an unfair competitive advantage that will ripple through the supply chain.

U.S. law looks to the economic consequences of business behavior. Identifying the cause and effect of anticompetitive behavior can be exceedingly complex at times, but the law seeks to preserve competition per se. The concentration of market power in one or more competitors is not illegal if it was earned fairly and maintained through the creation of superior goods and value-added services. However, such concentration will always be scrutinized closely to make sure that it is not being abused and unfairly depriving society of innovation and fair pricing.

Price issues represent a ubiquitous potential risk exposure because all goods and services have a price, all prices are prone to change, and goods and services are sold every day. The sheer volume of transactions increases the likelihood of a mishap *unless* companies have systems in place to vet the changes.

OTHER FORMS OF UNFAIR COMPETITION

The antitrust issues surrounding pricing are among the best-known forms of unfair competition, and some people think that's all there is to the topic. But there's more. Market advantages resulting from selling goods at less than fair market value or pricing subsidized by governments designed to drive competitors out of business are also unfair. Moreover, unfair business advantage is not limited to getting an unfair edge on pricing. Interfering with others' contract rights, stealing their employees or intellectual property, or disparaging competitors' products or services can also create unfair competitive advantage and land your company in hot water.

Dumped and Subsidized Goods

In the international arena, imports being sold at less than fair market value to gain a toehold in the marketplace or imports being subsidized by a competitor's government in a way that creates unfair pricing advantages are illegal. Affected industries are able to bring complaints before the U.S. International Trade Commission and the U.S. International Trade Administration to halt the flooding of unfair goods and impose duties that level the playing field. The advantage of bringing an action through one of these federal agencies is that a single disposition can result in exclusionary orders or duties being imposed that affect the goods at issue at all ports of entry. Such actions are therefore more cost-effective than seeking exclusionary orders at one port of entry and one jurisdiction at a time.

Tortious Interference of Contract

Tortious interference of contract is a less frequently occurring but nonetheless anticompetitive behavior. The idea behind this cause of action is that a third party has no right to interfere with or cause the breach of a contractual relationship. It's telling someone, for example, to terminate a contractual relationship with a supplier because you've got a better deal. *Wait, that happens all the time.* Does it?

There is an important distinction between a bidding process and a done deal. Once an offer has been accepted the parties have a right to expect performance according to the contract terms. If a third party comes in with a better offer that then is accepted and causes a breach of the contract, the first party to the contract is harmed.

A tortious interference of contract requires a special set of elements. The interfering third party must have *knowledge of the contract* and *intend to interfere* with it. The interference must be the actual *cause of the contract breach,* or it must make the contract more difficult to perform or lessen the benefits enjoyed from the contract. The interfering party must have *acted improperly* and the action must result in *damages.* All of the elements must be proved for a tortious interference of contract claim to prevail.

Disparagement

Disparagement of another's product is a form of anticompetitive behavior that dovetails with potential sales and advertising activities. It involves making untrue statements of fact or opinion regarding another company's products or services that place your product in a more favorable light at your competitor's expense. It creates legal liability if publishing the information is motivated by ill will, or is intended to interfere with the interests of another (which you're not privileged to do), if you knew or had reason to know that the information is a lie or is unsupported. Comparative advertising regulations have been created to govern what constitutes a fair characterization of competing products and services.

Employee Raiding

Employee raiding is another potentially anticompetitive practice. What distinguishes these actionable claims from the normal turnover of employees is the unfair advantage that is created as a result of breached legal duties. Several scenarios of employee raiding can create such results.

A group of existing employees who go into business on their own are not necessarily engaging in an unfair trade practice—even if the business they are starting competes with their former employer. But if they take the former employer's customer lists or trade secrets with them, the stolen information gives the new company an unfair head start. Such behavior may be actionable on more than one ground, particularly if the employees were bound by employee confidentiality agreements.

Take another example. If your business sells its goods through distribution networks and you decide to eliminate the middleman by bringing the accounts in-house, the loss of business hurts the distributor—but if the termination is done properly it's merely a part of a distributor's normal business risk. However, if in connection with the designation of house accounts you also solicit the distributor's employees to work for you to handle those accounts, the distributor suffers a double whammy and the employee raiding may be actionable.

Hiring away an entire team, division, or department can devastate a fierce competitor. The ploy carries legal risk exposure if the raid is orchestrated so everyone leaves at once, an unfair tactic such as disparagement is used to persuade employees to leave, you use inside information regarding salary and benefits, and an insider at the competitor is pitching for you in breach of the "do no harm" duty of employee loyalty. Again, all of the elements need to be present to prevail. When the same struggle manifests itself as a David-and-Goliath contest between small companies and large it can create an emotionally charged issue that can invoke the jury's sympathy.

Intellectual Property Infringement

The infringement of intellectual property rights capitalizes on ideas and goodwill developed at someone else's expense. It creates confusion and dilutes the value of the original asset by siphoning sales and tarnishing reputations. It is a form of theft and fraud upon the consuming public. It can manifest itself in the form of patent, trademark, copyright, or "trade dress" infringement, discussed further in the following section of this appendix.

The tremendous growth of world trading partners such as China whose rule of intellectual property law is not as developed as that of other industrialized nations, has contributed to a glut of counterfeit goods in world markets. Aided by Internet sales, counterfeiting has fast become the number one anticompetitive threat faced by many companies today. The type of goods being knocked off extends far beyond expensive designer label luxury goods and has penetrated the supply chain in a pernicious way. Worst of all, the substandard quality of these goods masquerading as genuine product represents latent legal issues ranging from warranty claims to safety and health issues and destroys the real value of the goods. It is by far the worst form of unfair competition.

Unfair Competition Questions to Think About

- How are pricing decisions made in the company? Do they take into account potential anticompetitive effects?
- What procedures are in place governing discussions or contacts with competitors? How are contacts handled at trade association meetings, conferences, in social settings?
- Are there any hybrid business relationships that turn competitors into partners for a range of business activities? If so, what rules or procedures are in place to avoid the appearance of collusion or conspiracy?
- When faced with a competing quotation, does the company meet it or beat it?
- Are price differentials based on actual cost justifications, changing conditions, or availability? Or are numbers selected to please a particular customer?
- Are the contractual obligations of third parties respected? Or does the company actively interfere with such rights?
- Is the company fairly and accurately characterizing its competitors' goods or services? Or are they being disparaged?
- Are employee relationships monitored to avoid employee raiding?
- Are intellectual property rights properly protected and diligently monitored to detect infringement? Are the intellectual property rights of third parties properly acquired and used within the permitted scope?

6. INTELLECTUAL PROPERTY

Intellectual property is an umbrella term that refers to patents, trademarks, copyrights, and trade secrets. These laws are territorial. Each country has its own requirements for establishing and securing these rights, which must be independently met. Protection in one country does not provide protection in another. When doing business in jurisdictions where such protection is not obtained, contract protections can be employed to offer a modest layer of protection.

Since the creation of intellectual property rights is jurisdiction-specific, the choice of law provision in international contracts dealing with intellectual property rights takes on a heightened level of importance, as do ownership rights. Splitting ownership fifty-fifty between you and a business partner may sound fair, but it means different things in different countries. In the United States, for example, profits are shared between joint copyright owners but not between joint patent owners. In France and Germany the rule is the exact opposite.

Substantive differences from country to country can affect the ability to control licensing and future development or commercialization. In the United States, joint patent ownership means joint and several ownership. Those owning 10 percent therefore have *full* ownership rights to do with the patent as they see fit. It means that if co-owners have dissimilar plans their paths could bring them into conflict. There is no legal duty requiring consistency. It is a benefit of ownership. Contracts help avoid such conflicts. But before you know what to incorporate in an agreement you need to know what substantive laws govern the subject matter and how those laws match your expectations.

PATENTS

Patents fall into three broad categories: utility, design, and plant patents. Utility patents are the most common type, requiring some kind of invention. Design patents protect the appearance, or nonfunctional features, of an article of manufacture. Plant patents protect the unique results of nature that occur through human intervention—certain types of genetically controlled seeds, for example.

The classification of utility patents can be further divided as follows:

- *Machines:* Any mechanical device or apparatus consisting of multiple parts that function together to achieve a particular function.
- *Compositions of matter:* Compositions or mixtures of naturally occurring substances that have properties different from those of their ingredients, for example, drugs or chemicals.
- *Manufactures:* Any manmade item not naturally occurring that is not a machine or a composition—buildings or bridges, for example.
- *Processes:* Ways of doing something or making something, such as the methods or steps necessary to make a drug or chemical.

In the United States, business processes have been patented, but this category has been hotly contested and is not recognized as legitimate subject matter for patenting in Europe. Other ineligible subject matters for patenting are laws of nature, products of nature, mathematical formulas, and printed material, the latter being arguably protected by copyright or trademark laws instead.

Being eligible for patenting is not enough for a patent to issue. Other requirements must also be met. An invention must be novel, nonobvious, and useful. In addition, the patent application imposes a duty of candor. It's a requirement of honest disclosure in the patent application process. It means you're telling the patent office the truth about the prior art and why the proposed invention is worthy of protection.

Claims of novelty, or newness, can be defeated in a number of ways. It's no longer "new" if the invention is already patented or if it was described in a printed publication anywhere in the world. That's one reason confidentiality agreements are so important. Keeping a development secret preserves its novelty until you're ready to unveil it.

Novelty can also be defeated if others used the idea before the inventor invented it or if it was someone else's idea altogether, an idea that was not abandoned, suppressed, or concealed. Basically, the law won't let you use the patent application process as a means of purloining someone else's concepts.

If *yours* is the idea needing protection, certain precautions must be taken to avoid inadvertently giving up fragile inventorship rights. The United States protects the first to invent as opposed the first to file a patent application, which is the rule in many other countries. Demonstrating the date of first invention requires good documentation and evidence of diligently pursuing the invention process.

Infringement

Patent infringement can occur in several ways. It can be direct or indirect. Competitors can unfairly compete by making, using, or selling products that trespass or encroach on the claims protected by patents. Similarly, individuals or businesses who import or otherwise distribute these infringing goods are viewed as infringing on the patents.

A party can also contribute to the infringement of a patent by another. One example would be what the law calls the *sale of nonstaples by third parties.* This refers to the supply of an ingredient that permits another to engage in impermissible behavior, if the material sold has no other use except as a component of the patented device or process and the selling party *knows* it. Basically it's a form of aiding and abetting the infringement.

Another form of contributory infringement occurs when a product embodying an improvement patent infringes the underlying patent. That occurs when the only way for the improvement to be practiced is in conjunction with the underlying patent. This form of patent infringement is called the *sale of nonstaples by a patentee.*

TRADEMARKS

Trademarks differ from patents. They are distinctive marks of authenticity that link goods and services to a particular source of origin and quality standard. The origin of trademark law is therefore rooted in the law of fraud. Trademarks serve as a guarantee of authenticity. The law protects consumers by assuring them they are getting what they paid for.

Four types of marks may be protected by law: trademarks, service marks, certification marks—denoting that goods meet certain standards or are manufactured in a certain way, for example, the UL Underwriters Laboratory mark—and collective marks, which are used by members of an organization to denote endorsement of a particular product, such as the appearance of the American Fine China Guild mark on a bottle of dishwashing detergent, or the International Association of Fire Chiefs' mark on a fire extinguisher. The authenticity and quality of the goods creates customer goodwill and brand recognition that are valuable marketing assets.

The strength of a mark and its eligibility for trademark protection rests with its *distinctiveness*. Trademarks are assigned by class of goods and must be distinctive to qualify for legal protection. Marks are *inherently distinctive* if they meet the legal criteria for being fanciful, arbitrary, or suggestive. They are *potentially distinctive* if they are descriptive, deceptively misdescriptive (such as glass wax), geographic, surnames, or slogans. In the United States potentially distinctive marks are incontestable after five years of continuous use, during which time secondary meaning has attached to these common words linking the mark to the source of origin.

Some countries do not recognize potentially distinctive marks. Thus if establishing global brand recognition of a single mark is the centerpiece of your brand strategy, potential brand names seeking trademark protection will need to be vetted against the trademark requirements of each jurisdiction where you wish to register. Language and culture issues will also need to be taken into account. Words in one language don't always translate well into another and can have a totally unintended meaning that detracts from your product or service.

Trademark protection has at times been used in novel ways. Package shapes, for example, can be protected by trademark once secondary meaning has attached to them. Similar to design patents, the legal protection secures distinctive nonfunctional characteristics. The Perrier water bottle is an example of a distinctive design that has earned trademark protection and is so noted on its label.

If design patents and trademarked shapes can both protect the package, what's the benefit of one over the other? Establishing secondary meaning takes at least five years of continuous use. Once established and continuously used, however, a trademark can last forever. A patent issues faster, thereby establishing legal protection sooner, but patents expire and cannot be renewed. Which route provides a bigger benefit depends on the long-term and short-term business objectives and an assessment of the competitive environment.

Using trademarks to protect color and trade dress are another unique use requiring the creation of secondary meaning. A distinctive shade of pink, for example, was successfully defended by Owens Corning Fiberglass, who used the shade to color its home insulation materials, setting itself apart from the traditional yellow used by the rest of the industry. The color pink combined with advertising campaigns featuring the Pink Panther cartoon character gave the color high visibility and firmly established Owens Corning as the source of origin for the goods.

Trade dress refers to the aesthetic look and feel of a package or design. The owner of a Mexican fast food franchise, for example, was able to enjoin a competitor from using the same restaurant layout, color theme, and design on the basis of trade dress. The look and feel of the two restaurants was too similar. Walking in the door, customers were unlikely to know which restaurant they had walked into. It was confusing. The places looked the same.

Infringement

The standard for deciding whether a trademark infringement has occurred is based on these issues:

- Similarity of the mark with respect to appearance, sound, connotation, and impression
- Similarity of goods or services
- Similarity of trade channels
- Conditions of sale (impulse purchase versus a considered buy)
- Strength of the mark (inherently distinctive versus potentially distinctive)
- Actual confusion
- The number and nature of similar marks on similar goods

Trademark holders have a legal duty to police their marks and use them properly on their goods and in their advertising and promotional materials. The failure to do so allows others to dilute the value and possibly tarnish the trademark.

The worst-case scenario is the mark's losing its distinctiveness altogether and becoming a generic term. Thermos, escalator, and cellophane are examples of trademarks that have fallen victim to genericide. That's why companies like Xerox go to great lengths to periodically advertise the fact that Xerox has two R's in it—one in the word itself and the other the R in a circle denoting federally registered trademark protection. They want people to ask for a Xerox copy, not a Xerox—or, worse yet, a xerox.

COPYRIGHT

Copyright protection extends to any original work of authorship fixed in any tangible medium of expression. In the United States it is no longer necessary to affix a C in a circle to denote copyright protection. The work is protected as soon as it is expressed in a tangible medium, including electronic form. Affixing the proper copyright notice is still important for enforcing copyright rights. It is therefore prudent practice to add the notation where appropriate, including the copyright owner and the year of publication.

Copyright protection extends to these categories:

- Literary works
- Pictorial, graphic, and sculptural works
- Sound recordings
- Architectural works
- Compilations
- Derivative works (as when a book is made into a movie, or a song gets a new musical arrangement)

Gray areas of copyright protection exist with respect to computer programs, computer user interface programs, typefaces, and titles, trademarks, commercial prints, and labels.

Copyright is an umbrella term that encompasses a bundle of rights. It conveys upon the copyright owner the exclusive right to control reproduction rights, derivative rights, distribution rights, performance rights, and display rights. Contracts are the preferred method of assigning and controlling these rights. Contract terms must therefore be carefully reviewed with respect to the scope and duration of the rights being transferred.

Infringement

Copyright infringement need not be intentional and it need not be outright plagiarism. It includes any unauthorized copying or sharing that falls outside the "fair use" exception.

The fair use standard casts a wide net. It is not always clear what constitutes permissible use. That's because the fair use standard balances four competing interests in determining whether a copyright violation has occurred. Courts look at the purpose and character of the use, including its commercial nature. The more academic the purpose and character of the use the more likely it will be deemed fair use. The totality of the circumstances must be examined, however. Research and development facilities do not count as "academic" even if their activities are in pursuit of science, if that science supports a business enterprise whose mission is to make a profit. The nature of the copyrighted work, the portion that was "taken," and the economic impact of the "taking" are all weighed to determine fairness and the economic impact on the parties vis-à-vis the public interest.

In the case of Napster, the Internet file-sharing system that allowed for the downloading of copyrighted musical works, the court held the balance weighed against Napster. New Internet business models are therefore being created to realign the interests of copyright holders with the new medium of commerce. In the old world of hard copies, for example, the business reality of routine photocopying of newspaper, magazine, and journal articles that constitute violations of copyright led to the creation of the Copyright Clearance Center, a clearinghouse for copyright permission requests that makes it easier for businesses to be in compliance with copyright laws. The Center offers licenses with reasonable fee schedules calculated by a formula designed to take into account the number of office workers most likely to photocopy or electronically share articles.

TRADE SECRETS

The term *trade secrets* refers to any information or data that has competitive value. The magic protection lies not in any formal filings with a government agency but in self-restraint and self-regulation. Trade secret protections are lost if the secrets stop being secret. We preserve secrets by not telling more people than necessary and by creating a duty of nondisclosure through contract. If the duty is breached it gives rise to breach of contract claims. If an employee shares a trade secret outside the organization without obtaining a duty of nondisclosure from the recipient, the employee has violated the common law duty of loyalty to the company.

The loss of trade secret status has implications for patent rights. U.S. patent applications must be filed within one year of the commercialization of the product *or* the public disclosure of the invention. The failure to recognize the one-year window could result in the loss of valuable patent rights if applications are not filed before the year expires.

CREATING VALUE

The power of ideas secured by legal rights is modern-day alchemy. Intellectual property takes on an increasingly important strategic role as companies become more cognizant of its value in asset creation and in protecting competitiveness. Intellectual property law confers a limited monopoly that can be used to expand and protect market share, enhance branding efforts and the company's reputation as an innovator, and reposition products. It can be used defensively as well as offensively.

The value hierarchy of intellectual property in Figure B.2 starts with the primary objective of staking and defending a claim. It moves to cost center management, where costs associated with maintaining and developing the portfolio are streamlined and prioritized according to their overall strategic value to the company. The next step examines how the business can extract value through licensing, royalty audits, or intellectual property donations that generate tax benefits. Aligning intellectual property with corporate strategy takes the ante up yet another notch allowing the law to be used tactically to position and protect products and services. Finally, embedding intellectual property into the corporate culture projects it into the future and allows for visionary applications of a long-term strategic nature.

Intellectual Property Questions to Think About

- What type of intellectual property does the business have? How are ownership rights being protected?
- What procedures are in place to protect trade secrets and keep them confidential?

FIGURE B.2. USES OF INTELLECTUAL PROPERTY:
MOVING FROM TACTICAL TO STRATEGIC USE.

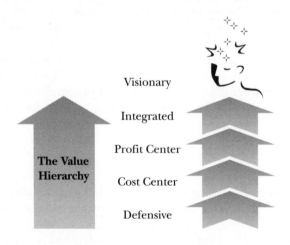

Source: Adapted from Davis and Harrison, 2001, p. 19.

- How are the intellectual property rights of others being respected?
- Are employees aware of the role confidentiality plays in the creation of patent rights?
- What role do trademarks play in the company's marketing strategy?
- Are trademark rights being adequately policed?
- How is the company extracting value from its intellectual property portfolio?
- Is the company's use of intellectual property tactical or strategic?

CONCLUSION

The foregoing synopsis is a taste of the law. It's an appetizer to the exciting menu of legal tools that are available to secure, advance, and promote legitimate business interests. Whether they are employed to optimize competitiveness or merely to plug unwanted risk exposure, they create value and put managers in the driver's seat of legal risk management.

APPENDIX C

THE LESSONS OF
SARBANES-OXLEY

For the past few years the Sarbanes-Oxley Act of 2002, affectionately known as SOX, has struck fear into the hearts of publicly traded corporations in the United States. It's also struck fear into the hearts of foreign corporations looking to do business in the United States and those who fear their own governments would enact similar legislation. The Act declares that its purpose is to "protect investors by improving the accuracy and reliability of corporate disclosures." In the aftermath of Enron, WorldCom, and other accounting scandals that blighted the business landscape by manipulating accounting rules and through outright fraud, the sanitizing effect of the Act would appear to be a good thing. Investor trust needed to be restored to financial markets.

On its face it doesn't look so bad. A look at SOX's table of contents (Appendix E) shows that the Act seeks to promote transparency, integrity, and independence. It enhances the authority of audit committees and corporate boards, restoring the watchdog function that was too often eroded by corporate politics. It also promotes corporate responsibility, requiring an assessment of internal controls and increased corporate disclosure. The Act backstops these legal duties with criminal penalties for failure to comply. It has teeth.

Despite its noble intentions, SOX has more than its share of detractors. Mere mention of the word is often met with groans, grunts, and guffaws. *Why? Aren't these prudent business practices that companies should be doing anyway?*

Yes, all the issues addressed by SOX represent sound public policy and prudent business practices. But as a practical matter, corporate growth spurts often lead to a patchwork of financial controls. Some of them are adequate. Some of them are not. Over time these casual practices cloud information and the transparency of disclosures, thereby contributing to suboptimal knowledge management. Along comes SOX and turns on a spotlight of accountability. Suddenly poor housekeeping practices are exposed for what they are. It's a painful and expensive process. Unfortunately, all the headlines surrounding these growing pains have drowned out the virtues of SOX and the broader business lessons it represents.

In many ways SOX is the poster child for legal literacy. We all know it's a cautionary tale of what happens when too many loopholes get stacked on top of each other, hollowing out the spirit of the law, and how exuberant overconfidence tricks executives into believing nothing is wrong. But what's not always clear is how the lack of legal literacy, the loss aversion bias, and the lack of available information have made the implementation of SOX more painful and costly than necessary.

THE IMPERFECT RULE OF LAW

The purpose of the rule of law is to drive and enforce behavior in conformance with society's core values. The law is a codification of public policy and ethics. It is not out to crucify business.

The rule of law, however, is not perfect. Once enacted, *any* new law poses the challenge of figuring out what it means for day-to-day business routines. *How will it change the way things are being done?* SOX does not go into tremendous detail. It leaves room for interpretation, and that is where the lack of legal literacy bred ignorance and fear. In the process we became our own worst enemy.

The Public Company Accounting Oversight Board (PCAOB), the private, nonprofit corporation created by SOX and entrusted with the responsibility of protecting investors by establishing auditing and related attestation, quality control, ethics, and independence standards for public accounting firms, took two years to adopt three rules and submit them to the SEC for approval. These rules dealt with three circumstances in which supplying tax services can impair an audit firm's independence. It's no doubt an important step toward protecting audit independence. But it is hardly an encyclopedic work product. There is much about SOX that is still left unsaid.

Nonetheless, in 2005 the infamous Section 404 of the Act took effect, requiring publicly traded companies with market capitalization of more than $75 million to assess the effectiveness of their internal financial controls. It requires auditors to determine whether the controls are adequate or are materially weak. This is a judgment call and it's being made in a highly charged environment.

DECISION MAKING LOSS AVERSION BIAS

The memory of Arthur Andersen's demise and its role as Enron's audit is still fresh. The wreckage of the 2001 scandals is still being picked over by trial lawyers in courtrooms packed with reporters, and the increased threat of zealous prosecutors casts a cold shadow that has dampened enthusiasm for aggressive risk taking. The net result is a touch of silent hysteria and a genuine fear factor that colors interpretation of the new law.

An unintended consequence of this fear factor and the lack of available rules and standards is that it has caused auditors to err on the side of extreme caution, making ultraconservative judgments to immunize themselves from risk and protect against losses of their own. In the process they have placed unnecessary burdens on their clients when determining what constitutes "proper business controls" under Section 404. Burdens that must be met before the auditors will sign off on financial audits. These gold-plated solutions have thereby increased the cost of some internal controls far in excess of the benefit they provide.

"It's made outside auditors regulators," laments one CEO. The shift in the balance of power and the impact on the bottom line, all wrapped in an intimating blanket of fear, have gripped the business community and sparked spirited debate. The chairman of the American Stock Exchange, Neal Wolkoff, for example, has gone on record saying the high compliance cost of SOX is a curse for small-cap companies. One academic study concluded that in 2003 the number of companies resisting compliance and delisting from public exchanges due to SOX tripled. They preferred to resist and delist than comply.

The president and CEO of the NASDAQ exchange, Bob Geifeld, had a different perspective. He also went on record about SOX, but in support of the law. He concedes that compliance is painful and time-consuming but maintains that the benefit of better information improves the way businesses are run and creates valuable competitive advantage. He further estimates that while the infrastructure start-up costs of Section 404 compliance are high, the expenses should drop sharply after the first year, once the control infrastructure is in place. He calls it the price of restoring trust.

Unfortunately, the compliance cost message has been louder and more frequent than the trust message. It's an amazing and sensational message, and it keeps being repeated at the expense of the spirit of the law. This imbalance has given SOX an undeserved black eye.

The chairman of the PCAOB acknowledged the unnecessarily high compliance cost concerns surrounding Section 404 compliance. He publicly stated that while the new financial controls have made financial disclosures more trustworthy, in some cases they have also led to overkill, causing too much work to be done to verify statements.

The SEC's chief accountant went even further when he encouraged auditors to exercise sound judgment and good decision making. In a staff report he noted that too many companies had turned implementation of Section 404 into a mechanical checklist with little thought as to whether the particular control made sense in a given application. They missed the point of the exercise, driving up costs unnecessarily in the process. The better approach, he counseled, was to devote resources to the greatest risk exposures, to evaluate and prioritize them rather than using a one-size-fits-all approach without regard to the magnitude of the risk.

DECISION-MAKING AVAILABILITY BIAS

The loss aversion bias that influenced SOX compliance efforts and led to ultraconservative implementation was further compounded by the availability bias. It reminds me of the office slacker who signed up for every available company training course. When asked why, he said because when it came time for his performance review he couldn't be criticized for not expanding his skill set. Rather than dig down and ask whether the courses would be relevant to what he did and cost-effective for the company, he took the concept of training at face value.

In the case of SOX, instead of asking *what controls will work or be effective*, the auditors looked no further than the lack of articulated standards. Few rules offer guidance on *how* the regulations are to be complied with. The lack of information drives *mindless*, mechanical compliance rather than *mindful* and thoughtful business practices that are effective. It invites doing what's necessary to protect the flanks instead of doing what's right. Had the auditors dug deeper and developed an understanding of the spirit of SOX they would have been better equipped to fill in the blanks and achieve the law's objective without exposing themselves to criminal liability or overburdening their clients.

But how many of these auditors have actually read the guidelines used by prosecutors for determining whether to indict? If all you know about criminal prosecution is summed up in the headlines, the perp walks of fallen CEOs on the ten o'clock news, and the occasional episode of *Law and Order*, the criminal process looks terrifying. It would make anyone steer a wide berth around issues that could remotely trigger such liabilities.

Yet why not make more information available about criminal risk exposure? If you know what's expected of you it's easier to stay out of trouble. You'll know what behaviors need to be managed and what actions need to be taken. Why not take an insider's look at the guidelines that influence the *prosecutor's* decisions of whether to indict?

The U.S. Department of Justice guidelines on the subject were set forth in the "Thompson Memo," which has been adopted in the *United States Attorneys' Manual* as Title 9 §162, "Federal Prosecution of Business Organizations." It starts off by saying corporations should not be treated more leniently *or more harshly* simply because they are an artificial legal entity. (See Appendix F.) It dispels the fear of what some executives believe is a corporate witch-hunt by overzealous prosecutors.

If we take a look at §27.220, the factors prosecutors consider when charging a corporation for example, the guidelines identify nine factors:

1. Nature and seriousness of the offense, including the risk of harm to the public
2. Pervasiveness of wrongdoing, including the complicity or condonation of the wrongdoing by management
3. History of similar conduct
4. Timely and voluntary disclosure of wrongdoing
5. Existence and adequacy of a corporate compliance program
6. Corporation's remedial actions, including efforts to implement or improve a compliance program
7. Collateral consequences including disproportionate harm to shareholders, pension holders, and employees not proven personally culpable, and the impact on the public arising from the prosecution
8. Adequacy of the prosecution of individuals responsible for the malfeasance
9. Adequacy of remedies such as civil or regulatory enforcement actions

The first point to be considered is the nature and seriousness of the offense, including the risk of harm to the public. If auditors would identify the weakest financial controls instead of treating all financial weaknesses the same they could eliminate the biggest risks first instead of spreading resources too thin or gold-plating their compliance efforts. This approach would be more in keeping with the spirit of the law while still protecting auditors from liability.

Going down the list point by point will generate a keener understanding of how the justice system's moving parts can touch the business and what we need to do to keep out of the way. Prioritizing and tackling the biggest problems reduces both the financial liability and the criminal liability.

Tipping Point

Ironically, for all the bellyaching about SOX, ample evidence suggests that the demand for transparency, integrity, and independence of audit committees and corporate boards has reached a critical mass and a tipping point. Noncompliance is increasingly no longer an option.

A number of U.S. states have enacted SOX-like laws that apply to public and nonpublic business enterprises alike and foreign governments are toying with the idea. Pressure to conform and meet the expectations of customers, competitors, bankers, suppliers, insurers, and auditors has also raised the bar on best practices regarding internal financial controls. Pressure from these stakeholders has even prompted some companies with no intention of going public to informally comply with SOX.

As a result, SOX has become a catalyst for better financial controls that create better financial knowledge management systems and lead to better decisions and better business. It is a testament to the value of proactively managing legal risk. It illustrates the importance of legal leverage to the decision-making processes, how loss aversion blinds us and increases the cost of compliance, and how better legal literacy promotes understanding and mindfulness, and drives cost-effective performance.

The law is not unknowable. Legal literacy is attainable. The time has therefore come to extend the lesson of SOX beyond financial controls and to build a corporate culture that is legally literate and ethically grounded—one that looks beyond compliance checklists and is strengthened and sustained by the ability and courage to do the right thing—both legally and ethically.

Excerpts from Federal Organizational Sentencing Guidelines, 2004

Chapter 8—Part B—Remedying Harm from Criminal Conduct, and Effective Compliance and Ethics Program

2. EFFECTIVE COMPLIANCE AND ETHICS PROGRAM

§8B2.1. <u>Effective Compliance and Ethics Program</u>

(a) To have an effective compliance and ethics program, for purposes of subsection (f) of §8C2.5 (Culpability Score) and subsection (c)(1) of §8D1.4 (Recommended Conditions of Probation—Organizations), an organization shall—

(1) exercise due diligence to prevent and detect criminal conduct; and

(2) otherwise promote an organizational culture that encourages ethical conduct and a commitment to compliance with the law.

Such compliance and ethics program shall be reasonably designed, implemented, and enforced so that the program is generally effective in preventing and detecting criminal conduct. The failure to prevent or detect the instant offense does not necessarily mean that the program is not generally effective in preventing and detecting criminal conduct.

(b) Due diligence and the promotion of an organizational culture that encourages ethical conduct and a commitment to compliance with the law within the meaning of subsection (a) minimally require the following:

(1) The organization shall establish standards and procedures to prevent and detect criminal conduct.

(2) (A) The organization's governing authority shall be knowledgeable about the content and operation of the compliance and ethics program and shall exercise reasonable oversight with respect to the implementation and effectiveness of the compliance and ethics program.

(B) High-level personnel of the organization shall ensure that the organization has an effective compliance and ethics program, as described in this guideline. Specific individual(s) within high-level personnel shall be assigned overall responsibility for the compliance and ethics program.

(C) Specific individual(s) within the organization shall be delegated day-to-day operational responsibility for the compliance and ethics program. Individual(s) with operational responsibility shall report periodically to high-level personnel and, as appropriate, to the governing authority, or an appropriate subgroup of the governing authority, on the effectiveness of the compliance and ethics program. To carry out such operational responsibility, such individual(s) shall be given adequate resources, appropriate authority, and direct access to the governing authority or an appropriate subgroup of the governing authority.

(3) The organization shall use reasonable efforts not to include within the substantial authority personnel of the organization any individual whom the organization knew, or should have known through the exercise of due diligence, has engaged in illegal activities or other conduct inconsistent with an effective compliance and ethics program.

(4) (A) The organization shall take reasonable steps to communicate periodically and in a practical manner its standards and procedures, and other aspects of the compliance and ethics program, to the individuals referred to in subdivision

(B) by conducting effective training programs and otherwise disseminating information appropriate to such individuals' respective roles and responsibilities.

(B) The individuals referred to in subdivision (A) are the members of the governing authority, high-level personnel, substantial authority personnel, the organization's employees, and, as appropriate, the organization's agents.

(5) The organization shall take reasonable steps—

(A) to ensure that the organization's compliance and ethics program is followed, including monitoring and auditing to detect criminal conduct;

(B) to evaluate periodically the effectiveness of the organization's compliance and ethics program; and

(C) to have and publicize a system, which may include mechanisms that allow for anonymity or confidentiality, whereby the organization's employees and agents may report or seek guidance regarding potential or actual criminal conduct without fear of retaliation.

(6) The organization's compliance and ethics program shall be promoted and enforced consistently throughout the organization through (A) appropriate incentives to perform in accordance with the compliance and ethics program; and (B) appropriate disciplinary measures for engaging in criminal conduct and for failing to take reasonable steps to prevent or detect criminal conduct.

(7) After criminal conduct has been detected, the organization shall take reasonable steps to respond appropriately to the criminal conduct and to prevent further similar criminal conduct, including making any necessary modifications to the organization's compliance and ethics program.

(c) In implementing subsection (b), the organization shall periodically assess the risk of criminal conduct and shall take appropriate steps to design, implement, or modify each requirement set forth in subsection (b) to reduce the risk of criminal conduct identified through this process.

Commentary

Application Notes:

1. *Definitions*. *For purposes of this guideline:*

"Compliance and ethics program" means a program designed to prevent and detect criminal conduct.

"Governing authority" means the (A) the Board of Directors; or (B) if the organization does not have a Board of Directors, the highest-level governing body of the organization.

"High-level personnel of the organization" and "substantial authority personnel" have the meaning given those terms in the Commentary to §8A1.2 (Application Instructions—Organizations).

"Standards and procedures" means standards of conduct and internal controls that are reasonably capable of reducing the likelihood of criminal conduct.

2. *Factors to Consider in Meeting Requirements of this Guideline.*

(A) *In General. Each of the requirements set forth in this guideline shall be met by an organization; however, in determining what specific actions are necessary to meet those requirements, factors that shall be considered include: (i) applicable industry practice or the standards called for by any applicable governmental regulation; (ii) the size of the organization; and (iii) similar misconduct.*

(B) *Applicable Governmental Regulation and Industry Practice. An organization's failure to incorporate and follow applicable industry practice or the standards called for by any applicable governmental regulation weighs against a finding of an effective compliance and ethics program.*

(C) *The Size of the Organization.*

(i) *In General. The formality and scope of actions that an organization shall take to meet the requirements of this guideline, including the necessary features of the organization's standards and procedures, depend on the size of the organization.*

(ii) *Large Organizations. A large organization generally shall devote more formal operations and greater resources in meeting the requirements of this guideline than shall a small organization. As appropriate, a large organization should encourage small organizations (especially those that have, or seek to have, a business relationship with the large organization) to implement effective compliance and ethics programs.*

(iii) <u>Small Organizations</u>. In meeting the requirements of this guideline, small organizations shall demonstrate the same degree of commitment to ethical conduct and compliance with the law as large organizations. However, a small organization may meet the requirements of this guideline with less formality and fewer resources than would be expected of large organizations. In appropriate circumstances, reliance on existing resources and simple systems can demonstrate a degree of commitment that, for a large organization, would only be demonstrated through more formally planned and implemented systems.

Examples of the informality and use of fewer resources with which a small organization may meet the requirements of this guideline include the following: (I) the governing authority's discharge of its responsibility for oversight of the compliance and ethics program by directly managing the organization's compliance and ethics efforts; (II) training employees through informal staff meetings, and monitoring through regular "walk-arounds" or continuous observation while managing the organization; (III) using available personnel, rather than employing separate staff, to carry out the compliance and ethics program; and (IV) modeling its own compliance and ethics program on existing, well-regarded compliance and ethics programs and best practices of other similar organizations.

(D) <u>Recurrence of Similar Misconduct</u>. Recurrence of similar misconduct creates doubt regarding whether the organization took reasonable steps to meet the requirements of this guideline. For purposes of this subdivision, "similar misconduct" has the meaning given that term in the Commentary to §8A1.2 (Application Instructions—Organizations).

3. <u>Application of Subsection (b)(2)</u>. High-level personnel and substantial authority personnel of the organization shall be knowledgeable about the content and operation of the compliance and ethics program, shall perform their assigned duties consistent with the exercise of due diligence, and shall promote an organizational culture that encourages ethical conduct and a commitment to compliance with the law.

If the specific individual(s) assigned overall responsibility for the compliance and ethics program does not have day-to-day operational responsibility for the program, then the individual(s) with day-to-day operational responsibility for the program typically should, no less than annually, give the governing authority or an appropriate subgroup thereof information on the implementation and effectiveness of the compliance and ethics program.

4. <u>Application of Subsection (b)(3)</u>.

(A) <u>Consistency with Other Law</u>. Nothing in subsection (b)(3) is intended to require conduct inconsistent with any Federal, State, or local law, including any law governing employment or hiring practices.

(B) Implementation. In implementing subsection (b)(3), the organization shall hire and promote individuals so as to ensure that all individuals within the high-level personnel and substantial authority personnel of the organization will perform their assigned duties in a manner consistent with the exercise of due diligence and the promotion of an organizational culture that encourages ethical conduct and a commitment to compliance with the law under subsection (a). With respect to the hiring or promotion of such individuals, an organization shall consider the relatedness of the individual's illegal activities and other misconduct (i.e., other conduct inconsistent with an effective compliance and ethics program) to the specific responsibilities the individual is anticipated to be assigned and other factors such as: (i) the recency of the individual's illegal activities and other misconduct; and (ii) whether the individual has engaged in other such illegal activities and other such misconduct.

5. *Application of Subsection (b)(6). Adequate discipline of individuals responsible for an offense is a necessary component of enforcement; however, the form of discipline that will be appropriate will be case specific.*

6. *Application of Subsection (c). To meet the requirements of subsection (c), an organization shall:*

(A) Assess periodically the risk that criminal conduct will occur, including assessing the following:

(i) The nature and seriousness of such criminal conduct.

(ii) The likelihood that certain criminal conduct may occur because of the nature of the organization's business. If, because of the nature of an organization's business, there is a substantial risk that certain types of criminal conduct may occur, the organization shall take reasonable steps to prevent and detect that type of criminal conduct. For example, an organization that, due to the nature of its business, employs sales personnel who have flexibility to set prices shall establish standards and procedures designed to prevent and detect price-fixing. An organization that, due to the nature of its business, employs sales personnel who have flexibility to represent the material characteristics of a product shall establish standards and procedures designed to prevent and detect fraud.

(iii) The prior history of the organization. The prior history of an organization may indicate types of criminal conduct that it shall take actions to prevent and detect.

(B) Prioritize periodically, as appropriate, the actions taken pursuant to any requirement set forth in subsection (b), in order to focus on preventing and detecting the criminal conduct identified under subdivision (A) of this note as most serious, and most likely, to occur.

(C) Modify, as appropriate, the actions taken pursuant to any requirement set forth in subsection (b) to reduce the risk of criminal conduct identified under subdivision (A) of this note as most serious, and most likely, to occur.

Background

This section sets forth the requirements for an effective compliance and ethics program. This section responds to section 805(a)(2)(5) of the Sarbanes-Oxley Act of 2002, Public Law 107–204, which directed the Commission to review and amend, as appropriate, the guidelines and related policy statements to ensure that the guidelines that apply to organizations in this chapter "are sufficient to deter and punish organizational criminal misconduct."

The requirements set forth in this guideline are intended to achieve reasonable prevention and detection of criminal conduct for which the organization would be vicariously liable. The prior diligence of an organization in seeking to prevent and detect criminal conduct has a direct bearing on the appropriate penalties and probation terms for the organization if it is convicted and sentenced for a criminal offense.

Historical Note: Effective November 1, 2004 (see Appendix C, amendment 673).

APPENDIX E

EXCERPTS FROM THE SARBANES-OXLEY ACT OF 2002

Table of Contents

116 STAT. 745 PUBLIC LAW 107–204—JULY 30, 2002
Public Law 107–204
107th Congress
An Act

To protect investors by improving the accuracy and reliability of corporate disclosures made pursuant to the securities laws, and for other purposes.

Be it enacted by the Senate and House of Representatives of the United States of America in Congress assembled,

SECTION 1. SHORT TITLE; TABLE OF CONTENTS.

(a) SHORT TITLE. This Act may be cited as the "Sarbanes-Oxley Act of 2002".

(b) TABLE OF CONTENTS. The table of contents for this Act is as follows:

Sec. 1. Short title; table of contents.
Sec. 2. Definitions.
Sec. 3. Commission rules and enforcement.

TITLE I—PUBLIC COMPANY ACCOUNTING OVERSIGHT BOARD

Sec. 101. Establishment; administrative provisions.
Sec. 102. Registration with the Board.

Sec. 103. Auditing, quality control, and independence standards and rules.
Sec. 104. Inspections of registered public accounting firms.
Sec. 105. Investigations and disciplinary proceedings.
Sec. 106. Foreign public accounting firms.
Sec. 107. Commission oversight of the Board.
Sec. 108. Accounting standards.
Sec. 109. Funding.

TITLE II—AUDITOR INDEPENDENCE

Sec. 201. Services outside the scope of practice of auditors.
Sec. 202. Preapproval requirements.
Sec. 203. Audit partner rotation.
Sec. 204. Auditor reports to audit committees.
Sec. 205. Conforming amendments.
Sec. 206. Conflicts of interest.
Sec. 207. Study of mandatory rotation of registered public accounting firms.
Sec. 208. Commission authority.
Sec. 209. Considerations by appropriate State regulatory authorities.

TITLE III—CORPORATE RESPONSIBILITY

Sec. 301. Public company audit committees.
Sec. 302. Corporate responsibility for financial reports.
Sec. 303. Improper influence on conduct of audits.
Sec. 304. Forfeiture of certain bonuses and profits.
Sec. 305. Officer and director bars and penalties.
Sec. 306. Insider trades during pension fund blackout periods.
Sec. 307. Rules of professional responsibility for attorneys.
Sec. 308. Fair funds for investors.

TITLE IV—ENHANCED FINANCIAL DISCLOSURES

Sec. 401. Disclosures in periodic reports.
Sec. 402. Enhanced conflict of interest provisions.
Sec. 403. Disclosures of transactions involving management and principal stockholders.
Sec. 404. Management assessment of internal controls.
Sec. 405. Exemption.
Sec. 406. Code of ethics for senior financial officers.
Sec. 407. Disclosure of audit committee financial expert.

Sec. 408. Enhanced review of periodic disclosures by issuers.
Sec. 409. Real time issuer disclosures.

TITLE V—ANALYST CONFLICTS OF INTEREST

Sec. 501. Treatment of securities analysts by registered securities associations and national securities exchanges.

TITLE VI—COMMISSION RESOURCES AND AUTHORITY

Sec. 601. Authorization of appropriations.
Sec. 602. Appearance and practice before the Commission.
Sec. 603. Federal court authority to impose penny stock bars.
Sec. 604. Qualifications of associated persons of brokers and dealers.

TITLE VII—STUDIES AND REPORTS

Sec. 701. GAO study and report regarding consolidation of public accounting firms.
Sec. 702. Commission study and report regarding credit rating agencies.
Sec. 703. Study and report on violators and violations
Sec. 704. Study of enforcement actions.
Sec. 705. Study of investment banks.

TITLE VIII—CORPORATE AND CRIMINAL FRAUD ACCOUNTABILITY

Sec. 801. Short title.
Sec. 802. Criminal penalties for altering documents.
Sec. 803. Debts nondischargeable if incurred in violation of securities fraud laws.
Sec. 804. Statute of limitations for securities fraud.
Sec. 805. Review of Federal Sentencing Guidelines for obstruction of justice and extensive criminal fraud.
Sec. 806. Protection for employees of publicly traded companies who provide evidence of fraud.
Sec. 807. Criminal penalties for defrauding shareholders of publicly traded companies.

TITLE IX—WHITE-COLLAR CRIME PENALTY ENHANCEMENTS

Sec. 901. Short title.
Sec. 902. Attempts and conspiracies to commit criminal fraud offenses.
Sec. 903. Criminal penalties for mail and wire fraud.

Sec. 904. Criminal penalties for violations of the Employee Retirement Income Security Act of 1974.

Sec. 905. Amendment to sentencing guidelines relating to certain white-collar offenses.

Sec. 906. Corporate responsibility for financial reports.

TITLE X—CORPORATE TAX RETURNS

Sec. 1001. Sense of the Senate regarding the signing of corporate tax returns by chief executive officers.

TITLE XI—CORPORATE FRAUD AND ACCOUNTABILITY

Sec. 1101. Short title.

Sec. 1102. Tampering with a record or otherwise impeding an official proceeding.

Sec. 1103. Temporary freeze authority for the Securities and Exchange Commission.

Sec. 1104. Amendment to the Federal Sentencing Guidelines.

Sec. 1105. Authority of the Commission to prohibit persons from serving as officers or directors.

Sec. 1106. Increased criminal penalties under Securities Exchange Act of 1934.

Sec. 1107. Retaliation against informants.

UNITED STATES ATTORNEYS' MANUAL: THE THOMPSON MEMO

Also known as Title 9, Criminal Resource Manual 162 Federal Prosecution of Business Organizations

Federal Prosecution of Business Organizations[1]

I. Charging a Corporation: General

A. General Principle: Corporations should not be treated leniently because of their artificial nature nor should they be subject to harsher treatment. Vigorous enforcement of the criminal laws against corporate wrongdoers, where appropriate results in great benefits for law enforcement and the public, particularly in the area of white collar crime. Indicting corporations for wrongdoing enables the government to address and be a force for positive change of corporate culture, alter corporate behavior, and prevent, discover, and punish white collar crime.

B. Comment: In all cases involving corporate wrongdoing, prosecutors should consider the factors discussed herein. First and foremost, prosecutors should be aware of the important public benefits that may flow from indicting a corporation in appropriate cases. For instance, corporations are likely to take immediate remedial steps when one is indicted for criminal conduct that is pervasive throughout a particular industry, and thus an indictment often provides a unique opportunity for deterrence on a massive scale. In addition, a corporate indictment may result in specific deterrence by changing the culture of the indicted corporation and the behavior of its employees. Finally, certain crimes that carry with them a substantial risk of great public harm, e.g., environmental crimes or financial frauds, are by their nature most likely to be committed by businesses, and there may, therefore, be a substantial federal interest in indicting the corporation.

Charging a corporation, however, does not mean that individual directors, officers, employees, or shareholders should not also be charged. Prosecution of a corporation is not a substitute for the prosecution of criminally culpable individuals within or without the corporation. Because a corporation can act only through individuals, imposition of individual criminal liability may provide the strongest deterrent against future corporate wrongdoing. Only rarely should provable individual culpability not be pursued, even in the face of offers of corporate guilty pleas.

Corporations are "legal persons," capable of suing and being sued, and capable of committing crimes. Under the doctrine of respondeat superior, a corporation may be held criminally liable for the illegal acts of its directors, officers, employees, and agents. To hold a corporation liable for these actions, the government must establish that the corporate agent's actions (i) were within the scope of his duties and (ii) were intended, at least in part, to benefit the corporation. In all cases involving wrongdoing by corporate agents, prosecutors should consider the corporation, as well as the responsible individuals, as potential criminal targets.

Agents, however, may act for mixed reasons—both for self-aggrandizement (both direct and indirect) and for the benefit of the corporation, and a corporation may be held liable as long as one motivation of its agent is to benefit the corporation. In *United States v. Automated Medical Laboratories*, 770 F.2d 399 (4th Cir. 1985), the court affirmed the corporation's conviction for the actions of a subsidiary's employee despite its claim that the employee was acting for his own benefit, namely his "ambitious nature and his desire to ascend the corporate ladder." The court stated, "Partucci was clearly acting in part to benefit AML since his advancement within the corporation depended on AML's well-being and its lack of difficulties with the FDA." Similarly, in *United States v. Cincotta*, 689 F.2d 238, 241–42 (1st Cir. 1982), the court held, "criminal liability may be imposed on the corporation only where the agent is acting within the scope of his employment. That, in turn, requires that the agent be performing acts of the kind which he is authorized to perform, and those acts must be motivated—at least in part—by an intent to benefit the corporation." Applying this test, the court upheld the corporation's conviction, notwithstanding the substantial personal benefit reaped by its miscreant agents, because the fraudulent scheme required money to pass through the corporation's treasury and the fraudulently obtained goods were resold to the corporation's customers in the corporation's name. As the court concluded, "Mystic—not the individual defendants—was making money by selling oil that it had not paid for."

Moreover, the corporation need not even necessarily profit from its agent's actions for it to be held liable. In *Automated Medical Laboratories,* the Fourth Circuit stated:

> [B]enefit is not a "touchstone of criminal corporate liability; benefit at best is an evidential, not an operative, fact." Thus, whether the agent's actions ultimately redounded to the benefit of the corporation is less significant than whether the agent acted with the intent to benefit the corporation. The basic purpose of requiring that an agent have acted with the intent to benefit the corporation, however, is to insulate the corporation from criminal liability for actions of its agents which be inimical to the interests of the corporation or which may have been undertaken solely to advance the interests of that agent or of a party other than the corporation.

770 F.2d at 407 (emphasis added; quoting *Old Monastery Co. v. United States,* 147 F.2d 905, 908 (4th Cir.), cert. denied, 326 U.S. 734 (1945)).

II. Charging a Corporation: Factors to Be Considered

A. General Principle: Generally, prosecutors should apply the same factors in determining whether to charge a corporation as they do with respect to individuals. See USAM § 9–27.220, et seq. Thus, the prosecutor should weigh all of the factors normally considered in the sound exercise of prosecutorial judgment: the sufficiency of the evidence; the Likelihood of success at trial,; the probable deterrent, rehabilitative, and other consequences of conviction; and the adequacy of noncriminal approaches. See id. However, due to the nature of the corporate "person," some additional factors are present. In conducting an investigation, determining whether to bring charges, and negotiating plea agreements, prosecutors should consider the following factors in reaching a decision as to the proper treatment of a corporate target:

1. the nature and seriousness of the offense, including the risk of harm to the public, and applicable policies and priorities, if any, governing the prosecution of corporations for particular categories of crime (see section III, infra);

2. the pervasiveness of wrongdoing within the corporation, including the complicity in, or condonation of, the wrongdoing by corporate management (see section IV, infra);

3. the corporation's history of similar conduct, including prior criminal, civil, and regulatory enforcement actions against it (see section V, infra);

4. the corporation's timely and voluntary disclosure of wrongdoing and its willingness to cooperate in the investigation of its agents, including, if necessary, the waiver of corporate attorney-client and work product protection (see section VI, infra);

5. the existence and adequacy of the corporation's compliance program (see section VII, infra);

6. the corporation's remedial actions, including any efforts to implement an effective corporate compliance program or to improve an existing one, to replace responsible management, to discipline or terminate wrongdoers, to pay restitution, and to cooperate with the relevant government agencies (see section VIII, infra);

7. collateral consequences, including disproportionate harm to shareholders, pension holders and employees not proven personally culpable and impact on the public arising from the prosecution (see section IX, infra); and

8. the adequacy of the prosecution of individuals responsible for the corporation's malfeasance;

9. the adequacy of remedies such as civil or regulatory enforcement actions (see section X, infra).

B. Comment: As with the factors relevant to charging natural persons, the foregoing factors are intended to provide guidance rather than to mandate a particular result. The factors listed in this section are intended to be illustrative of those that should be considered and not a complete or exhaustive list. Some or all of these factors may or may not apply to specific cases, and in some cases one factor may override all others. The nature and seriousness of the offense may be such as to warrant prosecution regardless of the other factors. Further, national law enforcement policies in various enforcement areas may require that more or less weight be given to certain of these factors than to others.

In making a decision to charge a corporation, the prosecutor generally has wide latitude in determining when, whom, how, and even whether to prosecute for violations of Federal criminal law. In exercising that discretion, prosecutors should consider the following general statements of principles that summarize appropriate considerations to be weighed and desirable practices to be followed in discharging their prosecutorial responsibilities. In doing so, prosecutors should ensure that the general purposes of the criminal law—assurance of warranted punishment, deterrence of further criminal conduct, protection of the public from dangerous and fraudulent conduct, rehabilitation of offenders, and restitution for victims and affected communities—are adequately met, taking into account the special nature of the corporate "person."

III. Charging a Corporation: Special Policy Concerns

A. General Principle: The nature and seriousness of the crime, including the risk of harm to the public from the criminal conduct, are obviously primary factors in determining whether to charge a corporation. In addition, corporate conduct, particularly that of national and multi-national corporations, necessarily intersects with federal economic, taxation, and criminal law enforcement policies. In applying these principles, prosecutors must consider the practices and policies of the appropriate Division of the Department, and must comply with those policies to the extent required.

B. Comment: In determining whether to charge a corporation, prosecutors should take into account federal law enforcement priorities as discussed above. See USAM § 9–27–230. In addition, however, prosecutors must be aware of the specific policy goals and incentive programs established by the respective Divisions and regulatory agencies. Thus, whereas natural persons may be given incremental degrees of credit (ranging from immunity to lesser charges to sentencing considerations) for turning themselves in, making statements against their penal interest, and cooperating in the government's investigation of their own and others' wrongdoing, the same approach may not be appropriate in all circumstances with respect to corporations. As an example, it is entirely proper in many investigations for a prosecutor to consider the corporation's pre-indictment conduct, e.g., voluntary disclosure, cooperation, remediation or restitution, in determining whether to seek an indictment. However, this would not necessarily be appropriate in an antitrust investigation, in which antitrust violations, by definition, go to the heart of the corporation's business and for which the Antitrust Division has therefore established a firm policy, understood in the business community, that credit should not be given at the charging stage for a compliance program and that amnesty is available only to the first corporation to make full disclosure to the government. As another example, the Tax Division has a strong preference for prosecuting responsible individuals, rather than entities, for corporate tax offenses. Thus, in determining whether or not to charge a corporation, prosecutors should consult with the Criminal, Antitrust, Tax, and Environmental and Natural Resources Divisions, if appropriate or required.

IV. Charging a Corporation: Pervasiveness of Wrongdoing Within the Corporation

A. General Principle: A corporation can only act through natural persons, and it is therefore held responsible for the acts of such persons fairly attributable to it. Charging a corporation for even minor misconduct may be appropriate where the wrongdoing was pervasive and was undertaken by a large number of employees or by all the employees in a particular role within the corporation, e.g., salesmen or procurement officers, or was condoned by upper management. On the other hand, in certain limited circumstances, it may not be appropriate to impose liability upon a corporation, particularly one with a compliance program in place, under a strict respondeat superior theory for the single isolated act of a rogue employee. There is, of course, a wide spectrum between these two extremes, and a prosecutor should exercise sound discretion in evaluating the pervasiveness of wrongdoing within a corporation.

B. Comment: Of these factors, the most important is the role of management. Although acts of even low-level employees may result in criminal liability, a corporation is directed by its management and management is responsible for a corporate culture in which criminal conduct is either discouraged or tacitly encouraged. As stated in commentary to the Sentencing Guidelines:

> Pervasiveness [is] case specific and [will] depend on the number, and degree of responsibility, of individuals [with] substantial authority . . . who participated in, condoned, or were willfully ignorant of the offense. Fewer individuals need to be involved for a finding of pervasiveness if those individuals exercised a relatively high degree of authority. Pervasiveness can occur either within an

organization as a whole or within a unit of an organization. USSG §8C2.5, comment. (n. 4).

V. Charging a Corporation: The Corporation's Past History

A. General Principle: Prosecutors may consider a corporation's history of similar conduct, including prior criminal, civil, and regulatory enforcement actions against it, in determining whether to bring criminal charges.

B. Comment: A corporation, like a natural person, is expected to learn from its mistakes. A history of similar conduct may be probative of a corporate culture that encouraged, or at least condoned, such conduct, regardless of any compliance programs. Criminal prosecution of a corporation may be particularly appropriate where the corporation previously had been subject to non-criminal guidance, warnings, or sanctions, or previous criminal charges, and yet it either had not taken adequate action to prevent future unlawful conduct or had continued to engage in the conduct in spite of the warnings or enforcement actions taken against it. In making this determination, the corporate structure itself, e.g., subsidiaries or operating divisions, should be ignored, and enforcement actions taken against the corporation or any of its divisions, subsidiaries, and affiliates should be considered. See USSG § 8C2.5(c) & comment. (n. 6).

VI. Charging a Corporation: Cooperation and Voluntary Disclosure

A. General Principle: In determining whether to charge a corporation, that corporation's timely and voluntary disclosure of wrongdoing and its willingness to cooperate with the government's investigation may be relevant factors. In gauging the extent of the corporation's cooperation, the prosecutor may consider the corporation's willingness to identify the culprits within the corporation, including senior executives; to make witnesses available; to disclose the complete results of its internal investigation; and to waive attorney-client and work product protection.

B. Comment: In investigating wrongdoing by or within a corporation, a prosecutor is likely to encounter several obstacles resulting from the nature of the corporation itself. It will often be difficult to determine which individual took which action on behalf of the corporation. Lines of authority and responsibility may be shared among operating divisions or departments, and records and personnel may be spread throughout the United States or even among several countries. Where the criminal conduct continued over an extended period of time, the culpable or knowledgeable personnel may have been promoted, transferred, or fired, or they may have quit or retired. Accordingly, a corporation's cooperation may be critical in identifying the culprits and locating relevant evidence.

In some circumstances, therefore, granting a corporation immunity or amnesty or pretrial diversion may be considered in the course of the government's investigation. In such circumstances, prosecutors should refer to the principles governing non-prosecution agreements generally. See USAM § 9–27.600–650. These principles permit a non prosecution agreement in exchange for cooperation when a corporation's "timely cooperation appears to be necessary to the public interest and other means of obtaining the desired cooperation are unavailable or would not be effective." Prosecutors should note that in the case of national or multinational corporations, multi-district or global agreements may be necessary. Such agreements may only be entered into with the approval of each affected district or the appropriate Department official. See USAM §9–27.641. In addition, the Department, in conjunction with regulatory agencies and other executive branch departments, encourages corporations, as part of their compliance programs, to conduct internal investigations and to disclose their findings to the appropriate authorities. Some agencies, such as the SEC and the EPA, as well as the Department's Environmental and Natural Resources Division, have formal voluntary disclosure programs in which self-reporting, coupled with remediation and additional criteria, may qualify the corporation for amnesty or reduced sanctions.[2] Even in the absence of a formal program, prosecutors may consider a corporation's timely and voluntary disclosure in evaluating the adequacy of the corporation's compliance program and its management's commitment to the compliance program. However, prosecution and economic policies specific to the industry or statute may require prosecution notwithstanding a corporation's willingness to cooperate. For example, the Antitrust Division offers amnesty only to the first corporation to agree to cooperate. This creates a strong incentive for corporations participating in anti-competitive conduct to be the first to cooperate. In addition, amnesty, immunity, or reduced sanctions may not be appropriate where the corporation's business is permeated with fraud or other crimes.

One factor the prosecutor may weigh in assessing the adequacy of a corporation's cooperation is the completeness of its disclosure including, if necessary, a waiver of the attorney-client and work product protections, both with respect to its internal investigation and with respect to communications between specific officers, directors and employees and counsel. Such waivers permit the government to obtain statements of possible witnesses, subjects, and targets, without having to negotiate individual co-operation or immunity agreements. In addition, they are often critical in enabling the government to evaluate the completeness of a corporation's voluntary disclosure and cooperation. Prosecutors may, therefore, request a waiver in appropriate circumstances.[3] The Department does not, how-ever, consider waiver of a corporation's attorney-client and work product protection an absolute requirement, and prosecutors should consider the willingness of a corporation to waive such protection when necessary to provide timely and complete information as one factor in evaluating the corporation's cooperation.

Another factor to be weighed by the prosecutor is whether the cor-poration appears to be protecting its culpable employees and agents. Thus, while cases will differ depending on the circumstances, a corporation's promise of support to culpable employees and agents, either through the advancing of attorneys fees,[4] through retaining the employees without sanction for their misconduct, or through providing information to the employees about the government's investigation pursuant to a joint de-fense agreement, may be considered by the prosecutor in weighing the extent and value of a corporation's cooperation. By the same token, the prosecutor should be wary of attempts to shield corporate officers and employees from liability by a willingness of the corporation to plead guilty.

Another factor to be weighed by the prosecutor is whether the cor-poration, while purporting to cooperate, has engaged in conduct that im-pedes the investigation (whether or not rising to the level of criminal obstruction). Examples of such conduct include: overly broad assertions of corporate representation of employees or former employees; inap-propriate directions to employees or their counsel, such as directions not to cooperate openly and fully with the investigation including, for exam-ple, the direction to decline to be interviewed; making presentations or submissions that contain misleading assertions or omissions; incomplete or delayed production of records; and failure to promptly disclose illegal conduct known to the corporation.

Finally, a corporation's offer of cooperation does not automatically entitle it to immunity from prosecution. A corporation should not be able to escape liability merely by offering up its directors, officers, employees, or agents as in lieu of its own prosecution. Thus, a corporation's willingness to cooperate is merely one relevant factor, that needs to be considered in conjunction with the other factors, particularly those relating to the cor-poration's past history and the role of management in the wrongdoing.

VII. Charging a Corporation: Corporate Compliance Programs

A. General Principle: Compliance programs are established by corporate management to prevent and to detect misconduct and to ensure that corporate activities are conducted in accordance with all applicable criminal and civil laws, regulations, and rules. The Department encourages such corporate self-policing, including voluntary disclosures to the government of any problems that a corporation discovers on its own. However, the existence of a compliance program is not sufficient, in and of itself, to justify not charging a corporation for criminal conduct undertaken by its officers, directors, employees, or agents. Indeed, the commission of such crimes in the face of a compliance program may suggest that the corporate management is not adequately enforcing its program. In addition, the nature of some crimes, e.g., antitrust violations, may be such that national law enforcement policies mandate prosecutions of corporations notwithstanding the existence of a compliance program.

B. Comment: A corporate compliance program, even one specifically prohibiting the very conduct in question, does not absolve the corporation from criminal liability under the doctrine of respondeat superior. See *United States v. Basic Construction Co.,* 711 F.2d 570 (4th Cir. 1983) ("a corporation may be held criminally responsible for antitrust violations committed by its employees if they were acting within the scope of their authority, or apparent authority, and for the benefit of the corporation, even if. such acts were against corporate policy or express instructions."). In *United States v. Hilton Hotels Corp.,* 467 F.2d 1000 (9th Cir. 1972), *cert. denied,* 409 U.S. 1125 (1973), the Ninth Circuit affirmed antitrust liability based upon a purchasing agent for a single hotel threatening a single supplier with a boycott unless it paid dues to a local marketing association, even though the agent's actions were contrary to corporate policy and directly against express instructions from his superiors. The court reasoned that Congress, in enacting the Sherman Antitrust Act, "intended to impose liability upon business entities for the acts of those to whom they choose to delegate the conduct of their affairs, thus stimulating a maximum effort by owners and managers to assure adherence by such agents to the requirements of the Act."[5] It concluded that "general policy statements" and even direct instructions from the agent's superiors were not sufficient; "Appellant could not gain exculpation by issuing general instructions without undertaking to enforce those instructions by means commensurate with the obvious risks." *See also United States v. Beusch,* 596 F.2d 871, 878 (9th Cir. 1979) ("[A] corporation may be liable for the acts of its employees done contrary to express instructions and policies, but . the existence of such instructions and policies may be considered in determining whether the employee in fact acted to benefit the corporation."); *United States v. American Radiator & Standard Sanitary Corp.*, 433 F.2d 174 (3rd Cir. 1970) (affirming conviction of corporation based upon its officer's participation in price-fixing scheme, despite corporation's defense that officer's conduct violated its "rigid anti-fraternization policy" against any socialization (and exchange of price information) with its competitors; "When the act of the agent is within the scope of his employment or his apparent authority, the corporation is held legally responsible for it, although what he did may be contrary to his actual instructions and may be unlawful.").

While the Department recognizes that no compliance program can ever prevent all criminal activity by a corporation's employees, the critical factors in evaluating any program are whether the program is adequately designed for maximum effectiveness in preventing and detecting wrongdoing by employees and whether corporate management is enforcing the program or is tacitly encouraging or pressuring employees to engage in misconduct to achieve business objectives. The Department has no formal guidelines for corporate compliance programs. The fundamental questions any prosecutor should ask are: "Is the corporation's compliance program well designed?" and "Does the corporation's compliance program work?" In answering these questions, the prosecutor should consider the comprehensiveness of the compliance program; the extent and pervasiveness of the criminal conduct; the number and level of the corporate employees involved; the seriousness, duration, and frequency of the misconduct; and any remedial actions taken by the corporation, including restitution, disciplinary action, and revisions to corporate compliance programs.[6] Prosecutors should also consider the promptness of any disclosure of wrongdoing to the government and the corporation's cooperation in the government's investigation. In evaluating compliance programs, prosecutors may consider whether the corporation has established corporate governance mechanisms that can effectively detect and prevent misconduct. For example, do the corporation's directors exercise independent review over proposed corporate actions rather than unquestioningly ratifying officers' recommendations; are the directors provided with information sufficient to enable the exercise of independent judgment, are internal audit functions conducted at a level sufficient to ensure their independence and accuracy and have the directors established an information and reporting system in the organization reasonable designed to provide management and the board of directors with timely and accurate information sufficient to allow them to reach an informed decision regarding the organization's compliance with the law. *In re: Caremark*, 698 A.2d 959 (Del. Ct. Chan. 1996).

Prosecutors should therefore attempt to determine whether a corporation's compliance program is merely a "paper program" or whether it was designed and implemented in an effective manner. In addition, prosecutors should determine whether the corporation has provided for a staff sufficient to audit, document, analyze, and utilize the results of the corporation's compliance efforts. In addition, prosecutors should determine whether the corporation's employees are adequately informed about the compliance program and are convinced of the corporation's commitment to it. This will enable the prosecutor to make an informed decision as to whether the corporation has adopted and implemented a truly effective compliance program that, when consistent with other federal law enforcement policies, may result in a decision to charge only the corporation's employees and agents.

Compliance programs should be designed to detect the particular types of misconduct most likely to occur in a particular corporation's line of business. Many corporations operate in complex regulatory environments outside the normal experience of criminal prosecutors. Accordingly, prosecutors should consult with relevant federal and state agencies with the expertise to evaluate the adequacy of a program's design and implementation. For instance, state and federal banking, insurance, and medical boards, the Department of Defense, the Department of Health and Human Services, the Environmental Protection Agency, and the Securities and Exchange Commission have considerable experience with compliance programs and can be very helpful to a prosecutor in evaluating such programs. In addition, the Fraud Section of the Criminal Division, the Commercial Litigation Branch of the Civil Division, and the Environmental Crimes Section of the Environment and Natural Resources Division can assist U.S. Attorneys' Offices in finding the appropriate agency office and in providing copies of compliance programs that were developed in previous cases.

VIII. Charging a Corporation: Restitution and Remediation

A. General Principle: Although neither a corporation nor an individual target may avoid prosecution merely by paying a sum of money, a prosecutor may consider the corporation's willingness to make restitution and steps already taken to do so. A prosecutor may also consider other remedial actions, such as implementing an effective corporate compliance program, improving an existing compliance program, and disciplining wrongdoers, in determining whether to charge the corporation.

B. Comment: In determining whether or not a corporation should be prosecuted, a prosecutor may consider whether meaningful remedial

measures have been taken, including employee discipline and full restitution.[7] A corporation's response to misconduct says much about its
willingness to ensure that such misconduct does not recur. Thus, corporations that fully recognize the seriousness of their misconduct and accept
responsibility for it should be taking steps to implement the personnel,
operational, and organizational changes necessary to establish an awareness among employees that criminal conduct will not be tolerated. Among
the factors prosecutors should consider and weigh are whether the corporation appropriately disciplined the wrongdoers and disclosed information concerning their illegal conduct to the government.

Employee discipline is a difficult task for many corporations because
of the human element involved and sometimes because of the seniority of
the employees concerned. While corporations need to be fair to their employees, they must also be unequivocally committed, at all levels of the corporation, to the highest standards of legal and ethical behavior. Effective
internal discipline can be a powerful deterrent against improper behavior by a corporation's employees. In evaluating a corporation's response
to wrongdoing, prosecutors may evaluate the willingness of the corporation to discipline culpable employees of all ranks and the adequacy of the
discipline imposed. The prosecutor should be satisfied that the corporation's focus is on the integrity and credibility of its remedial and disciplinary measures rather than on the protection of the wrongdoers.

In addition to employee discipline, two other factors used in evaluating a corporation's remedial efforts are restitution and reform. As with
natural persons, the decision whether or not to prosecute should not depend upon the target's ability to pay restitution. A corporation's efforts
to pay restitution even in advance of any court order is, however, evidence
of its "acceptance of responsibility" and, consistent with the practices and
policies of the appropriate Division of the Department entrusted with enforcing specific criminal laws, may be considered in determining whether
to bring criminal charges. Similarly, although the inadequacy of a corporate compliance program is a factor to consider when deciding whether
to charge a corporation, that corporation's quick recognition of the flaws
in the program and its efforts to improve the program are also factors to
consider.

IX. Charging a Corporation: Collateral Consequences

A. General Principle: Prosecutors may consider the collateral consequences of a corporate criminal conviction in determining whether to
charge the corporation with a criminal offense.

B. Comment: One of the factors in determining whether to charge a natural person or a corporation is whether the likely punishment is appropriate given the nature and seriousness of the crime. In the corporate context, prosecutors may take into account the possibly substantial consequences to a corporation's officers, directors, employees, and shareholders, many of whom may, depending on the size and nature (e.g., publicly vs. closely held) of the corporation and their role in its operations, have played no role in the criminal conduct, have been completely unaware of it, or have been wholly unable to prevent it. Prosecutors should also be aware of non-penal sanctions that may accompany a criminal charge, such as potential suspension or debarment from eligibility for government contracts or federal funded programs such as health care. Whether or not such non-penal sanctions are appropriate or required in a particular case is the responsibility of the relevant agency, a decision that will be made based on the applicable statutes, regulations, and policies.

Virtually every conviction of a corporation, like virtually every conviction of an individual, will have an impact on innocent third parties, and the mere existence of such an effect is not sufficient to preclude prosecution of the corporation. Therefore, in evaluating the severity of collateral consequences, various factors already discussed, such as the pervasiveness of the criminal conduct and the adequacy of the corporation's compliance programs, should be considered in determining the weight to be given to this factor. For instance, the balance may tip in favor of prosecuting corporations in situations where the scope of the misconduct in a case is widespread and sustained within a corporate division (or spread throughout pockets of the corporate organization). In such cases, the possible unfairness of visiting punishment for the corporation's crimes upon shareholders may be of much less concern where those shareholders have substantially profited, even unknowingly, from widespread or pervasive criminal activity. Similarly, where the top layers of the corporation's management or the shareholders of a closely-held corporation were engaged in or aware of the wrongdoing and the conduct at issue was accepted as a way of doing business for an extended period, debarment may be deemed not collateral, but a direct and entirely appropriate consequence of the corporation's wrongdoing.

The appropriateness of considering such collateral consequences and the weight to be given them may depend on the special policy concerns discussed in section III, supra.

X. Charging a Corporation: Non-Criminal Alternatives

A. General Principle: Although non-criminal alternatives to prosecution often exist, prosecutors may consider whether such sanctions would adequately deter, punish, and rehabilitate a corporation that has engaged in wrongful conduct. In evaluating the adequacy of non-criminal alternatives to prosecution, e.g., civil or regulatory enforcement actions, the prosecutor may consider all relevant factors, including:

1. the sanctions available under the alternative means of disposition;
2. the likelihood that an effective sanction will be imposed; and
3. the effect of non-criminal disposition on Federal law enforcement interests.

B. Comment: The primary goals of criminal law are deterrence, punishment, and rehabilitation. Non-criminal sanctions may not be an appropriate response to an egregious violation, a pattern of wrongdoing, or a history of non-criminal sanctions without proper remediation. In other cases, however, these goals may be satisfied without the necessity of instituting criminal proceedings. In determining whether federal criminal charges are appropriate, the prosecutor should consider the same factors (modified appropriately for the regulatory context) considered when determining whether to leave prosecution of a natural person to another jurisdiction or to seek non-criminal alternatives to prosecution. These factors include: the strength of the regulatory authority's interest; the regulatory authority's ability and willingness to take effective enforcement action; the probable sanction if the regulatory authority's enforcement action is upheld; and the effect of a non-criminal disposition on Federal law enforcement interests. See USAM §§ 9–27.240, 9–27.250.

XI. Charging a Corporation: Selecting Charges

A. General Principle: Once a prosecutor has decided to charge a corporation, the prosecutor should charge, or should recommend that the grand jury charge, the most serious offense that is consistent with the nature of the defendant's conduct and that is likely to result in a sustainable conviction.

B. Comment: Once the decision to charge is made, the same rules as govern charging natural persons apply. These rules require "a faithful and honest application of the Sentencing Guidelines" and an "individualized assessment of the extent to which particular charges fit the specific circumstances of the case, are consistent with the purposes of the Federal

criminal code, and maximize the impact of Federal resources on crime."
See USAM § 9–27.300. In making this determination, "it is appropriate
that the attorney for the government consider, *inter alia,* such factors
as the sentencing guideline range yielded by the charge, whether the
penalty yielded by such sentencing range . is proportional to the seriousness of the defendant's conduct, and whether the charge achieves
such purposes of the criminal law as punishment, protection of the public, specific and general deterrence, and rehabilitation." See Attorney
General's Memorandum, dated October 12, 1993.

XII. Plea Agreements with Corporations

A. General Principle: In negotiating plea agreements with corporations,
prosecutors should seek a plea to the most serious, readily provable offense
charged. In addition, the terms of the plea agreement should contain appropriate provisions to ensure punishment, deterrence, rehabilitation,
and compliance with the plea agreement in the corporate context. Although special circumstances may mandate a different conclusion, prosecutors generally should not agree to accept a corporate guilty plea in
exchange for non-prosecution or dismissal of charges against individual
officers and employees.

B. Comment: Prosecutors may enter into plea agreements with corporations for the same reasons and under the same constraints as apply to plea
agreements with natural persons. See USAM §§ 9–27.400–500. This means,
inter alia, that the corporation should be required to plead guilty to the
most serious, readily provable offense charged. As is the case with individuals, the attorney making this determination should do so "on the basis
of an individualized assessment of the extent to which particular charges fit
the specific circumstances of the case, are consistent with the purposes of
the federal criminal code, and maximize the impact of federal resources
on crime. In making this determination, the attorney for the government
considers, *inter alia,* such factors as the sentencing guideline range yielded
by the charge, whether the penalty yielded by such sentencing range . . .
is proportional to the seriousness of the defendant's conduct, and whether
the charge achieves such purposes of the criminal law as punishment,
protection of the public, specific and general deterrence, and rehabilitation." See Attorney General's Memorandum, dated October 12, 1993.
In addition, any negotiated departures from the Sentencing Guidelines
must be justifiable under the Guidelines and must be disclosed to the sentencing court. A corporation should be made to realize that pleading
guilty to criminal charges constitutes an admission of guilt and not merely

a resolution of an inconvenient distraction from its business. As with natural persons, pleas should be structured so that the corporation may not later "proclaim lack of culpability or even complete innocence." See USAM §§ 9–27.420(b)(4), 9–27.440, 9–27.500. Thus, for instance, there should be placed upon the record a sufficient factual basis for the plea to prevent later corporate assertions of innocence.

A corporate plea agreement should also contain provisions that recognize the nature of the corporate "person" and ensure that the principles of punishment, deterrence, and rehabilitation are met. In the corporate context, punishment and deterrence are generally accomplished by substantial fines, mandatory restitution, and institution of appropriate compliance measures, including, if necessary, continued judicial oversight or the use of special masters. See USSG §§ 8B1.1, 8C2.1, et seq. In addition, where the corporation is a government contractor, permanent or temporary debarment may be appropriate. Where the corporation was engaged in government contracting fraud, a prosecutor may not negotiate away an agency's right to debar or to list the corporate defendant.

In negotiating a plea agreement, prosecutors should also consider the deterrent value of prosecutions of individuals within the corporation. Therefore, one factor that a prosecutor may consider in determining whether to enter into a plea agreement is whether the corporation is seeking immunity for its employees and officers or whether the corporation is willing to cooperate in the investigation of culpable individuals. Prosecutors should rarely negotiate away individual criminal liability in a corporate plea.

Rehabilitation, of course, requires that the corporation undertake to be law-abiding in the future. It is, therefore, appropriate to require the corporation, as a condition of probation, to implement a compliance program or to reform an existing one. As discussed above, prosecutors may consult with the appropriate state and federal agencies and components of the Justice Department to ensure that a proposed compliance program is adequate and meets industry standards and best practices. See section VII, supra.

In plea agreements in which the corporation agrees to cooperate, the prosecutor should ensure that the cooperation is complete and truthful. To do so, the prosecutor may request that the corporation waive attorney-client and work product protection, make employees and agents available for debriefing, disclose the results of its internal investigation, file appropriate certified financial statements, agree to governmental or third-party audits, and take whatever other steps are necessary to ensure that the full scope of the corporate wrongdoing is disclosed and that the responsible culprits are identified and, if appropriate, prosecuted. See generally section VIII, supra.

February 2003 Criminal Resource Manual 162

Notes
1. While these guidelines refer to corporations, they apply to the consideration of the prosecution of all types of business organizations, including partnerships, sole proprietorships, government entities, and unincorporated associations.
2. In addition, the Sentencing Guidelines reward voluntary disclosure and cooperation with a reduction in the corporation's offense level. See USSG §8C2.5)g).
3. This waiver should ordinarily be limited to the factual internal investigation and any contemporaneous advice given to the corporation concerning the conduct at issue. Except in unusual circumstances, prosecutors should not seek a waiver with respect to communications and work product related to advice concerning the government's criminal investigation.
4. Some states require corporations to pay the legal fees of officers under investigation prior to a formal determination of their guilt. Obviously, a corporation's compliance with governing law should not be considered a failure to cooperate.
5. Although this case and Basic Construction are both antitrust cases, their reasoning applies to other criminal violations. In the Hilton case, for instance, the Ninth Circuit noted that Sherman Act violations are commercial offenses "usually motivated by a desire to enhance profits," thus, bringing the case within the normal rule that a "purpose to benefit the corporation is necessary to bring the agent's acts within the scope of his employment." 467 F.2d at 1006 & n4. In addition, in *United States v. Automated Medical Laboratories*, 770 F.2d 399, 406 n.5 (4th Cir. 1985), the Fourth Circuit stated "that Basic Construction states a generally applicable rule on corporate criminal liability despite the fact that it addresses violations of the antitrust laws."
6. For a detailed review of these and other factors concerning corporate compliance programs, see United States Sentencing Commission, GUIDELINES MANUAL, §8A1.2, comment. (n.3(k)) (Nov. 1997). See also USSG §8C2.5(f).
7. For example, the Antitrust Division's amnesty policy requires that "[w]here possible, the corporation [make] restitution to injured parties. . . . "

BIBLIOGRAPHY

Chapter 1

American Corporate Counsel Association. *In-House Counsel for the 21st Century,* 2001. Available online: http://www.acca.com/Surveys/CEO/. Access date: Oct. 28, 2005.

Flaherty, C. "Bottom Line." *Corporate Legal Times,* Oct. 2005, pp. 48–53.

Heidrick & Struggles International, Inc., and The Minority Corporate Counsel Association. *The Fortune 500 CEO Survey on General Counsels,* Apr. 2000. San Francisco: Heidrick & Struggles International, 2000.

Monty, L. L. "Creating a Compliance Culture in the Workplace." *Preventive Law Reporter,* 1994, *13*(4), 19–21.

Porter, M. "How Information Gives You Competitive Advantage." *Harvard Business Review,* 1985, *63*(3), 149–160.

"Quotation of the Day: Mike D'Angelo, jury foreman, on convicting A. Alfred Taubman of price fixing." *New York Times,* Dec. 6, 2001, p. A2.

Chapter 2

Adamson, J. *The Denny's Story: How a Company in Crisis Resurrected Its Good Name.* New York: Wiley, 2000.

Armstrong, J. S. Letter to the Editor. *Wall Street Journal,* Oct. 11, 2004.

Bazerman, M., Loewenstein, G. and Moore, D., "Why Good Accountants Do Bad Audits." *Harvard Business Review,* 2002, *80*(11), 96–102.

Fox, C., and Tversky, A. "Ambiguity and Comparative Ignorance." *Quarterly Journal of Economics,* 1995, *110*(3), 585–603.

Grimshaw v. Ford Motor Co. 119 Cal. App. 3d 757, 174 Cal. Rptr. 348 (Cal. App. 1981).

Heath, F., and Tversky, A. "Preference and Belief: Ambiguity and Competence in Choice Under Uncertainty." *Journal of Risk and Uncertainty,* 1991, *4*, 5–28.

Jennings, M. *Business: Its Legal, Ethical, and Global Environment.* Mason, Ohio: Thomson South-Western West, 2003.

Kahneman, D., Slovic, P., and Tversky, A. (Eds.), *Judgment and Uncertainty: Heuristics and Biases.* Cambridge, England: Cambridge University Press, 1982.

Kahneman, D., and Tversky, A. "Prospect Theory: An Analysis of Decision Under Risk." *Econometrica*, 1979, *47*, 263–291.

Martinez, B., and Lublin, J. "Why a Lawman Wields Authority Over Drug Maker." *Wall Street Journal*, June 20, 2005, p. B1.

Slovic, P., Fishhoff, B., and Lichtenstein, S. "Facts Versus Fears: Understanding Perceived Risk." In D. Kahneman, P. Slovic, and A. Tversky (Eds.), *Judgment and Uncertainty: Heuristics and Biases*. Cambridge, England: Cambridge University Press, 1982.

Stewart, J. B. *Den of Thieves*. New York: Simon & Schuster, 1991.

Tversky, A., and Kahneman, D. "Availability: A Heuristic for Judging Frequency and Probability." In D. Kahneman, P. Slovic, and A. Tversky (Eds.), *Judgment and Uncertainty: Heuristics and Biases*. Cambridge: Cambridge University Press, 1982.

Tversky, A., and Koehler, D. "Support Theory: A Nonextensional Representation of Subjective Probability." *Psychological Review*, 1994, *101*(4), 547–567.

Watkins, M., and Bazerman, M. "Predictable Surprises: The Disasters You Should Have Seen Coming." *Harvard Business Review*, 2003, *81*(3), 72–80.

Chapter 3

Coleman Parent Holdings v. Morgan Stanley, No. 2003 CA 005045 (Palm Beach Co. Cir. Ct. 2005).

Davidoff, G. "Jurors Distrust Corporate America." *Chief Legal Executive*, Winter 2003, p. 12.

Drucker, P. *The Practice of Management*. New York: HarperCollins, 1954.

Federal Trade Commission. *Online Profiling: A Report to Congress, Part 2 Recommendations*. Washington, D.C.: Government Printing Office, 2000.

France, M. "The Litigation Machine." *Business Week*, Jan. 29, 2001, pp. 114–123.

Himelstein, L. "Should Business Be Afraid of Juries." *Business Week*, Nov. 8, 1993, pp. 100–101.

"Juror Perception Survey Shows Distrust of Corporations." *ACCA Docket*, 2003, *21*(2), 12.

Loomis, T. "Scandals Rock Juror Attitudes." *National Law Journal*, Oct. 21, 2002, p. A30.

Orey, M. "Lawyers Find Jury Pools Polluted by Antibusiness Biases." *Wall Street Journal*, Aug. 12, 2002, p. B1.

Pulliam, S. "At Center of Fraud, WorldCom Official Sees Life Unravel." *Wall Street Journal*, Mar. 24, 2005, p. A1.

Van Voris, B. "Jurors Negative About Business." *National Law Journal*, Nov. 20, 2000, p. B1.

Yingshi, Y. "State Rules to Elevate Lift Safety." *China Daily*, May 4, 1995, p. 2.

Zubelake v. USB Warburg LLC, 220 R.F.D. 212, 2003 U.S. Dist. LEXIS 18771 (S.D.N.Y., October 22, 2003), *sanctions allowed* 2004 U.D. Dist. LEXIS 13574 (S.D.N.Y., July 20, 2003).

Chapter 4

Barber, F., and Strack, R. "The Surprising Economics of a 'People Business.'" *Harvard Business Review,* 2005, *83*(6), 80–90.

Baum, H. *The Transparent Leader.* New York: HarperCollins, 2004.

Berenson, A. "Merck Offering Top Executives Rich Way Out." *New York Times,* Nov. 30, 2004, p. A1.

Berenson, A. "The Nation: Oversight; The Biggest Casualty of Enron's Collapse: Confidence." *New York Times,* Feb. 10, 2002, Sec. 4, p. 1.

Brown, K. C. "The Value of a Good Reputation." *Chief Legal Executive,* Spring 2003, p. 14.

Covey, S. R. *The 7 Habits of Highly Effective People.* New York: Simon & Schuster, 1989.

Drucker, P. *The Practice of Management.* New York: HarperCollins, 1954.

Dumaine, B. "Mr. Learning Organization." *Fortune,* 1994, *130*(8), 147–152.

Fitz-enz, J. *The ROI of Human Capital.* New York: AMACOM, 2000.

Godin, S. *Wisdom, Inc.* New York: HarperBusiness, 1995.

Kaplan, R. "Corporate Value Creation: Integrating Intangible Assets and Regulatory Processes." (Lecture, Cornell University, Ithaca, N.Y., Nov. 11, 2003).

Kaplan, R. and Norton, D. *Strategy Maps.* Boston: Harvard Business School Press, 2004.

Martel, L. *High Performers: How the Best Companies Find and Keep Them.* San Francisco: Jossey-Bass, 2002.

Michaels, E., Handfield-Jones, H., and Axelrod, B. *The War for Talent.* Boston: Harvard Business School Press, 2002.

Morgan, N. "How to Overcome 'Change Fatigue.'" *Burning Questions 2001: A Special Report From Harvard Management Update,* July 2001, p. 1.

Nocera, J., and others. "System Failure." *Fortune,* June 24, 2002, p. 62.

Sharpe, R., Jr. "Taking Stock of Lawsuit Costs." *Chief Legal Executive,* Winter 2003, p. 20.

Simon, D. "Code of Conduct Training: Why Bother?" *Metropolitan Corporate Counsel,* June 2003, p. 37.

Thomas, L., Jr. "Another Top Executive to Leave Morgan Stanley." *New York Times,* May 24, 2005, p. C8.

Chapter 5

Brown, L., Kandel, A., and Gruner, R. *The Legal Audit*. St. Paul, Minn.: West Group, 1999.

Eichenwald, K. *Serpent on the Rock*. New York: HarperCollins, 1995.

Maitland, A. "GE Hotline Gives Workers Some Clout." *Financial Times*, May 19, 2005, p. 29.

Rivette, K., and Kline, D. *Rembrandts in the Attic*. Boston: Harvard Business School Press, 2000.

Senge, P. M. *The Fifth Discipline: The Art and Practice of the Learning Organization*. New York: Currency Doubleday, 1990.

Yoffie, D. B., and Kwak, M. *Judo Strategy*. Boston: Harvard Business School Press, 2001.

Chapter 6

Baldas, T. "New Data Used as Evidence." *National Law Journal*, Aug. 16, 2004, p. 1.

Dakin, S. (Ed.). *Skills for Practical Writing: A Workbook for Training in Work-Related Writing*. Chapel Hill: North Carolina Writers' Network, 1994.

Fox, A. T., Fertleman, M., Cahill, P., and Palmer, R. D. "Medical Slang in British Hospitals." *Journal of Ethics and Behavior,* 2003, *13*(2), 173–189.

Monty, L. L. "Creating a Compliance Culture in the Workplace." *Preventive Law Reporter,* 1994, *13*(4), 19–21.

Rambus Inc. v. Infineon Technologies AG, 220 F.R.D. 264 (E.D. Va., May 18, 2004).

Rooney, J. "Tylenol Settlement Based on Secrecy." *Chicago Daily Law Bulletin,* May 14, 1991, p. 1.

United States v. Philip Morris USA, 2005 U.S. Dist. LEXIS 5283 (D.D.C. March 25, 2005).

Wong, E. "A Stinging Office Memo Boomerangs." *New York Times,* Apr. 5, 2001, p. C1.

Yoffie, D. B., and Kwak, M. *Judo Strategy*. Boston: Harvard Business School Press, 2001.

Zubulake v. UBS Warburg LLC, 216 F.R.D. 280; 2003 U.S. Dist. LEXIS 12643 (S.D.N.Y., July 24, 2003) *aff'd* 2003 U.S. Dist. LEXIS 18771 (S.D.N.Y., Oct. 22, 2003).

Chapter 7

Arenson, K. "The Fine Art of Listening." *Education Life,* Jan. 13, 2002, p. 34.

Cialdini, R. "The Language of Persuasion." *Harvard Management Update,* 2004, *9*(9), 10–11.

Covey, S. R. *The 7 Habits of Highly Successful People.* New York: Simon & Schuster, 1989.

Fisher, R., and Ury, W. *Getting to Yes.* New York: Penguin Books, 1983.

Friedman, R. "Learning Words They Rarely Teach in Medical School: 'I'm Sorry'." *New York Times,* July 26, 2005, p. F5.

Gardner, E. "Older and Wiser." *Corporate Counsel,* 2004, *11*(6), 23–26.

Golann, D. *Mediating Legal Disputes.* New York: Aspen Law & Business, 1996.

Jerome, R., and Bane, V., "The Avenger: A Montana Woman Blows the Whistle on the Asbestos Mine That Killed Her Parents and Ravaged Her Town." *People,* Oct. 2, 2000, pp. 70–75.

Lind, E. A. "Litigation and Claiming in Organizations: Antisocial Behavior or Quest for Justice?" 1998. Available online: http://www.duke.edu/~alind/litagate.html. Access date: Oct. 28, 2005.

Maslow, A. H. *Toward a Psychology of Being,* 2nd ed. New York: Van Nostrand, 1968.

"Microsoft and Gateway to Settle Antitrust Suit." *New York Times,* Apr. 12, 2005, p. 7.

Nierenberg, G. I. *The Art of Negotiating.* New York: Cornerstone Library, 1968.

"Palm Handed Suit Over Colors," *Wired,* Aug. 24, 2002. Available online: http://www.wired.com/news/business/0,1367,54744,00.html. Access date: Oct. 28, 2005.

Salacuse, J. *The Global Negotiator: Making, Managing and Mending Deals Around the World in the Twenty-First Century.* New York: Palgrave Macmillan, 2003.

"Service, Not Suits." *National Law Journal,* May 14, 2001, p. B1.

Simons, J. A. *Psychology: The Search for Understanding.* New York: West, 1987.

"Tailhook: An Assistant Secretary's Message to the Fleet." *Ethikos,* 1994, *7*(6), 5–7.

Tanner, L. "Doctor Advised: An Apology a Day Keeps the Lawyer Away." Nov. 12, 2004. Available online: http://www.law.com. Registration required.

Zimmerman, R. "Doctors' New Tool to Fight Lawsuits: Saying 'I'm Sorry.'" *Wall Street Journal,* May 18, 2004, p. A1.

Chapter 8

Hammer, M., and Champy, J. *Reengineering the Corporation: A Manifesto for Business Revolution,* New York: HarperBusiness, 1993.

Kaplan, J. M. "Thinking Inside the Box: Risk Analysis in Three Dimensions." *Ethikos,* Sept./Oct. 2000, p. 1-3, 16.

Lisec v. United Airlines, 10 Cal. App. 4th 1500; 11 Cal. Rptr. 2d 689 (Ct. App. 1992), *aff'd* 1992 Cal. LEXIS 5753 (Cal. 1992).

Russo, J. E., and Schoemaker, P.J.H. *Winning Decisions.* New York: Currency Doubleday, 2002.

Weick, K. E., and Sutcliffe, K. M. *Managing the Unexpected.* San Francisco: Jossey-Bass, 2001.

Yoffie, D. B., and Kwak, M. "Playing by the Rules: How Intel Avoids Antitrust Litigation." *Harvard Business Review,* 2001, *79*(6), 119–122.

Chapter 9

Arthur Andersen LLP v. United States, 125 S.Ct. 2129, 161 L.Ed.2d 1008 (2005).

Burger, M. "From Metrics to Six Sigma." *Legal Times,* Aug. 21, 2000, p. 20.

Dietel, J. E. *Leaders' Digest: A Review of the Best Books on Leadership.* Chicago: American Bar Association, 1996.

Murray, S. "Bigger Profits Are the Prize for Education." *Financial Times,* Oct. 13, 2003, p. 7.

Parry, S. "Just What Is Competency? (And Why Should You Care?)" *Training,* 1998, *35*(6), 58–62.

Senge, P. M. *The Fifth Discipline: The Art and Practice of the Learning Organization.* New York: Currency Doubleday, 1990.

Singer, A. "GE Extends Its 'Quality' Effort to Compliance." *Ethikos,* 2001, *14*(4), 6–7.

Weidlich, T. "Miracle Gro-ing Compliance." *Corporate Counsel,* Mar. 2, 2004. Available online: http://www.law.com. Registration required.

Chapter 10

Baldas, T. "Big Business Turns to Plaintiffs Lawyers for Help." *National Law Journal,* July 17, 2005, p. 1.

Brown, L. *Manual of Preventive Law.* Upper Saddle River, N.J.: Prentice Hall, 1950.

Geyelin, M. "More Law Schools Are Teaching Students Value of Assuming Clients' Point of View." *Wall Street Journal,* Sept. 17, 1991, p. B1.

Hardaway, R. "Teaching Preventive Law." *Preventive Law Reporter,* 1997, *16*(4), 3–7, 36–39.

Krzyzewski, M. *Five-Point Play: Duke's Journey to the 2001 National Championship.* New York: Warner Books, 2001.

Lin, A. "Video Trains Lawyers Not to Be Boors." *Recorder,* Dec. 28, 2004, p. 1.

Prentice, R. "An Ethics Lesson for Business Schools." *New York Times,* Aug. 20, 2002, p. 19.

Raelin, J. A. *The Clash of Cultures: Managers and Professionals.* Boston: Harvard Business School Press, 1985.

Rivlin, G. "It's Not Google, It's That Other Big IPO." *New York Times,* May 9, 2004, Sec. 3, p. 1.

Rosenbaum, T. *The Myth of Moral Justice.* New York: HarperCollins, 2004.

Schmalensee, R. "The 'Thou Shalt' School of Business." *Wall Street Journal,* Dec. 30, 2003, p. B4.

Chapter 11

Argyris, C. "Skilled Incompetence." *Harvard Business Review,* 1986, *64*(5), 74–79.

Cross, R., and Parker, A. *The Hidden Power of Social Networks.* Boston: Harvard Business School Press, 2004.

Geneen, H., and Moscow, A. *Managing.* Garden City, N.Y.: Doubleday, 1984.

Hammer, M., and Champy, J. *Reengineering the Corporation: A Manifesto for Business Revolution.* New York: HarperBusiness, 1993.

Hammer, M., and Champy, J. *The Reengineering Revolution Handbook.* New York: HarperBusiness, 1995.

Securities and Exchange Commission v. Arthur Andersen LLP, Robert E. Allgyer, Walter Cercavschi, and Edward G. Maier, Civil Action No. 1:01CV01348 (J.R.) (D.D.C. June 19, 2001).

Serven, L.B.M. *The End of Office Politics as Usual.* New York: AMACOM, 2002.

Singer, A. "Changes at Teledyne: Installing a 'World-Class Ethics Program.'" *Ethikos,* 1994, *8*(1), 1–4, 16.

Singer, A. "DuPont's Daring Communications Formula." *Ethikos,* 2004, *17*(4), 1–3, 10–11.

Squires, S. E., Smith, C., McDougall, L., and Yeack, W. R. *Inside Arthur Andersen: Shifting Values, Unexpected Consequences.* Upper Saddle River, N.J.: Prentice Hall, 2003.

Chapter 12

Bennis, W. *The Unconscious Conspiracy Continues: Why Leaders Can't Lead.* New York: AMACOM, 1985.

Bennis, W. *On Becoming a Leader.* Reading, Mass.: Addison-Wesley, 1989.

Bravin, J. "Scared Straight, White-Collar Style." *Wall Street Journal,* Oct. 10, 2000, p. B1.

Covey, S. R. *The 7 Habits of Highly Effective People.* New York: Simon & Schuster, 1989.

Grove, A. *Only the Paranoid Survive: How to Exploit the Crisis Points that Challenge Every Company and Career.* New York: HarperCollins, 1996.

Hamburger, T. "Enron Official Tells of 'Arrogant Culture': Energy Firm Discouraged Staff Whistle-Blowing, House Panel Is Informed." *Wall Street Journal,* Feb. 15, 2002, p. A3.

Langer, E. *Mindfulness.* Reading, Mass.: Addison-Wesley, 1989.

Langley, M. "Flung into Top Job, Sullivan of AIG Learns on the Fly." *Wall Street Journal*, July 21, 2005, p. A1.

Martin, R. "The Virtue Matrix: Calculating the Return on Corporate Responsibility." *Harvard Business Review*, 2002, *80*(3), 69–75.

Schwartz, J. "Shuttle Inquiry Finds New Risks." *New York Times*, June 14, 2003, p. A1.

Schwartz, J. "Report Faults NASA as Compromising Safety." *New York Times*, Aug. 18, 2005, p. A15.

Schwartz, J., and Broder, J. "Loss of the Shuttle: The Overview; Engineer Warned About Dire Impact of Liftoff Damage." *New York Times*, Feb. 13, 2003, p. A1.

Thomas, L., Jr. "On Wall Street a Rise in Dismissal Over Ethics." *New York Times*, Mar. 29, 2005, p. A1.

Pulliam, S. "A Staffer Ordered to Commit Fraud Balked, Then Caved." *Wall Street Journal*, June 23, 2003, p. A1.

Pulliam, S., and Solomon, D. "How Three Unlikely Sleuths Discovered Fraud at WorldCom." *Wall Street Journal*, Oct. 30, 2002, p. A1.

Epilogue

Collins, J. *Good to Great*. New York: HarperCollins, 2001.

Gladwell, M. *The Tipping Point: How Little Things Can Make a Big Difference*. New York: Little, Brown, 2000.

Appendix B

Bamer, G., and Lansbury, R. *International and Comparative Employment Relations*. New York: Sage, 1998.

Davis, J., and Harrison, S. *Edison in the Boardroom: How Leading Companies Realize Value from Their Intellectual Assets*. New York: Wiley, 2001.

Goldstein, P. *International Intellectual Property Law*. New York: Foundation Press, 2001.

Merryman, J. *The Civil Law Tradition: Europe, Latin America, and East Asia*. Charlottesville, Va.: Michie, 1994.

Post, L. "Deferred Prosecutions on Rise in Corporate Bribery Cases." *National Law Journal*, Aug. 17, 2005. Available online: http://www.law.com/jsp/article.jsp?id=1124183109360. Access date: Dec. 1, 2005.

Rivette, K., and Kline, D. *Rembrandts in the Attic*. Boston: Harvard Business School Press, 2000.

Rosner, B., Halcrow, A., and Levins, A. *The Boss's Survival Guide: Everything You Need to Know About Getting Through (and Getting the Most Out of) Every Day*. New York: McGraw-Hill, 2001.

ACKNOWLEDGMENTS

To my agent, Bonnie Solow, for taking this project under her wing, giving it flight, and for being a joy to work with.

To my editor, Neal Maillet, and the excellent team at Jossey-Bass—Jessie Mandle, Carolyn Miller Carlstroem, Kasi Miller, Mary Garrett, Hilary Powers, and Matt Kaye—who turned my words into a book, made the editing process fun, and graciously answered the questions of a first-time author that they've no doubt answered a million times before.

To my dear friend Abby Greene, who translated my concepts into presentable artwork.

To Marty Orlowsky, Ron Milstein, and Bill Crump at Lorillard Tobacco Company for their willingness to accommodate my writing schedule.

To the Duke University Fuqua School of Business—including Marian Moore, who is now at the University of Virginia Darden School of Business—for opening its doors to my Legal Leverage course, and to all of my former students who came along for the ride and who continue to use the lessons learned in their day-to-day decision making.

To Sara Barbee, for her steadfast encouragement, and to Ann Quinlan, who reminded me to keep my sense of humor.

To all of the great management thinkers whose work has laid the foundation for this book, particularly Peter Drucker.

To all of the managers and executives whose actions illustrate the pros and cons of legal literacy. Your stories provide an endless source of material and an ongoing, albeit unwitting, endorsement. My deepest thanks.

THE AUTHOR

Hanna Hasl-Kelchner is a licensed attorney and former adjunct professor at the Duke University Fuqua School of Management. She earned her undergraduate degree from Duke University, an MBA degree from Cornell University, and her law degree from the Rutgers University School of Law—Camden, where she won awards for her advocacy skills.

Her legal career began in Washington, D.C., spanning private and government practice and including service at the U.S. International Trade Commission, where one of her cases was decided by President Reagan. She moved to in-house practice in 1984, developing a diverse portfolio of increasing responsibility at Degussa Corporation, a subsidiary of Frankfurt-based Degussa AG, and at Reichhold, Inc., a subsidiary of Tokyo-based Dainippon Ink and Chemicals.

She is currently associate general counsel at Lorillard Tobacco Company, where she serves as a member of the Brand Integrity Group and is national counsel for Lorillard's trademark infringement litigation. She also serves on the advisory board of WeComply, Inc., and the editorial board of the *Journal of Business Ethics Education*.

INDEX

A

Abacus Direct, 60
Accountability, admitting error and, 145, 147
Actors, as testimony readers, 49
Ad hoc internal investigations, 84–85, 86–88, 95, 252
Admissions: and apologies, 142–150; smoking-gun documents as, 101
Airline grief counseling, 142, 150
Allaire, P., 126
Allbritton, J. L., 41–42
Allbritton, R., 41–42
Allied Universal Corporation, 292–293
Alternative dispute resolution, 151–152
Altria Group, 131
American Fine China Guild, 306
American International Group (AIG), 53–54, 248
American Radiator & Standard Sanitary Corp., United States *vs.*, 339
American Stock Exchange, 314
Analysis paralysis, 22
Annals of Internal Medicine, 149
Anonymous hot lines. *See* Hot lines and ombudsman programs
Antibusiness bias, 46–47
Antitrust law: collaboration and, 141; complexity of, 298–300; costs of violating, 45; horizontal restraints and, 295–296, 298–300; international, 26–27, 37, 169, 262, 263; price discrimination and, 296–300; primer on, 295–300; proactive compliance program for, 91–92, 169, 190–192; vertical restraints and, 296–297, 298, 299. *See also* Thompson Memo; Unfair competition
Apologies, 142–150; impact of, on remedies, 147–149

Aptitude, in decision making, 172
Arbitrators, 151–152
Argyris, C., 224
Armstrong, J. S., 20
Arthur Andersen, 62; document retention/destruction policy of, 131, 179–186; Enron and, 126–127, 177–178, 179–186, 222, 240, 314; Enron-Andersen time line, 183–184; Waste Management and, 221–222; WorldCom and, 49
Asbestos claims, 33–34, 145–146
Asia, legal traditions in, 264, 266
Assignability, 278
Association of Corporate Counsel, 8
Assumptions, decision making based on, 19–20. *See also* Decision traps and bias
At-will doctrine, 288–289, 294
AT&T, 92
Attestation signature, 83
"Atticus Finch," 199
Attitude, in decision making, 172
Attorney-client privilege, 199
Automated Medical Laboratories (AML), United States *vs.*, 330, 331, 346*n*.5
Availability bias: characteristics of, 26; concept of, 21–25; by design, 26; legal consequences of un-, 26

B

Balanced scorecard, 70
Bank of America, 249
Banking industry scandals, 68, 247–248. *See also* Scandals, corporate
Barings, 247
Basic Construction Co., United States *vs.*, 338, 346*n*.5
Baum, H., 66–67
Baxter International, 267

Bayer, Baycol liabilities of, 71
Behavioral economics, 18–35; decision traps and, 21–35, 53; roots of, 21. *See also* Decision traps and bias
Benefield, G., 145–146
Bennis, W., 230
Berry Street Corporation, 117
Beutsch, United States *vs.*, 338
Bias, decision making. *See* Decision traps and bias
Bingham, J. F., 126
Black, C., 62
Blind spots: eliminating, 4–5; of leaders, 238–245
Boehner, J., 115
Boehner case, 115
Bondi, E., 48–49
Bondi *vs.* Citigroup, 48–49
Boston Legal, 199
Boyden, S., 128
Brand recognition, 92
Breach of contract, 273–274, 281, 301
Breach of duty, 135–137, 154, 282
Bribery, international law and, 265, 266–269
Bridgestone-Firestone tire defect, 68, 128, 283–284, 285
Bristol-Myers case, 58
Bristol-Myers Squibb, 58
Brown, L., 214
Bush, G. W., 177
Business education: focus of, 208–211; legal education *versus*, 5; legal training in, 6, 15, 19–20, 208, 213; risk perspectives in, 5, 208
Business hot spots, diagnosing, 84–94, 225
Business objectives: alignment of policies with, 179–186; defining, 165, 209–210, 253–254; identifying legal risks associated with, 165–166; lawyers' support for, 204–208, 210–211; measuring progress on legal risk management and, 245–247
Business policies: alignment of, 179–186; communications and, 215–229; employees' understanding of, 76–77; employment law and, 293; excellence and risk tolerance in, 170–173; latent legal liabilities in, 39–43

Business process reengineering (BPR) movement, 221
Business schools, 208–211

C

California Supreme Court, 169
Campbell's Soup, 72
Canada, employment laws of, 262–263
Candid Camera, 98–99
Carlyle Group, Korea, 104–105
Cartels, 147, 295
Case law, 264
Catholic bishops, 116
Cell phone communications, 109, 113, 114–115
Cellophane, 307
Cerner Corporation, 106–107, 108
Certification signature, 83
CGB Occupational Therapy, 51–52
Champions, 251
Champy, J., 221
Chat rooms, 112
Checkov, A., 288
Cheesecake Factory Incorporated, 46
Chief executive officers (CEOs): importance of legal risk management to, 8; time spent on legal issues, 209; trend toward prosecution of, 52–54
Child labor laws, 288
Chile, Riggs Bank scandal and, 41, 42
China: Citibank in, 247; Confucian tradition and, 264; elevator safety regulation in, 57, 59; intellectual property law in, 302; labor pool of, 73; one-child rule in, 123; telecommunications regulation in, 55
China Daily, 57
Cincotta, United States *vs.*, 330–331
Citigroup: Bondi *vs.*, 48–49; defections to, 69; regulatory problems of, 45–46, 248; scandals of, 247–248
Civil law model, 263–264
Civil liability, criminal liability and, 45
Civil Rights Act, 23
Civil Rights movement, 288
Clash of Cultures, The (Raelin), 199
Class action suits: in foreign countries, 45, 265; to get attention, 152; rise in, 44–45, 265
Classic economic theory, 4
Clayton Act, 296

Clinton, B., 11, 24
Closure management, 127–130
Coca-Cola, 116
Codes of conduct. *See* Ethics
Coleman-Sunbeam deal, 50–51
Colgate Palmolive, 66–67, 169
Collateral consequences, of criminal conviction, 341–342
Collective knowledge, 186. *See also* Knowledge management
Collective marks, 306
Color shade trademarks, 306–307
Columbia space shuttle disaster, 243–245
Comfort zones: employee, 218; loss aversion and, 31; preference for, 25, 31
Command-and-control approach, 221
Commitment: demonstrating, 216–222, 247–248; trust building and, 222–229
Common law: contract interpretation and, 274–275; employment law and, 288–289; international traditions of, 263–264
Communication channels: document retention and, 130–133; strengths and weaknesses of, 108–114
Communications: about compliance missteps, 221–222; and demonstrating commitment, 216–222; elements of, 218–219; empathic, 119, 136, 240; expectations management and, 134–155; in-person, 114; for internal compliance, 215–229; between lawyers and managers, 199–214; power of, 215–216; smoking gun, 98–133, 140; trust building and, 222–229; unmanaged legal risk and, 235. *See also* Documents; Electronic documents
Competent, preference for feeling, 25, 31
Competition laws. *See* Antitrust law; Unfair competition
Competitive advantage: decision making and, 162–163; legal leverage for, 17, 63–78; risk and opportunity assessment for, 92–93
Complaints: as legal risk metrics, 195–196; paying attention to, 140, 195–196
Compliance courses, 15
Compliance programs, criminal liability and, 338–340

Compositions-of-matter patents, 304
Computer backup tapes, 131–133
Computer cameras, 114
Confidence, 26. *See also* Overconfidence
Confidentiality: attorney-client, 199; of documents, 114–116, 125; as legal duty, 116, 249; rogue employees and, 289
Confidentiality agreements, in contracts, 163, 273
Conflict resolution provisions, 276–277
Conflicts: alternative dispute resolution of, 151–152; dissatisfaction and, 138–140; expectations management for, 134–155; hidden agendas and, 142. *See also* Lawsuits
Confucian tradition, 264
Consent decrees, 58
Constructive discharge, 107, 292
Context, loss aversion and, 29
Contingency fees, 264–265
Contingent commission arrangements, 86, 88
Continuous learning, 192–197
Contracts: conditional, 272–273; connecting, to bottom line, 14; for copyrights, 308; defined, 270; disclaimers in, 282–283; drafting control of, 278–279; enforceability of, 271–274; formation of, 270; "four corners of," 274–275; hot buttons in, 276–278; interpretation of, 274–278; legal literacy for signers of, 82–83; legal risk and opportunity assessment of, 90; metrics for, 194; overview of, 280; precise language for, 119; primer on, 269–281; remedies for, 279–280; standardized or boilerplate, 186–187, 273–278; statute of limitations for, 273–274; tortious interference of, 301; trade secrets and, 162–163, 277; written, 271–272
Copyright Clearance Center, 309
Copyright law, Internet piracy and, 192
Copyrights and copyright law, 307–309
Cornell University, 5, 70
Corporate governance, 8–9, 10
Corrupt business models, 121–122
Cost-benefit analysis: incentives and, 242; insufficiency of, 29, 31–33, 65

Counterfeiting, 302
Court TV, 47
Cover-ups, 88. *See also* Obstruction of justice
Covey, S. R., 63, 119, 136, 240
Cox-2 inhibitors, 285
Credit Suisse First Boston, 29–30
Criminal liability: civil liability and, 45; criminal intent and, 185; factors in, 329–346; Sarbanes-Oxley Act interpretation and, 315–316; Thompson Memo on, 316, 329–346. *See also* U.S. Federal Sentencing Guidelines for Organizations
Criminal proceedings: alternatives to, 343; Andersen's demise and, 178; increased prosecution and, 52–54; personal costs of, 17, 53–55
Crosby, P., 6
Cross-functionality: for legal risk assessment, 189; for product liability assessment, 90–91, 226–227; reframing for, 157–158; for regulatory compliance, 90
Cross-licensing arrangements, 141
CSI effect, 47
Customer complaint form, careless salesman and, 100–102, 119
Customer relations, 142

D

Damage awards: product liability and, 281; trend toward high, 51–52, 264–265, 282. *See also* Punitive damages
Damage control, 167
Data: defined, 186; developing, 187–190
Decision making: behavioral economics in, 18–35; ethical, 122–125; for legal leverage, 64, 156–173; legal literacy for, 94–97, 167–168; luck and, 158–161; rational *versus* irrational, 4, 20–21; risk tolerance and excellence in, 170–173
Decision-making processes: developing, 161–169; value of, 158–161
Decision traps and bias: of availability, 21–25; bad habits and, 87–88; denial and, 53; ethical leadership and, 238–245; in first level of legal understanding, 251; information

availability and, 27, 63; lawyers and, 200; legal literacy and, 87–88, 96; of loss aversion, 28–33, 157; noncompliance and, 217–218; of overconfidence, 25–28; Sarbanes-Oxley Act compliance and, 314–316; that sabotage legal leverage, 21–35. *See also* Availability bias; Loss aversion; Overconfidence
Deficiencies, documentation of, 195–196
Delivery date specification, 276
Demosthenes, 53
Denial, 53, 200
Denny's: availability bias applied to, 22–25; consent decree of, 58, 89
Design, lack of availability triggered by, 26
Deutsche Bank, 69
Deutsche Börse, 111, 114
Dial Corporation, 66–67, 169
Directors' insurance premiums, 34
Disclaimers, 282–283
Discovery: document product requests in, 124–125; electronic, 49–51; ethics and, 124–125; in United States, 265
Discovery space shuttle, 244–245
Discrimination, 289–291, 293. *See also* Racial discrimination cases; Sexual harassment
Disparagement, as anticompetitive behavior, 301
Disproportionate impact, 290
Disrespectful language, 105–108
Distributors, competition with, 298–300, 302
Documents: carelessness with, 99–102; clarity and accuracy in, 118–120, 140, 272; of closure process, 127–130; communication channels and, 108–114; confidentiality of, 114–116, 124–125; ethics and, 122–125; as latent legal liabilities, 49–51; legal leverage rules for, 103–133; legal literacy applied to, 116–118; legal *versus* illegal business practices and, 121–122; paper, 113; personal business in, 103–106, 131; respectfulness in, 105–108; retention of, 50–51, 130–133, 177–178, 179–186; shredding, 177–178, 179–186;

smoking gun, 98–133, 182; subject to pretrial discovery, 124–125; warnings in, 125–127. *See also* Contracts; Electronic documents; Smoking guns

Dolby Laboratories, 93

DoubleClick, 60–61, 68, 168

Dow-Corning breast implants, 29

"Dr Evil," 46

Drafting control, 278–279

Drucker, P., 19–20, 35, 77

Due diligence, 272

Duke University, 201

Dumped goods, 300–301

Duncan, D., 182, 183, 184, 185

Dunlap, T., 91–92, 190

DuPont, 222

E

E-mail. *See* Electronic documents

East Asia, legal traditions in, 264

Ebbers, B., 45

Edison, T. A., 156

Edison Schools, 52

EgyptAir, 142

Electronic documents and e-mail: disparaging *versus* respectful language in, 106–108; guidelines for using, 108–114; as latent legal liabilities, 49–51; maintenance of, 50–51, 130–133; misunderstandings in, 109–111; personal *versus* company business use of, 103–106, 131; privacy of, 104, 109, 116; saving draft forms of, 108; strengths and weaknesses of, 112. *See also* Documents

Electronic networks, 131

Electronic piracy, 192

Emotional weighting, power of, 21–22

Empathic communication, 119, 136, 240

Employee background checks, 289

Employee raiding, 301–302

Employee reporting metrics, 195

Employee satisfaction, 69–70

Employee suggestion plan, 168–169

Employee termination litigation, 139, 292–293

Employees: authority of, 98–102; collective knowledge and, 186; communications for compliance of, 215–229; documents and, 98–102;

fraternization of, 291–292; headroom for, 69–70; leaders' moral authority and, 232–244; legal competency requirements for, 95, 257–259; legal literacy for, 70, 76–77, 94–97; listening to, 219–221, 224, 240–245; managing and developing, 72–74; participation of, 225–229; as source of legal leverage, 13; trust building with, 222–229

Employment at-will doctrine, 288–289

Employment law: extraterritorial, 267; international, 93–94, 262–263, 294; organization size and, 88; primer on, 287–295; theories of, 293–294

Employment practices insurance, harassment claims and, 33

Enforcement: increase in, 52–54, 55, 57–58; proactive avoidance of, 58–62; rule of law and, 55, 57–58

Enron and Enron scandal, 26; Arthur Andersen and, 177–178, 179–186, 222, 240, 314; bankruptcy filing of, 59; document discovery in, 103–104; ethics policy of, 217; impact of, 46, 53, 68; insurance policies of, 34; internal warnings at, 126–127, 240, 241; *technically legal* defense of, 249–250

Enron-Andersen time line, 183–184

Environmental contamination or exposure claims, 33–34, 145–146

Equatorial Guinea, 41

Erin Brockovich, 47

Escalator, 307

Ethical dilemmas, 122–125; moral leadership and, 233–238

Ethical leadership: building moral authority and, 232–248; for legal leverage, 230–250

Ethics and ethics codes: communications and, 215–229; demonstrating commitment to, 216–222, 247–248; situational, 122–125, 233, 247; spirit of the law and, 248–250

Ethics Resource Center, 11

Ethics training, 6, 208

Europe: antitrust/fair competition laws in, 26–27, 169, 262; legal traditions of, 263; patent law in, 304

European Commission, 111

European Competition Commission, 26–27
European Court of First Instance, 111
European Union, hot line laws of, 94
Evidence, as litigation driver, 135–137, 154
Excellence, 170–173
Expectations management, 134–155; communication precision for, 118–120; international differences and, 265; knowledge management for, 192, 196; litigation dynamics and, 135–140; litigation prevention and, 140–153; risk assessment for, 91
Expert witnesses, 51
Extraterritorial laws, 266–269

F

Face-to-face communications, 114
Face-to-face training, 190–191
Fair use standard, 308–309
Fairness: employment law and, 294; expectations management and, 137–138, 143, 154–155; in negotiation, 154–155; reputation and, 66–67. See also Unfair competition
Family estate settlement case, 137–138, 142
Faxes, 111, 113, 114
Fear, employee, 223–224, 237–238, 241
Feurstein, A., 11–12
Fiduciary duty, 286–287
Final exam lesson, 236–238
Financial controls legislation. See Sarbanes-Oxley Act (SOX)
Financial performance: legal risk management for improving, 70–74, 253; obsession with, 71–72, 209–210, 216, 253–254
Financial reporting, benefits of transparent, 70–72
Fines, 89
Fishhoff, B., 22
Fitz-enz, J., 72
Five-Point Play, 201
Fleet Bank, 117
Force majeure provision, 271
Ford Motor Company: Ford Explorer tire problem of, 68, 128, 283–284, 285; Ford Pinto case of, 31–33, 169; Grimshaw vs., 31–33

Foreign Corrupt Practices Act (FCPA), 195, 266–267
Foreign languages, communication misunderstandings and, 111
Foreign laws. See International law
Fortune, 24, 107
Fox, A., 105–106
Fox, C., 31
Framing, availability bias and, 25
France: class actions in, 45, 265; intellectual property law in, 303
Franklin, B., 81
Fraud, obsession with financial performance and, 72. See also Criminal proceedings; Scandals, corporate
Frederick the Great, 134
Funt, A., 98

G

G-3 video phone, 114
Gandhi, M., 238, 242
Gateway, 141
Geifeld, B., 314
Gender discrimination, 290. See also Sexual harassment
Geneen, H., 224
General Electric (GE): in bribing Israeli military, 266; Honeywell merger deal of, 26–27, 37, 169, 262; Six Sigma in, 189, 195
Genericide, 307
Geneva Conventions, 261
George Washington University, 11
German Works Council Act, 94
Germany: antitrust law in, 263; intellectual property law in, 303; worker rights in, 94
Gingrich, N., 114–115
Globalization, 264
Goethe, 215
Golann, D., 146
Graco, 89
Grand Circle, 142, 149
Great Britain: Citibank in, 248; class actions in, 45, 265
Greenberg, G., 86
Greenberg, M. "H.", 53–54, 248
Grief counseling, 142, 150
Grimshaw vs. Ford Motor Company, 31–33
Grove, A., 91–92, 100, 190–192, 238

H

Hague Convention, 261
Hairdresser case, 134–135, 136–137, 142
Hammer, M., 221
Harassment claims: employment practices insurance and, 33; underestimation of, 33. *See also* Sexual harassment
Hardball tactics, 48–49
Harris, J. N., 48–49
Harvard Business School, 9
Hazardous products, 284
Health insurance, 34
Heath, 25
Hecker, J., 127
Helpline, 228
Hidden agendas, 142
High-reliability organizations, 170–171
High-tech bubble, 160
Hilton Hotels Corp., United States *vs.*, 338, 346*n*.5
Hindu Buddhist tradition, 264
Hollinger International, 61–62
Holtzman, E., 267
Honeywell: GE merger deal with, 26–27, 37, 169, 262; knowledge management system of, 189–190
Honeywell Law Web, 189–190
Hooters, 290
Horizontal restraints, 295–296, 298–300
Hostile work environment: disrespect and, 107–108; knowledge management and, 179; sexual harassment and, 291–292
Hot lines and ombudsman programs: benefits of, 93–94; communication about, 219, 220; foreign laws for, 93–94; metrics for, 195
House accounts, 299, 302
Houseman, J., 203
Human capital, 72–74. See also Employee headings
Human needs, 149–150, 233, 234–235, 241, 287–288
Huntsman Chemical Corporation, 10, 37, 90, 118, 169

I

IBM, 92–93
Ignorance: characteristics of, 26; legal consequences of, 26; as losing strategy, 14–16, 185–186, 252
Imclone, 30
Impossibility, contract, 271
Incentives: building, 233–238; characteristics of, 239; impacts of, 239; listening and, 242; negative, 233–235, 239; positive, 239
Indemnity provisions, 277, 282–283
India: legal tradition of, 264; personal jurisdiction in, 263
Information: availability of, and bias, 27, 63, 234–235; defined, 186; developing, 187–190
Initial public offerings (IPOs), 198–199
Injunctive relief, 279–280
Insider, The, 47
Instant messaging, 112, 131
Insurance, overreliance on, 33–35
Integration clause, 272
Integrity: contracts and, 272; demonstrating, 240–242
Intel, 100; antitrust compliance strategy of, 91–92, 169, 190–192; Pentium chip recall of, 238
Intellectual property rights and law: contracts and, 277; defined, 303; failure to secure, 36–38; international, 262, 302, 303–304, 306; primer on, 303–311; risk and opportunity assessment for, 90, 92–93; unfair competition and, 302; value creation and, 309–310. *See also* Copyrights and copyright law; Patent rights and law; Trade secrets; Trademarks and trademark law
Interests: legal rights and, 141–143; relationship, 142–150
International Association of Fire Chiefs, 306
International business, ethical dilemmas in, 123
International Convention on Combating Bribery of Foreign Public Officials in International Business Transactions, 267, 268–269
International law: on anonymous hot lines, 93–94; contracts and, 275–276; defined, 260; on employment, 93–94, 262–263, 294; extraterritorial, 266–269; on intellectual property,

262, 302, 303–304, 306; legal tradition differences and, 263–266;
primer on, 260–269; on product liability, 39–40, 262; on unfair competition and antitrust, 26–27, 37,
169, 262, 263, 300–301
Internet: copyright issues and, 309;
counterfeiting on, 302; piracy on,
192; privacy concerns and, 60–61,
116; spyware law and, 57. *See also*
Electronic documents and e-mail
InterTrust Technologies, 141
Intranets, 186
Islam, 264
Israel, international business dealings
and, 266, 267
Italy, class actions in, 45, 265
ITT, 224

J

Japan: Citibank in, 248; international
labor law and, 294; labor pool of, 73
Jeep Grand Cherokee plant, sexual ha-
rassment at, 292
Job functions: discrimination and,
290–291; matching legal compe-
tency requirements to, 95, 257–259
Johnson, S., 177, 198
Johnson & Johnson, 127–128
Joint and several liability, 284–285
Judges, unpredictability of, 51–52
Junk science, 51
Juries: antibusiness bias of, 46–47, 66;
CSI effect and, 47–48; and feigned
ignorance defense, 185
Justinian Code, 66–67, 263

K

Kahneman, D., 20, 21, 29
Kaplan, R. S., 70
Kellogg's, 72
Kennedy, J. F., assassination, 22
Key card entries, 109
Knowledge management: components
of, 186–192; document retention/
destruction and, 177–178, 179–186;
for expectations management, 192,
196; for legal leverage, 177–197;
quantifying, 193–197; strategic significance of, 179, 180; value of continuous learning and, 192–197
Koehler, D., 21

Kohler Company, 290
Korea, international labor law and,
294
KPMG, 147–148
Kraft Foods, 131
Krzyzewski, M., 201

L

Labor unions, 294
Language: clarity and accuracy in,
118–120, 140, 272; foreign, misunderstandings and, 111; respectful
versus disrespectful, 105–108
"Last in time rule," 274
Latent legal liabilities, 36–62; business
policies and, 39–43, 179–186; communications as, 98–133; costs of,
36–38, 55, 56; electronic documents as, 49–51; hostile legal climate and, 43–55, 56; intellectual
property rights and, 36–38; litigation forces and, 135–140, 154; litigation prevention and, 140–153;
personal costs of, 53–55; smoking-
gun communications as, 98–133, 182
Law and Order, 47
Law education: business training *versus,* 5; focus of, 203; preventive law
in, 214; risk perspectives in, 5, 204
Lawsuits: advantages and disadvan-
tages of, 140–141, 152–153; costs
of, 17, 48–49, 55, 56; employee,
basis for, 289–293; forces that drive,
135–140, 154; frivolous, 284; hostile
legal climate and, 43–55, 56, 284;
leveraging, 152–153; preventing
and managing, 140–153; risk metrics for, 194
Lawyer jokes, 201–202, 205, 210
Lawyers: contingency fees and,
264–265; discriminatory stereotypes
of, 199–200, 201–202; hardball tactics of plaintiffs', 48–49; legal leverage with, 198–214; mindset of,
203–205; need for, 198–199, 200;
relationship-building with, 211–213;
roles of, 211–213; timing of calling,
7–8, 18, 19; value-added billing for,
205–208
Lay, K., 126, 183, 184, 240
Leaders and leadership: blind spots of,
238–245; commitment of, 216–222,

225, 247–248; ethical, 230–250; integrity demonstrated by, 240–242; moral authority and, 232–248; organizational communications and, 215–229; oversight by, 247–248. *See also* Chief executive officers (CEOs); Managers

Leadership in Ethics Award, 11

Learning: continuous, 192–197; from mistakes, 94, 222; paradox of, 19–20, 179

Leeson, N., 247

Legal audits, 84–94; ad hoc internal, 84, 85, 86–88, 95, 252; categories of, 84–85; following up on, 225; knowledge management and, 187, 188–189; legal risk/opportunity assessment, 84, 85, 90–93; metrics for, 194; regulatory compliance, 84, 85, 88–90

Legal billing, value-added, 205–208

Legal competency requirements, 95, 257–259

Legal environment: hostile, 43–55, 56; scrutiny of, 8–9

Legal leverage: with business documents, 103–133; decision traps that sabotage, 21–35; factors in achieving, 63–65, 74, 76–78; failure of, example of, 11–12; rationale for, 74, 76–78, 253; value chain concept and, 9–10; for value creation and competitive advantage, 17, 63–78; winning with, 12–17

Legal leverage process portfolio: communications in, 215–229; decision making in, 156–173; document creation and retention in, 98–133; ethical leadership in, 230–250; expectation management in, 134–155; knowledge management in, 177–197; lawyers in, 198–214; legal literacy in, 63–65, 76–77, 81–97; overview of, 74, 76–78, 253

Legal leverage triage, 166–167

Legal literacy, 81–97; for business communications, 116–118; in decision making, 94–97, 167–168; employee performance and, 70; implementing, 94–97; lawyers and, 198–199; learning paradox and, 19–20, 179; legal audits and, 84–94; recogniz-

ing the need for, 82–83; role of, in achieving legal leverage, 63–65, 76–77, 251–255; for Sarbanes-Oxley Act interpretation, 313. *See also* Continuous learning; Knowledge management

Legal Literacy Tookit, 95, 257–259

Legal obstacles: identifying, 165; prioritizing, 166–167, 169–170; transforming, into strategic opportunities, 157–173

Legal primer, 260–311; on contracts, 269–281; on employment law, 287–295; on intellectual property, 303–311; on international law, 260–269; on product liability, 281–287; purpose of, 95–96, 260; on unfair competition, 295–303

Legal rights: focus on, *versus* relationships, 140–141, 142; interests and, 141–143

Legal risk and opportunity assessments, 84, 85, 90–93; decision-making processes and, 156–173; knowledge management and, 187, 188–189; metrics for, 193–197

Legal risk management: benefits of, 65–74, 75; best practice tools and procedures for, 232; business training in, 6, 15; case for, 3–17; costs of ignoring, 3–4, 18–19, 55, 56; financial benefits of, 70–74; latent liabilities and, 36–62; measuring progress in, 245–247; metrics for, 193–197; new environment for, 8–9; proactive approach to, 88–93, 251–255; reactive approach to, 86–88, 94–95; responsibility for, 6–7; unmeasurable benefits of, 65–70; value chain and, 9–10

Legal risk metrics, 193–197

Legal risk prioritization, 166–167, 169–170

Legal risk profile, determining, 84–94

Legal understanding, stages of, 251–252

Legalese, translating, 5–7

Leno, J., 23

Letter-of-the-law *versus* spirit-of-the-law, 248–250

Levitt, A., 71

Lexar Media, Toshiba suit of, 49–50

Liabilities. *See* Latent legal liabilities
Liability insurance, overreliance on, 33–34
Libya, 267
Licensing, 92–93, 141
Lichtenstein, S., 22
Lind, E. A., 139
Listening: to employees, 219–221, 224, 240–245; to internal warnings, 125–127, 240–245
Litigation-related metrics, 194
Liz Claiborne, 71
London Stock Exchange, 111, 114
Loss aversion: apologies and, 148–149; in customer collection case, 39; decision trap of, 28–33, 157; employee noncompliance and, 217, 223–224, 233; employment law and, 287–288; financial performance obsession and, 71–72; Sarbanes-Oxley Act compliance fears and, 314–315
Louisiana, 263
Lucent Technologies, 126
Luck, 158–161
Lundwall, R., 44

M

Malden Mills, 3, 11–12, 37, 92, 169
Malpractice, 286
Managers: lawyers' relationship-building with, 211–213; lawyers' views of, 200–201; mindset of, 208–211. *See also* Chief executive officers (CEOs); Leaders
Managing (Geneen), 224
Managing the Unexpected (Weick and Sutcliffe), 171
Manufactures patents, 304
Mark, R., 66–67
Mars, 107
Marsh & McLennan, 69, 86, 88
Martha Stewart case, 30, 131. *See also* Stewart, M.
Martha Stewart Living Omnimedia Enterprises, 30
Maslow, A. H., 150
Maslow's hierarchy of human needs: compliance and, 233, 234–235, 239, 241; concepts of, 149–150; employment law and, 287–288

Massachusetts Institute of Technology (MIT), Sloan School, 71, 209
McCombs School of Business, 209
McDonald's: coffee case of, 282; trademark of, 92
McNeil Consumer Products Company, 127–128
Media Vision Technologies, 46
Mediating Legal Disputes (Golann), 146
Mediators, 151–152
Medical charts, 105–106
Medical profession: apologies in, 143, 148–149; redundant procedures in, 170
Merck, Vioxx withdrawal of, 43, 69, 71, 285
Mergers and acquisitions case study simulation, 236–238
Merits of the case: factors in, 135–140; managing, 150–152
Merrill Lynch, 105
Metrics: for legal risk management, 245–247; for legal risks, 193–197
Michigan, State of, DoubleClick lawsuit of, 60
Michigan Lawsuit Abuse Watch (M-Law), 284
Microsoft: antitrust issues of, 45, 92, 141; litigation strategy of, 141, 142; Xbox cord recall of, 65–66, 166, 169
Mindfulness, 171–172
Miracle Bra, 36–37
Miracle-Gro, 188
Mistrials, jury misconduct and, 47–48
Mitsubishi Motor Manufacturing of America, 62, 292
Model Law on Electronic Commerce, 130
Moral authority, 232–248
Morgan Stanley, 50–51, 69, 132
Motion practices, 48–49
Motive to sue: factors in, 135–137, 139–140, 154; preventing and managing, 140–153
Movie and music industry, 192
Murphy's Law, 114–115
Myers, D., 54–55

N

Napster, 309
NASA, 243–245

NASDAQ, 46, 314

National Association for the Advancement of Colored People (NAACP), 23, 24, 25

National Highway Traffic and Safety Administration (NHTSA), 32, 128

Natural disaster, 271

Negligence, 281–282, 286, 293

Negotiation: contract creation and, 272; expectations management and, 139–141, 153–155; fairness in, 154–155; hidden agendas and, 142; international differences in, 265; *versus* litigation, 140–141; preparation for, 153–154

Netherlands, product shipped through, 39–40, 262

New York Attorney General's office, 52, 53, 69, 86, 88, 248

New York City hospitals, language complications in, 111

New York Times, 184, 198

Newell Rubbermaid, 89

9/11: impact of, on perceived risk, 21–22; Riggs Bank scandal and, 41; scrutiny of international business dealings and, 266

No Child Left Behind, 57–58

North Korea, 267

Nothing But Curves brand assimilation, 37

O

Objectivity, availability bias and, 25

Obstruction of justice: document shredding as, 177–178, 179–186; panic as cause of, 30; Sarbanes-Oxley definition of, 185–186

O'Connor, K., 60

Odom, M., 183

Old Monastery Co. *vs.* United States, 331

Ombudsman programs. *See* Hot lines and ombudsman programs

Online training, 190

Only the Paranoid Survive (Grove), 238

OPEC oil cartel, 295

Open secrets, 88, 224

Operational excellence, 170–173

Opportunity cost, 4; from bad implementation of policy, 180; from reg-

ulatory noncompliance, 45–46; sources of, 16

Order contracts, 275–276

Order shipping case, 39–40

Organizational infrastructure: communications and, 215–229; ethics and, 122–125; knowledge management and, 177–197; leadership and, 230–250; legal *versus* illegal business practices and, 121–122; role of, in achieving legal leverage, 64–65

Overconfidence: characteristics of, 26; decision trap of, 25–28; of leaders, 234, 238; legal consequences of, 26, 234; regression and, 27–28, 200

Owens Corning: breast implants of, 43; pink trademark of, 306–307

P

Package shape trademarks, 306

Pagers, 113

Palm, 152

Paper Chase, 203

Parmalat, Citigroup and, 46, 48–49

Parry, S., 193

Participatory management, 225–229

Past history consideration, 335

Patent rights and law: failure to secure, 11–12, 13–14, 18–19, 37, 162–163; infringement of, 117, 305; metrics for, 194; primer on, 304–305; security leaks and, 116; types of, 304. *See also* Intellectual property rights

Patterson, N. L., 106–107

Penalties, 89

Perelman, R., 50–51, 132

Performance evaluations, grade inflation in, 102–103

Perrier water bottle trademark, 306

Perry Mason, 199

Pervasiveness of wrongdoing, 334–335

Philip Morris, 131

Philip Morris case, 131

Physicians: class action suit by, 34; disparaging comments by, in medical charts, 105–106

Pink Panther, 307

Pinochet, A., 41, 42

Plaintiff's bar, 44

Plea agreements, 344–346

PNC Financial Services Group, 42–43
Polarfleece and Polartec, 10–11, 37, 92
Policies. *See* Business policies
Political risk, 261
Politics, organizational, 224, 225, 234–235
Porter, M., 9
Post-sale duty to warn, 285–286
Practice of Management, The (Drucker), 77
Prentice, R., 209
Preventive law, 214
Price discrimination, 296–300
Price fixing, 267, 296
Priceline.com, 126
Privileged information, 125
Process control technology, 195
Process patents, 304
Product liability: assessment of, 90–91; defects that trigger, 283–284; defined, 281; international law and, 39–40, 262; joint and several, 284–285; listening to customer complaints and, 195–196; negligence and, 281–282; post-sale duty to warn and, 285–286; primer on, 281–287; regulatory compliance and, 91; strict, 282–284
Product safety, reputation and, 65–66, 68
Product warnings: defective, 284; failure to include, 39–40; post-sale, 285–286
Promotion policies, 95
Property insurance, 33–34
Proprietary information, 116
Prosecution, increase in, 52–54
Prudential Insurance Company, 87
Public Company Accounting Oversight Board (PCAOB), 313, 314–315
Punitive damages: insufficiency of cost-benefit analysis and, 31–33; trend toward high, 51–52, 264–265, 282. *See also* Damage awards
Purchasing policy case, 156–158

Q

Quality: building, into processes, 6; legal risk metrics and, 193–197; of legal services, 207–208; risk tolerance and, 171–173

Quality control: product liability and, 283, 287; rule of law as, 57; Sarbanes-Oxley Act as, 59, 161
Quantum meruit, 280
Quattrone, F., 15, 26, 29–30, 121–122
Quattrone case, 29–30
Quid pro quo claim, 291–292

R

Racial discrimination cases: class action, 44; due to availability bias, 22–25
Raelin, J. A., 199
Rambus case, 131
Ratification, 293
Re-export laws, 267
Reactive approaches: learning and, 94–95; risk of relying on, 86–88, 94–95
Reasonable accommodation, 291
Reasonableness, 276
Reengineering Revolution Handbook, The (Hammer and Champy), 221
Reengineering the Corporation (Hammer and Champy), 221
Reformation, 280
Regression: bad decision making and, 160, 200; concept of, 27–28
Regulation, purpose and dynamics of, 88
Regulatory compliance: good intentions in, 158–159; inattention to, 40–43; increased enforcement of, 52–54, 55; lost opportunities and, 45–46; metrics for, 194; product liability and, 91; relying on, inadequacy of, 10, 85; tipping point for, 317
Regulatory compliance audits, 84, 85, 88–90
Relationship interests and management, 140–150
Remediation, 340–341
Remedies: apologies and, 147–149; contract, 279–280
Remorse, as partial remedy, 147–148
Repeatability, 160–161, 246
Reputation: financial performance and, 70; legal risk management for improving, 65–70
Resale price maintenance, 296
Rescission, 280

Research and development (R&D) case: leveraged decision making in, 163–168; poor decision making in, 162–163

Respectfulness, in business communications, 105–108

Respondeat superior, 289, 293, 338

Restitution, 340–341

Retribution, fear of, 237–238, 241

Rhone Poulenc, 147

Richardson, J., 23

Riggs Bank, 40–43

Risk perception: availability bias and, 21–25; context and, 29; loss aversion and, 28–33; overconfidence trap and, 25–28

Risk tolerance, 170–173

Rogers, W., 36

Rolling Stones, 138

Roman law, 263

Royal & Sun Alliance Insurance, 105

R.R. Donnelley & Sons, 105

Rule of law: international concepts of, 261; letter of *versus* spirit of, 248–250; purpose and dynamics of, 55, 57–58, 59; shortcomings of, 313

"Rule of reason" analysis, 296

Russo, E., 158, 159, 160, 161

S

Safety net procedures, 169–170

St. Mary's Hospital, London, 105

Sale of nonstaples, 304

Salesforce.com, 198

Sarbanes-Oxley Act (SOX): compliance efforts for, decision-making bias in, 314–316; costs of avoiding, 71; document retention and, 130; events surrounding the birth of, 59, 60, 125, 170; FCPA enforcement and, 267; going beyond, 10; grumbling about, 161, 231, 249, 312–313; impact of, on CEOs' views on risk management, 8; lessons of, 312–317; "obstruction" defined by, 185–186; process controls and, 228; purpose of business and, 77; as quality control mechanism, 59; Section 404, 313, 314–315; Table of Contents of, exerpted, 325–328; whistle-blower protections of, 241

Satisfaction and dissatisfaction, 138–140

Saudi Embassy, 41

Scandals, corporate: closure process for, 127–130; corporate governance and, 8–9, 10; directors' and officers' insurance premiums and, 34; ethics training in response to, 6; fiduciary duty and, 286–287; increased enforcement and, 53–54, 59; leadership message from, 230–232, 233, 247–248; legal risk management in response to, 8; negative incentives and, 230–231, 233, 234; reputation and, 68

Schmalensee, R., 209

Schoemaker, P., 158, 159, 160, 161

Scientific breakthrough, 160–161

Scorched-earth approach, 48–49, 141, 147–148

Scotts Company, 188–189

Seamlessness, 254

Security leaks, 115–116

Security surveillance cameras, 109

Self-actualization, 150

Self-dealing, 286–287

Self-esteem, 150

Self-regulation, 168

Senge, P. M., 71, 94, 95

Senior lawyers, 207

Service marks, 306

Service sector liability, 286–287

Settlements, advantage of, 140–141

7 Habits of Successful People (Covey), 119

Sexual harassment: admitting error in, 144–145, 150; company policies and, 62; law on, 291–292; smoking gun e-mail and, 102–103, 151

Sharks, 202

Sherman Antitrust Act, 338, 346n.5

Simulations, 191–192, 227

Situational ethics, 122–125, 233, 247

Six Sigma, 189, 195

Skilling, J., 183

Sloan School of Management, 71, 209

Slovic, P., 20, 21, 22

Smoking guns: business documents as, 98–133, 182; closure process and, 129–130; defined, 102–103; managing expectations and, 140; range of severity of, 102

Social needs, 150
Social networks, employee, 220–221
Socratic method, 203
Sony, 66, 169
Sotheby's, 15
Soviet Union, former, 217
SOX. *See* Sarbanes-Oxley Act (SOX)
Specific-performance remedy, 279
Spirit-of-the-law *versus* letter-of-the-law, 248–250
Spitzer, E., 52, 53, 69, 86, 88, 248
Spyware, 57
State Farm Insurance, 128
Stewart, M., 26, 30, 131
Stock value, transparency and, 70–72
Storage tank manual case, 203–205
Strategic opportunities, transforming legal obstacles into, 157–173
Strict liability, 282–284
Subsidized goods, 300–301
Suffolk University School of Law, 146
Sullivan, M., 248
Sullivan, S., 49, 54
Sumo wrestling match, 27
Sun Microsystems, 141
Sunbeam-Coleman deal, 50–51
Survival needs, 150, 233, 234–235, 241
Sutcliffe, K. M., 171
Sweden, class actions in, 45, 265
SWOT analysis, 165, 167

T

Tailhook Association convention, 144–145
Taubman, A. A., 15
Tax law, translating, into bottom line, 5, 6
Taylor, G., 126
Teledyne, ethics and compliance program of, 227–229
Teledyne Relays, 228
Telephone communications, 112–113; confidentiality and, 115–116
Temple, N., 183, 184
Termination provisions, contract, 276, 296
Terrorist attacks, risk perception for, 21–22
Texaco, 44
Text messaging, 113
The Real Yellow Pages, 38
Thermos, 307
Third-party suits, 289, 291

Thompson Memo (DOJ), 316; text of, 329–346
Time Warner, 141
Tipping point, 317
Title 9, Criminal Resource Manual, 316, 329–346
To Kill a Mockingbird, 199
Tollbooth cameras, 109
Tort claim, 282
Tort reform, 285
Tortious interference of contract, 301
Toshiba America Electronic Components, Lexar's suit against, 49–50
Trade dress protection, 306, 307
Trade secrets, 162–163, 170, 309
Trademarks and trademark law: benefits of, 92–93; failure to secure, 38; infringement of, 307; injunctive relief and, 279–280; licensing of, 92–93; primer on, 305–307; types of, 306. *See also* Intellectual property rights and law
Training: metrics for, 194; regulatory, 89; targeted, 84; types of, 190–192. *See also* Business education; Law education
Transparency: financial benefits of, 70–72; for trust and reputation building, 67–68, 70
Transparent Leader, The (Baum), 66–67
Treaties and conventions, 261
Trespass, 288
Trooper case, 146, 147, 150
Trust and trust building: with employees, 222–229, 235, 236–238; fear *versus*, 223–224; in lawyer-manager relationship, 201, 211; relationship of, to influence, 223; transparency and, 67–68
Tuesday Morning, 71
Tutors, regulation of, 58
Tversky, A., 20, 21, 25, 29, 31
TW Services, 23
Tylenol recall, 127–128

U

UBS Warburg LLC, Zubulake *vs.*, 50, 131–132
UL Underwriters Laboratory, 306
Uncertainty: decision-making biases and, 161; decision-making excellence for, 171–172; international

law on, 26–27, 37, 169, 262, 263, 300–301; loss aversion and, 30–31
Unfair competition: defined, 295; primer on, 295–303. *See also* Antitrust law
Unintended consequences, 39–40
United Airlines, 168–169
United States: high damage awards in, 51, 264–265; intellectual property rights in, 303, 304, 307–308; state law in, 281
United States, Old Monastery Co. *vs.*, 331
United States *vs.* American Radiator & Standard Sanitary Corp., 339
United States Attorneys' Manual, Title 9 §162 ("Federal Prosecution of Business Organizations"), 316; text of, 329–346
United States *vs.* Automated Medical Laboratories (AML), 330, 331, 346n.5
United States *vs.* Basic Construction Co., 336, 346n.5
United States *vs.* Beutsch, 338
United States *vs.* Cincotta, 330–331
United States *vs.* Hilton Hotels Corp., 338, 346n.5
U.S. Attorneys' Offices, compliance resources for, 340
U.S. Congress, 8, 170, 338
U.S. Consumer Product Safety Commission, 89
U.S. Court of Appeals, 104
U.S. Department of Defense, 340
U.S. Department of Health and Human Services, 340
U.S. Department of Justice (DOJ), 190; Antitrust amnesty program of, 147; Denny's and, 23, 24, 25; FCPA enforcement and, 267; Sarbanes-Oxley Act and, 316
U.S. Environmental Protection Agency (EPA), 336, 340
U.S. Federal Bureau of Investigation (FBI): criminal liability and, 54; Riggs Bank and, 41
U.S. Federal Energy Regulatory Commission, Enron investigation by, 103–104
U.S. Federal Reserve Board, Citigroup and, 45–46
U.S. Federal Sentencing Guidelines

for Organizations: compliance programs and, 217; excerpts from (Chapter 8-Part B), 318–324; management commitment and, 240; penalty calculations in, 158–159. *See also* Thompson Memo
U.S. Federal Trade Commission (FTC), 190; DoubleClick probe of, 60
U.S. Food and Drug Administration (FDA), 30
U.S. House Ethics Committee, Gingrich inquiry by, 115
U.S. International Trade Administration, 300–301
U.S. International Trade Commission, 300–301
U.S. Navy, 144–145
U.S. Office of Federal Contract Compliance Programs, 290
U.S. Secret Service agents, Denny's and, 24, 25
U.S. Securities and Exchange Commission, 71; appearance of impropriety and, 52; Arthur Andersen/Waste Management investigation of, 221–222; as compliance resource, 340; Enron investigation of, 127, 182, 183–184; foreign government bribery and, 267; official registration statements and, 198–199; Prudential and, 87; Quattrone investigation of, 121–122; restatement filing with, 46; Salesforce.com investigation of, 198–199; Sarbanes-Oxley Act and, 313, 315; voluntary disclosure programs of, 336; Xerox investigation of, 126, 148
U.S. Supreme Court, 177–178, 180
University of Hertfordshire, 117
University of Pennsylvania, Wharton School of, 20, 208
University of Texas, Austin, 209
Unselfishness, in lawyer-manager relationship, 200–211
USA Patriot Act, 266
Utility maximization, 4
Utility patents, 304

V

Value chain: business communications and, 117–118; concept of, 9–10; legal leverage and, 9–17; legal weakness in, 37–55

Value creation: intellectual property rights and, 309–310; lawyers' role in, 205–208; legal leverage for, 63–78
Value maximization, 4
Verification signature, 83
Vertical restraints, 296–297, 298, 299
Veterans' Affairs Hospital, Lexington, 148–149
Vicarious liability, 291
Victoria's Secret, 36–37
Video conferencing, 114
Vindication motive, 145–146
Vinson, B., 230–235, 241
Vitamin cartel, 147
Voice mail, 113
Voluntary disclosure of wrongdoing, 335–336

W

Wachner, L., 36
Wacky Warning Label Contest, 284
Wal-Mart, in Germany, 94, 263
War for Talent, The (Michaels et al.), 73
Warnaco Group, 36–37
Warning signs, costs of not heeding, 15
Warnings, listening and responding to, 125–127, 240–245. *See also* Product warnings
Warranties, 277, 281, 282–283
Waste Management, 221–222
Watergate, 267
Watkins, S., 126–127, 183, 240, 241
Web logs (blogs), 109, 112
Web sites, 112
Weick, K. E., 171
Welch, J., 26–27, 37, 189
Wellpoint Health Networks, 34
West Nile virus, 215, 216

"We've always done it" rationale, 86–87
Wharton School of Business, 20, 208
Whistle-blowers: and ad hoc internal investigations, 86; listening to, 240–242
White-knuckled stage, 251–252
Winning: loss aversion and, 28–29; through legal leverage, 12–17
Winning Decisions (Russo and Schoemaker), 158
Wiseman, R., 117
Witness testimonies, actors for reading, 49
Wolkoff, N., 314
World Trade Organization, 261
WorldCom and WorldCom scandal, 26; Arthur Andersen and, 49; B. Vinson at, 230–235, 241; bankruptcy filing of, 59; Citibank and, 247; criminal liability in, 45, 54–55; impact of, 53; insurance policies of, 34; negative incentives at, 230–231, 233, 234
W.R. Grace, 145–146
Writing. *See* Contracts; Documents; Language
Wrongful death cases, due to overconfidence, 27
Wrongful discharge, 292–293

X

Xerox, 126, 148, 307

Y

Yellow Pages, 38

Z

Zubulake, L., 50
Zubulake *vs.* UBS Warburg LLC, 50, 131–132